Economic and Financial Law & Policy – Shifting Insights & Values

Volume 2

Series editors
Koen Byttebier
Brussels, Belgium

Kim van der Borght
Brussels, Belgium

This book series focuses on presenting critical legal and interdisciplinary research regarding the tools and instruments of free-market-driven societies and their economies.

For the last few decades, the world markets have been in turmoil, to a large extent as a result of value and policy choices which have been made since the late middle ages. As a result, on a global scale, economies and the legal systems giving form to them, have mainly if not exclusively become based on selfishness and greed, a reality which is moreover explicitly propagated by the theories of economic neo-liberalism.

It has nevertheless become clear in the recent past that said free market tools and mechanisms – such as private money creation by banks, next to the way huge corporations in general function and determine the outcome of economic processes – result in disastrous consequences, especially when remaining uncorrected by law and when not being submitted to clear public policy intervention measures.

Despite the evidence and growing understanding of the causes and consequences of neoliberal policy, few alternatives for the capitalist model as currently implemented, have so far been proposed.

In order to meet these concerns, this book series aims at offering an outlet for various forms of scientific research output, both monographs and edited collections.

The objective of every book of the series will hereby be to look critically at the legal methods and mechanisms shaping the free markets, and even to suggest alternatives for these.

Although the book series is initiated by legal scholars, it nevertheless aims to be truly multi- and interdisciplinary. The books series therefor welcomes and will incorporate all relevant disciplines, including law, economics, philosophy, ethics, religion, psychology, sociology, anthropology etc.

More information about this series at http://www.springer.com/series/15643

Koen Byttebier

The Unfree Market and the Law

On the Immorality of Making Capitalism Unbridled Again

Springer

Koen Byttebier
Center for Economic Law and Governance
Free University Brussels
Brussels, Belgium

ISSN 2522-5243 ISSN 2522-5251 (electronic)
Economic and Financial Law & Policy – Shifting Insights & Values
ISBN 978-3-030-07347-3 ISBN 978-3-319-97382-1 (eBook)
https://doi.org/10.1007/978-3-319-97382-1

Softcover re-print of the Hardcover 1st edition 2018

This Springer imprint is published by the registered company Springer Nature Switzerland AG
The registered company address is: Gewerbestrasse 11, 6330 Cham, Switzerland

Preface

Building further on the insights which have led to my previous books *Nu het gouden kalf verdronken is*[1] and *Towards a New International Monetary Order,*[2] in this book, I have made an attempt to describe the system of values of capitalism.

It hereby appears that, particularly since the rise of economical liberalism in the eighteenth century, the values of "selfishness", "greed" and "egoism" have gradually succeeded in claiming a central position in socio-economic thinking and behaviour.

Although one could argue that these "values" of "selfishness", "greed" and "egoism" already started determining the shape of so-called indirect trade economies[3] since their very beginning, as of the seventeenth century, a philosophical theory later in history referred to as "economic liberalism" would succeed in offering an ideological justification for this choice of values, which have since then increasingly determined the outlook of the world economy.

Various capitalist mechanisms which are based on these values have since then contributed to the success of capitalism as the current dominant economic system on earth, such as (*i*) the prevailing monetary system, based on the power to newly create money to a large extent being handed over to private banks; (*ii*) the model of organizing enterprises through companies and corporations, as well as the financial markets stemming from this; and (*iii*) the liberal and later neo-liberal principle holding that business profits are more important than the labour of hard-working people, hence, of people themselves, in addition to (*iv*) less obvious mechanisms, such as the liberal doctrines of freedom and equality, which translate into a variety of legal techniques, among which is the theory of voluntary association that forms one of the main legal building stones of the capitalist economy.

It has not been until far in the twentieth century and after two devastating world wars that initiatives were taken to create certain elementary mechanisms which have

[1] See Byttebier (2015b). See also Byttebier (2015a).

[2] See Byttebier (2017).

[3] Referring to economies in which trading goods and services in a direct manner has mainly been replaced by trade based upon the payment of money.

aspired to counter (unbridled) capitalist practices. During the post-World War II era, this would lead to the introduction—at least in some countries—of the so-called welfare state model, which in substance is a collective term referring to mechanisms of socio-economic planning introduced by public authorities which aim at offering a certain type of protection to the working classes and, by extension, to the weak and poor within society, against the dominant capitalist exploitation mechanisms.[4]

Nonetheless it is a fact that, from the 1980s onwards, an economic ideology broke through which, in an even more aggressive way than the predecessing theories of economic liberalism, has attempted to reduce the entire world economy to one large "free market". Obviously, here reference is made to the theories of economic neo-liberalism,[5] which is in itself a collective term for a variety of doctrines in economical thinking which, summarized, advocate "more (so-called) free market" and "less state" and which, for that exact reason, oppose the mechanisms mentioned in the previous paragraph aimed at establishing a more just society than the one that resorts to a blind application of the free market system itself.

Since then, the implementation of the theories of economic neo-liberal thinking has taken a relentless rise which has been changing the appearance of the world more and more extensively. As a result, more than ever before in history, humanity is in the grip of the values of selfishness, greed and egoism, or, to make reference to the term used by Jesus Christ in the Gospels (see Matthew 6:24, and Luke 16:9-13), of "the mammon", the money devil which thus has obtained the status of the one god which is to be worshipped in accordance with the theories of economic neo-liberalism.

Meanwhile, the world is more and more in ruins, characterized, inter alia, by a threat to the ecosystem as a consequence of the interminable exploitation of the natural resources, a shameless exploitation of a major part of the human population, an increasing polarisation between the poor and the rich within society and, in general, a clearly unjust socio-economic order.

As a result, the world is increasingly becoming one where only money counts and where the rich dominate. Strangely enough, this has already been warned about for millennia, for instance by leading philosophers (such as Plato and Aristotle), next to prominent spiritual teachers from Buddha to Jesus Christ, whose doctrines, although being followed by billions, seem to have had little real influence on socio-economic structures, especially those preached by the contemporary gospel of economic neo-liberalism.

---

[4]Taylor-Gooby (2013), p. 2, defining the welfare state as follows:

> The welfare state, the idea that a successful, competitive, capitalist market economy can be combined with effective services to reduce poverty and meet the needs people experience in their everyday lives.

Taylor-Gooby refers to the welfare state model as "the great gift from Europe to the world". (See Taylor-Gooby (2013), p. 2.)

[5]According to Bouquin, the theories of economic neo-liberalism already date back to the years after World War II. (See Bouquin (2015), p. 88.)

The question arises as to whether there is still anything to be done to counter this, and if yes, what.

This book aspires to offer an incentive to reflect on this matter, not by providing yet another treatise on economics, but by, on the contrary, on one side undertaking an inquiry into the value scales that, throughout history, have determined the content of the two aforementioned main economic schools, namely the schools of economic liberalism and of economic neo-liberalism, and on the other side wondering if there can still be alternatives perceivable for the many dogmas with which these both economic schools have brainwashed mankind.

Ghent, Belgium
Brussels, Belgium

Koen Byttebier

References

Bouquin S (2015) Helemaal Anders. Critica, Brussel

Byttebier K (2015a) De onvrije markt. Garant, Antwerp

Byttebier K (2015b) Nu het gouden kalf verdronken is. Van hebzucht naar altruïsme als hoeksteen voor een Nieuwe Monetaire Wereldorde. Maklu, Antwerp

Byttebier K (2017) Towards a new international monetary order. In: Byttebier K and van der Borght K (eds), Economic and financial law & policy – shifting insights & values, vol I. Springer, Cham

Taylor-Gooby P (2013) The double crisis of the welfare state and what we can do about it. Palgrave Macmillan, Houndmills

Contents

Chapter 1
General Background

1.1 Introduction

It may be a witticism to hold that, during the past decades, the world economy has gradually evolved into a unitary capitalist system.

In contradiction to what the ideology of economic liberalism and later the very similar ideology of economic neo-liberalism, which are the main causes of this,[1] would like us to believe, this has hardly been a coincidence at all.

On the contrary, among prominent economists, next to scientists from other disciplines, the awareness has emerged that the domination of capitalism as a unitary global economic system has been mainly the result of a deliberate manipulation of human thinking itself, with all its known detrimental consequences.[2]

This awareness puts the central economic questions of our time immediately in the right perspective that, throughout the ages, the word economy has been the arena of an ongoing struggle of values and ideas, whereby one can but observe that, especially during the past decades, the doctrines of economic thinking and action which emphasize greed, selfishness and egoism as central economic values, have increasingly gained ground from the doctrines which have attempted to promote the opposite values of sobriety, sharing and altruism.[3]

---

[1] As a side remark, it can be observed that (economic) neo-liberalism is not much more than the contemporary manifestation of (economic) liberalism itself.

[2] See for instance Krugman (2008) and Akerlof and Shiller (2015).

[3] Fortunately, more and more people are meanwhile becoming aware of this.

A notorious example from the recent past has been Severn Cullis-Suzuki, a Canadian environmentalist who, since her youth, became famous for her commitment to the environment. According to Cullis-Suzuki, as a consequence of globalisation (and the world-wide copying of the Northern American consumer society model), people have started to live extremely artificial lives and are no longer connected to the environment. Cullis-Suzuki for instance gives as examples that people are totally disconnected from the production of their food, as well as from most other objects they use, and that they see unbridled consumption as the highest form of development. This has lead to the

K. Byttebier, *The Unfree Market and the Law*, Economic and Financial Law & Policy – Shifting Insights & Values 2,
https://doi.org/10.1007/978-3-319-97382-1_1

1.2 The Mystical World of Capitalism as Shaped by the Doctrines of Economic Liberalism and Economic Neo-liberalism

The notions "capitalism", "(economic) liberalism" and "(economic) neo-liberalism" all comprise terms which are often used, but which cannot easily be assimilated into a precise definition.

Capitalism[4] has been referred to as the economic system based on the way businesses operate through the investment of capital, hence of (surpluses of) (savings) money, and whereby these businesses above all aim at maximising profits which, in the end, are meant to enrich capital investors. To reach this goal, these businesses produce all kinds of goods or services at the lowest cost possible, in order to sell them on the market at the highest price possible.

In other words, capitalism is substantially an economic system stemming from the practice of an indirect trade economy based on monetary traffic.

It is hereby obviously not easy to determine[5] a precise starting date of capitalism.

The question even arises if capitalist practices are not as old as the use of money itself, at least as old as the emergence of savings activities based on the use of money.

Nevertheless, certain authors have placed the general breakthrough of pre-capitalist practices within Western society(ies) in the middle ages, more specifically at the revival of the (interregional and international) trade from the eleventh and twelfth century on, a period during which the acquisition of possessions became a way of life for many, and methods of circumventing religious-ethical barriers to capitalist principles, such as the ecclesiastical interest ban which had been prevailing for centuries before,[6] gradually became more and more accepted.[7]

In the world of ideas, one could be inclined to link the emergence of true "capitalist thinking" with some of the fathers of Protestantism, notoriously Calvin, as he opposed the classic medieval ecclesiastical interest ban, clearing the path for the idea that money in itself could yield new money (= interest). In a more general way, protestant doctrines produced a caesura with Catholic Christian thinking which up

---

fact that people have started to abuse the earth, whereby an individual is barely linked to the consequences of his selfish behavior. Another part of the problem is that politicians act in accordance with an alleged mandate that there should be unlimited economic growth, which has resulted in a set of values that needs to be completely modified again (see Kuin (2014), p. 218).

[4] Galbraith has indicated that (contemporary) adherents of capitalism prefer to avoid this term and rather refer to the "free-market"-system (see Galbraith (2004), p. 3).

[5] Bernstein (2004), p. 19.

[6] For a contemporary analysis of the interest-mechanism as a method through which the rich get richer to the detriment of the poor, see Stiglitz (2003), p. 81.

[7] Vandewalle (1976), p. 7; Ripert (1951), p. 13.

till then, under reference to the Scriptures themselves, had managed to resist the breakthrough of several capitalist practices. It is therefore probably not a coincidence that (pre-)capitalism as the general accepted economic system emerged first in the German territories (in the sixteenth century) and in Holland and the United Kingdom (in the seventeenth century) as these regions where among the first to embrace the ideas of Protestant Christian thinking. Since then, capitalism started to peak from the eighteenth century onwards, and especially in the nineteenth and twentieth centuries evolved into the dominant global economic system.[8]

Although the practices of capitalism for the first time in history gained a large degree of validation in Protestant Christian thinking, it has nevertheless been a number of at first philosophical, and later economic schools which would provide a strong ideological base which, in turn, has helped to contribute to the great success of capitalism as the dominating economic system of our times.

The most important of these schools are obviously the schools of "economic liberalism" (basically having installed capitalism) and of "economic neo-liberalism" (aiming at making capitalism "unbridled" again).

According to the theories of economic liberalism, dating back to the Scottish moral philosopher Adam Smith, private entrepreneurship (and more in general: private initiative) should play a central role within economies and public authorities should refrain from any action which could hinder their activities. Of central importance is individual property by which an individual can deploy his economic initiatives.[9] This goes hand in hand with the further idea that the capital providers of a business are seen as its (economic) owners, which is why it is considered normal that the profits resulting from businesses mainly should flow back to these "owners", i.e. the capital providers or shareholders, rather than to the labourers or to society in general.

It is evident that economic liberal thinking has, from its birth, been closely related to the interests of the bourgeoisie as the new prevailing class of the liberal society that took shape as of the eighteenth century, and mainly shaped capitalist economies in the course of the eighteenth, nineteenth and twentieth centuries in many European countries, as well as in their (former) overseas colonies.[10]

The doctrine(s) of economic neo-liberalism is (are) probably even harder to define than economic liberalism itself; to a certain extent, one could even define economic neo-liberalism in a broad manner as a collective name for contemporary philosophies and economic models in favour of capitalist practices.

---

[8] Ripert (1951), p. 14; Fromm (1979), p. 83 a.f.; Byttebier (2015), p. 129.

[9] Stiglitz (2010), p. 201.

[10] As a consequence of this, within liberal and neo-liberal thinking, one has traditionally advocated fiscal policies which serve the interests of the bourgeoisie, such as the idea that the operation of businesses should, as much as possible, be exonerated from substantial taxes; as a result, worldwide, taxes have mainly been impacting income from labour rather than income from capital. This will be discussed further in this book. (See, furthermore, especially under Sect. 4.6.)

Nevertheless, in terms of content, economic neo-liberalism is obviously very closely related to economic liberalism itself.

The doctrines of economic neo-liberalism have, for the most part, originated in a number of Western countries since the sixties of the twentieth century,[11] as a reaction to the breakthrough of the so-called "welfare state model" and the "mixed economy" to which this had led.[12]

The welfare state model hereby appeared to cause a serious challenge to members of the rich classes within society, as financing a welfare state was, in their view, undermining their business profits (of which, given the way capitalist economic model functions, indeed a part was needed for the financing of several welfare mechanisms).[13]

This opinion gradually led to the development of an ideological line of thought in which a central role was laid down for the myth of the free market. In this world view, anything hindering this free market should be eliminated as much as possible. In other words, in this neo-liberal approach, it is not the role of public authorities to work out a welfare state model, but their main task is to prevent the emergence of obstacles hindering free market operation, in addition to develop active policies of supporting such free market operation.

The implementation of neo-liberal thinking since then has in practice been accompanied by different governmental measures to achieve these goals, such as the economic theories and practices of "monetarism" and "consumerism", next to techniques such as the privatization of state owned businesses and the cutting down on several government expenses, such as those related to public education and social care.[14]

Particularly with effect from the 1980s, the ideas of economic neo-liberalism have exerted a strong influence in many countries to the extent that, up till this very date, a majority of the world countries is more or less pursuing a social and economic policy which heavily relies on the doctrines and ideas of economic neo-liberalism.[15]

One of the major consequences of this liberal and neo-liberal (economic) thinking has been that it has strongly contributed to the expansion of capitalism and to making it "unbridled" again, at the same time shaping the currently prevailing societal model in which greed, selfishness and egoism have become the leading mechanisms determining relationships on a socio-economic level.[16]

---

[11] According to Bouquin, the roots of neo-liberalism may already be situated in the period after World War II. (See Bouquin (2015), p. 88 a.f.)

[12] About the state welfare model, see Stiglitz (2010), p. 197.

[13] Compare, as regards the UK especially, Taylor-Gooby (2013), p. 2.

[14] Chomsky (2017), p. 68.

[15] Neo-liberal thinking links closely to political conservatism (mainly defending the interests of the rich and powerful within societies).

[16] Compare Congregation for the Doctrine of the Faith (2018), n° 9.

1.3 The Greed Is Good-Credo

As demonstrated in the previous Sect. 1.2, both economic liberalism and economic neo-liberalism are based on the belief that man is above all a selfish being who should behave in the most selfish way possible, especially in socio-economic relations.

This belief system is strikingly defined in the so-called "greed is good"-credo.[17]

Within this way of reasoning, selfishness is not only an end in itself, but also a means to give effect to socio-economic relations. This implies that, especially within a socio-economic context, every person has to make the best possible efforts to reach his own selfish goals, which will provide the economy with the necessary impetus for productivity and innovation resulting in the greatest possible level of prosperity for all economic players.

Moreover, as has been put forward by Skidelsky and Skidelsky, the ideology of economic neo-liberalism has been consistently hostile to the idea that any amount of wealth (or money) could ever represent "enough",[18] going hand in hand with the idea that the economy will and should keep on growing forever.

Through this belief system, economic liberalism and economic neo-liberalism obviously appeal to the lowest impulses of human behaviour.

As economic neo-liberalism has meanwhile become the predominant economic discipline on earth, both in every day practice and as the basic ideology determining government policies on a global scale, selfishness, individual greed and egoism also have gradually become the predominant moral values in socio-economic thinking and action.

This underlying thought implies that if every human being fully embraces the idea that he should behave as selfishly, greedy and egoistically as possible, everyone will act in an active and productive manner, causing economy to flourish and grow further, which in return will provide a breeding ground for a world where all people will be able to live a good and luxurious life (also referred to as the "trickle-down-economics").

---

[17] The quote "greed is good" (purportedly) goes back to tot Gordon Gekko, a character from the movie "Wall Street" (1987) (a role portrayed by Michael Douglas who received an Oscar for it).

The movie character Gordon Gekko is (even so purportedly) slightly based on financial investors Ivan Boesky and Carl Icahn. In the movie Gordon Gekko holds a speech with following quote (see http://nl.wikipedia.org/wiki/Gordon_Gekko; last consulted on June 16, 2018):

> The point is, ladies and gentlemen, that 'greed' — for lack of a better word — is good. Greed is right. Greed works. Greed clarifies, cuts through, and captures the essence of the evolutionary spirit. Greed, in all of its forms — greed for life, for money, for love, knowledge — has marked the upward surge of mankind. And greed — you mark my words — will not only save Teldar Paper, but that other malfunctioning corporation called the USA.

Since then, the quote has been repeatedly referred to, even in economic literature. (See for instance Tyler (2013), p. 36; Peterson (2011), p. 96; Krugman (2004), p. 110.)

[18] Skidelsky and Skidelsky (2013), pp. 40–41.

It is crystal clear that, like is the case for many ideologies, economic (neo-)liberalism is intrinsically based on a utopian world view which is completely out of touch with reality, and that it has hardly been fulfilled in practice.

As a result, over the past years, many human scientists have come to the conclusion that both economic liberalism and economic neo-liberalism are mainly based on a number of imaginary principles and, above all, through their impact on the socio-economic system, have given shape to a completely unjust world.

This will hereafter, step by step, be further demonstrated and illustrated, where our attention will first go to a number of so-called "obvious capitalist mechanisms" (see Chap. 2), secondly to a number of so-called "less obvious capitalist mechanisms" (Chap. 3) and finally to some reflections on the outlook of the contemporary capitalist system (Chap. 4). In Chap. 5, we will conclude with a number of lines of thought about how the socio-economic organisation could further evolve for the better towards the creation of a system that truly promotes social welfare and societal well-being.[19]

References

Akerlof G, Shiller R (2015) Phishing for phools. The economics of manipulation & deception. Princeton University Press, Princeton

Bernstein WJ (2004) The birth of plenty. How the prosperity of the modern world was created. McGraw-Hill, New York

Bouquin S (2015) Helemaal Anders. Critica, Brussel

Byttebier K (2015) Nu het gouden kalf verdronken is. Van hebzucht naar altruïsme als hoeksteen voor een Nieuwe Monetaire Wereldorde. Maklu, Antwerp

Chomsky N (2017) Requiem for the American dream. The 10 principles of concentration of wealth & power. Seven Stories Press, New York

Congregation for the Doctrine of the Faith – Dicastery For Promoting Integral Human Development (2018) Oeconomicae et pecuniariae quaestiones – Considerations for an ethical discernment regarding some aspects of the present economic-financial system. http://www.vatican.va/roman_curia/congregations/cfaith/documents/rc_con_cfaith_doc_20180106_oeconomicae-etpecuniariae_en.html. Last consulted 16 June 2018

Fromm E (1979) The sane society. Routledge & Kegan Paul, London

Galbraith JK (2004) The economics of innocence fraud. Houghton Mifflin Company, Boston

Krugman P (2004) The great unraveling: losing our way in the new century. W. W. Norton & Company, New York

Krugman P (2008) The conscience of a liberal: reclaiming America from the right. Allen Lane, London

Kuin F (2014) Severn Cullis-Suzuki liet de wereld vijf minuten zwijgen. In: van Straaten F, Kloek E (eds) Kinderen die de wereld hebben veranderd. PixelPerfect Publications, Den Haag, pp 211–221

Peterson R (2011) Inside the investor's brain: the power of mind over money. Wiley, Hoboken

Ripert G (1951) Aspects juridiques du capitalisme modern. Librairie Générale de droit et de jurisprudence, Paris

[19] Compare to Stiglitz (2002), p. 24.

Skidelsky R, Skidelsky E (2013) How much is enough. Money and the good life. Penguin Books, London
Stiglitz J (2002) Employment, social justice and societal well-being. Int Labour Organ 141(1–2):9–29
Stiglitz J (2003) The roaring nineties. W.W. Norton & Company, New York
Stiglitz J (2010) Freefall. Free markets and the sinking of the global economy. Allen Lane (an imprint of Penguin Books), London
Taylor-Gooby P (2013) The double crisis of the welfare state and what we can do about it. Palgrave Macmillan, Houndmills
Tyler G (2013) What went wrong: how the 1% hijacked the American middle class … and what other countries got right. BenBella Books, Dallas
Vandewalle G (1976) De geschiedenis van het economisch denken. Kluwer, Deventer

Chapter 2
On Some Obvious Capitalist Mechanisms and How They Evolved Under the Doctrines of Economic Liberalism and Economic Neo-liberalism

2.1 The Quasi Monopoly of the Private Bank Sector as Regards the Creation of Money

2.1.1 The Origin of the Western Banking System

The success of capitalism as the predominant economic system of our times is to a large extent the result of the way in which the prevailing monetary and financial system provides individuals, businesses, economies and even states with the means of financing their activities and operations.[1]

It is indeed especially through the monetary and financial mechanisms driving the money and capital markets that capitalism determines the distribution of global wealth, in a way that mainly expresses the motives of selfishness, greed and egoism which have been declared as the determining values by both economic liberalism and economic neo-liberalism.[2]

Although throughout history various systems of money creation have prevailed, and there even have been long periods of time during which money creation was mainly in the hands of public authorities, the breakthrough of capitalism from the seventeenth century on has completely changed the way (new) money is created, with itself caused money and capital, to a large extent, ending up in the private hands of a small elite of market players, in a process where practically all other social values have gradually been sacrificed to the hunger for ever money of a few individuals.

---

[1] Compare Kennedy (2013), p. 8, pointing out that "money", but also "capital", "labour", "credit" and "liquidity", all are "creatures of the law", implying that law not only regulates such things, but creates them. This implies that the history of political and economic life is at the same time also the history of institutions and laws.

[2] Chomsky (2015), p. 34.

K. Byttebier, *The Unfree Market and the Law*, Economic and Financial Law & Policy – Shifting Insights & Values 2,
https://doi.org/10.1007/978-3-319-97382-1_2

Indeed, since the rise of the modern Western banking system during the course of the second half of the Middle Ages, the power to create money has gradually ended up in the hands of a few private bankers.[3]

Private bankers getting hold of the power to create new money manifested for a first time when medieval money changers saw in the practice of deposits of coins issued by public authorities and cast from precious metals, an opportunity to issue so called "private paper money" for much higher sums than the underlying coins deposited by the general public with these money changers who, by doing so, themselves evolved into bankers. Such issuing of privately created paper money became in itself part of a practice by which bankers increasingly started to grant credit whereby, on each occurrence, new paper money was issued in excess of the reserves in precious metal coins which the banker held. This system was, hence, literally one where such a banker, totally "out of nothing" and "by doing (almost) nothing",[4] created new paper money.

The success of this practice supplied the economy of the western regions in which it occurred, with new money at a much faster rate and for far greater amounts than before in history had been possible in an economy based on coins cast from precious metals.

The upside of this (then) new mechanism of money creation by private market players "out of nothing" was that it provided a breeding ground for a much faster economic growth. The downside was that money became a synonym for credit, in which the initial borrower (who first received the newly issued money) was expected to produce a sufficient degree of economic wealth to be able to pay the credit back, implying that a very high pressure was placed on the collectivity of borrowers to aim for an ever-increasing economic growth that was needed to keep in pace with the increase of money that itself was issued in the form of a repayable credit.[5]

There is no doubt that this technique of creating privately issued new money out of nothing has played a crucial role in the development of capitalism, but, by extension, also in the way that man, as an individual, relates to his surroundings (which does not only include other people, but also the entire eco-system of planet).[6]

The expectation generated by this new monetary system was that the bank credits—representing money created out of thin air—would translate into true economic wealth that in its turn would enable the borrowers to pay the credit back.

As a result, this (at that time) new mechanism of creating new money would turn out to be of decisive importance in creating an economic setting in which, gradually, all society and, by extension, the whole planet, would be beholden to the objective

[3] Galbraith expressed this as follows (see Galbraith (1977), pp. 164–166):

> With banks came the power, given to few private citizens, to create money.

[4] On the still prevailing ease of creating new money, see Cole (1937), p. 206.

[5] See also Galbraith (1977), pp. 166–167.

[6] See also Turner (2016), p. 133 a.f.

that credit resulting in new money being created "out of nothing" needed effectively to be paid back.

Looking at this process rationally, it is somewhat astonishing that this mechanism has been able to have such an economic and societal impact, and moreover, that the collectivity of mankind has been seduced to embrace the whole idea that such a system could be even possible.

Indeed, from the viewpoint of a banker (creditor) partaking in such a monetary system, the mere agreeing upon such a credit agreement resulting in newly created money, requires little or no effort. Through a simple decision (in fact a simple "yes"), such a banker/creditor exercises the power to create new money out of thin air, sometimes for large amounts. Hence, without much effort, private bankers obtained the power to create huge sums of new (paper) money.

However, already from the start, the story of private money creation through bank credits sounded a bit more complicated from the borrower's end. Under a credit agreement, the credit taker is bound by the obligation to repay the money (which the bank/creditor creates out of nothing) at a future moment in time. Otherwise put: upon entering into the credit agreement, the credit taker gets a sum of money at his disposal, by means of which he can finance various expenses. However, this happens on the condition that, in the near future (determined by the terms of the credit contract itself), the credit taker will manage to repay the credit. This in itself has to be done on the basis of a return obtained from real economic efforts (as opposed to the effortless decision of a bank to grant a credit), implying that a credit taker submits himself to an expectation of gaining a sufficient amount of money out of his economic efforts in order to be able to comply with the credit agreement's repayment terms and conditions.

This way, a bank credit agreement links the relatively simple act of private money creation, which can so to speak be approved by a simple nod from a banker, to the expectation that real economic efforts will be made so that the credit taker obtains an income which at the very least will be sufficient to repay the credit (on occasion: increased with interests).

It can be easily understood that this mechanism would create an immense pressure on the economy. As the collectivity of bankers under such a system had a wide range of clients/credit takers, this system soon also implied an immense competition between economic players (in their capacity of credit takers) which in our times has even degenerated "into an (economic) war of everyone against everyone"[7] and whereby every participant in this play of economics attempts to extract enough wealth from economic activities in order to be able to pay back his bank credit(s) (where applicable: with interests), as well as keeping a sufficient amount of profits for himself.[8]

---

[7] Further reference can be made to Sect. 3.3 hereafter.

[8] For further details, see Byttebier (2015), p. 115 a.f.; Byttebier (2017), under Sect. 3.3.3.

2.1.2 *The (Medieval) Interest-Debate*

During the rest of the Middle ages, a second evolution took place further emphasising said impact of the at the time newly developing technique of private money creation through bank credit agreements.

This second development concerned the way society started dealing with the ability (or inability) of contracting parties to agree upon a so-called "interest" (to be paid in addition to the repayment obligation itself).

From a contemporary viewpoint, the idea of interest payments is, of course, generally accepted (at least in Western economies and/or economies based on Western thinking). Hence, it may even sound perplexing that, from a historical perspective, also in the West, the interest mechanism has during a large part of history been anything but evident.

Drawing on the importance of philosophers from the Classical Antiquity (among whom Plato and Aristotle), but also on the Old and New Testament[9] and on the teachings of certain early "church fathers" (for instance: the Saints Ambrose and Augustine of Hippo), from the fourth century on, a church doctrine started prevailing that strongly challenged the permissibility of interest charging. In a nutshell, this church doctrine also known as "the (medieval) clerical interest prohibition", stated that the levy of interest was sinful as it introduced a method by which the rich could appropriate ever more wealth at the expense of the poor within society. Hence, such behaviour was considered to be opposed to the teachings of Jesus Christ Himself who on the contrary called for handing out one's wealth.[10]

Based on this clerical doctrine, already early on in church history, clerical authorities, among which the famous councils of early Christianity that dealt with the fundamental issues of the Christian faith, but also worldly Christian monarchs such as Charles The Great and his son Louis The Pious, tried to introduce an overall ecclesiastical interest ban which would cover all Catholic territories.[11]

Along with the renewed emergence of trade and, through this, of (pre-)banking in the course of the eleventh and twelfth centuries, the ecclesiastical interest ban would gradually be challenged, initially through the development of practices enabling to "bypass" the interest prohibition (a typical example was the use of discount mechanisms in the context of the letter of exchange) and, later on, because credits were openly provided at interest rates. Through this, it got gradually advocated that the interest prohibition should be abandoned. The latter opinion would even become one of the main stakes in the clerical schism, as a result of which interest would become a legitimate Christian credit practice in the European protestant regions.[12]

---

[9] Including the words of Jesus Christ Himself, as recorded in the four Gospels.

[10] For a thorough (historical) analysis of this doctrine, see Byttebier (2017), p. 115 a.f.

[11] For a more detailed analysis, see Byttebier (2015), pp. 115–136; and Byttebier (2017), p. 115 a.f.

[12] Galbraith (1977), p. 164; Byttebier (2015), pp. 127–129.

2.1.3 The Evolution Towards a Credit Economy Dominated by Private Bankers

The emancipation process referred to at the end of Sect. 2.1.2 would have an important impact on medieval banking practices (especially in the second half of the Middle Ages).

As during this period, the levying of interest was deemed to be more and more legitimate, banking would increasingly base its practices of credit lending based upon the abovementioned new credit mechanism, where credit takers were increasingly expected not only to repay the principal, but also the agreed upon interests.[13]

It needs not much explanation that this interest mechanism increased the pressure on the economy even more. The levying of interest moreover made the granting of bank credits an increasingly lucrative activity. The simple granting of a credit by a private banker not only resulted in the issue of new paper money, but also created a (potentially very important) new source of income for such banker, at the first place due to the fact that the "out-of-nothing" created money had to paid back, given the fact that is was at the same time credit, and, secondly because of the interests the credit taker owed to the banker. In this way, very high profits were generated by the minor effort of saying "yes" to a credit request (hence: a decision to create new paper money).

Moreover, this mechanism allowed a considerable amount of freedom for speculative credit lending, where private bankers were increasingly tempted to provide high risk credits. Indeed, the losses from non-repaid credits could be borne by the interests effectively paid by "good" credit takers, especially when the interest rates were sufficiently high to take into account this risk margin of bad payers. This would not only lead to an increasing risk behaviour of the private bankers, but would also present global society with a new type of free riding behaviour (and even with "bad money"). As Western societies became increasingly dependent on private bankers for their supply of new money, good credit takers were also increasingly subjected to the risks created by bad payers, especially when private bankers started to base their calculations of the average interest rates they would apply on the risks imposed by these bad credit takers.

Probably one of the most important consequences of the new credit mechanism has been that both the continuous creation of new money it implied, as the interest mechanism it got based upon, above all created a high expectation of continuous economic growth. Credit takers were indeed not only expected to pay back the basic amount of the credit granted to them (which, as said, represented money that had been created out of nothing), but also the agreed upon interest.

In other words, the collectivity of credit takers within such an economic system were all more and more expected to generate enough income to pay back the credits

[13] On the history of (early) banking, see furthermore Ferguson (2009), p. 42 a.f.

themselves, as well as the agreed upon interest, obviously enhancing the prospect of economic growth even more.[14]

This historical evolution would eventually contribute to a fundamental shift of values. The expectancy of a continuous economic growth which was necessary to allow credit takers to pay back credits enhanced with interests, would already on itself create a breeding ground for the development of an economic system characterized by selfishness, greed and egoism. As more and more economic agents, among which even states and other public authorities, entered the capacity of credit takers who started existing and behaving under pressure to repay their credits and the agreed upon interests, this effect got over time more and more enhanced.

It is precisely this expectation of an ever-growing economy as implied by the private money creation mechanism that is based upon private bank credits that up till now has determined the shape of the capitalist world economy, with its many disastrous characteristics and consequences.

Nevertheless, notwithstanding the above, the path of private money creation has not always been a rosy one.

It is hereby crucial to be aware that the above explained medieval private paper mechanism model kept on presupposing an underlying commitment by the issuer of the new (paper) money, upon request, to exchange the paper money for an equivalent amount of money in precious metal coins. Earlier in history, coin money had indeed been the only type of money available, and it had been deposit agreements regarding such coin money which had brought private bankers to issue private paper money, initially as means of evidence of such deposit agreements, but later in excess of such deposits. Even after the private bankers were tempted to bring more and more paper money into circulation, as this provided them with high profits through the interests they started charging, the underlying exchange obligation indeed remained in place, enabling the holders of the paper money to exchange it back into precious metal coins at their convenience.

The more a private banker issued paper money, by definition above the amounts of precious coins he held in reserve, the more his ability to meet this exchange obligation decreased, as the amounts of precious coins held in cash by the banker remained relatively unchanged in comparison to the increasing amounts of paper money issued by the same banker.

It is evident (as is the case with any form of money) that such a mechanism implied a large degree of mutual confidence, which could only be maintained as long as a large number of holders of the newly created paper money expressed their confidence in the underlying exchange commitments of the private bankers. When, on the contrary, the holders of the new paper money lost their confidence that the issuing bankers would be able to meet the underlying exchange obligation, they got inclined to ask their coin money back, which of course made the new private money creation model inherently vulnerable.

[14] Galbraith (1990), p. 19.

2.1.4 *Inherent Flaws of the Medieval Banking System and the Search for Remedying Them*

In various parts of Europe (especially in large urban areas where banking activities were most prevalent), the risk of a confidence breach between the private bankers and the holders of paper money manifested repeatedly in the course of history and, in some cases even led to bank bankruptcies.

Moreover, these bankruptcies impacted highly on the rest of the economy when, due to the phasing out of a bank (who was per definition also a private issuer of paper money), the money issued by this bank became valueless (and through this, the purchasing power it had represented so far got lost), with all obvious consequences. To the extent that bankers were often also holders of each other's paper money, cascade effects could occur where, through the demise of one banker, other bankers were impacted as well; this could even have a highly disruptive effect on the whole of society.[15]

Especially when the inherent risks of this monetary system manifested, in the course of the seventeenth, eighteenth and nineteenth centuries, in many Western countries, governments started to look for ways to counter the flaws of this private money creation mechanism, which gradually resulted in the rise of an (early) central banking system.

Without the existence of a real blueprint—since the mechanisms described here have mainly been the result of a process of "trial and error", rather than the result of a well-thought upon system[16]—the central banking system in most European countries gradually adopted a similar structure, with as main characteristics: a prohibition on (or at least a strong restriction of) the ability of (ordinary) private banks to issue private paper money, next to the granting of the (exclusive) power to create paper money to a single central bank, which henceforward was not only given a monopoly to issue new paper money, but also usually was granted a role of supplying other (private) banks with the new (governmental) paper money, next to a role as lender of last resort for the benefit of these other (private) bankers.

2.1.5 *Further Evolution of the Western Banking System*

After these (early) government interventions referred to in the previous Sect. 2.1.4, it seemed for a while that a "monetary peace" had returned, be it that the private banking system, driven by its boundless hunger for ever more profits, would quickly

[15] Galbraith (1990), p. 20.

[16] One could even argue that, throughout all human endeavor, "trial and error" has been the usual "method" or rather "process" of creating societal systems, and for coming up with solutions to problems arising from living together (see Popper (1940), p. 403).

discover new opportunities of participating in the money creation processes which would gradually result in the monetary system prevailing up to this very date.

Looking back, it is difficult to avoid reaching the conclusion that mankind would, as a consequence of these evolutions, very quickly step into the same trap for a second time in history, whereby the real economy would be driven into a model of an expectation of continuous growth as a consequence of a hoax thought up by the private banking sector.

A determining factor of this evolution has probably been the willingness of many other market players to surrender to their own selfish profit motives, a willingness which was enhanced through new philosophies (such as "rationalism") that gradually took the place of former Church teachings as the guiding thought systems determining the outlook of European (and through Europe's colonialism, even global) civilisation.

The new technique of participating in the processes of money creation by the private banking sector which broke through in the course of the eighteenth century was all in all not very different from the earlier described processes of private creation of paper money.

As indeed, from the seventeenth to eighteenth centuries on (with certain differences between countries), private bankers could no longer issue newly created paper money themselves, they sought new mechanisms to facilitate bank credits. This led to the development of credit lending through methods of mere bookings on (banking) accounts. In simple words, this mechanism implied that a private banker granting a credit made the money available to the credit taker through means of a booking on a banking account held by this credit taker. As a result, the banker recognized a conventionally created debt, in particular the commitment to pay out the agreed upon credit amount to the credit taker, and, conversely, the credit taker obtained a claim for payment of the credit granted to him by the private banker. The credit taker could then make use of this claim on his private banker in various ways, either by a withdrawal in cash (i.e. the still also existing bank notes or coins), or by executing (scriptural) payment orders in the broad sense of the word. However (and obviously), at the same time, the banker also obtained a claim on the credit taker, as the credit taker had to repay the credit (usually enhanced with agreed upon interest payments).[17]

These in themselves fairly simple accounting techniques once more in history disguised what has probably been one of the most important findings in the development of the modern banking and financial system, notably the mechanism of private (scriptural) money creation through bank credits.

The new mechanism had in common with the method of the private creation of paper money as developed in the late Middle Ages that it led to the creation of new private money "from scratch" and "without any considerable effort": the simple granting of a credit led to a booking on an account of the credit taker which expressed a debt of the bank that could be honoured in different ways, among which cash withdrawals in bank notes or coins, next to techniques of scriptural transcribing the

[17] Ferguson (2009), p. 49.

obtained money to someone else's account. At the same time, the bank obtained a claim on the credit taker, as the credit needed to be paid back, enhanced with the agreed upon interests, so that private banks very easily could expand their wealth and fortune—and thus ultimately that of their shareholders—by simply granting new credit resulting in "out of nothing"-created new money.

The new mechanism ran even more smoothly than its historical predecessor, as new privately created scriptural money could be very easily brought into circulation by a simple booking on a bank account, thereby reducing the efforts of the banking system to issue new money (and, through both the repayment obligation and the interest mechanism, to make easy profits), to practically nothing,[18] without the banker (hence: private money creator) even needing to print paper money.

This technique of creating scriptural money out of nothing, bewildering simple as it were, nevertheless would generate one of the main drivers for the development of capitalism during the nineteenth and twentieth centuries, where the only (new) limitation was the conventionally agreed upon commitment a private bank issuing new scriptural money had to make to pay out the amount of the granted credit in the form of cash on the simple request of any owner of such a scriptural claim.[19]

As the private banks themselves were in most Western countries no longer authorized to issue (new) paper money (nor authorized to issue coin money), within the new system, they indeed needed to ensure that they always held a sufficient amount of cash money to meet their customers' possible exchange requests (regardless whether these were a consequence of an initial cash deposit, of benefiting from a scriptural payment by a third party, or of a credit booked to their account).

As, again, due to the way the credit mechanism on which scriptural money creation is based works, any bank started creating more scriptural claims for its customers than it held cash, a new precarious risk emerged (comparable to the position of the private bankers in the late Middle Ages that had developed private paper money), as such bankers could, by definition, never be able to honour all exchange requests from all of its creditors in case these would be made at the same time.

2.1.6 The Outlook of the Modern-Day Banking System and the (Excessive) Credit Economy It Has Created

Since then, the method of scriptural money creation resulting from the granting of credits (as referred to in the previous Sect. 2.1.5) has continued to be the most essential characteristic of the private banking industry.

---

[18] There was even no need any more of printing (paper money) and of taking noteworthy safeguarding measures. However, it should be remarked that, in present times, the efforts of the banking system to keep the scriptural money system safe, have become remarkable higher (e.g. due to the need of safeguarding measures against cyber crime). (See, for instance, Jones (2016).)

[19] It should however be pointed out that, during the nineteenth century until the second half of the twentieth standard, many countries made the creation of new (paper) money by their central bank conditional upon the central back holding a certain amount of gold as underlying coverage.

Within the monetary system that resulted from these evolutions, the abovementioned flaws of the system could, in theory, be countered by the central banking system. As central banks in most (capitalist) countries got themselves vested with the privilege to issue (and newly create) bank notes (which, along with the coins issued by public authorities, form "cash" money), they also got empowered to distribute newly created bank notes to private banks who are in need them (in order to prevent these private banks from suffering a shortage of cash). This distributing of bank notes (and coins) by the central banks to the private banks started happening within the context of granting credits to such private banks, which is classically referred to as the "lender of last resort function" of the central bank(s).

Based on this central banking function, from the eighteenth century on, a further policy would be pursued where private banks were encouraged to prevent an imminent lack of funds (for some of them), or cash surpluses (for others), by means of mutual credit agreements entered into on the so-called interbank market. Based upon its central interest rate policy, the central bank itself could also play a guiding role in the overall amount of money in circulation in order to achieve its monetary policy objectives.

Since then, the role of scriptural money has steadily increased over the past decades.

According to some estimations, the amount of scriptural money circulating in most (capitalist) countries represents at the very least 90% of the entire amount of money (and in some countries even far more). This itself may be explained by, on one hand, an increasing preference by the end users of money to use scriptural money instead of cash money and, on the other hand, by various policy measures which further enhance this preference for scriptural money use (e.g. the fight against black money, and the fight against organized crime and terrorism).

The downside of this evolution has been that the increased use of scriptural money went even further hand in hand with the development of a true credit economy and, moreover, with a gradual enhancement of the power of private banks, as the latter got entrusted with one of the main societal powers, namely the power to create new money (out of nothing) and, through this, the power to organise the distribution of the wealth brought forward by the economy as a collective system.

In spite of the many positive effects of the use of scriptural money which lied at the origin of these developments, such as an increased level of security (however, in present days, bearing in mind the vulnerability to hacking and cyber attacks with regard to, for instance, internet payment transactions), and the high level of transparency the use of scriptural money allows, the increasing success of scriptural money creation has also allowed private banks to transcend the steering role of the monetary authorities,[20] a problem that has gotten worse throughout time and for which no satisfactory policy answer has yet been found.

[20] These processes have also been described in more detail in Chapter I of Byttebier (2015) and in Chapter 2 of Byttebier (2017).

As a result, the outcome of this historical evolution[21] has been that the supply of money to the global economy has basically completely ended up in the hands of one private sector, i.e. the private banking system.

Through a variety of credit mechanisms, which almost all come down to the same conventional basic technique of granting a credit based upon an asset backed security (to a large extent: real estate),[22] private banks control the supply of money to any economic agent, whether an individual needing a credit in order to meet a consumer expenditure, a business in need of a credit for an investment or a payment, or even a state or other public authority for any of its projects.

This private money creation credit mechanism and the immense economic power it implies which took its shape in the course of the eighteenth and nineteenth centuries through a process of trial and error, has moreover never been the subject of a true democratic decision making process,[23] neither has it since then hardly ever been challenged, nor has it, strangely enough, barely ever been the subject of a thorough, or even elementary soci(et)al debate.[24]

Nevertheless, through the course of history, some (minor) shifts in emphasis have taken place, such as an ever increasing degree of (legal) sophistication in the credit mechanisms (both as regards bank credits to private credit takers, as in the field of credit techniques applied by the central bankers when granting credits to

---

[21] For a more extended historical analysis, see for instance Byttebier (2015), Chapter I; Byttebier (2017), Chapter 2. See also Galbraith (1975); Galbraith (1990); Bogaert et al. (2000).

[22] As expressed by Galbraith on this matter (see Galbraith (1990), p. 19):

> The rule is that financial operations do not lend themselves to innovation. What is recurrently so described and celebrated is, without exception, a small variation on an established design, one that owes its distinctive character to the aforementioned brevity of the financial memory. The world of finance hails the invention of the wheel over and over again, often in a slightly more unstable version. All financial innovation involves, in one form or another, the creation of debt secured in greater or lesser adequacy by real assets.

[23] With perhaps as rare exception the establishment of the IMF in 1944 that took some elementary reflection by the world community on the outlook of the global monetary system, albeit not even the IMF-system has managed to establish a true counterbalancing force to the power of the private bank sector.

On the website of the IMF, the reasons for creating the IMF are summarized as follows:

> This breakdown in international monetary cooperation led the IMF's founders to plan an institution charged with overseeing the international monetary system—the system of exchange rates and international payments that enables countries and their citizens to buy goods and services from each other. The new global entity would ensure exchange rate stability and encourage its member countries to eliminate exchange restrictions that hindered trade. [It was] believed that such a framework was necessary to avoid a repetition of the disastrous economic policies that had contributed to the Great Depression. (See https://www.imf.org/external/about/histcoop.htm; last consulted on June 16, 2018.)

[24] With as rare exception, some observations under Marxist doctrine.

For instance Karl Marx himself expressed the concern that capitalism, based on its own intrinsic laws, would head towards its own collapse, after which it would, amongst other things, advocate the return of money creation processes into public hands. (See Vandewalle (1976), p. 101. On the Marxist ideas about money, see also Mandel (1962), tII, pp. 252 a.f.)

private bankers), next to the development of a variety of financial derivatives (which in many cases stem from the operation of credit on the credit markets themselves).

2.1.7 *The Cherry on the Neo-liberal Pie: The Role of Credit Rating Agencies*

As if the monetary and banking system as described in the previous sections is not sufficiently undemocratic on its own, in recent times the intrinsically undemocratic nature of this system has even been further enhanced as a result of the increasing role of so-called "credit rating agencies", basically specialised private businesses that "judge" the creditworthiness of actual and potential credit takers.

At present, the importance of these credit rating agencies is immense, which to a large extent seems to be caused by the increasing globalisation of the financial world (which has as a result that credit positions got more and more based upon documentation, rather than on the classic "know thy customer"-principle).[25]

The role of said rating agencies is thus that it has even been held that, on one hand, a positive credit rating can provide a country more wealth than the availability of natural resources, such as commodities, and, on the other hand, that a negative credit rating can undermine the economy of a country completely.

A possible explanation for this lies in the fact that a credit rating by a credit agency translates into the interest rates applied by the bank sector. This implies that a credit taker with a good rating will be considered to cause a lower risk, and hence will be granted a lower credit interest rate. On the contrary, a credit taker with a bad rating will be seen as a higher risk, and will therefore have to endure a higher interest rate.

In case where the credit rating becomes all too low, the entire creditworthiness of the credit taker could get at stake, implying that, ultimately, such a credit taker will no longer be provided with new credit, with all the known adverse consequences.[26]

Through this, credit rating agencies have obtained much power, albeit being mere private institutions that have no democratic legitimation whatsoever, which forms yet another characteristic of the prevailing monetary and financial order as being completely submitted to the invisible hands of the private markets.

---

[25] During a conference, a colleague once had a scene from the movie "It's a Wonderful Life" (Frank Capra; 1946) projected in order to illustrate how far the present-day prevailing banking system has been removed from its historical roots of banks providing an elementary service to the local communities in which they are embedded.

[26] See also Stiglitz (2002), p. 22.

What has happened to Greece over the past years clearly illustrates the strong grip of the banking sector, through credit mechanisms, on the world economy, in other words, the disastrous consequences private bankers greed brings to the rest of society, and against which, almost ironically, philosophers from Ancient Greece, such as Plato, had warned.

2.1.8 Preliminary Conclusion

Since the development of the modern banking system (based upon a model of private money creation) in the late Middle Ages, numerous financial crises, the most recent being the severe one of 2007–2008, have painfully demonstrated the perverse nature of the above explained mechanism of private money creation.[27]

Notwithstanding the fact that the intrinsically immoral nature of this private money creation mechanism has been proven for centuries already,[28] one nevertheless has to observe how strongly capitalist societies, even on the level of their highest authorities, continue to cling to this mechanism, causing the sinister "danse macabre" of the model of private money creation to go on and on in all its negative shortcomings.

Thus, the mechanism of private money creation is above all responsible for the fact that the world economy game, in its endless pursuit of ever more economic growth, is mainly driven and controlled by the financial markets, but also for the fact that financial institutions globally have a much higher political power than can be deemed acceptable in so-called democratic societies, next to the fact that global societies are more and more characterised by an excessive polarization between (extremely) rich and poor people.

Nevertheless, the mechanism of private money creation is but one of the mechanisms that attributed to the determinant role of capitalism as the predominant world economic system, as will be further explored hereafter.

2.2 The Modern-Day Capital Company and the Financial Markets to Which It Has Become Subject

2.2.1 The Emergence of the Capital Company Model

In addition to the mechanism of private money creation described in Sect. 2.1, the success of capitalism has further been enhanced by a second legal technique which even so has been developed at the beginning of the capitalist era (and could hence, as is the case with the prevailing monetary and banking system itself, also be

[27] See especially Galbraith (1990).

[28] We can even make the philosophical observation that in the financial world, there is nothing new under the sun (see Ecclesiastes 1:9), as, already centuries ago, Ancient philosophers such as Plato and Aristotle, next to leading religious figures, such as Jesus Christ Himself, but also church fathers of early Christianity, such as Saint Ambrose and Saint Anthony, and later in time, the Scholastic school (with as a notorious representative Saint Thomas Aquinas) and the Franciscan movement (with as one of the most fervent adversaries of bankers greed Saint Anthony of Padua), all have rightly argued that the bank credit mechanism, and especially the technique of charging interests, is the ultimate method for the rich to become ever more rich to the detriment of the poor.

considered as a late-medieval societal construct), namely the so-called "(stock) corporation".

The way the (stock) corporation has been shaped legally from the start even more underlines the determining role of the values of selfishness, greed and egoism as the most important characteristics of the capitalist system.[29]

Historical literature mentions early forms of "capital companies" in certain German areas during the sixteenth century (especially in the mining industry), next to in Holland—with as striking example the notorious "East India company"—and the United Kingdom during the seventeenth century.

Very roughly speaking,[30] the technique of the capital company is such that its founders, in essence entrepreneurs seeking to develop a certain business project, receive legal authority to proceed with the creation of a so-called "legal entity", which becomes solely legally responsible for all legal consequences invoked by the operation of said capital company. To a more or less extent, the founders and/or later shareholders of such a company, but by extension also other "stakeholders" involved in its operation, such as managers, directors and employees, are not, or barely, legally responsible for the actions of the thus created legal entity.

This basic characteristic of the capital company is, from a legal point of view, also known under the description that it grants "(the advantage of) a limited liability", which essentially provides a free licence for an extremely de-responsibilized way of doing business.

The operation of such a capital company is, furthermore, often based on the idea that a large number of underlying shareholders (either individuals or other legal entities) bring together the (starting) capital needed for the basic operation of the enterprise it will conduct, without any of these capital providers being expected to have any kind of other input, or even interest, for the operation of the company.

The only expectation such shareholders have is that, at regular intervals, they can participate in an adequate profit distribution (a so-called "dividend") out of the activities of such a capital company, while, as a general rule, they show very little interest in how the company makes these profits.

Given the high lack of interest of the shareholders in the whereabouts of such a capital company, its management needs in many cases to be entrusted to a group of specially designated directors and managers, which in the course of the twentieth century resulted in the so-called CEO-mechanism which will be elaborated in more detail later. The main tasks of such managers of a capital company became to make as much company profits as possible on behalf of the capital company, so that its shareholders can be satisfied with on regular intervals paid dividends.

As of the seventeenth century, this legal formula started to provide the perfect recipe for legally organizing capitalist enterprises throughout the Western world.

Without encountering any major impediment, among other things because economic activities at that time were hardly subject to any form of government regulations, the capital company thus created also the private legal form for conducting

[29] Galbraith (1990), p. 18; Galbraith (1977), p. 257.

[30] In the awareness that books on this topic have filled entire libraries.

exploitation practices such as slavery, colonialism and imperialism. This further helps explaining why some capital companies grew to immense proportions, very often characterized by an absolutely de-responsibilized management and, because of this, in many cases attributed to a total immorality in the way capitalist businesses got conducted.

In order to continue to feed the shareholders of such capital companies with sufficient dividends, it became indeed necessary to advocate the maximisation of profit (for mere profit's sake) principle to its fullest extent, gradually causing the entire (business) world to sacrifice all other values to this pursuit of profits principle.

Very soon, this pursuit of profits principle resulted in the most harrowing practices of early capitalism, including massive raids in overseas territories in an endless search for new wealth and resources; the development of all types of tradable, often intrinsically useless or barely usable, products[31]; the establishment of the most inhumane systems of exploitation of entire social or ethnic groups, and finally even slave trading and slavery (where people themselves got reduced to mere merchandise).

2.2.2 The Emergence of Financial Markets

The mechanism of the capital company referred to in the previous Sect. 2.2.1 would, furthermore, lead to the development of more refined models of enterprise financing, among which the stock exchange markets (currently: the "organised" or "regulated" financial markets in financial instruments).

It indeed appeared that big enterprises organised in the form of a capital company had such a great need for (new) working capital that collecting it could in many cases no longer easily be organised on a small scale.

To deal with this problem, so called "stock markets" emerged, where capital companies were admitted in order to launch calls to the general saving public, thereby enabling a wide range of savers to subscribe to shares issued by these capi-

[31] As a result of this development, a first wave of "consumerism" emerged where industrial production started to create products by definition useless, and succeeded to convince entire nations of buying these products.

As an early example of the production of such intrinsically useless goods, the rise of Christmas decoration in the Victorian England can be mentioned.

The success of this Christmas decoration industry has later on in history expanded to many other seasonal products, where in the Western world initially mostly classic Christian holidays inspired the introduction of ever more intrinsically useless products. A contemporary illustration of this phenomenon is the practice of buying very expensive children's clothing and holding expansive parties to celebrate the receiving of the communion sacrament by young children. This is in itself a surprising development in light of the doctrine of Jesus of Nazareth who above all preached poverty and who Himself declared that He did not even have a stone to rest his head on (see Luke, 9:58, and Matthew, 8:20).

Later, commerce and industry even started inventing fictitious holidays (such as Valentine and Halloween) to create even more opportunities to produce seasonal nonsense articles.

tal companies (who by this got known as "(capital) corporations").[32] In addition to these "primary stock markets", also so-called "secondary stock markets" emerged where existing shares could be traded among the members of an interested investment public.

Up to this very date, the (primary) listing and (secondary) trading of shares issued by such public corporations are among the basic activities going on the (regulated or not) financial markets and continues to function as the main mechanisms of financing huge capitalist enterprises.

The emergence of these practices would even further enhance the characteristics of capitalism, especially the pursuit of profits principle,[33] next to an enhanced level of de-responsibilisation in the way such corporations were run. As shareholders were offered the opportunity of a smooth tradability of their shares, their intrinsic disinterest in the business activities of the capital companies was also even further enhanced.

In light of the foregoing, it is not a surprise that the shareholders of such stock quoted capital companies, to an ever-increasing extent, got only concerned with the dividends paid out by the company, without any concern for the practices required to generate those profits.

In case these dividend expectations were not sufficiently met, this type of shareholder had no scruples whatsoever in simply selling his shares and re-investing his money in the shares of a more profitable company (a practice which would later be described in the financial jargon as "voting with the feet").

This practice would in its turn cause an even larger degree of de-responsibilisation: the shares of such a capital company barely created a link with the issuing company other than the expectation that enough profit would be distributed (where, in some historical cases, capital companies even started to take up credit to cover the shareholders high dividend expectations, and thus avoid the prices on the stock exchange market of plummeting due to non-fulfilled profit expectations).

---

[32] Galbraith mentions the existence of very primitive stock markets in the Northern-Italian cities Firenze, Venice and Genoa of the fourteenth century. The modern stock markets as we know today arose in the course of the seventeenth century, where the city of Amsterdam played a pioneering role, not only developing the first modern stock market, but at the same time witnessing one of the first large speculative financial crises in history, namely the famous tulip bulbs crisis ("tulpenbollen crisis") (see Galbraith (1990), p. 27).

[33] As Galbraith has phrased it (see Galbraith (1967), p. 109):

> The market has only one message for the business firm. That is the promise of more money. (...) It must try to make money and, as a practical matter, it must try to make as much as possible. Others do. To fail to conform is to invite loss, failure and extrusion. Certainly, a decision to subordinate interest in earnings to an interest in a more contented life for workers, cows or customers would, in the absence of exceptional supplementary income, mean financial disaster. Given this need to maximize revenue, the firm is thus fully subject to the authority of the market.

See furthermore Galbraith (1992), p. 55; Bakan (2005), p. 256; Simonet (1970), p. 47.

These methods of financing enterprises as a result attributed to extreme forms of "short-term thinking" which has become one of the further basic principles of capitalism.

This pillar of capitalist thinking is up to this date widely determining the world economy, albeit again with certain further historical evolutions. Moreover, through the course of history, the former (stock) exchange markets became increasingly more complex, where in addition to the actual shares of capital companies, numerous other financial instruments were developed to address the financing needs of business enterprises, but also to feed the speculative needs of investors, as well as these of specialised financial institutions.

In the current post-industrial world, the financial markets have evolved to a world in itself, largely escaping any type of true government supervision and where with the stroke of a pen or the push of a button, or even in a fully automated way (without any human intervention), financial operations are taking place which determine the fate of large groups of people and even of entire nations.

In all of this, the world economy got more and more governed by a small number of large capital companies where all conceivable values—ranging from labour, ergo the human being providing labour,[34] to the planet itself—have been resolutely sacrificed to the massive pursuit of profits and where, especially since the neo-liberalisation wave which began in the 1980s, states themselves are barely capable of facing any of the detrimental consequences of these capitalist practices.

2.3 Some Final Thoughts on the Capitalist Financing Mechanisms

At present, and based on the different capitalist financing methods which all have their roots in the two abovementioned, medieval mechanisms of financing the capitalist economy (namely the power to create private scriptural money which is attributed to the private banking sector, next to the capital company model and the financial markets that were created to invite investors in financing such companies), over the course of the past two to three centuries, the world economy, and hence the world itself, has step by step been subject to the financial sector's control and the invisible hands directing it.

As a result, to an ever-increasing extent, people themselves have become the slaves of these financial mechanisms (as, in the real world, only people exist, companies and the likes basically being mere fictions of the law by means of which (some) people organise themselves).

The principles governing the financial markets have hereby evolved into so-called "economic laws" to which man is believed to owe a blind obedience.

[34] See the insights of Erich Fromm in this regard, referred to under Sect. 2.4 below.

In the past, it has been demonstrated repeatedly to what distressing situations this may lead, especially each time a (severe) financial crisis occurs. For instance, the last such financial crisis of 2007–2008 not only condemned millions of people to poverty, but it also put a heavy mortgage on the economy of many countries, next to bringing many companies and even entire nations to, or over, the brink of bankruptcy.[35]

Nevertheless, even such financial crises fulfil the true promise of (unbridled) capitalism, namely that the most egoistic, selfish and greedy people, by behaving in the most egoistic, selfish and greedy way possible and, through this, by demonstrating as few (ethical or other) scruples possible when aiming at enriching themselves to the detriment of everything and everyone else, are still able to generate even more profits even out of a financial crisis, a fact which is confirmed by many studies and reports dealing with said financial crisis of 2007–2008.

This for instance helps explaining why since the financial crisis of 2007–2008 the gaps between the rich and the poor have widened even more, and why the financial sector, more than ever, helps to generate the profits which make the very rich even richer, literally by the second. (See also below, under Sect. 4.7.)

2.4 The Subordination of Labour to (The Interests of) Capital

2.4.1 The Idea of Labour as a Mere Cost Factor as the Basis of the Iron Law of the Wages

It has already been briefly mentioned above and it probably goes without saying that capitalism—in addition to being based on the abovementioned mechanism of money creation by the private banking sector, on the capital company model, and on the techniques of financing economic activities through the financial markets—from the very start has also been based on a consciously defined hierarchy between "labour" and "capital".

In the capitalist economic model as it has developed over the centuries under the influence of "economic liberalism" (especially in the eighteenth and nineteenth centuries) and "economic neo-liberalism" (especially in the second half of the twentieth century and in the twenty-first century), enterprises organised as capital companies, or as groups of such companies, mainly focus on making the highest possible profits, to which all other values, including respect for the individual, for society and for the eco-system of the earth itself, have completely become subordinated.[36] (See already above, Sect. 2.2.)

[35] See especially Stiglitz (2010).

[36] On this topic: Byttebier and François (2015), pp. 221–250.

In particular "labour" that needs to be performed in order to, in the real world, make the activities of such enterprises possible, is as a consequence treated exclusively as a mere "cost factor" which needs to be kept as low as possible.[37]

Erich Fromm has in this regard rightly argued that the term "labour market" itself sums up the tragedy which has fallen upon humanity since the rise of capitalism: as a company buys resources, it also buys someone's ability to work to make economic production possible, resulting in the reduction of labour, hence of people performing labour, to mere merchandise.[38] Herbert Marcuse has in the past reached a similar conclusion and has moreover pointed out that this affects all forms of labour, not only hard manual labour which is traditionally used in the industrial sector, but any other form of labour.[39]

According to Fromm, this even has resulted in a complete "dehumanisation" of the people performing such labour being reduced to "hunted" and "bewildered" individuals.[40]

It needs not much further saying that ever since Fromm and Marcuse made these observations, not much has changed but that on the contrary, especially due to the

---

[37] See Stiglitz (2002), p. 10, qualifying this as one of the great "tricks" of neoclassical economies. Stiglitz furthermore points out the differences between labour and the (true) other production factors, with as most important such distinction labour's human aspect (see Stiglitz (2002), p. 10).

See furthermore Oxfam (2017), p. 18:

> Squeezing labour and production costs and minimizing taxes allow corporations to hand an ever-growing proportion of these profits to their owners.

One might even think that, more than a century after his death, the Catholic church has recently done justice to Karl Marx, to the extent that it has taken the following point of view in this ongoing debate:

> What was sadly predicted a century ago has now come true today. Capital annuity can trap and supplant the income from work, which is often confined to the margins of the principal interests of the economic system. Consequently, work itself, together with its dignity, is increasingly at risk of losing its value as a "good" for the human person and becoming merely a means of exchange within asymmetrical social relations. (See Congregation for the Doctrine of the Faith (2018), n° 15.)

[38] Fromm (1979), p. 93.

Fromm has indicated that the process of degradation of man ('s work force) to merchandise has completely eroded personal relations, illustrated by the fact that the only obligation of the employer consists in paying a financial compensation (as low as possible) to the thus "purchased" working man (without any further concern about his personal wellbeing). (Compare to Krugman (1998), p. 15; and to Stiglitz (2002), pp. 10–11.)

Fromm has also argued that, in doing this, capitalism has succeeded in convincing almost every human participating in its processes of the fact that any person only exists to produce labour (hence: to work), which, in economic science, is expressed by referring to labour as to a so-called "production factor". Through this, all interaction between humans has gradually been reduced (not to say: degraded) to merely mechanical socio-economic relations, which can only result in a large extent of alienation which is in present-day societies harrowingly visible, even under the form of cross border replacements of entire nations of people (see Fromm (1990), p. 91).

On qualifying labour as a (mere) production factor, see further Stiglitz (2002), pp. 10–11.

[39] Marcuse (1991), p. 59 a.f.

[40] Fromm (1990), p. 90.

globalisation of the world economy, the entire world is more and more confronted with this reality.[41]

This basic principle of capitalism which is clearly based on manifestly favouring capital above any other value is itself mainly derived from (neo-)liberal economic thinking and translates in several further working principles of capitalism, most notoriously the intent to keep the wages of the people performing labour as low as possible. As a result, any human being whose labour is used in the capitalist economic model is awarded the lowest possible compensation in return. The majority of the returns resulting from enterprises operating according to capitalist principles, indeed need to be "profits" which are primarily allocated to, traditionally, the capital providers of the capital companies (being the legal form under which said enterprises are conducted), and, especially since the twentieth century, the CEO's (and other managers) who are hired to take on the general management of said capital companies.

This basic capitalist principle is in traditional literature also known as the "Iron Law of the Wages".[42]

Particularly since the breakthrough of capitalism in the eighteenth century, this "Iron Law of the Wages" has started to strongly dominate labour relations in most capitalist countries, although through the course of history, some correction methods have been developed. For instance, under the impulse of trade unions and similar organisations (but also of economic doctrines which have attempted to give a more human slant to unbridled capitalism, such as socialism and Keynesianism), during the course of the twentieth century, in certain (especially western) countries, legal and procedural measures have been introduced to protect labour, thus establishing a certain easing of the application of free market mechanisms to labour relations. Obvious examples are the concept of a (by law imposed) minimum wage, in addition to granting all kinds of entitlement to replacement benefits for those who are unable to work, or unable to find a (suitable) job.

Nevertheless, since the seemingly unstoppable rise of neo-liberal thinking from the 1970s and 1980s on, as a result of which, practically on a global scale, a systematic dismantling of many of these correction mechanisms have been strongly advo-

[41] Fromm (1979), p. 80.

In recent times, reference can be made of the increase of mental diseases, such as depressions, burn-outs and similar psychological and mental sicknesses especially in highly capitalistic countries.

[42] See Ricardo (1957).

More on this topic: Byttebier (2015), p. 152, no 282; Byttebier (2017), p. 191.

The abovementioned awareness led John Kenneth Galbraith to the following statement (see Galbraith (1987), p. 84):

> This thought, as the Iron Law of the Wages, was to enter into a history extending far beyond formal economics; it established that those who worked were meant to be poor and were not to be rescued from their poverty by a compassionate state or employer or through trade unions or by other action of their own.

cated and implemented, the Iron Law of the Wages (yet again) controls the operation of the (world) economy more than ever.[43]

In addition to certain other mechanisms (such as the abovementioned private money creation mechanism, next to the inherently unjust character of fiscal policy in most capitalist countries),[44] the "Iron Law of the Wages" is in its different appearances one of the main causes for the increasing polarisation at a socio-economic level, where particularly since the last decades of the twentieth century, the traditional gaps between the "rich"—the small group of people building vast wealth from capital investments and from certain very rewarding forms of independent work (for instance in the entertainment industry and in the specialised consultancy industry)—and the "poor"—the very large group of people who rely on providing labour (in a broad sense of the word) in order to secure their daily needs—has reached unseen levels.[45] (See furthermore, in Sect. 4.7.)

2.4.2 *Some Further Manifestations of the Iron Law of the Wages*

As explained above (see Sect. 2.2), conducting an enterprise under the form a capital company is one of the main methods of legally achieving the (neo-)liberal idea of maximising profits, especially for the benefit of the shareholders of such capital companies and, in modern times, of its CEO (and, by extension, other top-managers).

This model of legally organising businesses also supports the keenest possible price setting of the labour needed to produce and commercialise the goods or services these companies offer on the market. These capital companies which, globally, represent the main category of employers hence strongly advocate and implement the (neo-)liberal principle that wages should be kept as low as possible, because the salaries to be paid are above all considered as costs that need to be kept as low as possible.

This legal working method has, both in the past, as in the present-day context, taken on extreme proportions with an enormous impact on global societies and how they are run.

The most extreme appearance of this economic model is obviously slavery, where the degradation of labour to the interests of capital even happens at the expense of the loss of liberty of the people performing labour who are, "manu militari", forced to provide labour for free.

Reference can obviously be made to some of the Ancient civilisations, with as notorious example the Ancient Roman Empire, whose economies to a large extent

[43] See Byttebier (2015), p. 17, n°s 2 a.f.; Byttebier (2017), p. 231 a.f.

[44] Byttebier (2015, 2017).

[45] Byttebier (2015, 2017).

were based on slave labour. It is hence no coincidence that the breakthrough of capitalism as of the seventeenth and eighteenth centuries has gone hand in hand with the formal reintroduction of slavery in (some of the Southern states of) the USA, albeit that the practices of the European colonial forces of that time were characterized by very similar systems of shameless exploitation of the local inhabitants of colonised areas.[46]

Those who would, nevertheless, be inclined to brush this expression of capitalist working methods under the carpet of historical oblivion should bear in mind that also in our modern world slavery still exists in many countries, where even young children are shamelessly used to serve the craving for ever more profits of (big) capital companies.[47] Furthermore it has to be observed that the American society itself has still not swallowed the bitter pill of slavery, which can be illustrated by the severe integration problems that Afro-Americans, and with them, the rest of American society, still experience today.

An equally alarming example of the capitalist principle that labour should be exploited as cheaply as is possible is obviously the migrant issue. In that sense, populist (political) opinion arguing that the failure to integrate migrants in many western countries has been caused by left-wing thinking (which has, above all, attempted to propagate that migrants should be given a worthy place within the Western societies[48]), whereas in reality the migrant issue directly stems from the capitalist principle that labour should be exploited as cheaply as possible, even if this implies importing cheap labour forces from other countries, is both factually and morally completely wrong.

This method of importing cheap labour forces from other territories, especially to perform hard and hazardous labour, has indeed been used on a massive scale by many capitalist companies in the period after WOII, often even with explicit governmental approval.

However, this mass import of cheap labour, mainly to carry out the less pleasant jobs, has in most cases not been accompanied sufficiently by appropriate measures to effectively integrate the people providing the labour into the societies to which they were artificially drawn, resulting in the known migrant issues which many Western countries are facing today.[49]

---

[46] Harari (2014), p. 368 a.f.

[47] In June 2018, still 40.3 million people were used as slaves in the strict sense of the word. (See www.globalslaveryindex.org; last consulted on June 16, 2018.)

[48] See also Van Lommel (2015), p. 7.

[49] See furthermore Vermeiren (2015), p. 13, containing an interview with Mohamed Benhaddou who, inter alia, stated:

> Look at the figures – I am not making them up – and you will learn that 52% of the Moroccans [in Belgium] live below the poverty line. Compared to the Flemish average: 8 to 10%. Is this a choice of the Moroccans? No, they inherit it. The first generation who came here, in the sixties, were true immigrant workers. Poor people, who had families here in the seventies which were exposed to a growing unemployment. When economy resurged, mainly the natives benefited from this. The second generation was unable to counter this because, meanwhile, discrimination related to work and housing had become a standard. So

Obviously, many other harrowing examples can be given of the inhumane degradation caused by reducing the human being to a mere work force to be used in the capitalist production process at the cheapest price possible.

We shall limit ourselves hereafter in the Sect. 2.4.3 to some such examples within the context of the present-day globalisation of the world economy.

2.4.3 The Iron Law of the Wages in the Modern-Day Globalised Economy

It is indeed even more harrowing that, as a consequence of the neo-liberalisation of the world economy since the 1980s and 1990s, (industrial) production relying on "hard" labour, for which in the period after WOII migrants were "imported" into Western countries, has largely shifted to (even poorer) countries, where labour can be provided at an even lower cost than by the labour forces which in the past were imported from poorer areas into the traditionally rich countries.

In its 2017 report "An economy for the 99%", Oxfam has pointed out how this basic principle of capitalism (in this report referred to as "squeezing wages at the bottom") is up to this very date still prevailing, even within some of the world's most successful and profitable enterprises[50]:

> In the short term, corporate profits are generated by keeping margins high, which means minimizing the cost of inputs like labour. Apple has been particularly successful at this (…). Squeezing wages drives inequality and has a major human cost. Apple is plagued by reports of exhausted workers in China working 12-hour shifts in punitive conditions to produce iPhones and iPads. Workers on low incomes across the world continue to see their wages squeezed, particularly through global supply chains where suppliers compete to provide consumers with the lowest prices. Women are the hardest hit, as they are the most likely to work in precarious and low-paid employment. Cocoa farmers in the 1980s received 16% of value of a chocolate bar; today they get 6%. Recent Oxfam research found poverty wages being paid in Malawi, Vietnam and Kenya by businesses that were supplying some of the UK's most profitable corporations. We calculated that Kenyan flower workers' wages could be doubled if just 5 pence were added to a £4 bunch of roses. In extreme cases, forced labour, also known as modern slavery, can be used to keep corporate costs down while inflicting immeasurable human cost. The ILO estimates that 21 million people are victims of forced labour, which generates an estimated $150bn of profits every year. There is evidence of forced labour from the cotton industry in Uzbekistan to the shrimp farms in Thailand. The world's largest garment companies have all been linked to cotton-spinning mills in India, which routinely use the forced labour of girls. Meanwhile, the gap between the lowest-paid workers and senior executives grows ever wider. Annual share dividends from Zara's parent company to Amancio Ortega –the world's second richest man – are worth €1,108m which is 800,000 times the annual wage of a worker employed by a supplier garment factory in India.

---

you try to get out of that valley. The third generation has something the previous one did not have: to speak fluent Dutch, the will to integrate. But discrimination on the professional and housing markets remains. Even highly educated people face that wall.

[50] See Oxfam (2017), pp. 16–17.

In other words, where previously the application of the (capitalist) "Iron Law of the Wages", in the period after WOII, resulted in massively "importing" labour(ers) to Western countries, this same "Iron Law of the Wages" has, particularly since the 1980s, caused the production of several industrial sectors to move to countries where even cheaper labour forces are abundantly available, thus mainly leaving the formal migrants in the Western world without employment.[51]

As a result, the "Iron Law of the Wages" has also been one of the main causes for the extensive de-industrialisation which, over the last few decades, has caused severe economic problems in many Western countries. The drain of economic production from Western countries to particularly Asian (and to some extent South American) countries is thus creating many and increasingly heavier economic problems for many Western countries. (See also below, Sect. 4.5.)

For instance, the painful financial situation of many Western countries for which it has become increasingly difficult to withdraw sufficient tax income from their collapsing economies, can be mentioned here, especially in light of the fact that the income from large capitals has de facto been granted a status of "fiscal invulnerability", as any real taxation of such income leads to a flight of large capitals to tax paradises.[52] This, in return, also explains that during the past decades many Western countries had to take refuge in debt financing mechanisms (which mainly enrich the financial sector).[53]

Next to other factors, this has also attributed to an ever increasing dismantling of public administrations in many Western countries, for instance characterized by an under financing and understaffing of numerous essential governmental services (such as justice, education, army, police, social security, etc.).[54]

A more thorough description of these particularities of the capital system will be dealt with later in the text (see Chap. 4).

Another as worrying illustration of the impact of the "Iron Law of the Wages" on global economies is the unemployment stemming from the de-industrialisation which is taking place in many Western countries, especially among the least skilled working classes, including to a large extent the descendents of the abovementioned migrant population,[55] resulting in a breeding ground for dissatisfaction and, through this, even extremism.

At the same time, the "Iron Law of the Wages" also results in the fact that businesses and other institutions vested in countries with a high level of unemployment, nevertheless advocate that people who are still employed should work as much as possible and that the highest results have to be achieved with the smallest possible

---

[51] Krugman (1998), p. 82.

[52] Stiglitz (2002), p. 13.

This problem is also extensively dealt with in Byttebier (2015), p. 206 a.f., and in Byttebier (2017), p. 249 a.f., with many further references and illustrations. See also further in Sect. 4.6.

[53] See the overview table in Byttebier (2015), p. 197 a.f., n° 347 and in Byttebier (2017), p. 235 a.f.

[54] See Byttebier (2015), p. 214 a.f., no 360, particularly the illustration "De impact van de afkalving van de overheidsfinanciering op het Vlaamse, academische weefsel".

[55] As regards Belgium, see more in particular Lippens (2015), p. 16.

staff, implying that the very often thinly spread personnel of capitalist enterprises, next to many other institutions, has to cope with an extremely high work pressure (= the modern-day "doing more with less (means)"-principle).

As a result, in many businesses and other institutions, "rationalisation exercises" have been taking place for many years now, practically always resulting in the fact that more work needs to be performed by fewer people, a phenomenon which goes hand in hand with an increase in work related mental health problems.[56] Meanwhile, there are even sectors, such as the aviation sector, where young workforces have to fund themselves to gain professional experience (= the so-called "pay to fly"-principle),[57] a practice that takes society back to the way Middle Age Guilds worked.

2.4.4 *Conclusion*

To summarize, the "Iron Law of the Wages" ensures that producers and merchants (in the widest sense of these terms), but increasingly also many other institutions employing people which have become subject to the neo-liberal logic (such as hospitals; universities…), have an ever growing tendency to make use of the cheapest labour possible, which in extreme cases results in actual slavery, in importing cheap labour forces from other countries or areas, next to other social migratory phenomena, and in the delocalisation of industries to low-wage countries, in turn having

[56] End March 2015, a plane crash became world news. An Airbus A320-200 of Germanwings crashed between the French Prads-Haute-Bléone and Barcelonnette. Psychological problems of the co-pilot Andreas Lubitz of the airplane were indicated as the main cause.

In an interview with a Belgian co-pilot in response to this disaster, this co-pilot witnessed the following (see Smout (2015), p. 3) (own free translation):

> Companies want as much work as possible done with the lowest number of people. Many studies of unions, as well as surveys are available – hard facts about pilots often being depressed or anxious – but no-one cares. During trade union negotiations, these facts are just ignored. (…) Fly, eat, sleep, that is all which is left in life. Your social support weakens. There is no more safety net. If you work full time, you barely have a private life. Especially in low cost, but everything is low cost these days. (…) In addition, many young pilots suffer from a huge burden of debt. 100 to 200,000 euro for a general training, plus 30,000 euro for training costs for a specific aircraft. It takes a long time to fill this gap and this generates stress. And nowadays, fixed contracts are very scarce.

See also Anonymous (2015a), pp. 4–5; Meeussen (2015), p. 17.

The tone of this testimony bears witness of very similar evolutions which during the past years have taken place in the Flemish academic world, but also in Belgian justice, probably next to many other sectors.

In 2018, similar press coverage on the working conditions of Belgian pilots furthermore demonstrated that the problems have in the mean time not been dealt with. On May 12th 2018, it was hence reported upon in the press that a large part of the Belgian pilots had underwritten an open letter, in which they massively complained about the appalling working conditions prevailing in the airway sector and in which they announced a strike for the next week. (See GJS (2018).)

[57] Meeussen (2015), p. 17.

resulted in a wave of de-industrialisation which has meanwhile been going on for decades in many Western countries and which in return poses a serious threat to the Western welfare state model.

It may even be feared that, as long as a worldwide uniform system of protecting labour, i.e. the human beings performing such labour, remains lacking, that the "Iron Law of the Wages", particularly in combination with the abovementioned capitalist financial models, will continue to contribute to the fact that a large portion of the world population lives on the edge of, or below, the poverty line, and that the ongoing polarisation between the (very) rich and the (very) poor will enhance even more. (See furthermore Sects. 4.7 and 4.9.)

2.5 The Questionable Hero Status of the CEO's of (Large) Capital Companies

In spite of the abovementioned (or, possibly, in order to keep applying the classic capitalist mechanisms, so especially the abovementioned "Iron Law of the Wages", in modern times as much as possible intact), particularly during the twentieth century, a very specific type of labour emerged which largely escaped becoming subject to the abovementioned "Iron Law of the Wages".

Implied is "labour" consisting of "managing" or "leading"[58] a capital company based on a de-responsibilised shareholdership and which operates by using the labour of others at the lowest possible prices.

It can hereby be observed that especially when the "founding father" of a capital company gets out of the picture, those who inherit the control over such a capital company often lack the (management) skills to lead the company as successfully, and are therefore inclined to attract a third person as its CEO. In other cases, a capital company simply becomes too large; and/or, as a result of how financial markets operates, is faced with a magnitude of small shareholders (institutional or not); and/or its organisation is being split into different subsidiaries, causing the company to no longer be able to be led efficiently by one single person.

Paul Krugman has argued that the CEO's of capital companies (especially the so-called "Berle and Means"-companies[59]), where the collection of capital takes place on the financial markets and as a consequence of which the highly dispersed shareholdership can no longer ensure effective corporate governance mechanisms itself, in essence determine their own working conditions, including their pay, and

[58] Or to a segment of such a business.

[59] In the field of law and economics, "The Modern Corporation and Private Property" is a famous book that was written by Adolf Berle and Gardiner Means and was published in 1932–1933. The book deals with the principles of American corporate law, more specifically with the evolution of big business under capitalism through a legal and economic lens. (See Berle and Means (1932–1933). See also https://en.wikipedia.org/wiki/The_Modern_Corporation_and_Private_Property; last consulted on June 16, 2018.)

face but one "brake", namely "external anger", for instance in case the media starts paying attention to the fact that their remuneration is way too high.[60]

This also explains why, especially in large capital companies, the general management is entrusted to specialised managers in exchange for very high management remunerations which in many cases are an excessively large multiple (in some cases hundreds of times more) of the wages paid to the other workers who in reality are as important for such companies to reach their objectives.

Through this, these managers avoid, to a large extent, being subjected to the abovementioned "Iron Law of the Wages" themselves, albeit that, at the same time, it becomes their duty, within the companies which they lead, to apply the "Iron Law of the Wages" as excessively and mercilessly as possible on the other people employed by these companies. As a result, the ratio between the remuneration of the (top) managers and the wages of the other workers can be identified as one of the main (further) causes of the increasing polarisation between the rich and the poor within global societies.

It can even be held that the model of a capital company led by an excessively expensive CEO who has, amongst other things, a mission to minimise the costs of his company, among which the wages of the other employees, seems to have globally conquered all segments of the economic environment—going from classic production enterprises, to mere service providers, such as for instance large consultancy and law firms[61]—through which it can even be stated that globally, the organisation of business is increasingly affected by a high level of injustice in the classic Aristotelian meaning of the word.[62]

---

[60] See Krugman (2005), pp. 125–126:

> In practice, modern C.E.O.'s set their own compensation, limited only by the "outrage constraint" – outrage not on the part of the board, whose members depend on the C.E.O.'s good will for many of their perks, but on the part of outside groups that can make trouble. And the true purpose of many features of executive pay packages is not to provide incentives but to provide "camouflage" – to let C.E.O.'s reward themselves lavishly while minimizing the associated outrage.

[61] See Byttebier (2015), p. 175 a.f., no 316, especially the illustration "Kapitalistische praktijken van bepaalde internationale advocatenkantoren". See also Byttebier (2017), p. 197, especially the illustration "Capitalist Practices of Certain International Law Firms".

[62] Byttebier (2015), pp. 242–243, no 416, making reference to the works of Aristotle who provided the following (relatively simple) and (probably because of this) up till today very convincing interpretation of the concept "justice":

> Injustice on the contrary is similarly related to that what is unjust, which is a disproportionate excess or deficiency of something beneficial or harmful. Hence injustice is excess and defect, in the sense that it results in excess and defect: namely, in the offender's own case, an excess of anything that is generally speaking beneficial and a deficiency of anything harmful, and in the case of others, though the result as a whole is the same, the deviation from proportion may be in either direction as the case may be. (See Aristotle (1996), p. 125.)

In this Aristotelian approach, a (disproportionate degree of) "inequality" – in the way it determines socio-economic relations world-wide today – is "unjust" by definition, where there is mention of "committing injustice" on the part of those who, disproportionately have too much (of what is good), and "suffering from injustice" on the part of those who, equally disproportionately, have not enough (of what is good) (see Aristotle (1996), p. 124 a.f.).

More and more it can be observed that the larger (in the sense of revenue, number of employees, profits, market share...) such a capital company becomes, the stronger the abovementioned principle applies, fully demonstrating a strong correlation between individualism, greed and selfishness and successful entrepreneurship under the premises of (neo-liberal) capitalism.

Within economic neo-liberal thinking, there has even been attempted to "rationalise" as far as possible this business model where an excessively paid CEO leads a large capital company. Especially during the second half of the twentieth century on, this has led to a blind belief in the so-called "genius principle".

This "genius principle" holds that a CEO (or another leading person leading a (large) capital company), who has succeeded in getting himself in the spotlight as a so-called "genius" within his or her sector—which in practice is often also the consequence of a lot of bravura and/or of a good couturier and marketing campaign, where being proclaimed "manager of the year" in one or other weekly magazine or journal is very often a good stepping stone—will later on hardly be questioned within the company that he or she leads. Out of a mix of admiration, fear and a pursuit to get ahead, but even so through flattery, most employees of the company led by such a genius CEO will hardly dare to question any plan or objective proposed by him or her (and this, obviously, up to the moment where everything goes really wrong, as for instance in the case of bankruptcy or, as regards private banks, in case of the need for a bail-out under which the failure of the genius of such a manager is passed on to public budgets, i.e. wider society, at a high social cost).[63]

Also the boards of directors of such capital companies which are assumed, under a theoretical corporate-governance model, to "monitor" (and where needed to "adjust" the management of) such a CEO, usually fail to really counterbalance the power of such a CEO.[64]

This alleged "genius" status of such CEOs (and other leading managers) in turn provides the so-called objective justification for the often extremely high fees granted to such CEO (or similar senior managers).

On the downside, it can be observed that, in order to justify their extremely high remunerations, this type of alleged "genius" CEOs will sometimes resort to an aggressive, rash, often megalomaniac, sometimes even truly idiotic management style, above all aimed at making short-term profits, of which the operation of the bank sector since the 1980s delivers an extreme example. As a consequence, according to for instance Galbraith (already in 1992 (!)), the worst mistakes in the banking industry are often made by the highest ranking managers (who no-one indeed dares to question) and also involve the largest thinkable amounts,[65] an observation which is thus the more striking in light of the heavy financial crisis of 2007–2008.

---

[63] Galbraith (1990), p. 16; Loizou (2012), p. 59 and 281 a.f.

[64] Krugman (2005), pp. 125–126; Galbraith (1992), pp. 59–61.

[65] Galbraith (1992), p. 60.

These findings relentlessly expose the core problem of capitalist economies, more precisely the rule of unbridled egoism since the works of Adam Smith.[66] Especially the positioning and behaviour of CEOs (of large capital companies)—in addition to those of other professional segments, for instance specialised consultants who claim similar excessive remunerations—should be reconsidered in light of the severe financial crisis of 2007–2008, as the latter itself was caused by the application of neo-liberal principles and working methods, including the principle that economic agents must behave as selfishly as possible, next to the abovementioned "greed is good"-credo.[67]

2.6 The State as Nemesis of the Free Market

2.6.1 The Viewpoint of Economic (Neo-)liberalism on the Role of the State in General

Since Adam Smith's writings, economic liberalism (and later in history: economic neo-liberalism) has strongly expressed an extremely high distrust towards states and other public authorities.

Under liberal and neo-liberal thinking, states entering the socio-economic order in order to establish more fair wealth distribution mechanisms are basically seen as collective organisation methods aiming at depriving individuals in general, and the (rich) entrepreneurs more specifically, of their freedom and of their legitimately earned wealth.

Based upon this starting premise, both the doctrines of economic liberalism and economic neo-liberalism argue that the socio-economic role of the state needs to be kept as moderate as possible.[68]

For neo-liberals more specifically, state organisation is only expected to create a framework in which the free market can achieve its full potential. It has even been held that states should not bear any consideration for the weaker within society at all; on the contrary, under the theoretical argument that everybody is equal and has equal opportunities, weaker members of society should be left to their fate, so that they are encouraged to look after themselves.

---

[66] Those who doubt this statement are advised to read "The virtue of selfishness" of the neo-liberal author Ayn Rand (see Rand (1992)), and to hereby consider that the line of thinking and the world views presented by this author have produced—and continue to produce—an important source of inspiration for many policy makers (e.g. former president of the Federal Reserve Alan Greenspan) and managers.

[67] See furthermore Byttebier (2015), p. 383, endnote 12; Byttebier (2017), p. 4.

[68] Compare Chomsky (2017), p. 71.

2.6.2 *The Aim of Economic Neo-liberalism of Dismantling (Welfare) States*

2.6.2.1 On Some of the Theoretical Neo-liberal Arguments for Dismantling the Welfare State Model

Already Adam Smith expressed an extreme degree of state aversion, especially in the socio-economic field, for instance when fostering the opinion that large infrastructure works need to be left to the private initiative and should not even be financed by the government and/or out of by public funds[69]; Smith also expressed the opinion that the work of state officials in organising collective life does not, or hardly, adds any added value,[70] an opinion which up till today provides a favourite "leitmotiv" among those advocating neo-liberal ideology.

Bearing this in mind, it is no surprise that, already in the nineteenth century, the application of economic liberalism would lead to a global restriction of state intervention in (socio-)economic life.[71]

This state aversion became even much stronger under the theories of economic neo-liberalism[72] that mainly consider states and governments as a "burden",[73] especially when they have the audacity to enter the field of socio-economic relations.

As a consequence, as of the 1970s–1980s, a large-scale neo-liberal offensive has kicked off aimed at reducing global state intervention to the minimum in socio-economic order areas, in order to scale down the social accomplishments of, in the USA, doctrines such as Keynesianism, and, especially in Western European countries, of trade unions and of socialism to establish mechanisms of social welfare.[74]

The ideal world of economic neo-liberalism is one where enterprises can freely act and remain unhindered by anyone or anything which could slow down their unbridled pursuit of profits and economic growth.

All this is condoned with reference to an approach towards economy dating back to the works of Adam Smith himself, also known as the "trickle down economics", a doctrine which assumes that entrepreneurs are the only positive forces within society, implying that only in a world where they can conduct their affairs freely and in an undisturbed manner, the highest possible welfare will be obtained and that the large masses of incompetent people will be able to benefit from this, even if the latter, by definition, do not express as much zeal to help progress humanity as entrepreneurs themselves do.

---

[69] Smith (1979), Volume II, p. 724.

[70] O'Rourke (2007), p. 73.

[71] Van Houtte (1942), p. 181.

[72] Rand (2008), p. 95; Rand (1992), p. 37.

[73] Galbraith (1992), p. 23.

[74] Krugman (1998), p. 29; Sterdyniak (2011), p. 21 a.f.

Among the most early examples of extreme neo-liberal governments were: the one of Ronald Reagan in the USA, and the one of Margaret Thatcher in the United Kingdom (both in the 1980s). (See, furthermore, Sect. 3.5.2).

This viewpoint would, as of the 1970s, lead to new state theories based upon the basic idea that markets should never be controlled by the state, but precisely the opposite.[75]

This has resulted in an environment where the state has a clear objective as regards making the free market performing optimal[76]:

- The state has (always) to respond to the needs of the market, whether through monetary, fiscal and labour policy, immigration policy, the treatment of criminals, organizing social care or providing public services, such as public education.

  Neoliberal rationality hereby indexes the state's success in accordance with its ability to sustain and foster the free market and, moreover, ties state legitimacy to such success.

  Needless to say that this presents a form of legitimation that clearly contrasts with the (historical) notion of the constitutional, democratic state as the universal representative of the people.
- The state can only be enfolded and animated by market rationality: that is, not simply "profitability", but moreover a generalized calculation of cost(s) and benefit(s) becoming the measure of all state objectives and practices.

  Political discourse on all matters gets hereby framed in mere entrepreneurial terms; the state must not simply concern itself with making markets as free as possible, but has itself think and behave like a (free) market actor across all of its functions, including law.
- Putting the foregoing points together, the health and growth of the economy becomes the (sole) basis of state legitimacy, both because the state is forthrightly responsible for the health of the economy and because of the economic rationality to which state practices have become submitted.

  As a result, the slogan "It's the economy, stupid" becomes the sole guiding principle of the state's legitimacy and the sole basis for all state action — from constitutional adjudication and campaign finance reform, to welfare and education policy, to foreign policy, including warfare and the organization of "homeland security."

Anything hindering this state's rational of making the economy grow is, by definition, considered detrimental, where it hence becomes the state's duty to eliminate such elements.

Under these premises, as of the 1980s, an unprecedented attack on the welfare state model emerged which is still ongoing as of today.

We shall deal with this further under Sect. 3.5.

[75] See Brown (2003).

[76] The arguments have been developed by Brown (2003).

2.6.2.2 Methods of Dismantling the Welfare State Model

Among the concrete measures promoted by the neo-liberal economics schools, as effectively implemented by many neo-liberal or neo-liberal inclined governments, from the 1980s and 1990s on until the present day, one may mention: the privatisation of public companies[77]; the deregulation of the economy[78]; the liberalisation of trade and industry; the liberalisation of the capital markets[79]; extensive tax reductions especially benefiting the richer classes (as taxes are seen as a an impediment to individual liberty and to entrepreneurship providing general welfare); monetary measures aimed at fighting inflation (even when causing an increase in unemployment); the constraining of trade unions (see especially the open war fought by Margaret Thatcher with the British trade unions, in addition to, for instance, in the current Belgian context, the ongoing conflicts of the neo-liberal government Michel I with different Belgian trade unions); a reduction of public expenditure (also when aimed at financing social services); the general reduction of the role of government in the socio-economic tissue of society; the expansion of the international markets, and the elimination of controls on global money and capital flows.[80]

A further central technique of "(neo-)liberalising" the economy has been so-called "monetarism". Amongst others, through the writings of Milton Friedman (1912–2006),[81] since the 1980s and 1990s, an important focus got placed on the operation of the money and capital markets, with a central role for central banking as a mechanism steering the economy.[82] Particularly during the period in which Alan Greenspan was the president of the American Federal Reserve, this would degenerate into an "era of an (uncontrolled) credit economy", often referred to as one of the main causes for the severe financial crisis of 2007–2008 (and the massive recession which has since resulted).[83]

Economic neo-liberalism, moreover, especially aims at reducing the number of people on the states' payroll. State officials, in the widest sense of the word, such as

---

[77] Bakan (2005), p. 117; Kruithof (2000), p. 205 a.f.

[78] Krugman (2009), p. 65; Stiglitz (2003), p. 143.

[79] For the effects thereof, see Stiglitz (2002), p. 13:

> Capital market liberalization enhances the bargaining power of capital: effectively, it gives "capital" the right to announce that if it is taxed unduly, or if other measures that it dislikes are adopted, it will leave the country. It enhances the threat point of capital, and therefore tilts the outcome more in its favour. In the extreme, it means that capital cannot be taxed at all.

[80] Steger (2013), p. 42.

[81] See Friedman (2002). See also Krugman (1994), p. 34 a.f.

[82] Galbraith, mentioning "the monetary illusion", had taken an opposite position on this topic already a long time before; see Galbraith (1974), pp. 187–197. See also Galbraith (1992), p. 88 a.f.; Galbraith and Salinger (1978), p. 86 a.f.

[83] Stiglitz (2010), pp. 9, 87–88 and 261, having held:

> Perhaps the worst outcome arose when the Chicago School and the wage-price rigidity school got together to shape monetary policy, in their fight against inflation.

(public) education teaching staff whose pay is financed out of tax money, are by definition, highly suspect: according to most neo-liberal thinkers, they are unproductive and only represent a cost for society, hence their numbers should be kept as low as possible.[84]

Under the theories of economic (neo-)liberalism, it can obviously never be the role of the state to set up mechanisms of redistributing wealth or of supporting the poor,[85] as these make "the competent"[86] within society unfree and subject to taxes which only serve "the incompetent" who do not deserve such support as their misery is caused by their own laziness.

This also helps explaining why only the poor and middle classes can be taxed (or subjected to social security contributions) in order to finance systems of mutual solidarity. On the contrary, the rich should remain as much as possible exempt from such taxation (or from paying social security contributions), in order to allow them to continue to focus on the creation of welfare for everyone (in accordance with the liberal and neo-liberal "trickle down economics"-doctrine). Economic neo-liberalism thus keeps on expressing the idea that poverty (bur for instance also the ongoing polarisation between rich and poor; see further Sect. 4.7), are but logical consequences of effort and responsibility, or a lack of them. Hence, such phenomena should not arouse concern and may certainly not lead to any type of state intervention to tackle them.

Putting these models in practice, the destructive state philosophy of economic neo-liberalism[87] has, in many countries, lead to a weakening, sometimes even a dismantling, of states under the further implicit reasoning that anything that can provide profits should, by definition, be taken away from the state (= so-called "privatization of gains").[88] In the wake of this implementation of neo-liberal doctrines, the state's authority has in many countries increasingly been usurped by the forces of large capital which, in this way, furthermore through the funding of electoral media campaigns, as well as through mechanisms of lobbying and (disguised) bribery, has been able to acquire a much greater hold on power than could

---

[84] This policy principle has by now been adopted by the Flemish government for decades already, having caused an underfinancing of Flemish education institutions at all levels. The neo-liberal ratio behind it has been bluntly (and in a most insulting manner) expressed by the former Flemish Minister of Education Pascal Smet when he defended the Flemish "doing more with less (means)"-policy by stating that university professors should finally start working a bit more like the rest of society. (See ILO (2010).)

[85] As Chomsky puts it (see Chomsky (2015), p. 34):

> in a society in which a "vigorous appetite for income and wealth" is extolled as the highest good (…), it is difficult – subversive of the prevailing ideology, in fact – to mobilize popular support for the public welfare or to meet human needs, however desperate they may be.

[86] The terminology is of Ayn Rand.

[87] Kruithof (2000), p. 58.

[88] Kruithof (2010), p. 73.

legitimately be expected from a democratic point of view. In more recent literature, this phenomenon has been described as "corporatocracy".[89]

Neo-liberal thinking thus also provides the theoretical justification for rich and large enterprises to behave in a totally tax-averse and tax-evasive manner,[90] which has resulted in completely unjust taxation systems on a global scale (= the so-called "great tax failure"). The methods of fiscal policy-making, based upon undemocratic methods of corporatocratic policy formation, are a further striking illustration of this phenomenon.[91] (See also further, under Sect. 4.6.)

To illustrate the latter, reference can, for instance, be made to the Oxfam 2017 report "An economy for the 99%",[92] in which it has been stated:

---

[89] On the way lobbying works, see Krugman (2008), p. 166.

Already in 1978, Galbraith described the problem of "corporatocracy" (albeit not yet using this term), in a very clear and blunt manner as follows:

> The American oil companies, large and small, control a certain number of members of the Congress and handle them pretty much as the performers in a puppet show manipulate their puppets. A squeeze there and the arms respond and the voice squeaks yes. It's very possible the greatest scandal in our political life, much more damaging to the public interest than Watergate. (See Galbraith and Salinger (1978), p. 142.)

[90] See already, next to the attention given to this topic in the present-day press, the analysis of Galbraith (1992), p. 26.

[91] Sachs (2011), pp. 116–117.

See even Congregation for the Doctrine of the Faith (2018), n° 30:

> Today, more than the half of the commercial world is orchestrated by noteworthy persons that cut down their tax burden by moving the revenues from one site to another according to their convenience, transferring the profits into fiscal havens, and the costs into the countries of higher taxation. It appears clear that all these have removed decisive resources from the actual economy and contributed to the creation of economic systems founded on inequality. Furthermore, it is not possible to ignore the fact that those *offshore* sites, on more occasions, have become usual places of recycling dirty money, which is the fruit of illicit income (thefts, frauds, corruption, criminal associations, mafia, war booties etc.)
>
> Thereby disguising the fact that the so-called *offshore* operations do take place in their official financial places, some States have consented to obtain profit even from crimes, thinking however of not being responsible as the crimes did not take place formally under their jurisdiction. This represents, from the moral point of view, an evident form of hypocrisy.
>
> And furthermore at n° 31:
>
> All this, while contributing grave damage to the good functionality of the actual economy, indicates a structure that, as it is formed today, seems to be totally unacceptable from the ethical point of view. Hence, it is necessary and urgent to prepare at the international level the suitable remedies to those unjust systems. Above all, practicing financial transparency at every level, (for example, the obligation of public accountability for the multinational companies of the respective activities and the taxes paid in each country in which they operate through their subsidiary groups) along with incisive sanctions, imposed on those countries that repeat the dishonest practices (tax evasion and avoidance, recycling of dirty money) mentioned above.

[92] Oxfam (2017), p. 5.

> Many of the super-rich also use their power, influence and connections to capture politics and ensure that the rules are written for them. Billionaires in Brazil lobby to reduce taxes, and in São Paulo would prefer to use helicopters to get to work, flying over the traffic jams and broken infrastructure below. Some of the super-rich also use their fortunes to help buy the political outcomes they want, seeking to influence elections and public policy. The Koch brothers, two of the richest men in the world, have had a huge influence over conservative politics in the US, supporting many influential think tanks and the Tea Party movement and contributing heavily to discrediting the case for action on climate change. This active political influencing by the super-rich and their representatives directly drives greater inequality by constructing "reinforcing feedback loops' in which the winners of the game get yet more resources to win even bigger next time.

Neo-liberal state aversion is, consequently, poignantly expressed in the chronic underfinancing of state operations in many countries, with as one of the main causes the fact that, within global societies, the rich and the very rich are too well treated from a fiscal point of view.

This even explains why, to a growing extent, states massively have to resort to debt financing in order to overcome budget shortages. (See furthermore, in Sect. 4.6.) Otherwise put, while some of the most basic methods of classic capitalism—among which the private money-making mechanism and the "Iron Law of the Wages"—are already on their own causing a small group of individuals to become ever more rich at the detriment of the rest of mankind, and while the same rich classes above all aim at instilling tax evasion techniques, states themselves are as a result forced to turn to skimming the (much lower) incomes of the poor and middle classes and to resort to debt finance in case taxing the low and middle classes does not generate a sufficient income. During the past decade, this traditional effect of neo-liberal economic policy has even been further enhanced due to the bailouts of financial institutions in the aftermath of the severe financial and/or bank crisis of 2007–2008, and since then numerous countries have found themselves in heavy financial problems,[93] causing them even more to turn to (expensive) debt financing.

By now, the debt burden of many (Western) countries has grown to almost unpronounceable proportions, where it has even become difficult to find precise data thereof (to the extent that one could even wonder if this is done deliberately).[94] (See furthermore, in Sect. 4.6.)

The neo-liberal answer to this problem has, at least in many European countries, been that states should reduce (even) more their expenditures, making the neo-liberal "wet dream" to further reduce social care systems and other services financed through public means even more turned into reality.

There are, however, certain roles for the state that may be enhanced in accordance with the doctrines of economic neo-liberalism.

---

[93] Stiglitz refers to the "bailouts" in the bank sector as one of the greatest schemes of redistribution of wealth (in favour of the rich to the detriment of the poor) of our times (see Stiglitz (2010), p. 200).

[94] See for instance the website http://www.nationaldebtclocks.org/ (last consulted on June 16, 2018).

For instance, a state must fully invest in security, on an internal level through police forces who are to protect the property and the interests of the rich,[95] and on an external level through the organisation of strong armies designed to defend the prosperous country's own position against the displeasure arising in (other) countries which, often due to their exposure to the capitalist principles of oppression and exploitation, have remained poor, or even to bring other country's wealth under the control of one's own enterprises.

Similarly, a state is expected to grant (even very large) subsidies to large enterprises, since they are the only institutions providing for welfare and prosperity, next to, for instance, when needed, to protect ailing banks from bankruptcy, since banks are deemed of absolute necessity within the capitalist economy.

It hereby is of no concern at all that such support measures have to take place in direct opposition to the most basic free market-principles themselves.[96]

In light of the foregoing, it may be obvious that the doctrines of economic neo-liberalism, especially when implemented in practice (see furthermore, under Sect. 3.5.), are increasingly endangering past achievements aimed at creating a more just society, especially in the field of socio-economic order.

On a more philosophical level, one has however to admit how well the attack on the welfare state model by economic neo-liberalism has been succeeding in accomplishing its general objective of completely turning around the historical hierarchy of values, and through this in shaping global societies in accordance with a world view where altruism is considered being "bad" and egoism is endorsed as the highest possible virtue (see in an extreme manner in Ayn Rand's book "The virtue of selfishness").

2.6.3 Conclusion

Probably more than ever in history, for the average person functioning within (unbridled) capitalist societies in an era where the theories of economic neo-liberalism are succeeding in eliminating, one by one, earlier in history developed

---

[95] The figures on the number of deaths in the USA following a police intervention are sobering (see Agorist (2015)):

> On average, US police kill people at a rate 70 times higher than any of the other first world countries as they "protect and serve" the American citizens. (…) The deaths follow a national pattern: suspects were mostly people of color, mentally ill, or both.

[96] Chomsky (2017), pp. 83–88. As Chomsky has phrased it:

> Each time, the taxpayer is called on to bail out those who created the crisis, increasingly the major financial institutions. In a capitalist economy, you wouldn't do that. In a capitalist system, that would wipe out the investors who make risky investments. But the rich and powerful, they don't want a capitalist system. They want to be able to run to the "nanny state" as soon as they're in trouble, and get bailed out by the taxpayer. They're given a government insurance policy, which means that no matter how often you risk everything, of you get in trouble, the public will bail you out because you're too big to fail – and it's just repeating over and over again. (See Chomsky (2017), pp. 84–85)

soci(et)al correction methods to unbridled capitalism, the banners of "equality" and "freedom" under which neo-liberal ideas are expressed (see below, in Chap. 3), are nothing more than an illusion, where in reality the average human being increasingly becomes the prisoner of a ruthless socio-economic exploitation model.

It can, hence, not come as a surprise that impoverishment is advancing, even in the Western world. For instance, since the financial crisis of 2007–2008, just in the USA, one out of six people are said to rely on food banks in order to meet their daily food needs, and also in neo-Thatcher United Kingdom food banks are among the fastest developing institutions in society. Elsewhere on the European continent, many public and social services are, to a growing extent, at stake, such as systems of public education[97] and public health care. (See furthermore Sects. 4.7 and 4.9.)

An extremely worrying example in the Belgian context could, for instance, be read in a press release of February 2015, reporting that pregnant women were at that time encouraged by social services to abort a foetus with Down-syndrome,[98] demonstrating that the neo-liberal opinion that the incompetent should be left to their fate, is gradually leading to eradication practices which earlier in history have been considered to be of a fascist nature. Also, the fact that in the Netherlands the treatment of certain diseases, such as cancer, are no longer financed by social insurance,[99] displays the same neo-liberal opinion that (profit) figures are more important than human lives.

In Chap. 4, it shall be further explained and illustrated to what kind of society the implementation of these neo-liberal principles is leading, but not after Chap. 3 will address a number of, at first glance, less obvious legal mechanisms than those referred to in this chapter which have attributed in shaping the (neo-)liberal capitalist socio-economic order.

References

Agorist M (2015) American cops just killed more people in March than the UK did in the entire 20th century (article of 6 April 2015). http://thefreethoughtproject.com/american-cops-killed-people-month-march-uk-entire-20th-century/. Last consulted 16 June 2018

Anonymous (2015a) Getuigenis. Jonge copiloot van lagekostenmaatschappij getuigt over de moeilijke werksituatie. Ik hou van job maar ik haat sector. De Morgen, 28 March 2015, pp 4–5

Anonymous (2015b) België kiest massaal voor uitroeiing kinderen met Down (article of 18 February 2015). http://www.knack.be/nieuws/gezondheid/belgie-kiest-massaal-voor-uitroeiing-kinderen-met-down/article-normal-534373.html. Last consulted 16 June 2018

Aristotle (1996) The Nicomachean Ethics (trans: Rackham H). Wordsworth Editions Limited, Hertfordshire

Bakan J (2005) The corporation. The pathological pursuit of profit and power. Constable & Robinson Ltd, London

[97] As a further illustration, reference can for instance be made to the objective of democratising higher education and universities in Belgium, which has not been reached according to a recent OECD report.

[98] Anonymous (2015b).

[99] de Vreede (2014).

Berle A, Means G (1932–1933) The modern company and private property. Macmillan, New York
Bogaert R, Brion R, Jurgan-Van Hentenryk G, Moreau LJ, Van Der Wee H (2000) A history of European Banking. Mercatorfonds and European Investment Bank, Antwerp (also: Bogaert R, Jurgan-Van Hentenryk G, Van Der Wee H (1991) De Bank in Europa. 25 eeuwen Bankgeschiedenis. Mercatorfonds, Antwerp; Bogaert R, Jurgan-Van Hentenryk G, Van Der Wee H (1991) La banque and Occident. Mercatorfonds, Antwerp)
Brown W (2003) Neo-liberalism and the end of liberal democracy. Theory Event 7(1). http://lchc.ucsd.edu/cogn_150/Readings/brown.pdf. Last consulted 16 June 2018
Byttebier K (2015) Nu het gouden kalf verdronken is. Van hebzucht naar altruïsme als hoeksteen voor een Nieuwe Monetaire Wereldorde. Maklu, Antwerp
Byttebier K (2017) Towards a new international monetary order. In: Byttebier K, van der Borght K (eds) Economic and financial law & policy – shifting insights & values, vol I. Springer, Cham
Byttebier K, François A (2015) For-profit or not-for-profit? That's the question. Profit maximization in company law: myth or (legal) reality? In: Cornelis L (ed) Finance and law: twins in trouble. Intersentia, Antwerp, pp 221–250
Chomsky N (2015) Masters of mankind. Penguin Random House UK
Chomsky N (2017) Requiem for the American dream. The 10 principles of concentration of wealth & power. Seven Stories Press, New York
Cole G (1937) Practical economics. Penguin Books, London
Congregation for the Doctrine of the Faith – Dicastery For Promoting Integral Human Development (2018) Oeconomicae et pecuniariae quaestiones – Considerations for an ethical discernment regarding some aspects of the present economic-financial system. http://www.vatican.va/roman_curia/congregations/cfaith/documents/rc_con_cfaith_doc_20180106_oeconomicae-et-pecuniariae_en.html. Last consulted 16 June 2018
de Vreede J (2014) In Nederland opgegeven, in België genezen van kanker (article of 19 April 2014). http://www.hln.be/hln/nl/957/Binnenland/article/detail/1858580/2014/04/19/In-Nederland-opgegeven-in-Belgie-genezen-van-kanker.dhtml. Last consulted 16 June 2018
Ferguson N (2009) The ascent of money. A financial history of the world. Penguin Books, London
Friedman M (2002) Capitalism and freedom. The University of Chicago Press, Chicago
Fromm E (1979) The sane society. Routledge & Kegan Paul, London
Fromm E (1990) Die Furcht von der Freiheit. Deutscher Taschenbuch Verlag, München
Galbraith JK (1967) The new industrial state. Houghton Mifflin Company, Boston
Galbraith JK (1974) The affluent society. Penguin Books, Middlesex
Galbraith JK (1975) Money. Whence it came, where it went. Houghton Mifflin Company, Boston
Galbraith JK (1977) The age of uncertainty. Houghton Mifflin Company, Boston
Galbraith JK (1987) Economics in perspective – a critical history. Houghton Mifflin Company, Boston
Galbraith JK (1990) A short history of financial euphoria. Whittle Books in association with Penguin Books, New York
Galbraith JK (1992) The culture of contentment. Houghton Mifflin Company, Boston
Galbraith JK, Salinger N (1978) Almost everyone's guide to economics. Penguin Books, London
GJS (2018) Piloten Brussels Airlines in open brief: 'Dit gaat niet alleen om geld, de citroen is genoeg uitgeperst'. De Standaard, 12 May 2018. http://www.standaard.be/cnt/dmf20180512_03509612. Last consulted 16 June 2018
Harari YN (2014) Sapiens – a brief history of humankind. Penguin Random House UK, London
ILO (2010) Vlaamse professoren verbolgen over uitspraak Pascal Smet. https://www.nieuwsblad.be/cnt/dmf20101207_141. Last consulted 16 June 2018
Jones A (2016) Cybercrime: the growing threat to global banking. https://internationalbanker.com/banking/cybercrime-growing-threat-global-banking/. Last consulted 16 June 2018
Kennedy D (2013) Law and the political economy of the world. Leiden J Int Law 26:7–48
Krugman P (1994) Peddling prosperity. W. W. Norton & Company, New York
Krugman P (1998) The accidental theorist: and other dispatches from the dismal science. W.W. Norton & Company, New York
Krugman P (2005) The great unraveling. Losing our way in the new century. Norton, New York

Krugman P (2008) The conscience of a liberal: reclaiming America from the right. Allen Lane, London
Krugman P (2009) The return of depression economics and the crisis of 2008. W.W. Norton & Company, New York
Kruithof J (2000) Het neo-liberalisme. EPO, Antwerpen
Kruithof J (2010) Het algemeen belang en de overheid. In: Jaap Kruithof – Teksten voor de toekomst. EPO, Berchem, pp 70–77
Lippens J (2015) Tewerkstelling allochtonen: in de EU scoort België het slechtst. Knack, 1 April 2015, p 16
Loizou A (2012) Het duivelspact. Een insiderverhaal over hoe het grote geld wordt verdiend. Zuidnederlandse uitgeverij, Aartselaar
Mandel E (1962) Traité d'économie Marxiste tII. Julliard, Paris
Marcuse H (1991) One-dimensional man. Routledge, London
Meeussen G (2015) Nepstatuten piloten gevaar voor veiligheid. De Tijd, 8 March 2015, p 17
O'Rourke PJ (2007) The wealth of Nations van Adam Smith. Mets & Schilt, Amsterdam
Oxfam (2017) An economy for the 99%. It's time to build a human economy that benefits everyone, not just the privileged few. Oxfam briefing paper, January 2017. https://d1tn3vj7xz9fdh.cloudfront.net/s3fs-public/file_attachments/bp-economy-for-99-percent-160117-en.pdf. Last consulted 16 June 2018
Popper K (1940) What is dialectic? Mind
Rand A (1992) The virtue of selfishness. New American Library (a division of Penguin Group), New York
Rand A (2008) Capitalism: the unknown ideal. New American Library (a division of Penguin Group), New York
Ricardo D (1957) The principles of political economy and taxation. J.M. Dent & Sons Ltd, London
Sachs J (2011) The price of civilization: reawakening American virtue and prosperity. Random House, New York
Simonet H (1970) La gauche et la société industrielle. Éditions Gérard & Co, Verviers
Smith A (1979) An inquiry into the nature and causes of the wealth of nations. As re-published by Campbell RH, Skinner A, Todd WB (eds) Clarendon Press, Oxford
Smout L (2015) Vlaamse co-piloot getuigt – Stress is extreem. Niet verbaasd dat piloot over schreef gaat. Het Laatste Nieuws, 28–29 March 2015, p 3
Steger M (2013) Globalization. A very short introduction. Oxford University Press, Oxford
Sterdyniak H (2011) Quelle politique économique? Morts et renaissances du keynésianisme" in Les Économistes atterés, Changer d'économie! Nos propositions pour 2012. In: Les liens qui libèrent, Paris, pp 21–42
Stiglitz J (2002) Employment, social justice and societal well-being. Int Labour Organ 141(1–2):9–29
Stiglitz J (2003) The roaring nineties. W.W. Norton & Company, New York
Stiglitz J (2010) Freefall. Free markets and the sinking of the global economy. Allen Lane (an imprint of Penguin Books), Londen
Turner A (2016) Between debt and the devil. Money, credit and fixing global finance. Princeton University Press, Princeton
Van Houtte JA (1942) Economische geschiedenis – de historische wording van de hedendaagsche wereldeconomie. De Haan, Utrecht
Van Lommel S (2015) Twitter laat zich niet dicteren. De Morgen, 28 March 2015, p 7
Vandewalle G (1976) De geschiedenis van het economisch denken. Deventer/Antwerp, Kluwer
Vermeiren S (2015) Iedereen moet verantwoordelijkheid nemen. Ook wij Berbers. Het Laatste Nieuws, 28–29 March 2015, p 13

Chapter 3
On Certain Less Obvious (Neo-)liberal Principles Shaping Capitalism

3.1 The Illusion of Equality

3.1.1 Why Men Are Not Equal, but Should Be Treated More Equally

One of the starting premises on which economic liberal and neo-liberal thinking, and through this, contemporary capitalist economies themselves, are based, is, at least implicitly, the idea that all man are equal.

Although nowadays anyone who dares to express an opposite opinion, runs the high risk of being misunderstood, the veracity of the thought that all men are equal nevertheless needs to be fundamentally questioned. This questioning of the idea that all men are equal hereby helps demonstrating that economic liberalism and economic neo-liberalism are clearly based on an erroneous wrong way of thinking and/or looking at reality.

It is of course obvious that, from a scientific viewpoint, especially the insights derived from (modern) biology, but one human species exists (and is left), namely "homo sapiens" to which all of mankind belongs. Genetically speaking, the differences between different "types" (whatever that word may mean) of men are indeed so small, that it cannot be assumed that there exists more than one human species.[1]

Otherwise put, every (living) human being belongs to the same human "species", which could indeed, at first sight, lead to the conclusion that all men are "equal".

However, in this approach one loses sight of the fact that the question whether or not two entities are "equal", is in essence a so-called "dichotomous" question. In

[1] This is moreover not different for many other species of animals, with as evident example the dog (Latin name: "Canis lupus familiaris"). However, many variations and breeds of dogs in size, look, type of hair and other defining characteristics, such as character and temperament, exist, there is still only one species "dog".

K. Byttebier, *The Unfree Market and the Law*, Economic and Financial Law & Policy – Shifting Insights & Values 2,
https://doi.org/10.1007/978-3-319-97382-1_3

other words, equality is only relevant in cases where there is a complete equality: this implies that something cannot be "a little", "a little more" or (even) "very" equal to something else. There needs to be a "complete equality" (where this way of phrasing the matter is, by definition, pleonastic).

This observation necessarily leads to the understanding that not many things are (entirely) "equal". On the contrary, the whole physical universe seems to be characterized by diversity: there are no two equal stars, or two equal planets, on earth there do not even exist two equal snowflakes, but also two people are never (completely) "equal". Even two persons (or other animals) who are "identical" twins, are never (completely) equal.

One can hereby barely doubt that nature is above all characterized by diversification because this optimizes the survival chances of living creatures, and hence also of a biological species.[2] In other words, many inequalities between human individuals from a same biological species stem from biological mechanisms which exist to optimise the survival chances of this species.

However, the main reason why the idea of equality between men can be fundamentally questioned is that, over the centuries, among others within the socio-economic order, but particularly within nearly all methods of organizing societies, many socio-economic and other societal inequalities have been (sometimes even: deliberately) developed, although it is obvious that these socio-economic and other societal inequalities have at the same time been severely challenged by numerous philosophical and ideological doctrines.

Hence, the idea of men being equal has in many ideologies become a (life) goal, whereas it needs to taken into consideration that this goal of achieving a society in which men become equal (or better: "are to be treated as being equal") has in practically none of these ideologies implied that nature itself is contested, so that the ideological thought of "men being equal" rather implies an "aspiration" (to be achieved when organizing society), than that it attempts to describe a reality (let alone a socio-economic or societal reality).

Otherwise put, to the extent that the abovementioned philosophical systems and ideologies put the idea of men being equal as a central value, this expresses the importance of striving for societal models in which all human beings would be treated in an equal way, or in a way as equally as possible.

This thought of equality as a philosophical or ideological goal, in return, translates, into (ideal) models of societal organisation, where the ultimate target becomes that all human beings, in the processes of regulating society—such as law, but even so economy—would be treated as equally as possible.[3]

---

[2] See for instance Dawkins (2009), p. 134, where he illustrates the phenomenon of "selection pressure" by explaining the colour differences of guppies.

[3] More in general, Skidelsky and Skidelsky have phrased this as follows (Skidelsky and Skidelsky 2013, p. 44):

> Men and women have always dreamt of a world without suffering, injustice and, above all, without work. (…) The prototype is Plato's Republic, an ideal city ruled over by an enlightened elite of guardians who share everything in common, including women, with whom they breed periodically on the order of the state.

3.1.2 *Illustrations of Societal Models Thriving on Inequality*

A few examples may further clarify the insight that has been dealt with in Sect. 3.1.1.

Let us first consider a number of human societal models, where the unequal treatment of human beings has been one of the corner stones of the societal order.

This has historically clearly been the case in many societies from Classical Antiquity, such as the (Ancient) Egypt, Greek and Roman civilisations. These Ancient societal models all had in common that they were based on the idea that different "castes" existed in society, hence that different people belonged to different groups all holding a different position in society, justifying a treatment of inequality.

For instance, in Ancient Egypt the pharaoh was considered to be a manifestation of God on earth, obviously implying that he was extremely high regarded, but also that all other people in society (mainly) existed to serve and obey him. This resulted into a societal model in which a large part of the population lived in serfdom, albeit that there were gradations in the unequal treatment between the pharaoh and the rest of the population. For instance, priests and administrators were more highly regarded and had more prerogatives than the rest of the population, even when they ultimately all had to serve the pharaoh.

Also classical Greek and Roman societies were based on a clear division of classes, where one of the main divisions, was the division between free people and the much larger class of slaves. Within the class of free people, there existed many subdivisions, all leading to an equal amount of systems of unequal treatment.[4]

A (striking) example of a present-day societal model which has already for many centuries been based on the division of society in castes, is obviously the Indian caste system.

As one may wonder if this cast system does not stem from a wrongly interpreted religious world view, it is worth while to look into it with a little more depth.

Hinduism already exists for millennia and there is probably no other religious system where so much thought has been given to the cycles that determine human life.[5] Hinduism in this regards states, amongst other things, that human life of man does not exist in itself, but on the contrary involves an endless cycle of rebirths where a soul, through history, takes different consecutive shapes until it will "realise itself" in its last life cycle. It is hereby believed that living the present incarnation in a virtuous way will be rewarded with an incarnation as a higher being, or that one will enjoy better chances in life—this expresses the so-called

[4] It is therefore very remarkable that, where a philosopher like Aristotle would raise himself as an advocate of more justice in the social order, he only had in mind the relations between the free people, but he never questioned the division of society in a class of free people and a class of slaves.

[5] Das (2012), p. xxxii.

"karma"-principle—where such a higher incarnation will also improve one's chances on reaching self-realisation.[6]

This "cyclical" concept of life provides in turn one of the elements justifying the Indian caste system based on the acquiescence about one's fate during a current incarnation in light of the hope on improvement in a next life, even to the extent that it has been argued that the caste system and traditional Hindu society are practically the same.[7]

As said, a rule of conduct stemming from this Hindu life view states that man should behave as virtuously as possible in order to improve his chances of enjoying a better incarnation in the next life, and hence his chances of being self-realised.

As the Hindu caste system has been in place since ages, its true origin is not entirely clear. One explanation is that the caste system stems from an ancient idea that a virtuous life runs in phases, so that man has to fulfil a role in life according to these life phases.[8] So during his childhood and youth, man will be driven by motives of learning, growth and development; life as an adult will be characterized by the aspirations to obtain a sufficient level of welfare for oneself and one's family, which obviously will go hand in hand with a sufficient level of socio-economic interaction with other people in society (for instance through providing labour, through trade, etc.); subsequently, a fully mature person will tend to take up a leading role in society, and, finally, at an older age, man will pursue contemplation and reflection, including preparing for one's death (and through this, the transition to a next incarnation). It may even be assumed that, in such a later phase of life, people in old Indian societies literally withdrew from society to go and live in the woods (or other solitary places) in order to devote their lives to contemplation and meditation, alone or in small groups.

One may hence wonder if the since then emerged Indian casts system is not a consequence of a wrongly interpreted implementation of such a life view, as a result of which groups of people got attributed a "static" set of tasks during their entire lives, hence getting divided in "casts", and where, gradually, such a division was not based on competence or personal preference, but got determined by birth (within such a cast).

Be that as it may, within the traditional Hindu cast approach typically four casts prevail, namely the "brahmins" or priests, the "kshatriya" of warriors/rulers, the "vaishya" or the independent craftsmen and traders, and finally the cast of the "shudra" or the working classes consisting of labourers and servants. Outside/next to these casts, there are also the "sannyasa" who withdraw from social life in order to devote their lives to meditation and asceticism. Lower than any other cast, there are the "chandala" or the pariah without cast.[9]

This traditional Hindu cast system has in turn helped shaping Indian society during centuries, albeit in modern times, it has increasingly been questioned, and later,

---

[6] See mainly the books of Meher Baba; see for instance Meher Baba (1955).

[7] Stoddart (2009), p. 47.

[8] Das (2012), p. xxxii.

[9] Stoddart (2009), p. 47.

to a certain extent, had to make place for the intrinsically even more unjust capitalist system that is mainly characterized by a sharp polarisation between a (small) elite of (very) rich people and a much larger group of poor proletarians.

In the Western world itself, so-called "feudalism" prevailed during the largest part of the Middle Ages, which was in practice also a cast system where a division in roughly three classes existed: the class of nobles or aristocrats (= the upper class), the class of the clergy (= also a high class) and a class of the serfs (= the majority of the population). Between these classes, a very high degree of unequal treatment (and unequal prerogatives) prevailed.

3.1.3 The Ongoing Struggle for More Equality

In light of the foregoing, it is remarkable that, especially in the further course of Western history, especially as regards the evolution of societal organization, subsequent emancipation battles seem to have taken place, often driven by a pursuit for an increased equal treatment (and hence also contrasting with the way in which the Indian population has, throughout time, continued to undergo the cast system in a more resigned way, which seems to illustrate that religion can indeed be "opium for the people").

The rise of the cities in Europe in the second half of the Middle Ages clearly may be seen as part of this emancipation battle of a new class of guilds and merchants which, as they became economically more successful, also started claiming increasing levels of social status (sometimes by combat, as during the French Revolution of 1789 which, to some extent, can hence be seen as the culmination point of this emancipation struggle of the class of merchants and traders). The emancipation of the class of merchants and traders would in itself gradually, from the seventeenth century on, and especially during the eighteenth and nineteenth centuries, result in the at present still prevailing capitalist (types of) societies, where the class of industrials and merchants would become the new top layer of society, which since then, in return, has started to exploit a large part of the rest of the world population.

It is indeed even the more striking that this type of social shifts, although they are mostly caused by a pursuit of a greater "equality", ergo "equal treatment", has in the past in many cases led to new systems of unequal treatment, a phenomenon which may be strongly witnessed in the current, modern (sometimes called "post-industrial") capitalist societal order.[10]

---

[10] It is therefore no coincidence that this process has been magnificently expressed, not to say criticised in world literature, so, for instance, by George Orwell in the satire "Animal farm". In this satire, at the end of a revolution of animals living on a farm, the initial slogan by which the revolution was led, namely: "All animals are equal", after the caste of pigs had taken a stand as the new elite on the farm, was changed to "All animals are equal, but some animals are more equal than others".

Although this satire, obviously mainly wanted to criticise the situation in the after the Russian October revolution of 1917, in 1922 established "Union of Socialist Soviet Republics", it is not

It hence appears that ideologies claiming that people are equal, do not describe a reality, but rather project an ideal image. Especially in societies characterised by far reaching inequalities between groups of people, the understanding will (rightfully) arise among members of the lower classes, but also with anyone willing to take an objective look at the processes of societal order, that such inequalities need to be avoided and that one should advocate social changes leading to a greater degree of equality.[11]

At the same time, groups of people which benefit most from prevailing inequalities will often be opposed to such soci(et)al changes, unless in case they would also benefit from the eventual outcome of these changes. The latter will, for instance, be the case when the fabric of society itself would be threatened when too large inequalities result in uproar, or even revolution. In that case, also the group of people belonging to the upper classes can be found willing to participate in social change processes to the extent that they put less at stake than in case of a total disruption of the prevailing societal order.

In other words, equality is neither a biological, nor a soci(et)al reality, even though the pursuit for more equal treatment between people can be perceived as a noble goal, which explains why many ideologies propagate equality as the leading principle of organizing societies, without any ideology ever having succeeded in effectively giving shape to a society (fully) based on this equality principle.

3.1.4 Inequalities Prevailing Within the Neo-liberalised Socio-Economic Order

It goes without saying that, in light of the foregoing, especially within the world dominating socio-economic system, namely (neo-liberal, unbridled) capitalism, vast inequalities between people and classes of people exist which in their own turn have a very high impact on the way how individuals are able to participate in (socio-) economic processes.

A first example of inequalities with a high impact on the way how someone can participate in the (socio-)economic processes are obviously the congenital talents of individuals.

It may be clear that not every person is born with the same talents. One person is e.g. from birth gifted with a very high IQ, another person may be not that fortunate

less applicable to what had happened in many Western countries after the different "civil" revolutions of the end of the eighteenth century and the beginning of the nineteenth century which, initially aimed at creating a more just societal system, have mainly contributed to the current (post) capitalist world, where the polarisation between the lower classes (= the poor and middle classes) and the rich classes (= the capitalists) has been stronger than ever before in recent history shaping a manifestly unjust society which, also in the West, more and more again resembles the society model of the feudal era.

[11] Compare Vivekananda (1989), p. 113 a.f.

(or, depending on the way how intelligence is looked at, not that unfortunate). One person may have a manifest congenital musical talent, where another person will not even succeed in deciphering an elementary clef. One person may be characterized by a flamboyant extrovert personality enabling him/her to make social contacts very easily, where another person may be more introvert and be inclined to avoid social interaction as much as possible.

There are obviously countless examples of similar, mostly congenital and genetically determined inequalities.

Furthermore, also physical characteristics can bring along large inequalities between individuals and, hence, also be of such nature to have an impact on (socio-) economic processes. For instance, one person may be born as a man, another as a woman, which immediately (and regrettably up to the present date) results in a manifest difference in the context of socio-economic life chances. People may be physically appealing or less appealing. The colour of one's skin, eyes, hair, to be tall or small, slim, athletic or obese, the amount of muscle mass, illness or health, almost all genetically determined characteristics, can even so highlight causes of differences that help determining the way how people participate in (socio-) economic processes.

Next to the abovementioned (rather obvious and mainly "biological" or "genetically determined") examples of inequalities that may have an impact on (socio-) economic processes, one can obviously also think about so-called "environmental" factors causing real inequalities between people. To start with, the place in the world where a person is born immediately may entail (potential) large inequalities. People born in prosperous countries will, by definition, face a completely different life situation than those born in poor(er) countries. Another distinctive factor may be the social class one is born into, implying that even someone who is born in a prosperous country can still end up becoming part of a poor family (and, vice versa, someone who is born in a poor country, can nevertheless belong to a rich family).

To put it in a more simple manner, one person will have (very) rich parents, another person will have very poor parents, and a third person can belong to the middle class, all different life situations creating different life chances and opportunities.[12]

Even one's mother tongue can be very determining for chances offered in life; for instance, in a world which is increasingly "Anglophone", those who have English as a mother tongue, will by definition in many professional situations have a head start as compared to people who speak another language and/or have learned the English language in a later stage of life. Furthermore, even up till this very day, many titles of nobility still exist (some of these even being of a hereditary nature) which also may entail socio-economic differences. The cultural context of a country where a person is born can also result in circumstances of distinction. For instance, in one country there may prevail a so-called "secular" society, which is increasingly the case in many European countries, while in another country the largest part of the population may be supportive to a certain religion, and where even the differences between religions can entail large socio-economic differences.

[12] The impact of such different life circumstances on one's personal development is even explored in literature, for instance in Paul Auster's recent successful novel "4321".

In short, the socio-economic-cultural characteristics of the society and the family in which a person is born, all may entail many factors which can incur a further inequality between individuals, also in the context of participating in (socio-) economic processes.

One of the main downsides of the manner in which economic liberal and neo-liberal ideologies have given effect to their ideological equality ideal is that the abovementioned "real inequalities" are not or barely taken into account, although they strongly influence the possibility of people to participate in socio-economic processes, and hence people's life chances.[13]

Indeed, both ideologies are to a large extent based on the belief that such true inequalities do not exist or should be completely ignored when implementing models or systems or organizing societies.

Although many illustrations of this observation can be thought off, the abovementioned can be illustrated in a striking way by means of the so -called doctrine of "the free expression of will", which is a clear example of the abovementioned "wrongly interpreted" thought of equality, although, most probably not by coincidence, it also is one of the corner stones of liberal and especially neo-liberal societies.

We shall address this doctrine in more detail in the next Sect. 3.2.

3.2 The Doctrine of the Free Expression of Will as the Product of a Mistaken Perception of Equality

3.2.1 Introduction

The distorted view on equality propagated by liberal and neo-liberal ideologies translates in present-day capitalist societies (ergo in quasi all countries where capitalism prevails, which in the current situation can be said about almost all countries

---

[13] On the correlation between "unequality" and "exploitation", see furthermore Osho (2011), p. 151:

> If mankind is one and equal, than the very basis of exploitation will be destroyed, because for exploitation to occur, inequality, sects and caste systems are essential.
>
> (…)
>
> A society without sects and casts is automatically against exploitation. To accept the equality of all people is to discard exploitation.

See also Oxfam (2017), p. 6, referring to the problem as to one of the false assumption's on which the capitalistic economy is based:

> **False assumption #3: Extreme individual wealth is benign and a sign of success, and inequality is not relevant.** Instead, the emergence of a new gilded age, with vast amounts of wealth concentrated in too few hands – the majority male – is economically inefficient, politically corrosive, and undermines our collective progress. A more equal distribution of wealth is necessary.

in the world) in a basic rule of law holding that all individuals (and by extension also all other legal subjects) can contract with one another on a so-called "free expression of will"-basis.

This "free expression of will"-doctrine—also referred to as the doctrine of "voluntary association"—is not by coincidence one of the corner stones of the (neo-) liberal societal order.

It is, hence, neither a coincidence that one of the "philosophers" most fervently having defended neo-liberal ideology, namely Ayn Rand, has referred to the principle of "voluntary association" as the one principle which should determine all interpersonal relations, and that no instance, especially no public authority, should be allowed to install models of societal order (for instance regulation) which could to any extent harm this "voluntary association".[14]

3.2.2 The True Meaning of the Free Expression of Will-Doctrine

What does this doctrine of the free expression of will (or: the doctrine of "voluntary association") mean? And furthermore, what is the link between an, in essence legal issue which any law student is likely to encounter during his or the first year of law studies, and the question of equality?

At the most general level, the doctrine of the free expression of will implies that all human beings—in some more civilised soci(et)al order systems: from a certain age on, referred to as the age of (legal) consent—but by extension also all other entities which have been granted an appropriate legal capacity (= the so-called "legal persons"), should be able to perform, on an equal and voluntary base, so-called "legal acts". By the notion "legal acts" is meant acts that, when undertaken, allow a legally capable individual to deliberately call upon the legal consequences that the law attaches to said acts. Otherwise put, the doctrine of the free expression of will basically holds that anyone with legal capacity can determine the legal consequences which he would like to call upon.

In case this would sound abstract, the further developed example will probably clarify the issue.

The doctrine of the free expression of will is most often called upon in the context of the so-called "freedom of contracting". Based on the doctrine of the free expression of will, every human being, but by extension every legal entity, is allowed to make legally enforceable commitments with any other person (or any other legal entity), about practically anything (except that what is legally forbidden).

The principle of free expression of will has meanwhile been generally[15] in use for (at least) three centuries in most countries in the world and has since then, at least in

[14] Rand (2008), p. 11; Rand (1992), p. 114.

[15] In many ancient societies, the freedom to contract was not as generally available to all layers of society. For instance, in societies based upon slavery, slaves themselves could not enter into

the private sector, determined most of the interpersonal relations (not taking into account a number of correction methods imposed by law), especially by entering into "contracts" (or "agreements").

The principle thus applies in almost all capitalist countries for any type of contracting, among others: the contract between an employer and an employee; renting contracts; any type of sale-purchase; agreements leading to the creation of a company or association… The list of further examples is obviously endless, as, within capitalism, an implicit invitation is made to all legal subjects to enter into as many contracts as possible. As a result, on a global scale, people and legal entities daily engage into numerous contracts, often without paying much consideration to the fact that by doing this, they are expressing their free will to be bound by the legal consequences of all these contracts they thus enter into.

3.2.3 The Free Expression of Will-Doctrine as a Breeding Ground for All Kinds of Injustices

As logic as the principle of the free expression of will may appear at first glance, it is nevertheless also a breeding ground for numerous injustices.

The reason for this is that the principle of free expression of will, as it prevails in most (capitalist countries) not only assumes that every person has the power to make such an expression of his will, but on top of that also assumes that any such expression of one's will is based on the idea of a presumed equality between all people (and other legal subjects) concerned.

Indeed, the free expression of will doctrine also implies that every capable person can participate in the contracting game on the basis of a full equality with any other capable person (natural persons, ergo people, as well as legal persons).

As a result, the doctrine of the free expression of will, which conceptually mainly aims at installing freedom in interpersonal relations, in practice fails in many cases in truly contributing to a just society, as the doctrine does not sufficiently take into account the manifest differences, mentioned earlier (see Sect. 3.1.4), prevailing between people (and by extension other legal entities).

These various differences between individuals (and, by extension, other legal entities) lead to the fact that, in reality, (legal) actions are almost never taken on a truly equal basis, especially in the game of the free expression of will (including the contracting game).

For instance, certain inequalities result in not everyone having access to all possible contractual opportunities. Some obvious examples speak for themselves. People who are not physically attractive enough will, in many cases, not be able to pursue a job as an actor or model. People who suffer certain illnesses, will often be unsuitable

---

agreements, but on the contrary could become the subject of such agreements among members of the higher classes.

for a career as a top athlete. People who lack a certain degree of intelligence, or did not enjoy a sufficient degree of education, will in many cases not be eligible for an employment requiring a certain level of intelligence or education. Although almost everything is for sale in this world, not everyone can buy everything, as the possibility to buy goods is determined by the financial capacity of the buyer, which is often, at least at the moment of entering socio-economic relations, stemming from one's familial or ethnical background,[16] hence dependent on mere coincidence.

These are obviously just a few manifest examples of how random, albeit important "true inequalities" result into an unequal access to contracting opportunities; further examples are numerous.

Other inequalities may cause a huge knowledge gap between the participants in the game of the free expression of will. A characteristic example concerns contracting between a large legal entity, e.g. a financial institution, and its average customers. A contract proposal of a similar (large) financial institution will in practice, in many cases, be the fruit of many years of expertise and specialisation, where maybe, for years, hundreds of people have been involved in setting out the contents of a given contract proposal (which, subsequently, very often takes the shape of long and complicated texts which are incomprehensible for the average person), while the average co-contractor engaging with such a financial institution will in many cases barely have any financial expertise and be inclined to blindly accept said proposal (by, in concrete terms, blindly signing the agreement without paying much attention to its contents).[17] This very fact explains why many people subscribe to financial products without any elementary awareness of the contents of the legal obligations which they commit to, but also why large legal entities can generously benefit from the incompetence of their co-contractors.[18]

---

[16] A remarkable case that made the news in May 2018 has been the one of "Nicolette", a spoiled rich girl who appeared on the US TV-show "Dr. Phil" as a class-school example of how rich young people get spoiled without meriting it. (See, for instance, http://www.wwlp.com/news/dr-phil-my-daughter-is-a-rich-spoiled-beverly-hills-brat-_20180501151031/1153176808; last consulted on June 16, 2018.)

[17] Compare Stiglitz (2010), pp. 253–254, who uses this phenomenon as an illustration of the many types of irrationality determining human economic behaviour.

See, similarly, even Congregation for the Doctrine of the Faith (2018), n° 14:

> For this reason, it must be noted that in the economic-financial world there are conditions in which some methods, though not directly unacceptable from an ethical point of view, still constitute instances of *proximate immorality*, that is, occasions that readily generate the kind of abuse and deception that can damage less advantaged counterparts. For instance, to commercialize certain financial instruments is in itself licit, but in a asymmetrical situation it would be possible to take advantage of a lack of knowledge or of the contractual weakness of either counterpart. In itself this amounts to a violation of due relational propriety, which is already a grave violation from an ethical point of view.

[18] One of the few parts of financial law by means of which one reacts against knowledge gaps are the regulations on the trade of financial instruments (for instance insider trading), albeit these regulations are often very complicated and as uncomprehensible for the common man as the practices they aim at regulating.

The same obviously applies to numerous other sectors, for instance the suppliers of social media instruments.

Even more inequalities impair the freedom on which a free expression of will is purportedly based itself. An extreme example would be that any person who is threatened by starvation, is likely to be willing to accept the most humiliating job at the most inhuman working conditions.[19] This in turn helps explaining why (especially) in poor countries, the application of the doctrine of the "voluntary association" often leads to the fact that very poor people accept work for a poverty wage, resulting in systems of modern slavery. However, also in Western countries, many examples can be mentioned where the ideal thought of freedom supporting the free expression of will is barely realistic, implying that also in the Western world many people end up in systems of nevertheless (so-called) contractually agreed upon exploitation.

It is hence no coincidence that the problem of unequal participating in the contracting game, is in some countries strongly visible in labour relations, given the manifest subordination of labour compared to capital, earlier in this text indicated as one of the main basic characteristics of the capitalist economies,[20] but also given the fact that working people, excluding cases of high specialisation, are abundantly available and nice jobs much less.

Next to many other examples, the abovementioned examples show that, in a world characterized by numerous "true inequalities", the assumption of an ideal equality as one of the main principles governing the societal order, as this idea legally translates, among others, into the doctrine of the free expression of will (also known as the "voluntary association"-doctrine), has above all many hazardous effects.

3.2.4 The Free Expression of Will-Doctrine as a Recipe for Exploitation

When, as is the case under economic neo-liberalism, the presupposed equality assumed within (neo-)liberal societies is linked to a "value thinking" where egoism, selfishness and greed are seen as the highest virtues, a perfect recipe to validate any type of unjust behaviour presents itself.

In such a belief system, the "strong(est)" co-contractor will be able to shamelessly take advantage of its "weak" co-contractor, where several factors can determine the relative positioning as a strong or weak co-contractor. Examples of such determining factors are undoubtedly the abovementioned causes of "true" inequality: financial capacity (not only because of the price of certain goods or services, but

[19] Marcuse (1968), p. 105; see also Stiglitz (2006), p. 67.
On the economics of job insecurity, see furthermore Stiglitz et al. (2010), p. 84 a.f.

[20] Fromm (1979), p. 83.

for instance also due to the (in)ability to pay for legal or other consultancy and guidance in contracting[21]); economic strength (a large multinational is for instance not an equal contractor to a simple individual); level of knowledge; level of intelligence; the nature of offsetting measures (those who can only offer a good or a service which is barely or not scarce, hold by definition a weaker contract position than those with a monopoly position)…

Hence, to the extent that the doctrines of economic neo-liberalism claim to be based on the "principle of equality", this appears in essence to be aimed at allowing the rich and powerful to abuse the different manifest true inequalities between persons/legal entities which are in reality present all over the world.

As a result, such a wrongly conceived thought of equality forms a perfect instrument for creating many new inequalities and has par excellence assisted in creating a breeding ground for a completely unjust world, especially on a socio-economic level.

It will probably not come as a surprise that, in the evolution of capitalism into the overpowering economic system on earth, the doctrine of the free expression of will has, notwithstanding its abovementioned intrinsic flaws, itself evolved into one of the main corner stones of the free market economy.

Said principle is in this way even yielding an (academic) licence by means of which the strong economic players shamelessly exploit the weak players, under the cloak that the weak players (have) agree(d) with the systems of socio-economic exploitation on a purportedly equal basis.

It is in this regard even often argued that people being unhappy with their resulting living conditions, for instance with a current job, can always test their luck elsewhere.

Neither astonishing is the fact that, as the ongoing neo-liberalisation of the world economy, and through this of global societies in general, is continuously expanding, also the set of exploitation mechanisms developed under the umbrella of the free expression of will, is as continuously growing, with as manifest examples: credit agreements with bankers; insurance agreements; rental agreements (for people not owning their own house); all types of contracting between an individual and a monopolist or an oligopolistic (for instance telecommunication providers; energy providers, water providers;…); the cost of food for the end consumer; the price charged by suppliers from third world countries for agricultural products and other resources…

Again, the further examples are numerous.

---

[21] A recent, very worrysome example is the increasing cost students have to pay for accessing higher education. As a result, many students all over the world have to enter into expensive student loans, which has in the recent past even been reported as a high competitive disadvantage which the entire generation of millennials has to face to an ever increasing extent. (See Crédit Suisse Research Institute (2017), p. 39. See also further under Sect. 4.7.1.5.)

3.2.5 Deregulation and (Neo-)liberalisation as Tools of Reinstalling the Free Expression of Will-Doctrine to Its Fullest Extent

In light of the foregoing, it does not come as a surprise that neo-liberal authors inveigh when a legal intervention, for instance a legal measure aimed at protecting consumers or investors, threatens to impair the scope of the field of the free expression of will.

Neither surprising is the zeal expressed by neo-liberal authors (and managers inspired by their doctrines), to advocate, among others, measures of (neo-)liberalisation and deregulation, where regulating systems that were in the past installed for different reasons (often with the intention to counter imbalances stemming from the abovementioned societal inequalities), but which limit the free expression of will, are systematically eliminated by neo-liberal governments all over the world.

In this way, the legal domain has itself to an ever-increasing extent become a part of the battlefield of the free market economy. Even more frightening is that, especially since the 1980s, it seems that economic neo-liberalism has hereby largely won the battle for dominating the legal system of almost all countries in the world.

Typical examples of countries where the techniques of (neo-)liberalisation and deregulation have on a large scale been used to avoid any deterioration of the free expression of will are obviously the United States of America and the United Kingdom, where already early in the 1980s "Reaganomics", respectively "Thatcherism", had a devastating impact on all types of social protection measures to the benefit of the free market. (See furthermore Sect. 3.5.2.2.)

It is even worse that, since that period, many other countries and other jurisdictions have followed these examples of extreme neo-liberalisation (with all obvious consequences).

A typical further example are the neo-liberal policies by which the European Union has attempted to "liberalise" (read: "neo-liberalise") several of its markets, often with a very disruptive impact. One may for instance refer to the reform operations of the previous decades of the financial and insurance market and the energy markets.

It hereby has to be further observed that European Union policies are most often deployed reluctant to any form of democratic legitimation, mainly being the result of lobbying by strong economic market players and, consequently, forcing member states to align their socio-economic order with neo-liberal thinking.

In the context of Belgium, this for instance has even led to the fact that governments in which traditionally "left oriented" (socialist and/or green) parties have over the past decades participated, nevertheless resorted to strongly neo-liberal flavoured policies (with as a striking example the alignment of the organisation of higher and academic education with the (in)famous Bologna—declaration,[22]

---

[22] See The Bologna Declaration (1999).

For more on the European policy related to this "Bologna declaration" (as regards higher education), see http://europa.eu/legislation_summaries/education_training_youth/lifelong_learning/c11088_nl.htm (last consulted on June 16, 2018).

a typical neo-liberal declaration which mainly aims at dismantling earlier efforts to democratise higher education).

Especially since the implementation of the WTO-treaty (and its subsequent amendments), as of the 1990s, even the global world economy has to an ever growing degree been submitted to neo-liberal principles, which has in many markets and for many economies, led to large disruptions (see also further in Chap. 4).

3.2.6 Conclusion

It may be clear that the neo-liberal, deliberately wrongly conceived principle of equality itself has produced one of the corner stones of many capitalist exploitation mechanisms and therefrom resulting inequalities.

Although this may at first glance seem heretical, people are not equal.

On the contrary, as is the case with anything in nature, also the human species is characterised by diversification.

This helps explaining why any given two people are never entirely equal, let alone that they would participate to the socio-economic order based on equality.

Consequently, the (harsh) truth is that the game of life opportunities as determined by numerous (among which biological and soci(et)al) factors, runs completely arbitrary.

It is even more harrowing that the different real-life inequalities which are caused by this, translate into unequal chances within the socio-economic order often resulting in further inequalities. Hence, an unbridled application of the neo-liberal "free will" (or "voluntary association")-doctrine, as it inherently leads to situations where the economic stronger dominates the economic weaker, can only result into an unjust societal order, as already for ages now, is constantly expressed by (unbridled) capitalism.

Any advocation for of a more just world for all people, should, hence start by accepting this basic reality and by abandoning the wrongly interpreted (neo-)liberal idea of equality as fast as possible and by replacing it by the thought that one should above all advocate the highest possible equal treatment of all human beings (amongst others by creating a level playing field of life opportunities).

See also Terry (s.d.), pp. 107–228.

3.3 The War of All Against All

3.3.1 On the (Neo-)liberal Competition Principle

The starting premise of (neo)liberal thinking that every individual should advocate his own selfish needs as much as possible, combined with the abovementioned true inequalities which distinguish people, has, already for centuries, been shaping an extremely aggressive socio-economic order.

Within this (neo-)liberal socio-economic order, people do not see themselves as a part of a collectivity,[23] in extreme cases not even as belonging to a same human species,[24] but only as each other's competitors in an ongoing battle to get the largest possible part of the metaphorical neo-liberal pie.

Under the doctrines of economic (neo-)liberalism, more noble motives such as mutual care or helpfulness have resolutely been pushed into the background, even to the extent that those who dare to plea for more altruism or solidarity, irrespective of any pursue of money goal, are, in the best case, seen as naive eccentrics lacking all sense of reality.

Centuries of blind application of the doctrines of economic liberalism (and later in history economic neo-liberalism) have thus resulted in a socio-economic order where almost all echelons of society have ended up in a cut-throat competition.

As a specific manifestation of the "spirit of selfishness", this "spirit of competition" which is widely welcomed under (neo-)liberal thinking ever since started determining all imaginable interpersonal relations, both on a macro as on a micro level.

Hereafter, we shall explore some striking examples of this sad reality.

3.3.2 Competition Between Countries

3.3.2.1 Introduction

At a macro level, the spirit of competition to an ever-growing extent dominates the way in which states behave towards each other.

---

[23] See again Ayn Rand who in her book "The virtue of selfishness" makes a fierce plea against any type of altruism or collectivism as socio-economic (or even general societal) ordering principles. (See Rand (1992).)

[24] See, for instance, the American President Donald Trump's remark that (some unauthorized) immigrants are animals. (See Davis (2018).) During a round-table discussion with state and local leaders on California's so-called sanctuary laws that took place in May 2018 and that reporters were allowed to document, President Trump was indeed reported to have stated:

> We have people coming into the country, or trying to come in — we're stopping a lot of them. You wouldn't believe how bad these people are. These aren't people, these are animals, and we're taking them out of the country at a level and at a rate that's never happened before. (See Davis (2018).)

The economy of another state (including its inhabitants) is hereby mainly perceived as a competitor of the own economy (and the own economic welfare). As a consequence, states, even those pretending to collaborate economically (as is purportedly the case for the members of the European Union) are in reality mainly each other's fierce competitors in many economic fields.

In this approach, socio-economic policy, including fiscal, labour and social policy, is mainly considered as a competing method in the battle to create as much economic welfare for the own state.

3.3.2.2 Competition on the Level of Fiscal Policy

A first striking example of the extent to which countries are each other's competitors concerns the fierce competition at a fiscal level which on a global scale has resulted in the development of a vast variety of tax-related favourable mechanisms aiming at stimulating large capital to either remain to be vested in the own territory of the state, or to migrate towards this own territory. It is hereby argued that one should attract (big) enterprises and their capital providers to one's own territory because of the wholesome effects, for instance as regards the level of employment, the attracting of business for subcontractors, or the providing of a source of tax revenues…[25]

As large capitalists can, furthermore, afford the most expensive consultancy and lobbying services, this attitude of economic neo-liberalism has degenerated into a true "race to the bottom", with as a consequence that, globally, the rich and their (large) corporations barely pay any taxes. Consequently, under the doctrines of economic neo-liberalism, states mainly need to turn to the poor and middle class for their tax income, where the main focus lies on income from labour (independent

[25] Within Europe, Luxembourg is a clear example of a state deploying this policy. (See, for instance, Neugarten (2018).)

As Neugarten puts it:

> Luxembourg draws the largest corporations from around the world that are seeking asylum from large corporate taxation, specifically in countries such as the United States where the corporate tax rate of 35% was once the third-highest in the world. In comparison, Luxembourg has a corporate tax rate of 21%. Although, as of 2018, that's now the maximum U.S. corporate tax rate as well, Luxembourg offers other tax advantages.
>
> For example, Luxembourg charges foreign corporations an extremely low tax rate to send money into and out of the country. Corporations that funnel profits through Luxembourg are charged around 1%. This is a huge incentive for large corporations that have the opportunity to save billions in corporate tax bills by moving cash to Luxembourg at such low rates.
>
> (…)
>
> Luxembourg is the most notable tax haven around the world. The country offers secrecy and advantageous tax laws for large corporations. U.S. corporations such as PepsiCo, Inc., American International Group, Inc. and Wal-Mart Stores, Inc. are well-known for creating subsidiaries and branches in offshore tax havens such as Luxembourg to cut taxes. (See Neugarten (2018).)

labour, as well as labour of employees), next to common transactions of goods needed to provide the basic needs of life. (See furthermore, under Sect. 4.6.)

This leads to the fact that, in many countries, the lower and middle classes are more and more challenged to reach an acceptable level of economic welfare, while at the same time the rich see their capital increase by the second. In this way, the fiscal policy[26] of many countries, rather than as a mechanism of redistribution of wealth, has degenerated into a mechanism contributing to the ever-increasing polarisation between the rich and the poor within society, where in some countries the middle class is even gradually disappearing.

Some rightfully claim that, on a global scale, tax systems have, hence, largely failed and so far no proposals to truly counter the intrinsic injustice of the currently prevailing tax systems have been made.[27]

As this fundamental problem of government funding is created due to the fierce competition between states, dealing with it will only be possible in the context of a global fiscal convention-based treaty (or set of treaties). Such an international treaty should achieve a true fiscal harmonisation in the context of which (at the very least) a resolute end would come to tax paradises and otherwise fiscal appealing countries, as well as the different tax mechanisms enabling the flight to such tax paradises.[28]

3.3.2.3 Competition on the Level of Labour and Social Policy

A second illustration of how the spirit of competition determines interstate behaviour concerns the regulation of labour relations in a broad sense of the word, next to the regulation of collective social care mechanisms.

Especially since the severe (and almost global) economic and financial crisis of the 1930s and in the aftermath of the second World War to which this crisis had led, in many Western countries, under different impulses—most notably including so-called "left-oriented" economic thinking, next to the doctrines of socially inspired economists, such as the British economist John Maynard Keynes (1883–1946), but also under the impulse of trade unions and similar organisations—policy measures were advocated which aimed at providing an elementary level of protection to the working classes, for instance the principle of granting a replacement income to those who are unable to participate in the working processes due to unfortunate life circumstances, such as unemployment and illness.

As long as the group Western countries in which such measures were taken could enjoy the comparative advantage of certain types of industrial production, these social measures would more or less succeed in, temporarily, giving a more human slant to capitalism.

---

[26] On the economics of fiscal policy in general, see Galbraith and Salinger (1978), p. 104 a.f.

[27] See Oxfam (2014), p. 16 a.f., referring to "the great tax failure". See also Sachs (2011), p. 118 a.f.

[28] Needless to say that such an alternative approach would be completely opposed to the present-day prevailing (neo-)liberal competition model.

However, from the 1980s on, a large neo-liberal offensive has taken off, in the context of which, globally, a large part of these social measures to an ever-growing extent got jeopardised.

Indeed, the theories of economic neo-liberalism, amongst others, advocate the dismantling of any hinder to the free market, including systems of labour protection[29] and collective social care mechanisms. (See already above, Sect. 2.6.)

In the process of implementing these theories, a leading role was played, as mentioned earlier, not by coincidence by two countries where capitalism had, since long, fully flourished for the first time, namely the United Kingdom and the United States of America.

As a result, the then prevailing leaders of both countries, respectively Margaret Thatcher and Ronald Reagan, affirmed themselves as the faces of said neo-liberal policy aiming at dismantling the social welfare state.

Unfortunately, many Western countries have later followed this example.

Furthermore, even international treaty systems which were originally created in order to establish certain global balances on an economic and financial level, have themselves increasingly been exposed to the influence of this ever increasing neo-liberalisation, which has undoubtedly been the case for the WTO treaty and the IMF treaty.[30]

The (neo-)liberalisation and deregulation of international trade- and capital markets resulting from these adaptations would mainly have a further catalyst effect on the already ongoing dismantlement of the social protection mechanisms in the countries where they were once installed.

As a result of the (neo-)liberalisation and deregulation of the international trade and capital systems, it, for instance, became increasingly simple and appealing for (large) companies to move their industrial production to so-called "low-wage countries",[31] traditionally also countries where the protection of labour and social care mechanisms had in the past remained underdeveloped.

This so-called "re-allocation" of many forms of economic productions has, in turn, gone hand in hand with an increasing de-industrialisation within the countries which, in the period after the second World War, had themselves succeeded in implementing an elementary set of social and labour protections rules. As a result, the increasing loss of industrial production in these countries resulted in a growing dismantlement of their economic tissue, which would, among others, in some of

[29] On the necessity of these due to market imperfections, see Stiglitz (2002), pp. 11–12.

[30] On the policy change that occurred within the IMF, see Stiglitz (2002), p. 22.

[31] In his book "Freefall" Stiglitz mentions the economic success of China in the (relatively) recent past. Stiglitz puts this success down not only to the massive presence of cheap labour forces, but also to the fact that these have a high education degree (higher than in other developing countries), next to the massive investments in infrastructure and a great attention to cost-efficient production of different products responding to the Western taste and needs (see Stiglitz (2010), p. 195).

Building on Ricardo's classical doctrine of the comparative advantages, Stiglitz makes the still valid remark that the Western countries urgently need to think about and focus on fields of economic production where there own comparative advantages are still present (see Stiglitz (2010), p. 196).

these countries lead to a high degree of unemployment, as a further consequence of which the systems of labour protection and social care, became even harder to finance.[32]

Inspired by the theories of economic neo-liberalism, the solution which most governments of these types of Western countries, among which many of the member states of the European Union, have thus far applied, has in most cases been based on a so-called "remediate- or save principle". This principle by definition implies an even further dismantling of the models of labour protection and social care installed in the past.

In the margin of this evolution, mainly from the side of the financial markets, the message got to a growing extent propagated that instead of relying on social care systems, individuals should resort to private insurances against any type of social risks (such as old age, but also illness), which has allowed the financial and insurance sector to massively sell all kind of new financial and insurance products in order to make (even more) profits.[33]

By doing this, the implementation of economic neo-liberalism results in a vicious circle: everything increasingly must be left to the operation of the free market mechanisms and states increasingly need to withdraw from the socio-economic order. As a result, a vicious race to the bottom also has emerged in the field of regulating labour protection and collective social services, which can be identified as one of the further other causes of the ever-increasing polarisation between the very rich and the poor and middle classes on a global scale.

---

[32] For an interesting illustration, see an opinion piece that appeared in the Belgian newspaper "De Morgen" about the replacement of the "care state" by the so-called "inclusive social model" (see Peeters (2015), pp. 4–5).

Like many of the policy measures propagated by economic neo-liberalism, this idea also stems from the United Kingdom and has from there, through a detour in The Netherlands, also reached Flanders. The idea behind the formula developed in the United Kingdom has in the quoted opinion piece been explained as follows:

> Many care responsibilities of central government have been pushed on to the municipality and the civilians. Four years later municipalities are crumbling under the retrenchments and they can no longer fulfill their basic care responsibilities. A similar movement took place in the Netherlands (see Peeters (2015), esp. p. 4).

In the same opinion piece, a renowned sociologist from the University of Leuven, Luc Huyse, was quoted as follows:

> This tempting understanding hides what is really happening: the government is rejecting care and passing it on to the civilians. In a coalition agreement of the Flemish and the federal government this is referred to as 'self-reliance', but in reality, it implies: do it yourself' (…) As it is no longer possible to provide the most basic care, the market will need to take over. (…) By definition this means an unequal access to care, while it just seemed that we were trying to create more equality. (see Peeters (2015), pp. 4–5).

[33] Stiglitz (2010), p. 195.

3.3.2.4 Impact on the Policy of the European Union

It is hardly a coincidence that the European legal treaties shaping the European Union strongly emphasise the organisation of free markets—pillars of the operation of the European Union being the "free movement of capital" and the "free movement of workers", which in reality come down to a freedom for the rich and powerful to have access to the cheapest possible labour forces—while at the same hardly paying any significant attention to questions such as fiscal harmonisation, or the protection of labour and/or the organisation of mechanisms of collective social care.

In this way, the European treaties are above all systems of implementation of the doctrines of economic neo-liberalism, which may also further be demonstrated by the many European measures that have been taken during the past years to "(neo-) liberalise" several European markets, with as striking examples the (neo-)liberalisation of the financial markets, the insurance markets, the energy markets…

Meanwhile, it has become clear that these (neo-)liberalisation techniques themselves have become one of the further causes of the increasing polarisation between the rich and the poor, while at the same time the European member states, even in their mutual relations, are increasingly engaged in a fierce competition battle in the fiscal and social field.

The fact that the European Union itself is still hosting several fiscal tax paradises (for instance Monaco) and fiscal refuge countries (for instance Luxembourg), or that within the European Union large migrations of cheap labour forces from East to West are taking place, are striking examples thereof.

One of the basic axioms of economic neo-liberalism holding that the average inhabitant of the countries which base their socio-economic policies on this belief system is benefiting from this, is hence contradicted by all facts, to the extent that one even could say that the (neo-)liberal dictate of the "triple-down-economics" clearly belongs in the realm of science fiction. On the contrary, it needs not much further arguing that, on a global scale, people who have to endure neoliberal governments, are to an ever-growing extent paying a large price, be it in the capacity of consumer (under the impulse of economic neo-liberalism almost everything has become more expensive over the past years), as well as in the capacity of labourer, civil servant or small business entrepreneur.

3.3.3 Competition Between Enterprises

The throat-cutting competition battle to which the (neo-)liberal creeds of greed and selfishness have led, not only characterizes the relationships between countries, but it is equally determining for the way in which (private) economic agents behave mutually towards each other.

Obviously, on the free markets, a fierce competition is going on between enterprises, which in a broad sense, is a collective term for anyone or any entity providing goods or services on a given market, generally, against payment of an amount of money.

Worldwide such enterprises take different legal shapes, going from the (mostly small) business ran by an individual, through large-scale capital corporations or groups of such corporations.

A small enterprise run by an individual will often remain small-scale and will mostly operate very local. Capital corporations however, can take very large proportions and can even become so-called "multinationals" or "transnationals" with an economic impact superseding the boundaries of countries.[34]

In the (neo-)liberal free market model, the expectation is that all these enterprises engage in a fierce competition battle with as objective maximising their own profits. In many cases, the ongoing existence of such enterprises depends on this, as enterprises who do not behave aggressively enough, risk to be forced out of the market by a market player who is willing to go to extremes in his own unbridled pursuit of profit.

One of the capitalist methods to make the biggest possible profits consists in many cases in acquiring the largest possible market share. This method often prevails in case of the production of goods which are easily reproducible and which can count on a large (potential) buyers public, a typical example being the providing of IT services. It is, hence, not a coincidence that the players in these markets are in many cases the largest companies in the world and that their mutual competition is extremely sharp. But even the many arguments between pop stars, to give but a random example, are in their own way an expression of the same capitalist principle that one should eliminate one's competition as much as possible in order to maximise one's own personal profit.

In this ongoing battle between enterprises for a larger market share with as ultimate goal to harvest as much profit as possible, it barely any longer comes down to improve

[34] The legal model on which the operation of such a capitalist enterprise is based, is in most capitalist countries the same: the enterprise is mostly set up in the legal format of a so-called "capital company" with as main objective to provide the highest profit possible to a small group of capital providers, the so-called "shareholders". In many cases, a large part of the shares, or even all of these, remain in the hands of the original founders of the company and/or their heirs, in which case the profits are often mainly used to increase the family fortune of the founding fathers. In other cases, for instance as a result of a stock market listing, the shareholdership has come in the hands of a wider public of investors which also, proportionally, obtains rights to participate in the profits generated.

In this matter, there is however no true dogma, implying that the shareholdership of companies (or corporations) can also have ended up in other hands, such as states or state funds, next to institutional investors, among which pension funds, insurance companies, investment funds…

The fierce competition between such big enterprises in some cases takes results in take-overs or acquisitions, implying that the shareholdership of a given company or corporation, entirely or partially, can end up in the hands of one of its competitors, sometimes even through aggressive methods which characterise the so-called "takeover market" where the capitalist game takes one of his most aggressive shapes. (For further reading, see Byttebier (1994) and Byttebier (1996)).

the wellbeing of others by providing quality goods or services[35]; on the contrary, the only goal is the pursuit of one's own profit which remains nevertheless, under the doctrines of economic liberalism and neo-liberalism, indicated as the main mechanism bringing societal welfare and lifting humanity to a higher level of civilization.

Typical examples of enterprises which function at the mercy of the abovementioned capitalist principles, may be found in the pharmaceutical and weapon sectors, not coincidently industries which have been marked by leading economists as sectors which have the most prominent lobbyists.

It needs not much further saying that a weapon producer is by definition barely concerned with the wellbeing of the human race, as his products by definition serve the opposite goal. Consequently, weapon producers obtain high profits thanks to the ongoing armed conflicts all over the world, and in some cases, they are even shamelessly willing to provide opposite fighting sides with their (ever more ingenious, efficient, destructive and through this, ever more expensive and profitable) products.

---

[35] Present-day production processes are also referred to as being based on the "disposable society" model. (See Tulipano (2013).)

Under this model, it has become almost impossible to have any broken product repaired, as the whole economic system incites people to replace broken products by simply buying new ones. It has even been argued that producers make products deliberately with a shorter life span than technically possible, in order to have bigger sales figures (which is a modern-day appearance of the "production for production's sake"-economy). This is obviously the case for most household appliances, next to more in general all kinds of electronical devices. For the rich, even cars have become throw-away-articles to be replaced by more fancy models every so many years.

As Tulipano (2013) has argued:

> Out with the old, in with the new. This is a classic motto recycled over and over again throughout generations, often used to justify the changes permeating throughout society and our own lives. This motto, though, is recycled far more often than the material items we deem as "garbage" in America. With the amount of goods we claim as broken or useless, America is collectively renowned as a "throw-away society."
>
> (…)
>
> During the 1920s and 1930s, the manufacturing philosophy of "planned obsolescence" was discovered. As mass production became popular and widespread, this viable business strategy was refined. Manufacturers made it a goal to produce products, or parts of goods, that break, fail, or become less desirable after a certain amount of use or time. This manipulation in the production of goods pressures consumers to replace their broken and/or less-desired products. This trend became profitable for manufacturers and is a process still used today.
>
> Think about how this trend plays out in your life. Cell phones and computer software are updated on an at least annual basis. How many times have you found yourself abandoning your current phone for a newer, more desirable replacement? Similarly, how often do you find yourself updating your computer software? I speak for myself when I say in the four years I have been a loyal customer of Apple products, my MacBook Pro software has been upgraded nearly three times. So far, it's an annual update because newer is deemed better.
>
> Manufacturers are compelled to build low quality products in hopes of earning higher profit margins. Throw-away materials guarantee customers will repurchase the same items in newer models, which is cost efficient and pure profit for manufacturers. Planned obsolescence may be manipulative against consumers, but is a smart business strategy for capitalists.

The fact that in many countries, with as notorious example the USA—the country which was probably the most involved in all types of armed conflicts over the last 50 years—next to the financial sector, the pharmaceutical sector, and the oil sector, the weapon industry is qualified as one of the four sectors which mostly influences government policy, hence puts the world-wide continuation of the most inhuman armed conflicts in a questionable perspective.

However, the underlying goals of the pharmaceutical industry are hardly any better. As is the case for the weapons industry, this sector is also dominated by a limited number of very large market players which are much more concerned with their market share and/or profit figures, than with the health of mankind. In the past, this has begged the question as to if the sector truly benefits from the discovery of a certain medication, or in case of a certain type of medication already invented, the question whether it should or should not be commercialised, especially in cases where the sector makes much more money on other medication which, instead of curing a disease, controls its symptoms. As questionable are the practices applied in many Western countries where pharmaceutical manufacturers approach physicians and other people working in the health industry, with all kinds of favours and presents in order to persuade them to preferably prescribe their products to patients. Therefore, sick people who are being prescribed a certain medication or therapy, may often have reasons to doubt if the prescription behaviour of their physician is indeed meant to make them better, or to maximise profits.

It is in this regard at the very least remarkable that in the Western World, according to a cautious estimate, at least 10% of the population is addicted to tranquilizers and/or stimulants, especially knowing that the effects of these, in many cases, are not that different than those of illegal drugs or stimulants.[36]

These observations, furthermore, place the setup of many legal systems which enhance the position of huge market players in a very specific perspective.

A typical example of such a legal system are the so-called "intellectual rights". Intellectual rights systems have purportedly been designed as mechanisms to protect an "inventor" (in a broad sense of the word) of a given contribution to the development of culture, science or technology (also in a broad sense of the word), especially by financially rewarding such an inventor. However, in reality, the possession of such intellectual rights has evolved into one of the main methods used by large enterprises to obtain unbridled profits by monopolising the proceeds of the inventions protected by such intellectual rights. In extreme cases, the invention which is under an intellectual rights protection, or the products based upon it, will no longer, or under difficult conditions, be accessible for a large a part of mankind which will not be able to pay the price for accessing said products.

Again, the pharmaceutical industry provides a typical example of this phenomenon. Especially the patent policy of large pharmaceutical enterprises illustrates the extent to which the objective of preventing people from suffering from a disease has become subordinated to the (neo-)liberal credo that greed needs to be the driving

[36] Wolffers (2010), 240 a.f.

force behind human behaviour. Consequently, many medicines have only become accessible to those who can afford to pay their high price.

Where traditionally this worry mainly concerned the inaccessibility of several modern medicines and other therapeutical products and methods for sick people in poor countries, one must observe that even so in the contemporary neo-liberalised Western world, a growing number of patients can no longer afford certain forms of medical care, especially in case of rather rare diseases of which the treatment cannot economically be commercialised in a purportedly "rational"—or better put: profitable enough—manner[37] (occasionally resulting in fundraising initiatives in the hope of obtaining access to medical products which have become too expensive, through means of charity).

In such cases where a seriously ill person does not have access to an effectively existing and working medicine, only because it is too highly priced, the capitalist principle that selfishness leads to the highest possible welfare for everyone, as it is fiercely defended under neo-liberal thinking, obviously but leaves a bitter taste.[38]

These practices illustrate how the unbridled pursuit of profit principle, as it is aggressively defended under the doctrines of economic neo-liberalism as the ultimate method for providing welfare, often enables the most harrowing injustices.

This truth in itself emphasises another manifest characteristic of the way free markets operate, namely how the merciless competition between enterprises has above all resulted in a moral system under which no longer any reward is given to elementary human values such as compassion and solidarity. Being obsessed by reaching the highest possible market share and/or the highest possible profits, enterprises (but hence: also the people who man said enterprises) are on the contrary

---

[37] Put otherwise: as a result of patent protection resulting in extremely high prices, many types of medicines exist which are not accessible to a large part of the world's population, often poor people who are mostly in need of them.

[38] In the (recent) Belgian context, the so-called "Soliris-dossier" serves as an illustration of this phenomenon.

In 2013, the pharmaceutical enterprise "Alexion" drew press attention when it appeared that its (at the time only commercialised) medicine "Soliris" could save the life of a 7-year-old boy ("Viktor"), but that the treatment with this medicine costed ±18,000 Euro per month and was therefore unaffordable for both the parents of the boy as for his health insurer. This eventually led to difficult negotiations between Alexion and the former minister of health Laurette Onkelinx who ultimately came to an agreement. Only at the end of 2015, the content of this agreement was made public and it turned out that said minister had to agree with a price of one ampule of Soliris amounting to 4278.14 Euro, a price which, according to the agreement, "could never be revised". An ex- co-worker of the minister later witnessed on how the said agreement was reached: "It was all or nothing", and another source confirmed: "The practices of Alexion defy all imagination. This was pure blackmail." (see Vandekerckhove and Van Garderen (2015a), p. 1).

That these practices are highly profitable, can be concluded form the turnover and profit figures of "Alexion". In the financial year 2013, Alexion was reported to make a net profit of 252 million USD, on a turnover of 1.5 billion USD, a turnover which had doubled over the past 2 years. It is thus the more remarkable that Soliris was at the time the only medicine marketed by Alexion, and that according to Forbes the price of an Alexion share was higher than a share of Apple (see Vandekerckhove and Van Garderen (2015b), pp. 12–13).

especially engaged in a competitive behaviour which is often mainly aimed at eliminating competitors active in the same market.

These are, obviously, but a few examples of how the doctrines of economic neo-liberalism drive enterprises to conduct an ongoing power struggle in order to, within their respective markets, be number one and, as a result, obtain the largest possible slice of the "neo-liberal pie" (a classical metaphor for the economy and its wealth).

Especially in the course of the past two centuries, the abovementioned capitalist mechanisms have through this resulted in the shaping of "mega-enterprises" whose power and wealth even surpasses the power and wealth of entire countries and which are mainly concerned with an ongoing growth in size and profit. It is hereby hardly surprising that any individual, except for the CEO or (large) shareholder of such a mega-enterprise, should be wary when acting with it, given the high risk he is running to be exploited as an employee or to be cheated as a customer.

Again, the examples of legal and other battles in which this type of mega-enterprises have become entangled are numerous.

One of the most notorious examples is undoubtedly the tobacco industry which, although having been aware of the extreme (to the health of both "active" and "passive" smokers) risks its products cause, the industry is known to have hidden this knowledge from the outside world for years, and to nevertheless have continued to strive for enlarged market shares, hence for an increase of the sale figures of its dangerous products, amongst others through aggressive advertising campaigns often deliberately targeting vulnerable groups of the population, such as young people, in order to make them addicts of their products. It probably will never be precisely determined how many people have died from cancer as a consequence of this immoral behaviour, but there have, luckily, been some cases where the victims of the tobacco industry, or their descendents, have called the tobacco producers to account by legal means.[39]

Most probably the tobacco sector is but the metaphorical top of the iceberg, and many other industries engage in the same strategy of keeping the dangers to public health of many of their products which are known for a very long time already hidden to the outside world and continue to produce and trade these products, thereby sacrificing public health in general and the wellbeing of their own customers more specifically to their (unbridled) pursuit of profits.

A further prominent example of such behaviour characterises the industrial food industry which continues to produce pre-manufactured products of which a long-term use may have disastrous consequences for people's health (with as a typical example the production of candy and similar products which are rich in sugar, such as sugar-rich soft drinks, attributing to, amongst others, diabetes and cardiovascular diseases).

From the abovementioned illustrations, it becomes obvious that business enterprises are continuously engaged in a fierce competition struggle to make ever more

[39] See for instance Lepew (2011).

profits, but that they hereby also demonstrate a great willingness to sacrifice all other values to this endless pursuit for profits.

3.3.4 *Competition Between Individuals*

3.3.4.1 The Classical Competition Model Within Enterprises

Especially under the impulse of economic neo-liberalism, the spirit of competition in a blind subjection to the pursuit of money principle, has contaminated numerous other levels of society, including by no means least the relations between individuals employed within the abovementioned types of business enterprises.

In a classical approach, the operation of a(n) (large) enterprise is often based on a "piriform" structure, admittedly with variants. Such an enterprise is, in many cases, led by a CEO, who, albeit mostly in a theoretical way, operates under the authority of a higher governing body, such as the board of directors of the company given legal form to such an enterprise (which in practice often barely provides but a theoretical monitoring of the actions of such a CEO).[40] Below the CEO, there are often different executive managers and, under these, there are the further employees of said enterprise.

Most typically, such an enterprise is run in strictly hierarchical way where employees from a lower echelon account for their operations to managers (or other employees) from higher echelons. The differences between the level at which a manager or employee operates within the enterprise often appear in many areas, most notably the financial reward one gets in return for one's employment, next to other reward mechanisms, such as the possibility to participate in the profits the enterprise is making (going from incentive mechanisms based on a targeted turnover, to true participations in the share capital—and through this in the company profits—of the company which gives legal shape to said enterprise).

The doctrines of economic neo-liberalism have added a further dimension to this cocktail of incentives determining the interpersonal relations within such an enterprise by holding that, even within the scope of such an enterprise, individuals should behave in the most competitive way possible in order to be successful.

As a result of this, the labour relations within many of these enterprises are governed by a continuous competitive battle among its employees, where everyone mainly strives to get promoted and to be financially rewarded as high as possible (see, for instance, the struggle to obtain ever higher bonuses and profit participation).[41]

More noble human values, such as the concern of doing good to others or to help one another, barely stand any chance in these types of aggressive working environments.

---

[40] See the discussion earlier in the previous Chap. 2.

[41] On the extent to which a bonus policy influences short term thinking and the taking of extreme risks, see Stiglitz (2003), pp. 142–143.

Although this neo-liberal competitive spirit is determining the working methods of almost all enterprises which operate in accordance with (neoliberal) free market principles, there have been cases where the model has become completely derailed.

Obvious examples hereof have been the collapse of the worlds former largest energy producer "Enron" and the decay of, through similar causes, one of the largest former banks in the United Kingdom, "Barings Bank".

More in general, reference can furthermore be made to the mechanisms characterising interpersonal labour relations between people employed in the entire financial sector, not by coincidence one of the fastest growing sectors under the implementation of neoliberal doctrines.

3.3.4.2 The Contamination of Other Work Environments

Unfortunately, even so under the impulse of the doctrines of economic neo-liberalism, the (extreme) competitive working model that is based on internal competition and on remuneration mechanisms and promotion systems which encourage internal competition as much as possible, has since a couple of decades expanded to almost all other domains of the socio-economic order than the business world in the strict sense of the word itself.

As a result, numerous other sectors have to an ever-increasing extent been forced to adopt this competition model as well. It goes without much further saying that in many cases, this has been in sheer contradiction with the underlying values of such other types of organisations and, in some cases, even with their historical or other reasons of existence.

In this way, the neo-liberal competition model nowadays determines the whereabouts of the so-called consultancy industry in a broad sense of the word (for instance also referring to large law firms), even to an extent that these large consultancy firms have in many cases lost touch of their underlying reason of existence. The objective to help others in need, has in many cases completely made way for a perception that a person in need seeking assistance is but an "account" by means of which high turnovers (and through this profits) are to be generated. Also, between the partners and other employees of such consultancy firms, a fierce competition is taking place often resulting in a behaviour aimed at attracting, by means of tricks and gimmicks, the most interesting "accounts" possible (and if needed, to steal them from a fellow colleague).

Similarly worrying is the fact that during the past decades said neo-liberal competition model has expanded to even more "soft" sectors, such as the liberal professions, the care sector and the education sector, which have as a result increasingly become subject to the free market principles.

As a result, in the present age and in almost all echelons of socio-economic life, the (neo) liberal competition model determines practically all interpersonal relations.

The result of this evolution is that, stemming from the idea that such a competitive spirit encourages productivity and initiative, on a global scale a socio-economic organisation model prevails where people are mainly deployed as each other's competitors. As said, the stakes of this competition model concerns issues such as the size of one's remuneration, career- and promotion opportunities, all types of incentive mechanisms which are granted in return for one's so-called productivity, the extent to which an employee can (or cannot) gain esteem from his or her "boss"…

The fact that, in the wake of this evolution, for instance physicians have completely lost track with the oath of Hippocrates in cases where they refuse to treat poor patients, is hardly surprising, as long as they make good profits from treating their richer (or better "(socially) secured" or "(privately) insured") patients.

It is in this context illustrative that, in 2015, Dutch cancer patients were reported to no longer receive treatment in their home country and, hence, increasingly looked for help in Belgium where, at that time, the treatment of poor cancer patients was still considered feasible.[42] Nevertheless, it was in the same period also reported that many Belgian hospitals had started refusing to provide certain types of treatment to patients who did not book a single (hospital) room, as under the Belgian social security system, physicians can not charge high enough fees for patients not having booked such a single room.[43]

Since the already abovementioned Bologna-declaration, the neo-liberal competition model has meanwhile also struck the operation of universities and similar institutions of higher education, entailing all of the already dealt with disastrous consequences in the field of scientific research and higher education.

Micklethwait and Woolridge have in this regard reported that "in Europe […] in many universities it is a mess because directors have cut in the provisions",[44] which is a statement that may be experienced on a daily base by any academic working at a Flemish university.

The fact that research areas stemming from different scientific disciplines have barely anything in common, has hereby not been cumbersome for Flemish policy makers to make their respective financing dependent on streamlined measurement systems which mainly set out a high degree of mutual competition, where for instance researchers from the psychological academic field are measured in accordance to the same standards as their colleagues working in natural sciences. This has mainly resulted in measurement systems where the output from any academic research field is only based on intrinsically pointless quantitative parameters, rather than still looking at the overall quality of one's performance.

It hereby barely seems to cause any societal turmoil that, as a consequence, especially in human sciences, less and less funding is available and that between academics a fierce battle is going on to obtain at least a small stake of this funding.

---

[42] de Vreede (2014).

[43] See Debackere (2015).

For a formal reaction of the Belgian Order of Physician, see https://ordomedic.be/nl/adviezen/advies/persbericht-weigering-van-enkele-artsen-om-patinten-te-behandelen-die-een-tweepersoonskamer-kiezen (last consulted on June 16, 2018).

[44] Micklethwait and Woolridge (2014), p. 121.

It moreover seems to pose as little societal reflection that the excessive neo-liberal savings policy which has been conducted in the aftermath of the Bologna declaration increasingly affects past democratisation efforts in the field of higher education. For instance, in more and more European countries, entrance fees of universities and other higher education institutions are, year by year, increasing. The only occasional expression of dissatisfaction in this regard stems from a newspaper columnist, or, on occasion, at the start of an academic year, from a student movement of which the members start feeling the financial impact of this policy.[45]

A colleague of mine once compared the career path of an academic at a university to the game "snakes and ladders", where everyone has to be willing to make more and more efforts to progress in their careers at the detriment of others, hereby metaphorically trying to avoid getting bitten by a snake which is a reference to any colleague maliciously trying to prevent someone else to progress in order to safeguard one's own career chances. In an environment where, as a result of a wide variety of ((neo)liberal) reorganisation and rationalisation policy measures, financing has gotten more and more scarce, one can as a result no longer speak of a normal career path which runs based on merits, but on the contrary, one has to observe that one's career path goes in full accordance with the nineteenth century capitalist principle referred to as the law of the jungle.[46]

3.3.4.3 Some Further Consequences of the Model of Workfloor Competition

In his book "De neoliberale waanzin – Flexibel, efficiënt en… gestoord", Paul Verhaeghe[47] has argued in detail how, since the breakthrough of the doctrines of economic neo-liberalism, the abovementioned processes have usurped in practically all socio-economic echelons interpersonal relations, with disastrous mental, and through this also physical, health consequences as a result.

Meanwhile it is as clear that those who, by nature, least tend to behave in the egoistic and over-competitive manner the theories of economic neo-liberalism presuppose and, on the contrary, tend more to solidarity and collaboration, most

---

[45] See furthermore the frame illustration: "the impact of the skimming of government financing on the Flemish academic tissue" in Byttebier (2015), pp. 215–218.

[46] For a recent illustration, see a press release of 2015 on "the culture of fear" prevailing at the University of Ghent (see Soenens (2015)):

> At the university of Ghent, there is a true climate of fear where bullying and burn-outs are an important problem, says the student magazine "Schamper" based on different testimonies, and it is confirmed by different testimonies and confidential documents, which were uncovered by "De Morgen" on the bullying behavior by one dean that has been going on for years. "The university is not doing enough at all for the wellbeing of its staff", is how it the problem was summarised by an important source.

The question is however if the situation is any better at the other Flemish universities…

[47] Verhaeghe (2011).

strongly suffer under this neo-liberal competition model (even running serious health risks of a burn-out or similar mental condition), while those who, by nature, are more selfish and competitive (or, otherwise put, or willing to go at any lengths to achieve their selfish career goals), often flourish, although one can seriously doubt if this also implies that they are performing better.

The extent to which the application of the neo-liberal competition model on the workplace is shaping entire sectors of economies and this on a global level, is evident.

Reference can again be made to the typical example of the financial sector, where especially employees in a commercial position will be pushed, at all cost, to the highest productivity and competitivity, resulting in the fact that even different branches of a same bank more and more compete with each other, amongst others in order to poach each other's customers. It has hereby become a widespread practice that individual employees of a financial institution (or other enterprise), where (part of the) remuneration is based on the turnover one makes, will openly chase their colleagues to win each other's customers (in jargon often no longer referred to as to (other) people, but as to (mere) "accounts", or by making use of any similar description indicating that interpersonal relations are only referred to in terms of their economic relevance).

As a result, in such a working environment, everyone needs to be especially wary of their colleagues who thus are given the proverbial role of (a fierce) enemy.[48]

It needs not much further arguing that the so-called bonus policy culture which has been characterising the financial sector for decades already and which is mainly also but an expression of the fierce competition model that has been deployed under the doctrines of economic neo-liberalism, has been one of the main causes of the financial crisis of 2007–2008.

Based upon these mechanisms (and many more), the neo-liberal competition model, has as of the 1980s, degenerated into a true "war of all against all". Any attention to the values of elementary human and civilized behaviour, let alone to these of mutual love and affection for one's fellow human beings, has hereby gradually and completely been banished and sacrificed to the values of egoism, selfishness and greed which prevail under the doctrines of economic neo-liberalism.

In this neo-liberal set of values, the fellow man has thus above all been reduced to a competitive creature, with which any other person is in an ongoing struggle.

Any society adopting these creeds of economic neo-liberalism in such an extensive manner can barely be surprised if the mutual competition spirit, where anyone only perceives his fellow man as a competitive being whose sole purpose is to hinder the fulfilment of one's own selfish goals, is gradually taking more violent proportions. In such a socio-economic environment, there is indeed an increasing risk that those who do not fully fulfil their selfish ambitions, especially in cases where this is caused by objective elements such as a lower social background or

[48] Next to the practices within certain financial institutions, the practices applied by many (large) consultancy and law firms form but another harrowing illustration of the same phenomenon.

similar social disadvantages, will express his frustrations by means of other methods than competing in the socio-economic sphere.

One may wonder if the occasional outburst of anger as witnessed in several Western societies over the past years provide more harrowing illustrations of these insights.

It is even more remarkable that the adherents of the doctrines of economic neo-liberalism at least still do see one important role for governments which they, by definition, otherwise denounce, more specifically the role of installing police forces needed to safeguard the economic interests of the higher classes. (See also above, Sect. 2.6.)

As has already been pointed out by Gailbraith decades ago, it is in this regard very remarkable that the biggest supporters of neo-liberal/conservative economic thinking, are often also the largest advocates of a maximum support to defence and army, and it is as remarkable that (past) American governments which were at the forefront of implementing the doctrines of economic neo-liberalism (such as those of Ronald Reagan and George Bush sr. and jr.), although having announced in their election campaigns that they would decrease overall government expenditure, mainly succeeded in substantially increasing the American public deficits, among others as a consequence of excessive expenditure for defence and safety.

In these cases, the unbridled competition spirit which has meanwhile been promoted by liberal thinking for centuries, and by neo-liberal thinking for decades, is taking terrible dimensions.

Notwithstanding the foregoing, it may perhaps because of some modest hope that, to a growing extent, the false optimist idea of the doctrines of economic liberalism and neo-liberalism that economic growth can be unbridled forever, is in some minds, slowly making way for a genuine concern about the future of mankind under a continued application of said liberal and neo-liberal doctrines.

3.4 The Illusion of Freedom

3.4.1 On the Ideological Promise of Freedom

Since the seventeenth and in the eighteenth century, the doctrines of economic liberalism promised liberty to any individual, a promise which has resounded even stronger in the belief declarations of economic neo-liberalism, which, from the 1960s, on have gradually succeeded to garner the minds of people all over the planet.

Indeed, both the doctrines of economic liberalism and economic neo-liberalism highly prioritise the idea of individual freedom, from which both belief systems have even derived their names, as the words "liberal" and "neo-liberal" are derived from the Latin word "liber" which literally means "free".

By stressing the importance of individual freedom (and, by extension, individual initiative on all societal levels), economic liberalism originally positioned itself against former economic movements such as sixteenth and seventeenth century mercantilism, under which economic processes were strongly steered by states, but as much against the as too ontologically perceived late-Middle Age predominance of religious doctrines such as Catholicism and even Protestantism.

Under this at the time new societal approach, man was invited to "liberate" himself from all these influences and to contribute to a new socio-economic order based on the principles of individualism, egoism, selfishness and greed, and by doing so, to make use of the then newly developed legal mechanisms which helped shaping this new societal order.

It has, therefore, hardly been a coincidence that economic neo-liberalism (which is to a large extent a new version of classical economic liberalism that manifested itself during the second half of the twentieth century) first appeared as a reaction against a variety of correction mechanisms to unbridled capitalism, which, especially by the rich and powerful within Western societies, were more and more perceived to be too collectivist or, otherwise put, as an obstacle against their own individual freedom.

This opposition concerned a wide variety of publicly funded mechanisms correcting (unbridled) capitalism, such as public education which was seen as deleterious for society, but also all possible social security systems that were even so perceived as an impairment to individual freedom.[49]

In this approach of both economic liberalism and economic neo-liberalism, there can be no room for any socio-economic mechanisms based on collectivism, even not to the extent that these aim at making corrections to the numerous injustices to which the blind application of the capitalist principles lead. The extent to which American neo-liberal authors such as Milton Friedman and Ayn Rand have been attacking all kinds of public or collective systems (a.o. based on Keynesian thinking) is of particular importance in this context.[50]

It is, therefore, hardly surprising that the efforts to "neo-liberalise" the socio-economic order which, under the cloak of restoring a greater degree of individual freedom, have been deployed since the 1980s, mainly had the objective to eliminate mechanisms which in the previous time periods had been installed in an attempt to create a more just socio-economic model than that of unbridled capitalism itself.

As a result, the attempts of realizing the neo-liberal promise of individual freedom have, among others, led to the decay of many mechanisms which in previous time periods had been installed by (national) governments in order to create a more just society. (See already under Sect. 2.6.)

[49] On the economics of privatizing social security, see Stiglitz (2002), p. 15.

[50] See also Stiglitz (2010), p. 257 a.f.

3.4.2 *The Many Chains of Capitalism for the Working Classes*

The question obviously arises if the implementation of the doctrines of economic liberalism and economic neo-liberalism have effectively achieved their goal of creating a free society.

This is obviously not, or barely the case for a large part of humanity which is being involved in the capitalist production processes.

The value hierarchy upon which capitalism is based has indeed, as was already explained in the second chapter of this book, mainly led to a before unseen application (or not to say: degradation) of human labour (force) into the capitalist production and trade processes, in a manner which is basically aimed at making a few people (especially the driving forces behind enterprises, or in terms of company law: the capital providers, and/or the C.E.O's appointed by them) as rich as possible to the detriment of the rest of mankind.

Already decades ago, Erich Fromm has pointed out the inherent value-inversion which thus emerged: within (unbridled) capitalism, labour (so in essence: "man" himself) has been completely subjected to capital (the "economic processes"). Man, a living being, hereby sees himself continuously degraded to a means that should serve a purpose, i.e. to fulfil the unbridled pursuit of profit of the enterprises which employ him (and ultimately of their ultimate capital provider(s)), as efficiently as possible.[51]

The capitalist value hierarchy which is since then relentlessly defended under the doctrines of economic liberalism and neo-liberalism, has become one where capital (and its objectives) has been completely prioritised as compared to labour (i.e.: man), a principle which in modern-day societies determines interpersonal relations on a global scale and where two sets of value scales continuously collide, namely the pursuit of money versus life (and its intrinsic value) itself.[52]

In this (neo-) liberal vision, human labour, hence man himself, has mainly been reduced to a (mere) cost for the enterprise (or other institution) exploiting it—or, on a macro-level, to a mere "production factor"[53]—ensuring that it preferably should be remunerated as low as possible (see also the earlier mentioned "Iron Law of the Wages"[54]). Indeed, the higher the compensation spent on labour, the lower the profit remaining for the enterprise that makes uses of labour (and ultimately: for the capital providers behind such an enterprise).

Under the doctrine of economic neo-liberalism, the only hinder left to further decrease the wages to even lower minima than the ones which are currently

[51] Fromm (1979), p. 85 a.f. See also Stiglitz (2002), p. 10, having pointed out that it has been one of the great "tricks" of neoclassical economics to treat labour like any other factor of production.

[52] Fromm (1979), p. 85 a.f.

[53] Stiglitz (2002), p. 10.

[54] Galbraith (1987), p. 84 a.f.

prevailing, forms the insight that the working classes (in the broad sense of the word)[55] should still have some purchasing power in order to continue to be able to buy the products generated by the capitalist machinery.

According to Michel Foucault, this expresses another basic idea of economic neo-liberalism, namely that "inequality is equal to everyone" which helps explaining that it cannot be the role of government to make efforts to level income or fortune.[56] On the contrary, the only thing that government can do is to ensure that a part of the over-capacity of the purchase power of the rich, is being transferred to those layers of the population experiencing a state of under-consumption (for instance because they are permanently unemployed, or because they meet unexpected challenges, such as sickness or injury making them unsuitable for the labour market). In other words, the only type of "social policy" which is deemed acceptable is one that contributes itself to economic growth (especially by stimulating consumption).[57]

Erich Fromm has rightfully indicated that the "subordinance" (one could even say: "degradation") of the (personal) life of any working person as a mere means to achieve economic goals, strikes the fundaments of the capitalist production, where the accumulation of capital has become the main, not to say only function and objective of economic activity. The working person who is subordinated to the capitalist production processes, works for the benefit of (someone else's) profit, but on top of that also for profit which is not mainly intended to be spent, but to serve for new capital investments. This increased capital, in turn, needs to generate new profits, through the allocation of the labour of other people. These new profits need to be re-invested again, and this cycle needs to continue infinitely (given the underlying objective that the economy needs to grow continuously, and this also to ensure the repayment of the enormous creation of private money under the capitalist private banking system).[58]

Fromm does not contradict that this has contributed to a certain degree of material progress for a part of humanity (but not for all people), but at the same time argues that this has happened to the detriment of a fundamental "dehumanisation" of (the working) man who, being reduced to a slave of the proprietary capitalist machinery, only lives for impersonal and extra-personal objectives and, as a result, is filled with a voidness and a meaninglessness.[59]

---

[55] Implied is the large group of people who depend on personal labour in order to fulfil their daily needs, thus not only employees in the strict sense of the word, but for instance also small business owners.

[56] This is clearly a liberal/neo-liberal way of looking at the role of government, going back to the works of Adam Smith himself. This viewpoint was already in Smith's time contested by other authors, such as the French social school of rationalism that on the contrary held that it is one of the main tasks of the government to install just mechanisms of redistributing wealth. (See further, in Sect. 5.9.4.2. See also Stiglitz (2002), p. 27.)

[57] Foucault (2013), pp. 192–193.

[58] Fromm (1990), p. 87.

[59] Fromm (1990), p. 87.

Still according to Fromm, the result of the inherent dehumanisation caused by the abovementioned turnabout of values is that man has been reduced to a "chased", "alienated" and "bewildered" individual.[60]

In this regard, there is in practice clearly very little achieved in terms of the theoretical freedom as predetermined by economic liberalism and neo-liberalism (except for the very limited class of very rich people who have gotten so extremely rich due to the application of the capitalist exploitation principles as described above that they themselves manage to escape from the chains of being employed by rich people themselves).

Next to Erich Fromm, a similar insight was reached by, for instance, Herbert Marcuse, who speaks of a "true negation of life"[61] which has become the driving force behind economic processes, with as extreme risk starvation for the dispossessed who are excluded from participating in these processes.[62]

In more economic terms, Paul Krugman has similarly pointed out that although classical economic handbooks may qualify the employment contract as one of the most basic "commercial transactions", but that the underlying truth is that where a merchant can trade several goods, a working man can only provide "one (amount of) labour" at a time, creating an extreme vulnerability as moreover the providers of such labour are usually available in much larger quantities than the demand to employ them. This author rightly states that "an unsold commodity is a nuisance, an unemployed worker a tragedy".[63]

In a similar way, also Stiglitz has pointed out one of the main differences between employment contracts and other contracts providing commodities needed for production, is the human aspect: individuals need to decide how hard they work and with what care, and, moreover, the environment affects their behaviour, including the incentives with which they are confronted.[64]

3.4.3 Some Last Examples of Capitalist Exploitation Techniques

From one's courses of history, one will probably remember the harrowing working conditions of the working classes in Europe and in the USA during the nineteenth until far in the twentieth century,[65] where the application of the theoretical liberal thought of freedom, in combination with the capitalist "Iron Law of the Wages", in

[60] Fromm (1990), p. 91.

[61] Marcuse (1968), p. 105.

[62] Marcuse (1968), p. 105.

[63] Krugman (1998), p. 15. On the mechanisms determining wages, hence the price for labour, see furthermore Galbraith (1979), p. 19.

[64] Stiglitz (2002), p. 10

[65] See Fromm (1956), p. 91.

reality led to a socio-economic model of exploitation which in essence was not better than the model of slavery from Classical Antiquity. It has even been argued that the living conditions of slaves from Ancient Greece and Rome may have been far better than those of the working classes in the nineteenth and during the first half of the twentieth century.

At present, this gives rise to the concern that the evergrowing implementation of the doctrines of economic neo-liberalism threatens to turn the clock back to these times.

This fact earlier brought historians to the observation that the success of industrial capitalism during the nineteenth century, especially in Europe and the USA, is to a very large part to be attributed to the cruel exploitation of the working classes by the leading captains of industry of that time, for instance in the textile industry, the metal industry and the mining sector.[66] However, also in the contemporary context, the abovementioned approach of labour as a mere production factor has continued to characterize the most harrowing abuses, such as the shameless exploitation of young children in several capitalist production and trade process as still taking place in many countries in the world.

Even in (traditionally) rich countries, the "Iron Law of the Wages" still rises in many debates, providing an ever-increasing catalyst effect on the worldwide dismantling of measures protecting labour (hence the working classes) and of other social protection mechanisms, and more recently, in the notorious pension debate where adherents of the theories of economic neo-liberalism all over the world unanimously start proclaiming that the working man should keep on working until an ever later age in order to keep economies ongoing.

3.4.4 The Duty to Consume

For most people, the ideal of freedom under the doctrines of economic liberalism and neo-liberalism is not only in their capacity of supplier of labour an absolute illusion, but also in many other domains of societal life, for instance in their capacity of consumer in the broadest sense of the word.

Given one of the most basic beliefs of economic liberalism and neo-liberalism that economic growth should continue endlessly, capitalism is characterized by a continuous pursuit of increasing production for the sake of production and, through this, also by a continuous pursuit of increasing consumption for the sake of

[66] Beaud (1994), p. 131.

consumption.[67] Skidelsky and Skidelsky have, furthermore, added to this that capitalism thus inflames the love of money for money's sake.[68]

The combination of the myths that enterprises should make ever more profits and that private banks should bring ever more newly created money (i.e. banking credit) into circulation in order to stimulate economic growth, has indeed led to an economic model where, as of the seventeenth century, ever more goods need to be produced and through this, also consumed (by the large masses).

In this economic model, all the resources available on earth (and as soon as this will be feasible: even beyond earth) need to be discovered and extracted as efficiently as possible in order to make them part of the capitalist production processes. All forests, wherever in the world, must be grubbed-up, in order to produce wood which can serve economic production, and new woods should only be planted if, for the same reason, they can be grubbed-up as soon as possible. Any scientific discovery should, without delay, serve the same capitalist production processes and should consequently translate into the production of goods which are sufficiently "marketable". As a result, in the contemporary purportedly "free" world, barely any independent scientific research is still taking place, but on the contrary, all scientific research is driven by, or in collaboration with, capitalist industry.[69] Almost every living creature on earth is studied to discover how it can be reduced to a method of entrepreneurial profit, be it as exhibition objects in a zoo (in essence one of the many "beneficent" findings of early capitalism), as pets (also in the case of exotic animals which do absolutely not fit that role), as a testing object, or as an ingredient for potential human consumption in the widest sense of the word. It is in this regard striking that the capitalist human being is even provisioning the exploitation of other planets (as witnessed by the contemporary intention to colonise the planet Mars, with the open question on what to do or to find there).

Put otherwise, the production for production's sake which derives from the capitalist principle driving economy towards an ever-increasing growth, necessarily translates in an everlasting and ever-expanding model of consumption for consumption's sake. As a result, man has in the period after World War II been exposed to the most aggressive advertising methods thinkable, going from classical advertisements and commercials inciting people to more and more consumption through "catchy" tunes and appealing images, to even more aggressive methods of influencing the

---

[67] See Galbraith (1992), p. 109. See also Sachs (2011), p. 144 a.f., referring to:

> the marriage between mass media and hypercommercialism.

According to Erich Fromm, Karl Marx has been one of the first to fight this intrinsic characteristic of capitalism. According to Marx, the aim of society should not be the mere production of things as an aim on itself. What since Marx' writings has been completely neglected by even left-wing political parties (such as socialist and communist parties), is that for Marx, maximum production and maximum consumption should not be the unquestionable aims of society. Society should be about the conquest of poverty and about putting an end to unjust levels on inequality, not about production and consumption as a supreme end. (See Fromm (2013), p. 31.)

[68] Skidelsky and Skidelsky (2013), p. 41.

[69] On this, see Debusschere (2015), p. 15.

human mind (such as the use of subliminal messages, but also the use of artificial colours and smells), which place the idea that (capitalist) man is free, in a very specific perspective.[70]

In modern days, Asian economies which have caught up, or are catching up, on their own economic growth model, among which China and India, are reported to be increasingly hit by this same urge for over-consumption.[71]

In their striving for ever more growth and profits, producers of a variety of consumption articles show no shame at all to make their goods as addictive as possible, with as typical example the one of the tobacco industry, next to that of the beverages and industrial food industry. All types of strategies are hereby tried to persuade people to consume more and more.

This has in recent times led to an excess of so-called "created wants", goods and services which are massively bought by consumers even if they serve no purpose or if they are intrinsically useless.[72] A typical illustration is the output of the entertainment industry, next to the variety of useless gadgets which have been made available especially in the Western world, going from decoration articles, luxury perfumes and design clothing, to all kinds of electronic and other useless gadgets.

How many of us have under the influence of advertising or otherwise, not been tempted to purchase one or another very promising article which, after a few uses, ends up somewhere deep in a cabinet to consequently, at the occasion of a clean-up, find its way to the dump, or, in the best case, to a garden or similar sale.[73]

In contemporary times, the very fast aging process of many types of consumer articles is in this regard of a particular notice, as the production for production's sake needs to evolve faster and faster and the preferences of consumers need to stay in pace.

In the music industry, this process is demonstrated by the swift rise and equally swift fall of contemporary pop stars: those who rise high today can as soon be forgotten, as the taste of the consumer needs to permanently evolve in other directions in order to ensure that the capitalist machinery will never stop.

As a result, the average human being is not only a modern slave who has to provide labour for his entire life to the capitalist production processes which are increasingly merciless; also in his capacity of a consumer, he is expected to continuously purchase new products and in this regard also be the slave of industrial production.

---

[70] See also Galbraith and Salinger (1978), p. 162.

[71] Not coincidentally one of the largest stock market listings of recent times has been the one of the large Chinese webshop "Alibaba" (see Westcott (2015)).

In a similar sense, recent press mentioned the increase of alcohol consumption among the members of the upcoming Chinese middle class (see Ferdman (2015)).

[72] Compare Skidelsky and Skidelsky (2013), p. 40.

[73] Where the same cycle may be repeated all over again.

In economic literature, this is also referred to as characterizing the "disposable society" (also: the "throw-away society"). (See above, in footnote 35.)

It is in this latter regard remarkable, but certainly not a coincidence, that one of the former American presidents has explicitly spoken of "a duty to consume" in order to sufficient stimulate the capitalist economy.[74]

The condemnation to "eternally have to work" and "eternally have to consume" are hereby obviously closely linked. Labour needs to be performed in order to provide a sufficient income to be able to continue to consume, and consumption is needed to continue to sustain production of the several goods to be consumed, thus ensuring employment, hence that a sufficient amount of people dispose of a sufficient income to keep on consuming.

3.4.5 The Rise of Consumer Credit

As if the capitalist "strait-jackets" of "eternal wage slave" and "eternal consumer" are not enough, modern capitalism has added yet another "golden cage" to these, namely the one of consumer credits (in the broadest sense of the word).[75]

The underlying "logic" is that man, when being placed before a (consumer) need without disposing of the financial means to immediately fulfill such need, should not be denied access to fulfilling this need (as economy would suffer from this). This dilemma has found its solution in another of the many "blessings" of the capitalist economic model, namely the consumer credit (in a broad sense of the word).

As is the case for enterprises aspiring to grow and states who do not recover enough means from taxing the poor and middle classes, also an individual who is facing a need without disposing of the financial means to immediately fulfill such a need, has access to all types of credit allowing him to participate in the consumption process.

It is not a coincidence that the rise of both the theories of economic neo-liberalism and their implementation in practice as of the 1980s have gone hand in hand with an increase of "credit economy thinking".

As a result, especially since the 1980s, taking up credit by individuals in order to be able to meet a consumption need has massively been stimulated (both by the private banking sector itself, as through the monetary policy of central bankers[76]). As a result, in Western countries, individuals have massively started to take up credits for all types of spending, going from a house, or even more than one, to the purchase of luxury cars, next to all types of other useful and less useful consumer goods and consumables, often with very marginal added value.

---

[74] See Reich (2001). See also Bacevich (2008), pointing out how this consumerism was based upon (banking) credit, thus having attributed to the severe financial crisis of 2007–2008.

[75] This is also a consequence of the capitalist mechanisms as discussed in Chap. 2, especially the so-called private money creation based on interest-generating credits provided by banks, and the subordination of labour to capital in enterprises which are legally organised as capital companies.

[76] About the failure of the central banking policy in the years before the financial crisis of 2008, see Stiglitz (2010), p. 261 a.f. It may be as interesting to read Greenspan (2007) in this regard.

In this way, the slave status as a consumer started supporting the slave status as a worker even more, as people do not only need to work in order to be able to finance their participation in unbridled consumption, but also in order to pay back (from their same income from labour) the consumer credits (in a broad sense of the word) which they take up in order to be able to consume sufficiently.

As a result, the fate of the average human being is not very different from the one of a caged rodent spending its life in a treadmill. It continues endlessly to run to nowhere, until it will finally drop dead, as indeed, in current neo-liberal societies, it is expected that everyone needs to undergo this hopeless participation in the capitalist socio-economic order till the highest age possible, as may, for instance, be illustrated by the present-day pension debate where neo-liberal governments all over the world, to an increasing extent, unanimously dictate that everyone (else) should work as long as possible.

This also implies that the hope to ever escape from the capitalist treadmill, for many people is procrastinated further and further in time, i.e. to an age where the health condition of a person will no longer allow to do anything else than wait the hour of death, probably wondering if the way how life has run within neo-liberally organised capitalism, has led to any form of true happiness.[77]

3.4.6 *Conclusion: Freedom As One of the Many Unfulfilled Myths of Capitalist Economies*

From the foregoing, it may be clear that the (classical) capitalist principles (as reshaped by the theories of economic neo-liberalism) do not at all fulfil their promise of freedom, in this way failing to achieve one of their main goals of creating free societies.

Only the happy few who can get excessively rich through said capitalist principles and mechanisms, will find themselves in a better position, as they at least will acquire enough money to, at least to a certain extent, escape from the compulsive processes of capitalism. Those who are rich will indeed need to work less, or need to perform less hard or boring labour, will be less inclined to turn to credit mechanisms in order to fulfil their consumption needs, and will therefore be less a slave of the abovementioned capitalist processes.

Nevertheless, there is still a hope that such rich persons may at least start to wonder whether his acquired wealth has been worth shamelessly exploiting a large part

[77] See also further under Sect. 3.5.4, where it is described how elderly people under the systems of capitalism often end up in miserable retirement homes.

Countless are the blogs and newspaper articles that sum up the things people regret on their death bed, having to have worked too hard in blind obedience of a boss being one of the five things people regret the most. (See recent https://elkedagenergie.be/sterfbed/; last consulted on June 16, 2018.)

of his fellow human beings and subordinating them to his own unlimited hunger for ever more money.[78]

We hence can but conclude that economic liberalism and economic neo-liberalism have not at all fulfilled their promise of shaping a world of freedom. On the contrary, their ideas have subordinated most people to neverending mechanisms of socio-economic suppression and exploitation, implying that economic liberalism and economic neo-liberalism may claim to intend to make the world freer, where in reality they have caught the largest part of humanity in the capitalist machinery, in which freedom is for most people on earth but an utter illusion.

3.5 Making the Neo-liberal Wet Dream of Dismantling the Welfare State Model Come True in Practice, Especially by Applying the Neo-liberal Techniques of Deregulation and Neo-liberalization

3.5.1 The Neo-liberal Agenda of Dismantling States Briefly Revisited

It has already been mentioned under Sect. 2.6.2: driven by its inherent aversion of state involvement in socio-economic life, economic neo-liberalism has the ambition to free the world from the methods of correcting unbridled capitalism which have been developed especially in the period after World War II and which under its doctrines are deemed to be disastrous.

In this neo-liberal approach, it is believed that anything which can hinder the free market, is economically disastrous and needs to be eliminated as much and as fast as possible.

It is obviously well known that, especially in the period after World War II, many methods of correcting unbridled capitalism were introduced in socio-economic life, mainly as a consequence of interventions by national governments.

A typical example are the several types of regulations which aimed at offering an elementary degree of social protection to the weaker members of society, such as, obviously, social security systems, next to system of public services which are financed by governments based upon tax money.

It however also concerned regulations which aim(ed) at streamlining certain economic processes, going from the so-called prudential, financial regulation urging financial institutions to exercise more reason and caution than they are inclined to by nature, to all types of regulations with as objective the protection of consumer interests or the environment.

[78]As did happen to the young prince in the fairy tale "The Young King" by Oscar Wilde (1854–1900), as well as (eventually) to Ebenezer Scooge in the famous Christmas story "A Christmas Carol" of Charles Dickens (1812–1870).

Under the doctrines of economic neo-liberalism, to the extent that all these methods of correcting unbridled capitalism were deemed to be an obstacle for the working of the free market, it got assumed that they needed to be eliminated as much and as quickly as possible, a doctrine that resulted in the neo-liberal agenda of "de-regulating" and "(neo-)liberalising" the economy.[79]

3.5.2 The Implementation of the Neo-liberal Agenda in Some Territories

3.5.2.1 General

Among the main propagated methods by means of which economic neo-liberalism has attempted to create its ideal world where states completely withdraw from socio-economic life in order to leave it as much as possible in the care of the invisible hands of the free markets were: the legal techniques of "(neo-)liberalisation" and "deregulation", which in itself are rather vague terms describing a diversity of interventions by which neo-liberal governments, especially as of the end of the 1970s, have expressed a paramount zeal to make markets as free as possible from any type of state interference. Although the differences between the two techniques are in practice often not that clear, one could state that the technique of deregulation aims at removing, or at the very least softening, rules and regulations that are perceived as hindering the way enterprises operate, while the technique of (neo-)liberalisation more in general aims at removing all types of (other) obstacles that purportedly impair the operation of the free market.

As a result of applying these techniques on a massive scale, and somewhat paradoxically, economic neo-liberalism has in reality expressed itself as an ideology deploying state authority as a means of resolutely reducing all forms of soci(et)al progress which had been accomplished in the period after World War II.[80]

A blueprint of (neo-)liberalisation and deregulation measures which could have been unilaterally applied in all countries, was hereby obviously not available.[81]

One of the reasons hereof has been that in the different Western or capitalist countries where economic neo-liberalism has struck during the past decades, the variations in the social protecting tissue and in other regulations which attempted to correct the free market mechanism, were obviously too large.

Therefore, in order to comprehend how economic neo-liberalism works, one has to look on a country-by-country base in which way a given neo-liberal government has attempted at purifying that country of the consequences of the mixed market

---

[79] See also Brown (2003).

[80] Stiglitz (2003), p. 143.

[81] The working methods of (neo)liberalisation and deregulation will be furthermore illustrated in the next Sects. 3.6 and 3.7 by means of two striking examples which affect us all on a daily base, namely the financial and the electricity sector.

economy, the constant in the underlying goals of such a policy making being the achievement of the freest markets possible.

3.5.2.2 The Attacks on the Welfare State Model by Ronald Reagan and Margaret Thatcher

For the purposes of academic research (albeit only for that), it has been a blessing in disguise that in the 1980s, there have been two major economic powers which were among the first ones to attempt to achieve the goals of economic neo-liberalism, which allows us to get a general idea of the working methods of economic neo-liberalism, but also of its disastrous consequences for society.

These two economic powers where the recipes of economic neo-liberalism have (early in history[82]) been tested during (a) considerably long government term(s) of strongly neo-liberal tainted governments, were obviously—as has been mentioned earlier—the United States of America (where the doctrine of economic neo-liberalism then deployed has also been indicated as "Reaganomics") and the United Kingdom (where the doctrine of economic neo-liberalism deployed has also been indicated as "Thatcherism").

Both neo-liberal governments were moreover active during more or less the same time period, namely the 1980s, and applied similar (albeit not entirely the same) methods of creating free markets, even to the extent that it is possible to understand the way the minds of fervent neo-liberal government leaders work by simply taking the biographies of the two heads of government of said governments, being the late Ronald Reagan and the late Margaret Thatcher, at hand.[83]

The fact that neo-liberal thinking especially in these two countries has struck such a significant chord, has probably not been a coincidence, knowing that both countries have throughout history been among the ones most notably endorsing unbridled capitalism and among the ones least inclined to take initiatives towards a "mixed economy".[84]

In these countries, both abovementioned governments eagerly addressed the invitation of the schools of economic neo-liberalism to purify capitalism (or the free markets) from the disastrous effects of the mixed economy. This would in both countries lead to a profound implementation of said doctrines of economic neo-liberalism which, on its own turn, would later on have an important inspiring effect on the rest of the world. As a result, in the course of the 1990s ultimately, even world

---

[82] Armstrong mentions that:

> neo-liberal strategies began in Latin America in the late 1970s as a result of the great economic imbalances they had. Other pioneering countries in neoliberalism are the United States, Germany and England. (See Armstrong (2017).)

[83] See for instance Thatcher (1993).

[84] See also Pauli (2014), p. 33; van Oudheusden (2012), p. 132.

trade and global payment and capital traffic itself would get almost entirely based on the theories of economic neo-liberalism.

One of the central measures taken by the American Reagan-government (1981–1989) has been the application of the so-called "consumerism"-theory.[85] This doctrine of consumerism aimed at answering a then prevailing economic crisis by stimulating demand within the economy.[86] The implementation of the doctrine of consumerism went, in the financial field, hand in hand with an extensive deregulation of the financial sector, along with an unprecedented stimulation of all types of (consumer) credit mechanisms.[87]

It goes without saying that this policy has been one of the main causes for the rise of the so-called "credit economy" (on its own turn, one of the main factors attributing to the severe financial crisis of 2007–2008).[88]

A further method, inspired by neo-liberal thinking with which Ronald Reagan attempted to boost the American economy, has been military expenditure.[89] Galbraith has indicated this as almost the only domain where, according to the doctrines of economic neo-liberalism,[90] a state may interfere in economic life (next to by (over)subsidizing the agricultural sector, as well as large enterprises in general, and by bailing out large financial institutions).[91]

After the far more peaceful administration of Jimmy Carter (president from 1977 to 1981), the Reagan-administration thus made its only, albeit very distorted application of Keynesian thinking (i.e. the call for stimulation economy through government spending). This resulted in an unprecedented increase of the expenditure on weapons of the USA (mainly benefiting the rich class of weapon producers).[92] Galbraith has indicated that, since then, the spending for weapons has been one of

---

[85] See Krugman (1994), p. 157.

[86] A policy also conducted by former president George Bush jr. (see http://www.washingtonpost.com/wp-dyn/content/article/2008/10/03/AR2008100301977.html; last consulted on June 16, 2018).

[87] See also under the previous Sect. 3.4.

[88] For further reading, see Steger (2013), p. 40; Steger (2014), p. 53; Lloyd (2012), p. 374; Harari (2014), p. 388; Bruckner (2002), p. 20; Sterdyniak (2011), p. 27; Pesendorfer (2012), pp. 414–434.

[89] Galbraith (1992), p. 122. See already before Galbraith and Salinger (1978), p. 157.

[90] And of its political counterpart: conservatism. (See also http://lchc.ucsd.edu/cogn_150/Readings/brown.pdf; last consulted on June 16, 2018).

[91] Galbraith (1992), p. 122. See also van Oudheusden (2012), p. 133.

In a comparable manner, Chomsky also mentions "the grotesquerie of the space race" as a "transfigured, transmuted and theoretical substitute for an infinite strategic arms race". (See Chomsky (2015), p. 35.)

About the impact of neo-liberalism on agricultural politics especially, see also Foucault 2013, p. 189 a.f.

[92] Ronse (1992), p. 74.

the few examples of government spending on which the American rich and middle classes seem to agree that the state is allowed to perform them.[93]

Unfortunately, since then, the consequent entanglement of political power and the weapon industry has only grown in importance.[94]

As an obedient servant of the schools of economic neo-liberalism which hold that mainly the rich within society—especially (large) enterprises and their underlying capital providers, next to their CEO's and other leading managers—may not be slowed down in their operations by having to pay taxes, so that they can ensure the pursuit for general prosperity for the global society, the Reagan-administration also implemented a number of "tax-shifts" which, obviously, mainly benefitted the rich in society[95] (a recipe that, in our times, has in the mean time been repeated by the Trump-administration[96]).

Driven by a spirit of unbridled consumerism which was, as mentioned, propagated by the Reagan-administration, the rich would massively spend the money saved by these tax reductions to what since then has been described as "an ever-increasing obscene orgy of consumption".[97]

As a result, and following the American example, the globalised world would be more and more drawn into an unprecedented "hyper consumption", thus underlining the classical characteristic of capitalist economy as a model of "consumption for consumption's sake" even more.[98]

One of the further consequences of the several measures the Reagan-administration resorted to has been that all levels of society—enterprises, consumers and governments—would massively take up credits "as if they would never need to be paid back".[99] This even further set the tone for the currently still prevailing "credit economy".

One should hereby, as argued before, bear in mind that this has been one of the main causes for the disruption of the monetary and financial system which would result in the severe financial crisis of 2007–2008.[100]

It has been disastrous that the largest part of this credit was not invested in a sustainable manner, such as to enhance beneficial forms of production, e.g. clean

---

[93] Galbraith (1992), p. 23:

> Specifically favored also have been military expenditures, their scale and fiscally oppressive effect notwithstanding.

[94] Sachs (2011), p. 117 a.f. See already before Galbraith (1992), p. 23 a.f.

[95] Galbraith (1992), p. 26.

[96] See, for instance https://www.thebalance.com/donald-trump-economic-plan-3994106 (last consulted on June 16, 2018), summarizing this classical neo-liberal fiscal policy as follows:

> Trump said that cutting [especially corporate] taxes will increase growth enough to offset the loss of revenue.

For a more detailed overview of Trump's 2017–2018 tax reform plans, see Bird (2017).

[97] Ronse (1992), p. 74.

[98] Sachs (2011), p. 144 a.f. See before also Ruyver (1969).

[99] Ronse (1992), p. 74.

[100] Regretfully, this problem has up to this very date not yet been tackled with in a serious manner, public and private debt since then having reached levels unseen ever before in history.

energy, or to renew infrastructure, but that it has mainly been used for further consumption. This in its own turn caused the USA (next to numerous other Western countries) to become ever more dependent on import,[101] an effect which would even be reinforced during the 1990s.[102]

According to some, this would ultimately lead to the fact that, already in 2014, the USA had to concede their leading position in the world economy to China.[103]

The Reagan-administration, furthermore, aimed at dismantling several social care systems, among which access to medical care and public education, next to de-regulating numerous sectors of economic life, among which the financial sector.[104]

---

[101] Ronse (1992), p. 74.

[102] Especially after the application of the techniques of (neo-)liberalisation and deregulation would be adopted by many other countries and regions (such as the member states of the European Union), and finally be applied at the occurrence of the creation of the new architecture of the global free trade and the global free traffic of payments and capital (especially within the context of the WTO).

[103] See already Van der Borght (2014), p. 2. See, furthermore, Carter (2014).

> For the first time in more than 140 years, the US has lost the title of the world's largest economy – it has been stolen by China, according to the IMF. But how reliable are the statistics underpinning this claim? The BBC's economics editor, Robert Peston, explains lower down why China matters to all of us.
>
> The Chinese economy is now worth \$17.6tn, slightly higher than the \$17.4tn the International Monetary Fund (IMF) estimates for the US.
>
> So for the first time since 1872, when it overtook the UK, the US has been knocked off the top spot. (See Carter (2014).)

Also in 2016, both the IMF and the World Bank continued to rank the Chinese economy on the first place (before that of the USA). (See Willige (2016).)

> Both the IMF and the World Bank now rate China as the world's largest economy based on Purchasing Power Parity (PPP), a measure that adjusts countries' GDPs for differences in prices. In simple terms, this means that because your money stretches further in China than it would in the US, China's GDP is adjusted upwards. (See Willige (2016).)

[104] Galbraith (1992), p. 49; Ronse (1992), p. 154 a.f.

Under president Donald Trump, a very similar neo-liberal policy has been deployed, i.a. also leading to a new deregulation of the financial sector. (See DM/RC (2018).) More precisely, the US House voted on 22 May 2018 legislation aimed at rolling back regulations imposed by the so-called Dodd-Frank Act (= an Act that was voted in 2010, under the presidency of Barack Obama, in response to the financial crisis of 2007–2008). The newly voted law loosens capital requirements for both major and smaller banks and was reported to mark yet another marquee "pro-business" triumph for president Donald Trump. (See DM/RC (2018).)

> The new bipartisan legislation will roll back several of the 2010 Dodd-Frank rules that raised capital requirements for banks, including several smaller lenders. The bill also raises the threshold in assets at which banks are considered risky and subject to stricter oversight from \$50 billion to \$250 billion (€42.5 billion to €212.5 billion). (See DM/RC (2018).)

For the text of this bill, after it having been approved by the American Senate on 14 March 2018, see S. 2155: Economic Growth, Regulatory Relief, and Consumer Protection Act, at: https://www.govtrack.us/congress/bills/115/s2155/text/es. For the text as of 24 May 2018, after having

Also in the 1980s, the doctrines of economic neo-liberalism similarly inspired the subsequent governments led by Reagan's close friend and kindred spirit Margaret Thatcher. The policy of her government(s) mainly focused on dismantling public institutions and social care mechanisms. Special attention was hereby paid to breaking the influence of trade unions, as well as to privatising a variety of government institutions and services.[105]

As has been the case for the Reagan-administration in the USA, the efforts of the subsequent Thatcher-administrations above all resulted in a fundamental decrease of the involvement of the British state in socio-economic life (which today still characterises the socio-economic order of the United Kingdom).[106]

3.5.2.3 The Global Application of the Doctrines of Economic Neo-liberalism

By the end of the 1980s, the doctrines of economic neo-liberalism would even further triumph thanks to the fall, in the Soviet-Union and its vassal states, of communism, which up till then had provided at least some counter weight to the since then ever predominant capitalist market model.[107]

As a result, especially in a socio-economic context, the power of capitalism would not be countered anymore in a meaningful manner. It is hereby hardly surprising that (especially by neo-liberal authors) the collapse of the communist economies has often been upheld as an argument that there are no alternatives for the free markets (= the so-called "TINA-argument").[108]

Since then, the belief in the myth of the free market has become ever more fanatic, even resulting into the idea that the free market is an essential prerequisite for a free society, and a condition for individual prosperity and societal progress.[109]

The overall success of the doctrines of economic neo-liberalism in the 1990s thus paved the way for an unprecedented globalisation of the world economy—to be understood as the increasing degree of mutual interdependence between countries economically, due to an increasing international traffic of goods, services,

---

passed Congress, see https://www.govtrack.us/congress/bills/115/s2155/text. (last consulted on June 16, 2018).

[105] Krugman (1994), p. 172 a.f.

[106] For some of the consequences thereof, see further, under Sects. 4.7.2 and 4.9.2.

[107] On the collapse of communism, see for instance Eyskens (s.d.), p. 107; Menasse (2012), p. 78. See also Stiglitz (2002), p. 26:

> The interplay between politics and economics has been most dramatically in Russia, where the privatization process resulted in the devastation of the middle class, and the creation of huge inequalities and an oligarchy which, if it seeks to establish a rule of law, will use its wealth and power to try to ensure that that rule of law favours itself.

[108] See for instance Rand (2008), p. 26.

[109] Pauli (2014), p. 33.

capital and labour[110]—based on the neo-liberal principles of liberalisation and deregulation.

Furthermore, already during the 1980s, many individual countries started following the example of the USA and the UK, causing that, on a global scale, the doctrines of economic neo-liberalism got more and more implemented in socio-economic policies. This translated into a worldwide dismantling of public socio-economic structures in fields as public services (for instance education and justice) and social care (in a broad sense of the word).

Already the first initiatives towards an economic (but not social, fiscal or political) European integration dating of the early 1950s, were inspired by liberal doctrines. It thus hardly came as a surprise that the European Economic and Monetary Union itself would, to an increasing extent, also embrace the principles and working methods of economic neo-liberalism. Illustrative hereof is the great enthusiasm the European Union has demonstrated to "(neo-)liberalise" and "de-regulate" many European markets.[111] As illustrative is the absence of any serious intent to stop the ongoing race to the bottom between member states in the field of social care protection and taxation.

3.5.3 Some Further Consequences of the Dismantling of the Welfare State Model

It is impossible to map the current socio-economic situation of every country in the world in order to further illustrate the abovementioned. Probably only international institutions such as the OESO and the IMF could be capable of performing such task, the question being if they would ever show a sufficient willingness to do so, as also their own operation has during the past decades been increasingly contaminated by the spirit of economic neo-liberalism which grips the entire world.

Nevertheless, the anecdotic proof speaks for itself, even by merely reading (local) press reports.

From the many possible examples, reference is here made to an article which appeared in the Belgian newspaper "De Morgen" of March 18th, 2015, containing an analysis of the socio-economic situation in Israel that was based on an interview with economics professor Bernard Avishai.

Obviously, Israel often draws the attention of the international press with regards to the Palestine question, implying that we rarely get (other) news about the socio-economic and political situation of the country. Although said article obviously does not qualify as a thorough analysis of the socio-economic whereabouts of Israel, it

---

[110] Stiglitz (2006), p. 4.

[111] See http://europa.eu/pol/pdf/flipbook/en/internal_market_en.pdf (last consulted on June 16, 2018).

nevertheless raises the assumption that the doctrines of economic neo-liberalism have hit hard in that country.

The article for instance mentions that Israel is particularly marked by an increasing socio-economic injustice, which already in 2011 has led to civil protest by hundreds of thousands of people. The article furthermore mentions that, to an increasing extent, the Israeli economy is strongly dominated by a small number of large conglomerates holding monopoly positions which are artificially boosting prices of all kinds of products (resulting in prices that are up to 33% higher compared to other countries). It is, furthermore, reported that the economic added value of the past 6 years has mainly been translated into profits flowing to the capital providers of large corporations, causing serious difficulties for (public) sectors such as education and health care. The article concludes with the observation that the condition of Israel is a result of the socio-economic policy of successive governments, where the open question rises what the near future will offer to Israel it this trend will go any further.[112]

3.5.4 *The Global Contamination of the Human Mind by the Virus of Economic Neo-liberalism*

It is very remarkable that, on a global scale, the huge success of economic neo-liberalism has only been possible because a sufficient large part of the population of the countries which have adhered its doctrines have empowered political parties who (explicit or less explicit) aimed at implementing it.[113]

This is thus the more surprising as, by implementing the doctrines of economic neo-liberalism, a socio-economic order has been established which is basically detrimental for the general public having elected said governments, due to, among others, the reduction of general public services and the under-financing of general good "sectors" such as health care and justice.

Nevertheless, on occasion, the same general public having elected said neo-liberal governments does not hesitate to express public indignation in cases were society is faced with the disastrous consequences of such neo-liberal policies, not rarely in the context of an individual, or a group of people, who suffer from some form of injustice caused by the neoliberal societal order.

In the period that an earlier Dutch version of this book was drafted, there was, for instance, a huge turmoil in Flanders about a 17-year old girl suffering from mental problems who was refused admittance by a hospital who instead delivered the girl

[112] Descamps (2015), p. 4.

[113] For instance, in Belgium, the "N-VA" party joined the federal government of Michel I in 2014. This government strongly conducts a neo-liberal course. This has been somewhat surprising to the extent that the N-VA, during the foregoing elections, had announced that it would mainly work on a community agenda, without having made any noteworthy allusion whatsoever of so strongly adhering the doctrines of economic neo-liberalism.

to the justice department, which ultimately resulted in the girl having to spend a night in prison. This was obviously a harrowing event, but nevertheless, the large indignation the event met in the Flemish press[114] is to a large extent incomprehensible, and even somewhat hypocrite, knowing that the Flemish, and by extension, the European population, by bringing neo-liberal governments to power, have massively supported a political ideology that holds that the least possible financial means (if any at all) should go to public services and social care, in order to ensure that the added value generated by the economy should as much as possible translate in maximised business profits, to the extent that, also in Belgium, many public and social sectors services are to an ever growing extent completely underfinanced and are no longer functioning properly.[115]

When writing the English version of this book, a similar indignation arose in the Belgian press about the harrowing living conditions in private homes for the elderly.[116] Based upon an investigation of the living conditions in several of such private homes for elderly, it was reported that most such homes were completely understaffed, resulting in the elderly people living there not receiving the basic care and attention they were supposed to have. Many of the elderly people living in such homes were reported to feel miserable, and in an interview with the investigating reporter, one of them even told that she would rather die than continue to live in the home she was staying in. From the investigation, it appeared that the lack of care and attention people receive in said homes for the elderly, was in no way justified given the large monthly amounts people had to pay for staying in such homes.[117]

The conclusion of the press articles sounded that the main cause for this atrocity is the pursuit of profits principle that governs such private homes for elderly, resulting in a general policy whereby as little as costs possible are made to provide a good service (resulting in, among others, cutting back in staff and cutting down in expenses for food, personal hygiene and health products).[118]

In this regard, reference can also be made to the ill fate of Rebecca Zeni, a former renowned model and US TV star who was eaten alive by scabies in her Georgia care home,[119] illustrating how also in the USA, the living conditions in some retirement homes may be qualified as dreadful.

---

[114] See for instance Desmet (2015), the title of the press article by this reporter in English literally to be translated as "Shameful".

[115] In the referred case of the 17-year old girl who ended up in prison, caregivers interviewed by a journalist of the newspaper "De morgen" called for a health care policy where the patient would take a central role, instead of financial matters. (See De Cuyper (2015).)

[116] See for instance Calluy and Nasser (2017) and Messiaen (2017).

[117] Which, according to the press reports, were on average between 2000 and 7500 euro per month, additional medical costs not included. (See Calluy and Nasser (2017) and Messiaen (2017).)

[118] Calluy and Nasser (2017) and Messiaen (2017).

[119] See Rogers (2018).

3.5.5 Conclusion

An ancient biblical saying goes that "one will reap what one has sown" (see Galatians, 6:7), which in the context of the socio-economic organisation of society translates in the observation that, when a societal order gets more and more based on the many witticisms of economic neo-liberalism, the resulting society will be the one which is at present increasingly experienced on a global scale. Such a society will be characterized by an extreme polarisation between the rich (= basically those who reap the business profits, ergo the largest part of the added value of economy) and the poor (= those who do not share in business profits, but are instead mainly drained in order to contribute to these business profits of the rich), with all known consequences. (See, furthermore, under Sect. 4.7.)

Such a society will, furthermore, be characterized and by an ongoing dismantling of the tissue of the public care mechanisms which have shapen the welfare state model in the period after World War II, at least in Western countries, such as justice, social care in a broad sense of the word and public education.[120]

Moreover, egoism, selfishness and greed will, in full accordance with the dictates of economic neo-liberalism, be the driving forces of such a society which, as a consequence, will be as remote as possible from the ideal Kingdom of God that Jesus Christ earlier on in history has strived for.

As a result of the ongoing implementation of the doctrines of economic neo-liberalism, such a neo-liberal society will also perfectly start mirroring the doomsday image which already Plato warned about ages ago[121]:

> The further they go in the process of accumulating wealth, the more they value it and the less they value goodness. For aren't wealth and goodness related like two objects in a balance, so that when one rises the other must fall. (…) So the higher the prestige of wealth and the wealthy, the lower that of goodness and good men will be. (…) And so there is a transi-

[120] Even a member of parliament of N-VA, albeit a political party fervently adhering the doctrines of economic neo-liberalism, has, in the abovementioned case of the 17-year old girl, reached the conclusion that the health care sector is being confronted with chronical capacity shortages (see Anseeuw (2015), p. 3), however without making the link with the underlying causes of this, being the fact that, for decades already, the application of the doctrines of economic neo-liberalism (to a large extent: by his own political party) has increasingly resulted in a dismantling of Belgian public and social services.

[121] Plato (1987), p. 306.

See also the rebuttal of neo-liberal authors such as Yaron Brook and Don Watkins (see Brook and Watkins (2012), p. 77):

> In Plato's Republic, Socrates declares "the more men value moneymaking, the less they value virtue." Rand's view is exactly the opposite. The value of virtues is its role in promoting your own welfare – including your economic welfare. The more men value money making, the more they value virtue.

The purported "rebuttal" by Brook and Watkins is a textbook example of the complete turnaround of values (in comparison to, for instance, the value scale of Classical Antiquity, or the one of Jesus Christ) that characterizes (economic) neo-liberal thinking.

tion from the ambitious, competitive type of man to the money-loving businessman, honor and admiration and office are reserved for the rich, and the poor are despised.

3.6 Further Illustration I: The (Neo-)liberalisation of the European Financial Sector

From the many conceivable examples of sectors which, under the influence of the doctrines of economic neo-liberalism, Europe has been "deregulating" and/or "(neo-)liberalising" since the 1980s, the case of the (neo-)liberalisation of the European financial sector is obviously very striking.

This is thus the more the case, given the fact that the correlation between the far-reaching degree of (neo-)liberalisation and deregulation the European financial sector as of the 1980s underwent, and the extent to which this has attributed to the severe financial crisis of 2007–2008, has hardly been investigated, let alone debated upon.

On the contrary, it seems that this theme is anxiously being avoided in political debate.

Indeed, since the end of the 1980s, through a variety of financial regulatory directives, the different components of the European financial markets were, one by one, subject to the European objective of harmonising said financial regulation, with as underlying goal a steady (neo-)liberalisation (and unification) of all levels of the European financial markets in order to bring them in line with the principles of free marketism.[122]

In this process, the so-called "second banking directive"[123] aiming at harmonising the rules on banking services and, at the same time, at creating a free (liberalised) market for such services, has undoubtedly been a milestone, as it, since then, has stood model for similar harmonisation and (neo-)liberalisation directives in several other fields of financial law.

The impact of this type of neo-liberal European directives to the landscape of European banking in general (and of banking in Belgium more specifically) has been paramount.

In order to prepare thoroughly for the challenges they faced as a result of the creation of the single and (neo-)liberalised European banking market, credit institutions all over Europe were, more precisely, strongly invited (not to say: "de facto" forced) to undergo an unprecedented upscaling of their working models, which resulted in an unprecedented wave of mergers, acquisitions and similar types of extensive partnership agreements.[124]

---

[122] See for instance De Grauwe (2014), p. 183 a.f.; Peersman and Schoors (2012), p. 4.

[123] See Dehousse and Dirick (1992), p. 826.

[124] See Commissie voor het Bank- en Financiewezen, Jaarverslag 1997-'98, p. 42 a.f. See furthermore the several case studies analysed in Byttebier and Verroken (1995).

The wave of mergers and acquisitions in the financial sector of the late 1980s, early 1990s was already initiated by the European preparatory works of creating an internal market for financial

By the end of the 1990s, this extreme degree of consolidation in the financial sector would dominate the entire European landscape, notably in countries such as France, Italy and Spain, next to the Benelux, where in many cases the bank sector had been very fragmented before.

More specifically in the Benelux, the banking landscape underwent very drastic changes as a consequence of this consolidation operation. For instance in Belgium, within a period of only 3 years, 9 out of the 10 largest Belgian banks of that time underwent fundamental changes in the field of their shareholdership, or got involved in a merger or an acquisition.[125] Most striking was the (massive) involvement of (the largest) Belgian credit institutions in international mergers and acquisitions which, among others, led to the creation of so-called trans-national, financial groups (such as "Fortis" and "Dexia"), or in local mega-mergers (such as the merger between KB and Cera Bank) or acquisitions (such as the acquisition of BBL by the Dutch ING).[126]

These M&A-operations obviously entailed important repercussions on the working models deployed by the banking sector of said territories. Up till the appearance of the mergers and acquisitions that took place in the 1990s, the Belgian banking landscape was more specifically mainly populated by a large amount of small institutions (of different variety), and some (at least in the context of Belgium), larger market players, who, thanks to the immense savings tissue generated by the Belgian population, based their workings on a strong deposit constitution and, for the remainder, conducted a conservative banking policy, which for over half a century—dating back to the previous severe financial and banking crisis of the 1930s—had succeeded in keeping the Belgian banking sector at peace and, basically, even out of problems.[127]

As a result of the M&A-operations of the 1990s, the Belgian bank sector would suddenly find itself in a much more insecure situation.

Most bank groups which arose from said M&A-operations in which the Belgian banks got involved—with as notable exception KBC bank—were moreover of a strong transnational nature (which was notably the case for Fortis, Dexia and ING-Group), and got more and more driven by the prospect of large short term profits, ergo by the capitalist principle that an enterprise should above all aim for profits. These transnational banking groups soon hereby showed themselves very keen to face the challenge set out by Europe of conquering the (neo-)liberalised European

services, especially the so-called "White Paper **on completing the internal market which was adopted by the** Milan European Council of 28th June 1985" [COM/85/0310], as well as by the several European banking directives of a later date.

[125] Commissie voor het Bank- en Financiewezen, Jaarverslag 1998-'99, p. 183.

[126] For detailed data, see Commissie voor het Bank- en Financiewezen, Jaarverslag 1997-'98, p. 176 a.f. and Commissie voor het Bank- en Financiewezen, Jaarverslag 1998-'99, pp. 183–217.

See also Byttebier and Verroken (1995), p. 215 a.f., as well as Byttebier and Verroken (Deel I) (1997), pp. 243–255, and (Deel II) (1997), pp. 401–413.

[127] Hulpiau et al. (2011), p. 430 a.f.

markets for banking services, and hence started to pursue very ambitious European, and later on global policy goals.

In many cases, over the time period of merely a decade, these policy goals degenerated into sheer megalomania[128]; the "Belgo-European" financial institutions were hereby witnessed to develop global business strategies based on an ever-increasing diversification in foreign markets, often resulting into an increase of investments in more and more high-risk financial products (such as derivatives).

As a consequence, and after only a mere decade of operating in the (initially European, and later on globalised) (neo-)liberalised financial markets, not much remained of the traditional, banking prudency which had characterised the Belgian banking sector before.[129]

As a consequence, during the financial crisis of 2007–2008, most "Belgian-European" financial groups would ultimately face severe financial difficulties. In this, the Belgian society ultimately had to pay a very high price for the megalomania of financial mega-groups such as Fortis[130] and Dexia,[131] due to costly bail out-operations which have been reported to negatively influence the Belgian public budgets for decades to come.[132]

3.7 Further Illustration II: The (Neo-)liberalisation of the European Electricity Markets

A second example of a sector that had to endure the consequences of European interventions of deregulation and (neo-)liberalisation has been the electricity sector.[133]

Already in the early 1990s, the European commission had the ambition to "(neo-) liberate" the electricity market which was considered to be (too) paralysed.

This policy goal resulted, among others, into the liberalisation directive of 26 December 1996,[134] which aimed at "unbundling" the electricity markets of the European member states, as a result of which the production, transmission, distribution and sale (delivery) of electricity had to be split up between different market players.

---

[128] See for instance the failed acquisition of ABN Amro by Fortis; on this: Smit (2013).

[129] See Hulpiau et al. (2011), p. 430 a.f.

[130] See Michielsen and Sephina (2009).

[131] See Ardaen (2012).

[132] Hulpiau et al. (2011), p. 430 a.f.

[133] Sachs (2011), p. 201.

[134] See in general Deconinck and Gillard (2004–2005); Deridder (2003).
See also https://eur-lex.europa.eu/legal-content/EN/TXT/?uri=CELEX%3A31996L0092, consulted on June 6, 2018.

As regards the impact on the Belgian electricity market specifically, one can indeed observe that, as a result of these European liberalisation efforts, new players have emerged on the Belgian electricity market, but one can wonder if this has been beneficial for consumers.

When considering the impact of these (neo-)liberalisation efforts on the Belgian electricity market, one has to take into account that, since this (neo-)liberalisation of the Belgian electricity market: (1) the price of electricity (for the average consumer) has strongly increased[135]; (2) many Belgian cities and communes (which traditionally had high stakes in the electricity sector) have since then been experiencing chronical funding shortages; (3) green electricity production has suffered strongly[136] and (4) the Belgian population has, in the recent past, on occasion been strongly alarmed by press reports that during winter season, especially at times of cold weather, the electricity supply is no longer guaranteed[137] which in the past has already led to the announcement of controversial contingency plans[138] (which have at least on one occasion been received as being hilarious by at least one neighbouring country[139]).

Moreover, the Belgian political world is since recent completely at loss on what to do with Belgium's decaying nuclear power plants, which in the recent past has on several occasions caused huge concern in some of Belgium's neighboring countries.[140]

It has been even more perplexing that, in spite of all European (neo-)liberalisation efforts which were aimed at installing a unified, free (electricity) market, it has apparently yet not been (sufficiently) possible to make use of an overcapacity of electricity production in The Netherlands in order to remedy impending shortages in Belgium.[141]

---

[135] See Elektriciteitsprijs stijgt: Electrabel en Co toch recht in hun schoenen? (article of 7 June 2014) at: http://redactie.radiocentraal.be/Home/?p=6390 (last consulted on June 16, 2018); Stroomfactuur op 1 januari tot 35 procent duurder (at: http://www.hln.be/hln/nl/943/Consument/article/detail/2156121/2014/12/18/56-plussers-massaal-weg-bij-Belfius.dhtml; last consulted on June 16, 2018).

See furthermore Adriaen (2014), p. 3. See also OIVO (2011).

[136] Heilbron et al. (2014), p. 30; Adriaen (2014), p. 3.

[137] Heilbron et al. (2014), p. 30.

[138] See Noodplan voor stroomvoorziening deze winter. Knack 18 July 2014 (also at http://www.knack.be/nieuws/belgie/noodplan-voor-stroomvoorziening-deze-winter/article-normal-265951.html; last consulted on June 16, 2018).

[139] See Nederland zamelt wokken in voor België (article of 5 November 2014). http://m.hln.be/hln/m/nl/31822/Dossier-Stroomtekort/article/detail/2112460/2014/11/05/Nederland-zamelt-wokken-in-voor-Belgie.dhtml?originatingNavigationItemId=1; last consulted on June 16, 2018.

See also Smout (2014), p. 4.

[140] See for instance Delbeke and Eckert (2018), pp. 4–5, reporting on protest actions in Aken (Germany), attended by both German and Holland concerned citizens, that were held on May 10th 2018 against the Belgian nuclear policy. The concern is however not new, but has already been present in Belgium's neighboring countries for years already.

[141] Heilbron et al. (2014), p. 29.

The messed-up situation on the Belgian electricity market is certainly not unprecedented: one will remember that in the years 2000–2001, similarly as a consequence of the (neo-)liberalisation and deregulation of the Californian electricity market, the electricity supply in California was reported to have been as problematic for many months. In the aftermath of the notorious Enron-scandal, it even appeared that there had been manifest manipulations of the electricity supply aiming at influencing the price for electricity in order to generate higher corporate profits.[142]

Not surprisingly, the press has in general been rather pessimistic about the effects of the (neo-)liberalisation of the European electricity market:

> The liberalisation has mainly ensured a concentration of power in multi-billion corporations which are meanwhile too big to fail.[143]

The same press moreover mentions as further effects of the (neo-)liberalisation of the (Belgian) electricity market: a substantial decrease of the wholesale prices, which however do not translate into a proportional decrease of the consumer prices which, on the contrary, have considerably risen (also as a consequence of different additional costs, such as a higher VAT, custom duties and increased transport costs, all costs from which, thanks to successful lobbying, only large energy consumers are mostly exempt).[144]

3.8 Towards a Society Even More Deprived of Solidarity

3.8.1 Solidarity as the Soon To Be Completely Forgotten Third Principle of the Liberal Societies that Broke Through in the Course of the Nineteenth Century

"Liberté" (= "freedom"), "Égalité" (= "Equality") and "Fraternité" (= "Fraternity" or, more freely translated: "Solidarity") were the societal ideals reflecting in the motto of the French Revolution of 1789, and under this motto, the revolutionary forces of that time wanted to counter the societal model of the "Ancien Régime".[145]

Also in other countries of the world, in the same time period, similar revolutions (or less violently occurring societal changes) helped shaping new civil societies, to a large extent based on the same (or similar) liberal theories of the eighteenth century.

Where the civil societal model stemming from this revolutionary era—with the emergence of capitalism as its counterpart in the economic sphere—at least still

---

142 See Krugman (2004), p. 299; Stiglitz (2003), p. 260. See also Leopold (2002).

143 Heilbron et al. (2014), p. 37.

144 Heilbron et al. (2014), p. 37.

145 See further at https://en.wikipedia.org/wiki/Libert%C3%A9,_%C3%A9galit%C3%A9,_fraternit%C3%A9 (last consulted on June 16, 2018).

attempted to pay lip service to the objectives of creating an "equal" and "free" society,[146] it would on the contrary very soon completely negate the idea of "solidarity".

This happened without much societal debate on the matter, under the implicit arguments that solidarity mechanisms cause too much of an impairment to individual freedom, but also that inequalities are the same for everyone, so there is no reason to deal with these on a political or policy level.

3.8.2 The Absence of Solidarity in the Main Legal Instruments Shaping Nineteenth Century Liberal Societies: The Example of the French Code Civil of 1804

As it had mainly been the third class of society (the so-called "bourgeoisie") which had taken the lead in combatting the societal model of the "Ancien Régime", and as this third class had moreover been prominently active in France as the driving force behind the French revolution, it may not be surprising that France also took the lead in the development of a set of legal instruments by means of which the nineteenth century civil (liberal) society has been shaped.

Later on, these "French" legal instruments of shaping the civil society functioned as an important source of inspiration in many other countries.

Already at the beginning of the nineteenth century, France thus issued a whole set of new (revolutionary) laws, among which several "codes" (or: "law books") in different branches of the law.

The most important among these "codes", which is up till today still in force in many countries all over the world, has obviously been the "civil code" (in French: "le Code civil") of 1804. This civil code was in its turn strongly influenced by the liberal ideas which had also inspired the French revolution itself, with, as main starting points, the new societal principles of "freedom" and "equality", but not of "solidarity".

Not surprisingly, the abovementioned idea that all human beings are equal and free lies at the base of said "Code civil", among others implying that French citizens became totally equal and free to perform legal acts in the civil context (see already the earlier Sect. 3.2, dealing with the "voluntary association"-theory). In the said "Code civil", this equality and freedom to perform legal acts, furthermore, applied to everyone, regardless of his social status or position within society, and moreover applied in the most absolute terms.

As demonstrated before (see Sect. 3.1), human beings are nevertheless not equal, as they are characterised by many differences stemming from both biological (genetic) and societal factors, such as the socio-economic conditions of the family one is born into. Up till today, in most (Western) countries, legal rules (such as the

[146] See also above, under Sects. 3.1 and 3.4.

liberal, French civil code of 1804 itself) still barely consider these effective inequalities between individuals, thus not taking into account that the legal idea that people are equal is merely an illusion, this notwithstanding some rare exceptions of legal systems aiming at protecting weaker contracting parties (for instance, in some countries, labour law and consumer law).

The consequence of this legal approach deployed by the French civil code of 1804 has thus been that all individuals are supposed to participate in the civil organisation of society on an equal base, especially when contracting with one another.

Appealing as such an approach may sound, it has already been demonstrated in Sect. 3.1 of this book that, in practice, it mainly provides a legal licence by means of which the stronger members of society (in our times, these are mainly belonging to the richer classes of society), when contracting with others, in most cases can impose their will on the weaker members of society in a practically unhindered way.

As a result, this starting premise of legally organising the liberal societies of the nineteenth century did not at all bear witness of any tendency of "solidarity", but rather resulted in the opposite, namely in creating a society model depraved of all forms of such solidarity.

It has moreover taken till far in the twentieth century before the legal systems of some (mainly Western) countries have been willing to make certain corrections to this starting premise of civil law that people are legally acting with one another on a presupposed equal basis.

These corrections resulted in certain imperative regulating systems granting the weak members of society some elementary degree of protection against the contractual exploitation mechanisms deployed by the stronger members of society, with as most typical examples "labour law" and "consumer law", next to other legal systems such as financial, prudential law which, at least in theory, next to serving numerous other goals—most notably the protection of financial institutions against the impact of free market mechanisms in case risks they have taken would lead to financial (or other) problems—aims at protecting the interests of deposit holders and investors.

In a similar manner, also the principle that (individual) freedom serves as a second basic starting point of contract law, has in practice appeared to be an illusion (see Sect. 3.4).

Indeed, a further reasoning of civil law systems such as the French Civil code of 1804 is that everyone is free to either contract, or not, or otherwise put, that no one can be forced to conclude a contract.

It needs not much further explanation that also this underlying starting point, more often than not, strongly collides with daily practice. Reference can for instance be made to authors such as Herbert Marcuse, who has righteously pointed out that the fear of starvation will by definition force people, especially the weakest members of a given society, to conclude the most adverse contracts. Again, the labour contract forms a typical illustration of this insight.[147] In practice, numerous labour

[147] Marcuse (1962), p. 71 a.f. See also Marcuse (1964), p. 300 a.f.

contracts would, most probably, not be concluded and/or continued by reasonable persons who would be given a true freedom of choice.

In present-day societies, a similar example concerns so-called "student loans" which poor(er) students are forced to enter into in case they still want access to a university training (or to a similar form of higher education).

Moreover, also in this case, it has taken up till far in the twentieth century before the legal systems of a (limited) number of countries have recognised this conundrum to at least some extent, resulting in labour and social protection mechanisms aimed at setting out a minimum standard of protection to the benefit of employees against malicious contracting practices of employers, be it that under the doctrines of economic neo-liberalism, these have come under severe scrutiny during the past decades.

3.8.3 Inquiry of Some of the Further Reasons Why Economic Neo-liberalism Keeps on Opposing Solidarity

In present times, it is thus the more remarkable that, under the cloak of re-installing the idea of freedom, over the past decades, economic neo-liberalism has given high priority to the dismantling of all types of legal systems protecting the weaker against the stronger members into society, so noticeably in the contractual domain.[148]

Chomsky has phrased the aversion of the adherents of economic neo-liberalism to the principle of solidarity as follows[149]:

> Solidarity is quite dangerous. From the point of view of the masters, you're only supposed to care about yourself, not about other people. This is quite different from the people they claim are their heroes, like Adam Smith, who based his whole approach to the economy on the principle that *sympathy* is a fundamental human trait – but that has to be driven out of people's heads. You've got to be yourself and follow the vile maxim – "don't care about others" – which is okay for the rich and powerful, but devastating for everyone else. It's taken a lot of effort to drive these basic human emotions out of people's heads.

It does not need to surprise that, in light of the foregoing, the (neo-)liberalisation and deregulation efforts deployed in many legal domains during the past decades, basically all have come down to the getting rid of the legal protective systems which, in earlier times, had been developed to protect the weaker members of society against abuses by the stronger members of society.

Next to the already mentioned examples of (neo-)liberalisation and deregulation of the financial markets and the electricity market, further typical examples within the Belgian context are the several initiatives which were taken during the past years to tighten the conditions under which a replacement income is granted to those who do not find a(n) (adequate) employment.

---

[148] See also Chomsky (2017), p. 65 a.f.

[149] Chomsky (2017), p. 65.

Above all, such legal initiatives pay lip service to the (neo-)liberal idea of freedom, which under the doctrines of economic neo-liberalism implies that the weaker members of society have no other choice than to engage in any type of employment contract, be it for the hardest, most cumbersome and often most unhealthy labour, at the risk of no longer being able to provide in their own basic needs or those of the family they are taking care of.[150]

More and more the fear rises wither through such (neo-)liberal(isation) efforts, economic neo- liberalism is not trying to reduce the labour relations to those of the pre-World War II era, when the members of the working class had in many cases no other choice than to work for a pittance in order to make the capitalist classes even richer.[151]

Moreover, this reality has, throughout time, remained very widespread in many poor countries, where the lower classes never succeeded in enforcing any of the correction systems to the unbridled capitalist principles of exploitation that were reached in the past in some Western countries, among which even the abovementioned very basic legal principles of contractual freedom and equality themselves, implying that, in such poor countries, even in our times, systems of socio-economic slavery, even of children, are still very common.

It is thus the more remarkable that in supposedly "rich" countries such as the USA and the UK, where the doctrines of economic neo-liberalism have probably been implemented the furthest, meanwhile large groups of the population depend on food stamps or other systems of charity to meet their own needs. (See further in Sect. 4.9.)

This raises the rhetoric question if the theory of the "voluntary association", which under the doctrines of economic neo-liberalism is the only principle permitted to govern private relations,[152] can offer any form of relieve to the unfortunate within these societies.

---

[150] See also the insights of Galbraith, having pointed out that in present-day societies, more than ever in history, the principle remains that any "unpleasant work" (especially so-called "hard" and/or "dirty" labour), is increasingly gravitated to the poorer classes of society. The idea is that the most repulsive possible work should be done by the poor for the lowest possible wages, whereby the workers performing this type of hard and/or degrading work need to be replenished over and over again. (See Galbraith (1992), p. 33. See also Krugman (1998), p. 15.)

As phrased by Galbraith (see Galbraith (1992), pp. 33–34):

> From the foregoing comes one of the basic facts of modern economic society: the poor in our countries are needed to do the work that the more fortunate do not do and would find manifestly distasteful, even distressing. And a continuing supply and resupply of such workers is always needed. That is because later generations do not wish to follow their parents into physically demanding, socially unacceptable or otherwise disagreeable occupations; they escape or seek to escape the heavy lifting to a more comfortable and rewarding life. This we fully understand and greatly approve, it is what education is generally meant to accomplish. But from this comes the need for the resupply or, less agreeably, for keeping some part of the underclass in continued and deferential subjection.

[151] See also Chomsky (2017), p. 65 a.f.

[152] One should bear in mind that, most likely dating back to the works of classical liberal authors such as John Stuart Mill (see Byttebier (2017), p. 168, n° 138), neo-liberal authors consider the principles of "individual property" and "individual freedom" almost as sacred, and consistently try

When considering the foregoing, one can but reach the conclusion that, while the ideas of "freedom" (= "liberté") and "equality" (= "égalité") from the revolutionary era of the late eighteenth century still have been—and continue to be—translated to some elementary extent into the legal systems of the Western capitalist countries, be it in the distorted meaning given to these notions by the theories of (economic) (neo-)liberalism themselves, the idea of "fraternity" or "solidarity" (= "fraternité") from that same era has, on the contrary, during most times been completely neglected.

This conclusion is both astonishing and not.

The complete absence of the idea of solidarity in capitalist thinking is to a certain extent understandable as it obviously collides with some of the basic starting points of the doctrines of both economic liberalism and economic neo-liberalism themselves (that, as explained above, have determined the outlook of unbridled capitalism).

As has already been elaborated upon before, one of these basic starting premises of the doctrines of economic liberalism and economic neo-liberalism states that, on an economic plain and more specifically in the pursuit of their own individual objectives and selfish desires, people should behave as selfishly as possible. The reasoning of both doctrines further goes that (only) through this, economy will be fed with sufficient impulses of productivity and innovation, which will ultimately be beneficial to everyone. It is argued that an "invisible hand" (being a metaphorical reference to the free market forces) will ensure that those who are economically successful, will raise the less successful to a higher level of welfare, an approach which has also been known as the "trickle down-economics".

In this, these "unsuccessful" should not receive more than what they, based on their position as partner/co-contractors of the "successful", are granted by the latter, even if this for instance would lead to miserable labour circumstances or conditions.

Higher ethical values such as "compassion", "altruism" or "solidarity" are obviously values which do not match this paradigm; as a result, within the doctrines of economic liberalism and economic neo-liberalism, little or no attention is paid to such values.[153]

---

and justify all excesses of capitalism by referring to this type of abstract concepts of societal organization; for instance, Ayn Rand herself has vigorously defended the doctrine of the "voluntary association" as being the sole principle that may determine human relations. (See Rand (2008), p. 11; Rand (1992), p. 114.)

[153] Except for, literally, qualifying these higher values as "devious" and "evil".

For instance, Ayn Rand has argued that (see Rand (1992), p. 38):

> altruism holds death as its ultimate goal and standard of value – and it is logical that renunciation, resignation, self-denial, and every other form of suffering, including self-destruction are the virtues it advocates.

According to his author, a so-called "altruistic" person shows the following characteristics: (1) a low self-esteem; (2) a lack of esteem for other human beings; (3) a perception of life as being a nightmare, i.e. a hostile happening where disasters occur all the time, and (4) a complete lack of ethics (see Rand (1992), p. 49).

See also Rand (2008), p. 19; Rand (1982), p. 27.

Compare Szalavitz (2012), who herself has observed that:

> to claim, as Rand does, that "altruistic morality" is a "disease" is to misrepresent reality.

The obvious incorrectness of this (neo-)liberal approach needs no further explanation.

By means of a further illustration, it suffices to further refer to the working and living conditions of workers in Western societies up till deep in the twentieth century. It should hereby be very clear that, as long as correction mechanisms to the (neo-)liberal ordering principles of "freedom" and "equality" in the contractual sphere remained lacking, a large part of the population of the Western countries suffered in appalling working and living conditions, while a small elite of rich capitalists spend their lives in the highest luxury.[154]

This, along with many other examples, illustrates that the blind application of the doctrines of economic (neo-)liberalism above all provides a breeding ground for a strong polarisation between a large group of poor and a small elite of rich. Through this, said doctrines do not at all fulfil the promise of the "trickle down-economics" holding that, under the application of "unbridled" capitalism (or: "entirely free markets") everyone will flourish and prosper.[155]

It is therefore hardly surprising how strongly the agendas of those in favour of the doctrines of economic (neo-)liberalism have, already for decades now, been advocating that capitalism should again become as "pure" or "unbridled" as possible, implying that all social and other correction mechanisms should be abolished as much as possible. In this, obviously, trade unions, and by extension socialist and other left-wing political parties, have been proclaimed to be the biggest enemies imaginable of economic prosperity and progress.

Otherwise said, the doctrines of economic liberalism and economic neo-liberalism are by definition opposed to any type of solidarity. At least one of the merits of Ayn Rand has been that she herself has made no attempts to hide this basic truth of (neo-)liberal thought good. On the contrary, for instance in her book "The virtue of selfishness", she bluntly stated that altruism is a bad thing and that social protection mechanisms are pernicious because they force the "competent" within society to concede their rightful earnings to the "incompetent".

With these blunt statements, Ayn Rand has strikingly summarised the essence of neo-liberal thinking.

It will, hence, not come as a surprise that, under the impulse of the doctrines of economic liberalism and economic neo-liberalism, during the past decades, a societal model has been advocated in which the least possible room is left for solidarity. It is hereby believed that the poor and needy are but to blame themselves and can hence not make any rightful claim to public services or mutual solidarity mechanisms.

---

[154] In literature, this theme is, for instance, explored in the works of F. Scott Fitzgerald.

[155] See also Skidelsky and Skidelsky (2013), p. 67, mentioning the collapse of the idea of "immanent abundance" for everyone.

See, in recent times, the works of many prominent economists, such as Thomas Piketty, but before him Joseph Stiglitz and Paul Krugman and, going back even further in time, John Kenneth Galbraith, all having questioned this paradigm.

In line with the neo-liberal viewpoints referred to under Sect. 2.6.2.1 above, states themselves should abstain as much as possible from organising such public services or mutual solidarity systems.[156]

At most, there may be some room left for individual charity, as the rich and powerful, according to the theories of economic liberalism and economic neo-liberalism being the noblest members of the human species, should at least be given the opportunity to demonstrate the nobility of their souls by, on occasion, giving alms to the less fortunate and, by doing so, bear witness of a modern-day approach of the trickle-down-economics. This explains the success of all kinds of charity, especially in those rich countries where capitalism prevails in its purest form and where it has barely or not been corrected through means of state organised social security or other public services.[157]

As indicated above, the fact that the theories of economic liberalism and economic neo-liberalism so strongly oppose solidarity could however also be considered bewildering. We shall address the reasons hereof in the next Sect. 3.8.4.

3.8.4 Why the Complete Lack of Solidarity of the Doctrines of Economic (neo-)liberalism Could, from a Rationalistic Point of View, Also Be Deemed Bewildering

3.8.4.1 On the Fundamental Incompatibility of the Doctrines of Economic Neo-liberalism with the Christian Roots of Western Civilisation

The insight that, especially since the era of rationalism and even more especially under the impulse of the theories of economic liberalism and economic neo-liberalism themselves, solidarity has been so strongly banned to the background may to some extent also be considered bewildering.

---

[156] These thoughts literally resonate in the works of Milton Friedman: see especially Friedman (1993).

Chomsky in this regards speaks of “the attack on Social Security”. (See Chomsky (2017), p. 65.)

[157] See, for instance, the opinion of Bill Gates on this matter:

> Philanthropy also can be an important part of the solution set. It’s too bad that Piketty devotes so little space to it. A century and a quarter ago, Andrew Carnegie was a lonely voice encouraging his wealthy peers to give back substantial portions of their wealth. Today, a growing number of very wealthy people are pledging to do just that. Philanthropy done well not only produces direct benefits for society, it also reduces dynastic wealth. Melinda and I are strong believers that dynastic wealth is bad for both society and the children involved. We want our children to make their own way in the world. They’ll have all sorts of advantages, but it will be up to them to create their lives and careers. (See Gates (2014).)

Capitalism is namely an economic system that has been developed in the Western world.

Adam Smith who has provided many ideas for the rise of capitalism[158] was himself Scottish, and most of the other early "liberal economists" were even so Europeans.

The fact that the European world of the seventeenth, eighteenth and nineteenth centuries provided such a fertile breeding ground for their ideas, may hence be considered somewhat astonishing, given the fact that (some of) these countries (at least at that time) also claimed to be "Christian", thus pretending be organised in accordance with the message of Jesus Christ, who, in his teachings as witnessed by the Gospels, had mainly taken positions which are completely opposite to the values of egoism, selfishness and greed which prevail under economic liberalism (and later in time: under economic neo-liberalism).

According to the Gospels, one of Jesus Christ's basic societal message has been that one should, above all, love one's neighbour, which basically makes his message one of altruism, rather than of selfishness, egoism and greed. Jesus Christ thus, for instance, thought that those who "possess" (too much) should be willing to share their wealth with those "who do not possess", calling for a society in which it is not the main purpose to get as rich as possible, but to ensure that the sick, the weak and the poor are even so cared for.

Jesus Christ furthermore invited the rich to sell their possessions and to donate the revenues of these sales to the poor. It have also been His words that it is practically impossible for a rich person to enter into the Kingdom of Heavens, and that one should not make it one's life purpose to gather treasures on earth, as everything is transitory there.[159]

Bearing these (and many other similar) words of Jesus Christ in mind, it is very surprising that, to the extent that the doctrines of economic liberalism and economic neo-liberalism are basically a set of ideas which are completely opposite to the messages of Jesus Christ, they have nevertheless so strongly resonated in the Western world as of the eighteenth century who, in the mean time, kept calling itself (and, in some cases, has even, at least in part, continued to do so ever since) "Christian".

One of the main questions in this is to what extent Protestantism has been (co-) responsible for the emancipation of the Western world from the message of Jesus Christ,[160] next to the question why the Catholic Church itself has also embraced capitalism and keeps on supporting liberal and neo-liberal ideas, but conversely also

---

[158] Galbraith (1983), p. 111.

[159] One just has to read the four Gospels of respectively Saint Marc, Saint Matthew, Saint Luke and Saint John.

See also Byttebier (2017), p. 94 a.f., with more detailed references to the relevant Gospel verses.

[160] See especially Tawney (1942), p. 71 a.f.

For further reading, see also Byttebier (2017), p. 131 a.f., with further references.

has been strongly condemning ideologies who kept on supporting the poor and oppressed, such as communism and socialism.[161]

It is thus the more significant that, especially in Europe, economic liberalism and, later, economic neo-liberalism themselves have at the same time called for an ever-increasing secularisation of society. As a result, in present times, Christianity in Europe, to the extent that it still exists, has essentially been reduced to the practice of rituals, such as Christian marriage and baptism, without any significant attempts still being made to aim for a society based on the true teachings of Jesus Christ.[162]

It is probably even more surprising that in the United States of America, some of the most "Christian" movements fully support neo-liberal (and also: conservative) thinking, where the question arises to what extent this can be related to the words of Jesus Christ as recorded in the Gospels, and to the extent that this can impossibly be the case, why no-one is prepared to see this, let alone admit it.[163]

The reason for all this may very well be that the true religion which reaches the core of the Western soul has, according to some,[164] become economic neo-liberalism itself, a religion which teaches us that we should all work exhaustively (and often literally until we drop dead[165]) to earn as much money as possible, in its own turn enabling us to buy everything which is artificially placed as a desire in our hearts through publicity and other types of capitalist brainwashing methods. All this is done to ensure that the wheels of the capitalist machinery will continue to turn on forever, so that the immense—and literally immeasurable—sums of credit which have been brought into circulation by private banks, will perhaps—or perhaps not—ever be recouped, that economic growth will continue endlessly, and that business

[161] Especially in and since the Papal Encyclical "Rerum Novarum" ("Of/about new things") of 1891.

[162] See in this regard, for instance, the works of Charles Gore (1853–1932), a renowned Anglican theologian (and bishop) of his time. (See Byttebier (2017), p. 141, with further references.) Gore blamed modern society for not having striven to bring the word of God truly to life, and that it even has accepted a widely spread violation of true justice, for example by having agreed to the exploitation of the poor and by approving "monstrous and unfounded" property rights which allow people to ignore the wellbeing of society and to focus more on personal possessions than on other people. Gore also blamed society for the fact that the systems it created, such as housing and employment and education politics, in a fundamental way ignore Christian ideals. Hence, Gore argued for a fundamental turn-around in society, where both the principles of capitalism, as well as those of socialism, were to be ignored. On the contrary, charity should become the leading principle of societal organization.

See, more recently, some similar viewpoints of the Catholic church expressed in: Congregation for the Doctrine of the Faith (2018).

[163] See also Tolstoj (2012), p. 95.

[164] See for instance Harari (2014), p. 391.

[165] Reference can here be made to the so-called "pension debate", where the adherents of the doctrines of economic neo-liberalism have started spreading the idea that every one (at least the lower 99% of the human race) should embrace the idea of having to work as long as possible, so that the free market economy can keep on thriving to make the rich of the planet ever more rich. (See also the further topics dealt with under Sect. 5.15.2.)

profits, and through this the fortunes of the rich of powerful of the planet in their capacity of capital providers of the big enterprises dominating the economic scenery, will continue to increase ever more.[166]

Those who can or will not adapt to this "free" market system, under this doctrine, do most certainly not deserve solidarity from those who are among the greatest advocates of this religious system, namely the rich and powerful in society (whose craving for ever more wealth, in the teachings of Jesus Christ Himself, was on the contrary severely condemned).

3.8.4.2 Why Solidarity Could Also Be Considered "Rational"

There may even be a second reason why it may be called surprising how, under the umbrella of rationalism, the idea of solidarity has been abandoned in many capitalist countries.

On the eve of the breakthrough of capitalism, namely in the pre-revolutionary era of the eighteenth century, there was indeed a second philosophical school of rationalism dealing with the matter of what the outlook of the socio-economic order should be.

Next to the school(s) of economic liberalism, which stemmed from the writings of Adam Smith and similar authors, there was more precisely in France another school of enlightenment, with as one of its main antagonists the French philosopher Jean Jacques Rousseau who, even so based on rationalism, advocated a "social society" instead of, as Adam Smith and the likes did, a society based on egoism, selfishness and greed.[167]

The "rationalistic" theories of this "French" school of enlightenment, most probably in a manner which was far more convincing than the teachings of Adam Smith and the likes, basically held that one should aspire for a global society which would be intrinsically solidary and just, and would thereto be organised by states implementing mechanisms of redistributing wealth. (See also further, Sect. 5.9.4.2.)

Although one could have expected that this other school of enlightenment should at least have been resonating in the collective thought world of the West in the same manner as the school of (economic) liberalism has been doing since, this has obviously hardly been the case.

History has indeed shown that it has been the (Scottish) school of (economic) liberalism which advocated selfishness rather than solidarity as the main force that

---

[166] Compare Harari (2014), p. 391, having summarized economic neo-liberalism as follows:

> The new ethic promises paradise on condition that the rich remain greedy and spend their time making more money, and that the masses give free rein to their cravings and passions – and buy more and more. This is the first religion in history whose followers actually do what they are asked to do. How though, do we know that we'll really get paradise in return? We've seen it on television.

[167] For further reading, see Arenas (2016).

should be shaping the socio-economic world order, which would resonate the most in Western thinking, especially in the field of economics. In present times, this debate basically comes down to the question how long what is still left of the social correction mechanisms which have been installed in the era after World War II up till the 1970s, will be able to withstand the ever-increasing pressure of economic neo-liberalism.

In an even more contemporary approach, one could also refer to the insights of the renowned biologist Richard Dawkins who has raised an argument for more solidarity which may very well be among the most convincing of all.

Dawkins more precisely developed the argument, that what seems "altruistic" can also be considered "selfish", where the conviction of self-preservation (not of an individual, but of the entire human race, and, by extension, of life in general, and even of non-living matter), itself bears witness of the only acceptable level of selfishness, namely the self-preservation of everything that "is" (in other words, of existence in its broadest meaning, of which mankind forms a part).[168]

With the latter idea, the insights of Dawkins even come very close to the Buddhist idea that everything is "one", as it sets one of the highest possible ethical standards for man's relationship with everything surrounding him. (See furthermore, in Sect. 5.5.)

3.8.5 Towards a Global Socio-Economic System Ever More Deprived of Solidarity: Lessons from Andersen's Fairy Tale "The Little Match Girl"

The events that happened after the financial crisis of 2007–2008, even though this crisis has clearly been caused by the failure of the free market mechanisms themselves, leave at present not much room for hope.

Not paying any consideration whatsoever to the fact that it have been both the doctrines and the implementation, in practice, of economic neo-liberalism that have caused the financial crisis of 2007–2008, the adepts of economic neo-liberalism have since then on the contrary expressed, louder and more unanimous than ever, that the collapse of the financial system in 2007–2008 was not caused by the blind forces of the invisible hand, and neither by financial and other economic mechanisms determined by greed, egoism and selfishness, but by what is left of the still prevailing systems of societal solidarity, thus adding one more excuse to the long list of excuses why society should get rid of these systems as quickly as possible.

The world-famous fairy tale-writer Hans Christian Andersen (1805–1875) has written many wonderful fairy tales which, alas, are too seldom known or read in their original literary format.

[168] See Dawkins (2006), pp. 4–5.

Unfortunately, albeit in full accordance with the free market principle that entrepreneurs should above all make mind-numbing products which please the broadest possible public, the (capitalist) cartoon animation industry has adapted many of said fairy tales in a completely distorted way.[169] This, again obviously in full accordance with the principles of capitalism, in its own turn helps generating huge business profits for the production enterprises involved (that are often transferred to tax paradises).[170]

One of these beautiful fairy tales that, at least for the moment, fortunately still seems to have escaped the interest of said animation-industry, is the story "The Little Match Girl".[171] It is a highly recommendable (and short) story, especially for those who only know Andersen's work from the adaptations by said animation-industry, as it clearly bears witness of the strong social concern and ethical values which also appear from many of the author's other fairy tales.

In the fairy tale, a little poor girl is selling matches on New Year's Eve to earn a bit of money, most probably to add to the lamentable income of her parents, as it appears from the story that the little girl is extremely poor. This undoubtedly fits the logic of economic neo-liberalism that we all should become entrepreneurs and that, if we fail to be successful, this is only due to our own stupidity. At a given moment, the little girl can no longer continue to walk (as she is barefoot in the snow) and, starving from hunger and cold, she stops in front of a window behind which a rich family is having a luxurious meal. Bearing neo-liberal thinking in mind, the little girl is most probably in this situation because of her own laziness and incompetence. No-one, and certainly not the rich people celebrating behind said window, notices the little girl who, as she failed in selling any matches at all, does not dare to go back home. To get some warmth, she starts lightning a few of her matches, but this does not help much, and so, the little girl ultimately dies from cold and hunger under a window where the members of a rich family stuff themselves with festive food which they certainly do not wish to share with others.

It is hard to imagine a better story to illustrate the intrinsic hypocrisy of the doctrines of economic (neo-)liberalism.

In said fairy tale, through the light of the matches, the spirit of the little girl's grandmother appears to her, as is suggested to take the little girl to heaven.

In real life, it is most probably highly questionable if man will ever be able to escape from the bitter reality of neo-liberal capitalism that only leaves room for a devastating experience and blind adoration of the free market powers and of the money devil steering them, and to an ever-decreasing extent, hardly at all for more ethical values, such as altruism and solidarity.

---

[169] These products of the animation industry have not only often a totally different story line than the fairy tales that inspired them, but, even worse, often also an entirely different moral message.

[170] About the fiscal evasive behaviour of, for instance, the Disney Corporation, see for instance Bové (2014), pp. 8–9.

[171] See http://www.andersen.sdu.dk/vaerk/hersholt/TheLittleMatchGirl_e.html (last consulted on June 16, 2018).

3.9 Embracing Elitist Thinking

3.9.1 The Classical Elitist Approach of Economic Liberalism

Notwithstanding the idea of equality to which the doctrines of (economic) liberalism and (economic) neo-liberalism provide lip service (see Sect. 3.1), and taking into further consideration the abovementioned exploitation mechanisms these doctrines propagate and which already in themselves shape a manifestly unjust world, both doctrines also express, as the proverbial cherry on the cake, a strong degree of elitist thinking.

Since Adam Smith, the idea rules that the classes of entrepreneurs and capital providers of large enterprises are the ones to whom society owes all progress and prosperity and this thanks to their presupposed extra-ordinary intelligence and other qualities which are presumed to be above average.

This line of thinking has been further enforced in the course of the nineteenth century by means of witticisms which have, among others, been derived from biological science, such as Darwin's notion of the "survival of the fittest" and, in the cause of the twentieth century, Dawkins' notion of the "selfish genes".[172]

In this (neo-)liberal approach, the rest of the people are mainly taking advantage of the efforts of these exceptional beings, namely said entrepreneurs and capital providers of (large) enterprises, and should hence be very grateful and certainly not complain that said exceptional beings claim the largest part of the metaphorical economic pie.

As explained by Galbraith, one of the most ultimate cases for capitalism came thus into existence, namely the idea that capitalism is nothing else than the manifestation of Darwin's teachings in the socio-economic order, whereby the principle of the "survival of the fittest" gets applied to (all) economic and, in general, societal interactions. Capitalists are in this way believed to be "great" or "extra-ordinary" because they are biologically superior. The poor are poor because they are biologically inferior. Wealth is the reward of those who are inherently better, and the effort to cost what cost attain it both reveals and further develops this superiority. In this

---

[172] The principle of "natural selection", in addition to the idea of "the survival of the fittest", as derived from the works of Charles Darwin (see especially his book "The Origin of Species" (1859)), and, more recently, the idea of "the selfish genes" taken from Richard Dawkins (see Dawkins (2006)), are concepts that have become extremely popular among (neo-)liberal scholars.

The misuse of the teachings of biology is moreover not a contemporary phenomenon, but is reported to date back to the end of the nineteenth century, when business tycoons, such as John Davison Rockefeller (1839–1937) and James Jerome Hill (1838–1916), already adhered to the idea of the "survival of the fittest", by expressing their opinions that the strongest and most efficient enterprises would automatically become market leader and, through this, would be best suited to further stimulate economic prosperity. (See Galbraith (1983), p. 117; Browne (2008), p. 101.)

This way of thinking even obtained a validation in pseudo-scientific works by writers such as Herbert Spencer (1820–1903).

reasoning, even the poverty of the poor can be accepted as socially good, as it provides man with a motivation to aim to do better.[173]

In this line of reasoning, the fact that entrepreneurs and capital providers of (large) enterprises are themselves but a small part of a larger society which, furthermore, but build on the efforts from the past (including all past inventions and realisations of the human mind which make contemporary businesses possible), is to a large extent neglected.

Obviously, in this way, the doctrines of economic liberalism (and later also: economic neo-liberalism) are strongly ignoring the fact that large enterprises, as is the case for practically all societal institutions, but exist and flourish thanks to the efforts of societies as a whole.

What in reality seems to be mostly distinguishing entrepreneurs (and capital providers of large enterprises) is, hence, not their moral, intellectual or biological superiority, but rather a total lack of scruples to reserve for themselves a magnitude of compensations, much more than they are willing to share with all other persons who help shaping their businesses.

There is undoubtedly a certain persuasiveness in the argument that an entrepreneur is in many cases the initiator and the driving soul behind the business which he leads, but especially when these businesses reach a certain degree of economies of scale, this starting premise is often but a relative truth. Even when considering the abovementioned argument that an entrepreneur, as the driving force behind the business he leads, merits a higher than average compensation for his efforts, it is not clear why such an entrepreneur should receive a compensation which forms a multitude of what other people employed by this business earn, and moreover why the ownership of said business should (forever) remain in the sole hand of said entrepreneur (and his offspring). The persuasiveness of this argumentation fails even more in cases where the largest part of the profits made by such a business flows to its capital providers who often attribute in no way whatsoever to said business, except for having contributed to the (starting) capital, not even taken into consideration that very often capital providers have obtained their capital shares from past inheritances or gifts from a relative.[174]

There is, otherwise put, no conclusive argument why entrepreneurs, business men or capital providers of (large) enterprises should receive a much higher compensation from the business operation than the other "stakeholders", among which the multitude of its employees.

In reality, the mechanisms which are enabling the remuneration gaps currently prevailing between, on one hand leaders and capital providers of (large) enterprises

---

[173] See Galbraith (1983), p. 117.

[174] See already Tolstoj (2012), p. 95:

> He who has inherited millions, or tens of thousands of hectares of land, thinks, because he has a large house, horses, automobiles and servants, that he is very special. He is surrounded by such luxury that it makes him drunk, causing that he is not able to have empathy for the life of the working man who organises a strike in a factory, or the poor farmer who cuts a tree in his woods. He is that drunk of his wealth that without conscience, he will punish the worker and the farmer as soon as he can lay his hands on them.

and, on the other hand the large multitude of employees and other stakeholders of such enterprises, are but the result of the principles and working methods of (unbridled) capitalism itself, such as the subordination of labour to capital (as this undeniably lies at the basis of the capital company model), next to the "Iron Law of the Wages", which have mainly allowed a limited elite of rich entrepreneurs within society to get extremely rich to the detriment of those who, under the logic of the "trickle down economics" are expected to be happy with the proverbial breadcrumbs that fall from the table.

3.9.2 Elitist Thinking Within Economic Neo-liberalism

In modern times, the doctrines of economic neo-liberalism keep continuing to aggressively defend the prevailing large inequalities resulting from the abovementioned capitalist principles by referring to present-day reasonings of elitist thinking.

For instance, Ayn Rand herself has bluntly stated that there are two types of people, namely "the competent" and "the incompetent"[175] (in this way defending a society model not that different from the one appearing in Huxley's famous novel "Brave New World").

In this approach, those who are successful, owe this to their own competence, even more as under the logic of (neo-)liberal thinking everyone by definition gets equal chances in life. Consequently, it comes down to effectively exploiting one's life opportunities, in which the competent in society succeed and in which the incompetent fail.

The idea that two types of people are participating in the socio-economic processes, namely "the competent" and "the incompetent", has in the mean while been resonating in capitalist (or free market) societies all over the world.

This approach, for instance, clearly resonates in the generally accepted idea that wealth and material prosperity are a synonym for competence and that poverty is a synonym for incompetence, and even so in the belief that every individual is fully responsible for his own life circumstances, implying that the poor only should blame themselves and, hence, cannot expect help from other echelons in society, and certainly not from the fortunate competent.[176]

It needs not much further arguing that this oversimplified way of reasoning completely ignores the fact that economic success does not only depend on ability or "competence" (whatever this term may mean), but as much, or probably to an even bigger extent, on many other factors, such as ancestry (and the many advantages or

[175] Rand (2008), p. 23. See also Rand (1982), p. 79 a.f.

[176] Ayn Rand has expressed this as follows (Rand 2008, p. 23):

> altruïsm seeks to rob intelligence of its rewards, by asserting that the moral duty of the competent is to serve the incompetent and sacrifice themselves to anyone's need.

disadvantages from being born in a wealthy, respectively poor family), inborn talent(s), physical appearance and physical or mental health, but also from factors such as coincidence and luck, next to innate characteristics making someone or more selfish or more altruist, all factors that are not taken into consideration in the abovementioned (neo-)liberal approach towards life.[177]

3.9.3 The Impact of Elitist Thinking on Public Policy Making

The neo-liberal premise that every human being is the sole responsible for his success or failure in the socio-economic field, is meanwhile dominating many social and societal discussions all over the world, going from discussions on the question whether or not substitute income forms are justified, up to discussions on how much tax money should still be invested in all forms of public services or social security systems.

In this way, neo-liberal thinking translates into an endless list of witticisms which govern political debate for decades already,[178] such as:

- unemployment is but a consequence of laziness;
- long-term illness cannot be real, implying that long-term ill should remain productive in the capitalist production processes[179];
- officials and public servants are mainly redundant,[180] or at least there are too many of them, leaving the suspicion that, given their magnitude, they are lazy and underperforming, where the solution for this horrible problem is that, from time to time, a sufficiently large amount of such officials and public servants should get fired and their workload should be re-distributed among the remaining ones, ensuring that finally they all have something to do[181];
- …

[177] See furthermore Galbraith (2004), p. 23.

[178] In the context of Flemish politics, these arguments—albeit sometimes phrased differently—are often used by members of the NVA or the OVLD, both political parties that are extreme adherents of the doctrines of economic neo-liberalism.

[179] This policy principle of economic neo-liberalism is (at present) very strongly adhered and implemented by Belgium's neo-liberal government Michel I.

[180] The only civil servants which neo-liberal thinking seems to accept, are those who yield more money than they cost (in salary). This leads to the observation that the only civil servants with whom neo-liberal thinking truly sympathises are tax officials (on the condition that they leave the rich and very rich unburdened, and only tax the poor and middle classes within society). (See also Wauters (2015), pp. 4–5.)

It goes without much further saying that this is a strange, although typical neo-liberal logic which explains why one needs to continuously cut in expenses for public sectors, such as education and justice, as the people employed in these areas only "cost" to society and, at least in financial terms, "do not yield anything".

[181] Blomme (2015), p. 3.

Through the methods of influencing (or even: usurpatory) public authority, meanwhile also known as "corporatocracy", the rich and powerful have during the past decades succeeded in obtaining a decisive influence on political programs and on the outcome of political decisions, in a way which is not justifiable in light of democratic principles which are nevertheless still said to prevail in capitalist countries.[182]

Through this, the world as shaped under the doctrines of economic liberalism and economic neo-liberalism, has become the one which was already described by Plato over two and a half millennia ago, as quoted before at the end of Sect. 3.5.5.

The question is, hence, no longer how to prevent that the abovementioned Platonic doomsday prophecy will be fulfilled now that, on a global scale, capitalist societies already for a long time have been shaped in full accordance with Plato's description, which earlier made Galbraith conclude in a similar manner that, within capitalism, money has become the (only) measure for social success.[183]

The only question still remaining is if it is even conceivable that this will ever be remedied, and whether or not there can still be room to advocate a societal model revisiting the abovementioned (neo-)liberal starting premises which in essence mainly express a degree of elitism that does not deserve a place within civilised societies.

3.10 The Network Economy

As a logic consequence of the importance of elitism characterizing the doctrines of economic neo-liberalism, networking of like-minded prominent people from the business and related world plays a completely underestimated role in the present globalised neo-liberal world order.

This is, nevertheless, completely in line with the abovementioned neo-liberal principles, such as the idea that the rich and powerful are the best what humanity has to offer, furthermore implying that society as a whole should be very grateful about the many benefits these rich and powerful keep on bestowing to the rest of the world.[184]

It thus is hardly surprising that the visible and invisible associations and institutions which help steering society in general and the global economy more specifically, the membership of which is more often than not reserved to those who are sufficiently successful economically, are countless.

It has even been suggested that the role and importance of these different types of networking associations and institutions in many cases overshadows the democratically more legitimate types of authority, such as (national) parliaments

---

[182] See Oxfam (2014).

[183] Galbraith (1990), p. 14.

[184] See also Galbraith (1990), pp. 14–15.

and governments and/or more local public authorities (e.g. cities and communes). This finding is meanwhile of such nature that prominent academics have deemed it necessary to, in more or less covered terms, contest the different types of influencing authority resulting from the foregoing to the extent that they are considered not to be legitimate from a democratic point of view.[185]

An example in the international context of such an influential networking organisation is the "World Economic Forum (WEF)",[186] a (networking) club which was established in 1971 by prominent leading people from the political and business world, as well as other "leaders from society".[187]

A similar eye-catching example from the financial sector is the famous "Basel Committee on Banking Supervision",[188] which is, in essence, a forum of financial supervisors organised in the context of the "Bank for International Settlements", which periodically develops initiatives aimed at steering the content of financial regulation.

Next to these types of eye-catching fore from where the decision making processes of countries and supra-national organisations are steered, there is also a large tissue of all types of open and occult national and international societies which also help determining the outlook of the capitalist economy, going from national and international chambers of commerce, in essence institutions of merchants and industrials which, through all kinds of methods advocate their own interests, to rotary and lion clubs, and the like.

It is hard to determine the precise impact of this type of organisations; the way they operate is often too intransparent to determine such. At the very least, it may be concluded that their influence is without any doubt a fact and that this does not bear witness of a high degree of democracy, especially given the elitist character of a lot of these organisations and institutions, the membership of which is most often reserved to the economic, financial or political elite of society.

As a result, this type of networks also provides one of the further ingredients of the breeding ground on which capitalism thrives and may hence be qualified as one of the further causes of the manifestly unjust world which unbridled capitalism has been shaping for centuries now.

[185] See for instance Sachs (2011).

[186] See http://www.weforum.org/ (last consulted on June 16, 2018).

[187] See http://www.weforum.org/world-economic-forum (last consulted on June 16, 2018).
This networking club has annual meetings mainly aiming at examining how the agenda's of political decision making can be influenced.

[188] See http://www.bis.org/bcbs/ (last consulted on June 16, 2018).

3.11 Preliminary Conclusion: The "Supremacy" of the "Free" Market

It may be clear from the foregoing that after more or less four decades of implementing the doctrines of economic neo-liberalism, the world and its socio-economic order is more than ever at the mercy of one dominant totalitarian economic system, being the free market system in all its different appearances.

As a result, during said previous decades, practically every human activity has gradually become subject to the logic and the mechanisms of the free market.[189]

It has already been explained above to what extent human "labour", otherwise put human beings and their lives themselves, have been completely subordinated to the free market mechanisms.[190]

As a result, all over the world, practically every human being—with exclusion of the rich and powerful of the planet—is every day waking up with as sole life purpose to produce as much labour as possible, and this from early in the morning until (late in) the evening when one is allowed to go to sleep.

The limited amount of leisure which is left for the working classes (and this only in the rich parts of the world) can, furthermore, only be devoted to participate in the consumption of products with which the free market is flooding humanity.

Within the capitalist economic system, the average man, hence, only exists for two main purposes, namely (1) to produce (as much) labour (against the cheapest possible remuneration) and (2) to consume.

In this process, man has to an ever increasing extent become more and more forced to serve one overall dictate, namely the dictate of making profit(s) (for the benefit of the rich).

Everything undertaken by man mainly needs to provide such profit(s) for the benefit of business owners, and anything which hinders the making of such profits should be abandoned or eliminated as efficiently as possible.

It is, hence, hardly a surprise that one of the most important points on the agenda of economic neo-liberalism is that every human activity should be deployed within the dictates of financial and accounting logic.

---

[189] As Lipman phrased it:

> Neoliberalism reframes all social relations, all forms of knowledge and culture in the terms of the market. All services established for the common good are potential targets of investment and profit-making. In the discourse of neoliberalism, the society becomes synonymous with the market, democracy is equated with consumer choice, and the common good is replaced by individual advantage. (Lipman (2006), p. 51.)

[190] In the writings of Erich Fromm as of the 1940s, it has been analysed to what profound extent labour, but through this man himself, has been subjected to the objectives of capitalism. Over half a century later (especially as a result of the world wide implementation of the doctrines of economic neo-liberalism), this plea may be more convincing than ever. Indeed, more than ever has the average man become enslaved by the goals and objectives of the free markets and the forces of the invisible hand(s) steering them.

A recent striking example of this way of reasoning is to be found in the very severe budget policy which the neo-liberal European Union has imposed on its different member states. The entire organisation of countries has, through this, become function of the free market mechanisms, amongst which the engagement in huge bank debts (at high interest rates). Through this, not only countries have become puppets in the hands of the financial system, but even so their entire economies. (See, furthermore, under Sect. 4.6.)

Most probably as an intended side-effect of implementing the doctrines of economic neo-liberalism, the achievements of a painful process of social emancipation that has been going on for ages, have almost completely been reversed over the course of a single generation. A result, the model of the welfare state, which mainly in the period after the second World War, until the end of the 1970s, took tremendous efforts to achieve, is under the impulse of the doctrines of economic neo-liberalism gradually being nullified. This often happens under reference to financing problems the welfare state purportedly faces, without paying any consideration to the fact that these financing problems themselves are mostly caused by the unjust free market mechanisms which shape the financial system, among which the private money creation model by the bank sector and the (neo-)liberal principle that all added value generated by the economic system should only benefit the entrepreneurs (and the shareholders of enterprises).

Through this, economic neo-liberalism is gradually succeeding in realising its wet dream of free markets controlling and steering everything, where state authority itself is more and more used to install mechanisms to further emphasise the operation of said free markets. This highlights one of the findings of Michel Foucault, namely his observation that economic neo-liberalism, although by nature striving for the least possible state influence, nonetheless shamelessly uses state authority to realise its objective of a unified, so-called free world market.

All this is to an ever growing extent achieved through mechanisms which more than ever before in history incite a polarisation between two groups within society, with on one side a small group of very rich people continuously—and literally by the second—increasing their immense wealth, and on the other side the large masses of workers who, with every victory of the doctrines of economic neo-liberalism, are forced to abandon earlier in history installed mechanisms of correcting unbridled capitalism and of ensuring a more just distribution of wealth than is possible under the above-explained systems and mechanisms of capitalism itself.[191]

This way, economic neo-liberalism is not only ensuring the gradual dismantling of the welfare state model, causing that the neo-liberal dictate that everyone should work for the benefit of capitalists until death, even gets to an ever-increasing extent applicable to the more vulnerable members of society, such as the sick and elderly.

Through its fiscal policies, economic neo-liberalism, furthermore, implements, in an extremely cynical way, its belief that enterprises and their rich capital providers,

[191] See Stiglitz (2002), p. 27, more specifically this author's call for the promotion of an equitable, sustainable and democratic development that promotes societal well-being and conforms to basic principles of social justice.

purportedly being the great inspiring powers of prosperity and progress, should also in the fiscal context not be hindered by any form of state interference. Through this, paying taxes, next to providing labour and consuming, has become (3) the third life duty of the working man, while the rich and very rich who take advantage of this, themselves transfer their fortunes to tax paradises, or, as is meanwhile happening, increasingly enjoy tax exemptions from their own home states themselves being faced with a seemingly endless race to the bottom in the field of taxation.

As a result, states have gradually been turned into mechanisms that above all contribute to the supremacy of the free markets, where, on a global scale, the majority of mankind has become but a means of pursuing ever more profits to serve the greed of the rich and powerful.

Thus, over the past half century, the warning of historical enlightened beings, such as Plato and Jesus Christ, seems to have reached its fulfilment, as under the impulse of economic neo-liberalism, in the words of Jesus Christ, the whole of mankind has been chained in servitude to what He called "the money devil" (= "the mammon").

It is hence hardly surprising that over the past decades also sectors of the socio-economic order which were until recently still seen as "soft", have even so been subjected to the dictates of the free market mechanism. Typical examples thereof are hospitals (and similar institutions of health care) and (public) schools (going from primary schools to universities). Whereas this type of institutions has historically grown from the power of altruism,[192] within contemporary societies they increasingly find themselves at the mercy of the profit logic of free market thinking.

It is hereby more and more argued that public schools and hospitals should receive the least possible amount of government funding, and should, on the contrary, "pay off". This also helps explaining the often excessive fees which doctors charge to their patients. Also the profit expectations to which many schools and universities have become subject during the past decades, fit the neo-liberal picture that everything should either generate profits or disappear.

Meanwhile, recent press even cheered for a teenager with obviously great business instinct who has succeeded in turning babysitting from what was in the past essentially a friends favour into a million dollar business, implying that even (older) children babysitting (younger) children only want to do so provided this is sufficiently profitable.[193]

Even supra-national institutions, such as the IMF and the OECD, which were historically established as institutions aiming at avoiding distortions between countries,[194] are at present, more than ever, themselves subject to the logic of

[192] In the Western world, the genesis of both public education and hospitals and similar institutions, can be found in early Christianity where, because of motives of Charity (and explicitly not driven by motives of profit pursuit), already in the time of the Roman Empire, initiatives were taken which have been the predecessors of our current schools and hospitals. (See Ortberg (2014), pp. 49–51.)

[193] See Lewak (2015).

[194] See Stiglitz (2002), pp. 22–23, on the original intent of the IMF and how this got distorted by the doctrines of economic neo-liberalism.

economic neo-liberalism, thus contributing to the efforts of turning the world economy into a single globalised free market system. For instance the way in which the IMF has handled the financial problems which Greece has been facing in the aftermath of the financial crisis of 2007–2008, clearly demonstrates the anti-solidarity principle to which free market doctrines are subjecting the entire world.

In short, the historical choice made by the Western world since the late Middle Ages of proclaiming selfishness, egoism and greed as leading socio-economic principles, has, but a few ages later, resulted into the current socio-economic world order where almost every human being, with exception of a limited amount of very rich people, as well as every form of human activity, has become unilaterally subject to the harsh reality of the free markets.

Objectives such as advocating more justice, but also the pursuit of personal happiness and personal development,[195] have in this all become subjected to the "money devil".

Especially for those who, after having read the abovementioned, are still not convinced of the way in which capitalism, as constructed by the doctrines of economic liberalism, and as made "unbridled" again by the doctrines of economic neo-liberalism, has developed into an oncologic system which is running the world, the next Chap. 4 of this book will present an overview of some more typical peculiarities of the outlook of the present-day capitalist society(ies).

References

Adriaen D (2014) Wegwerken groenestroomput begint in januari. De Tijd, 18 December 2014, p 3

Anseeuw B (2015) Geef Sylvie een bed in de kinderpsychiatrie. De Morgen, 18 March 2015, p 3

Ardaen B (2012) Tijdbom – de inside story. Own publication by the author, Ghent

Arenas L (2016) Rousseau. L'homme est bon par nature. C'est la société qui le corrompt. In: Apprendre à philosopher. RBA, Paris

Armstrong J (2017) 5 causes and consequences of neoliberalism. https://www.lifepersona.com/5-causes-and-consequences-of-neoliberalism. Last consulted 16 June 2018

Beaud M (1994) Geschiedenis van het kapitalisme van 1500 tot heden. Het Spectrum (Aula), Utrecht

Bacevich A (2008) He told us to go shopping. Now the bill is due (article of 5 October 2008). http://www.washingtonpost.com/wp-dyn/content/article/2008/10/03/AR2008100301977.html. Last consulted 16 June 2018

Bird B (2017) The GOP tax plan: breaking down the winners and losers – this tax proposal has many moving parts. https://www.thebalance.com/gop-tax-plan-winners-and-losers-4154293. Last consulted 16 June 2018

Blomme P (2015) Belastingen of snoeien in sociale zekerheid? De Tijd, 20 March 2015, p 3

[195] See the way how Stiglitz describes the general purpose of economy activity:

> The purpose of economic activity is to increase the well-being of individuals, and economic structures that are able to do so are more desirable than those that do not. (Stiglitz (2002), p. 9.)

Bové L (2014) Nieuw datalek zet Luxemburg helemaal in zijn blootje. De Tijd, 10 December 2014, pp 8–9
Brook Y, Watkins D (2012) Free market revolution – how Ayn Rand's ideas can end big government. Palgrave Macmillan, New York
Brown W (2003) Neo-liberalism and the end of liberal democracy. Theory Event 7(1). http://lchc.ucsd.edu/cogn_150/Readings/brown.pdf. Last consulted 16 June 2018
Browne J (2008) Over het ontstaan van soorten van Darwin. Een biografie (trans: Ruitenberg J). Mets & Schilt, Amsterdam
Bruckner P (2002) Misère de la prospérité – la religion marchande et ses ennemis. Bernard Grasset, Paris
Byttebier K (1994) Protective and defensive measures against hostile take-overs. In: Wymeersch E (Ed) Further perspectives in financial integration in Europe. W. de Gruyter, Berlin, pp 181–192
Byttebier K (1996) Hostile take-overs: economic (dis)functions and legal policy questions. In: Bouckaert B, De Geest G (eds) Essays in law and economics II. Maklu Uitgevers, Antwerp, pp 77–134
Byttebier B, Verroken A (1997) De bi-nationale, horizontale groep Gemeentekrediet – Crédit local de France (Deel I). V&F; De bi-nationale, horizontale groep Gemeentekrediet – Crédit local de France (Deel II), V&F
Byttebier K, Verroken A (1995) Structuring international co-operation between enterprises. Graham & Trotman/Martinus Nijhoff, London
Byttebier K (2015) Nu het gouden kalf verdronken is. Van hebzucht naar altruïsme als hoeksteen voor een Nieuwe Monetaire Wereldorde. Maklu, Antwerp
Byttebier K (2017) Towards a new international monetary order. In: Byttebier K, van der Borght K (eds) Economic and financial law & policy – shifting insights & values, vol I. Springer, Cham
Calluy K, Nasser L (2017) "Pano" undercover in woonzorgcentra: minimale zorg, maximale winst (article of 11 October 2017). https://www.vrt.be/vrtnws/nl/2017/10/11/-pano-undercover-in-woonzorgcentra%2D%2Dminimale-zorg%2D%2Dmaximale-wins/. Last consulted 16 June 2018
Carter B (2014) Is China's economy really the largest in the world? http://www.bbc.com/news/magazine-30483762. Last consulted 16 June 2018
Chomsky N (2015) Masters of mankind. Penguin Random House, UK
Chomsky N (2017) Requiem for the American dream. The 10 principles of concentration of wealth & power. Seven Stories Press, New York
Congregation for the Doctrine of the Faith – Dicastery For Promoting Integral Human Development (2018) Oeconomicae et pecuniariae quaestiones – Considerations for an ethical discernment regarding some aspects of the present economic-financial system. http://www.vatican.va/roman_curia/congregations/cfaith/documents/rc_con_cfaith_doc_20180106_oeconomicae-et-pecuniariae_en.html. Last consulted 16 June 2018
Crédit Suisse Research Institute (2017) Global Wealth Report 2017. http://publications.credit-suisse.com/tasks/render/file/index.cfm?fileid=12DFFD63-07D1-EC63-A3D5F67356880EF3. Last consulted 16 June 2018
Das G (2012) The difficulty of being good: on the subtle art of dharma. Penguin Books, New Dehli
Davis J (2018) Trump calls some unauthorized immigrants 'Animals' in Rant (article of 16 May 2018). https://www.nytimes.com/2018/05/16/us/politics/trump-undocumented-immigrants-animals.html. Last consulted 16 June 2018
Dawkins R (2006) The selfish gene. Oxford University Press. (30th anniversary edition, Oxford
Dawkins R (2009) The greatest show on earth. The evidence for evolution. Black Swan, London
Debackere J (2015) Klassengeneeskunde loert: "Waarom in eenpersoonskamer extra betalen voor behandeling?" (article of May 2nd 2015). https://www.demorgen.be/lifestyle/klassengeneeskunde-loert-waarom-in-eenpersoonskamer-extra-betalen-voor-behandeling-bb7b1d73/. Last consulted 16 June 2018
Debusschere B (2015) Wetenschap als wingewest. Bedrijven palmen 'onpartijdige' wetenschapscontrole. De Morgen, 1 April 2015, p 15

Deconinck E, Gillard W (2004–2005) De liberalisering van elektriciteitsmarkt in België. Jura falconis 2004–2005, n° 3, pp 453–538
Dehousse F, Dirick B (1992) Le marché unique des services financiers. In: J.T., pp 825–828
Delbeke K, Eckert M (2018) Trillen voor Tihange. Duitse angst voor Belgische kerncentrales. De Standaard, May 12th–13th 2018, Economic Section, pp 4–5
Deridder L (2003) Handboek gas- en elektriciteitsliberalisering in Energie en recht. Intersentia, Antwerpen
Descamps F (2015) Israël hoopt op een messias. De Morgen, 18 March 2015, p 4
Desmet Y (2015) Beschamend. De Morgen, 18 March 2015, p 1
De Cuyper R (2015) Geen plaats voor moeilijke gevallen. De Morgen, 18 March 2015, pp 2–3
De Grauwe P (2014) De limieten van de markt. De slinger tussen overheid en kapitalisme. Lannoo, Tielt
De Vreede J (2014) In Nederland opgegeven, in België genezen van kanker'. http://www.hln.be/hln/nl/957/Binnenland/article/detail/1858580/2014/04/19/In-Nederland-opgegeven-in-Belgie-genezen-van-kanker.dhtml (article of April 19th 2014)
DM/RC (2018) US House votes to dismantle crisis-era banking rules. http://www.dw.com/en/us-house-votes-to-dismantle-crisis-era-banking-rules/a-43888065. Last consulted 16 June 2018
Eyskens M (s.d.) Is verandering vooruitgang? De maatschappelijke gevolgen van de derde industriële revolutie. Davidsfonds, Leuven
Ferdman R (2015) China drinks a surprising amount of alcohol (article of 20 March 2015). http://www.washingtonpost.com/blogs/wonkblog/wp/2015/03/20/the-rise-and-fall-of-alcohol-consumption-around-the-world-charted/. Last consulted 16 June 2018
Foucault M (2013) De geboorte van de biopolitiek. Boom, Amsterdam
Friedman M (1993) Why government is the problem. Stanford University, Hoover Institution on War, Revolution and Peace
Fromm E (1956) (Vert. Claude J) Société aliénée et société saine - du capitalisme - du socialisme humaniste - psychoanalyse de la société contemporaine. Le Courrier du livre, Paris
Fromm E (1979) The sane society. Routledge & Kegan Paul, London
Fromm E (1990) Die Furcht vor der Freiheit. Deutscher Taschenbuch Verlag, München (also: Fromm E (s.d.) Escape from Freedom. Open Road, Integrated Media, New York)
Fromm E (2013) Marx's concept of man. Bloomsbury, London
Galbraith JK (1979) The nature of mass poverty. Harvard University Press, Cambridge
Galbraith JK (1983) The anatomy of power. Houghton Mifflin Company, Boston
Galbraith JK (1987) Economics in perspective – a critical history. Houghton Mifflin Company, Boston
Galbraith JK (1990) A short history of financial Euphoria. Whittle Books in association with Penguin Books, New York
Galbraith JK (1992) The culture of contentment. Houghton Mifflin Company, Boston
Galbraith JK (2004) The economics of innocence fraud. Houghton Mifflin Company, Boston
Galbraith JK, Salinger N (1978) Almost everyone's guide to economics. Penguin Books, London
Gates B (2014) Why inequality matters (article of 13 October 2014). https://www.gatesnotes.com/Books/Why-Inequality-Matters-Capital-in-21st-Century-Review. Last consulted 16 June 2018
Greenspan A (2007) The age of turbulence. Adventures in a new world. The Penguin Press, New York
Harari YN (2014) Sapiens – a brief history of humankind. Penguin Random House, London
Heilbron B, Mommers J, Muntz T, De Zeeuw H (2014) De zon en de wind zijn Europees. Knack, 19 November 2014, pp 28–37
Hulpiau S, Lierman F, Vermaut J (2011) Solvabiliteit en rendabiliteit van het Belgisch financiewezen 1970 – 2010. Bank.Fin., 2011, p 430
Krugman P (1994) Peddling prosperity. W. W. Norton & Company, New York
Krugman P (1998) The accidental theorist and other dispatches from the dismal science. W.W. Norton & Company, New York

Krugman P (2004) The great unraveling: losing our way in the new century. W. W. Norton & Company, New York
Leopold J (2002) Enron linked to California blackouts (article of 16 May 2002). http://www.marketwatch.com/story/enron-caused-california-blackouts-traders-say. Last consulted 16 June 2018
Lepew P (2011) How big tobacco got away with the crime of the century. https://theloungeisback.wordpress.com/2011/03/28/how-big-tobacco-got-away-with-the-crime-of-the-century/. Last consulted 16 June 2018
Lewak D (2015). Meet the 15-year-old babysitting boss poised to make millions. http://nypost.com/2015/02/19/meet-the-15-year-old-babysitting-boss-poised-to-make-millions/. Last consulted 16 June 2018
Lipman P (2006) "No Child Left Behind". Globalization, privatization, and the politics of inequality. In: Ross E, Gibson R (eds) Neoliberalism and education reform. Hampton Press. Inc., Cresskill, pp 35–58
Lloyd C (2012) What on earth happened? The complete story of the planet, life & people from the big bang to the present day. Bloomsbury, London
Marcuse H (1962) Eros and civilization – a philosophical inquiry into Freud. Vintage Books (A division of Random House), New York
Marcuse H (1964) Reason and revolution. Beacon Hill, Bosto
Marcuse H (1968) Geweld en Vrijheid. Politieke opstellen (trans: Boukema H). De Bezige Bij, Amsterdam
Meher Baba (1955) God speaks – the theme of creation and its purpose. https://www.ambppct.org/Book_Files/godspeaks_p1.pdf. Last consulted 16 June 2018
Menasse R (2012) De Europese koerier. De woede van de burger en de vrede van Europa. Een prachtig en prikkelend pleidooi pro Europa. De Arbeiderspers, Utrecht
Messiaen G (2017) Vermarkting van de zorg is niet de oplossing (article of 13 October 2017). http://www.dewereldmorgen.be/artikel/2017/10/13/vermarkting-van-de-zorg-is-niet-de-oplossing. Last consulted 16 June 2018
Michielsen S, Sephina M (2009) Bankroet – hoe Fortis al zijn krediet verspeelde. Lannoo, Tielt
Micklethwait J, Woolridge A (2014) De vierde revolutie. Op zoek naar de overheid van morgen. De Bezige Bij, Antwerp
Neugarten J (2018) Why is Luxembourg considered a tax haven? https://www.investopedia.com/ask/answers/100115/why-luxembourg-considered-tax-haven.asp. Last consulted 16 June 2018
OIVO (2011) Evolutie energieprijs versus evolutie gezinsbudget. OIVO, Brussels. http://www.agripress.be/_STUDIOEMMA_UPLOADS/downloads/1818.pdf. Last consulted 16 June 2018
Ortberg J (2014) Impact – Jezus. Geen mens heeft de wereld zo ingrijpend veranderd. Ark Media, Amsterdam
Osho (2011) Earthern lamps. 60 parables and Anecdotes to light up your heart. Osho Media International, New York
Oxfam (2014) Even it up – time to end extreme inequality. Oxfam GB, Oxford
Oxfam (2017) An economy for the 99%. It's time to build a human economy that benefits everyone, not just the privileged few. Oxfam briefing paper, January 2017. https://d1tn3vj7xz9fdh.cloudfront.net/s3fs-public/file_attachments/bp-economy-for-99-percent-160117-en.pdf. Last consulted 16 June 2018
Pauli W (2014) De kloof in de democratie – Het historische belang van Thomas Piketty. Knack, 10 December 2014, pp 32–35
Peersman L, Schoors K (2012) De perfecte storm. Hoe de economische crisis de wereld overviel en vooral: hoe we eruit geraken. Borgerhoff & Lamberigts, Ghent
Peeters T (2015) Hoe insluiting tot meer uitsluiting kan leiden. De Morgen, 1 April 2015, pp 4–5
Pesendorfer D (2012) Goodbye neo-liberalism? Contested policy responses to uncertain consequences of the 2007–09 financial crisis. In: Alexander K, Dhumale R (eds) Research handbook on International Financial Regulation. Edward Elgar, Cheltenham, pp 414–434
Plato (1987) The Republic (trans: Lee D). Penguin Books, London

Rand A (1982) Philosophy: who needs it. New American Library (a division of Penguin Group), New York
Rand A (1992) The virtue of selfishness. New American Library (a division of Penguin Group), New York
Rand A (2008) Capitalism: the unknown ideal. New American Library (a division of Penguin Group), New York
Reich R (2001) How did spending become our patriotic duty? Article of 19 December 2001. http://prospect.org/article/how-did-spending-become-our-patriotic-duty. Last consulted 16 June 2018
Rogers J (2018) 'Eaten alive' Who was Rebecca Zeni? Former model and US TV star 'eaten by scabies in her Georgia care home' (article of 30th April 2018). https://www.thesun.co.uk/news/6169196/rebecca-zeni-model-eaten-alive-scabies-mites-georgia-lafayette/. Last consulted 16 June 2018
Ronse T (1992) Rambo op lemen voeten – Amerika in de jaren negentig. Kritak, Leuven
Ruyver R (1969) Éloge de la société de consommation. Calmann-Lévy, Paris
Sachs J (2011) The price of civilization: reawakening American virtue and prosperity. Random House, New York
Skidelsky R, Skidelsky E (2013) How much is enough. Money and the good life. Penguin Books, London
Smout L (2014) Black-out is erg slechte publiciteit. HLN 29–30 November 2014, p 4
Smit J (2013) De prooi. Blinde trots breekt ABN Amro. Prometheus, Amsterdam
Soenens D (2015) UGent wankelt: na financiële kater ook angstcultuur aangeklaagd. De Morgen, 30 March 2015
Steger M (2013) Globalization. A very short introduction. Oxford University Press, Oxford, p 40
Steger M (2014) Globalisering. In: Elementaire deeltjes – 8, Amsterdam University Press, Amsterdam
Sterdyniak H (2011) Quelle politique économique? Morts et renaissances du keynésianisme. In: Les Économistes atterés, Changer d'économie! Nos propositions pour 2012, Les liens qui libèrent, Paris
Stiglitz J (2002) Employment, social justice and societal well-being. Int Labour Organ 141(1–2):9–29
Stiglitz J (2003) The roaring nineties. W.W. Norton & Company, New York
Stiglitz J (2006) Making globalization work. Penguin Books, London
Stiglitz J (2010) Freefall. Free markets and the sinking of the global economy. Allen Lane (an imprint of Penguin Books), London
Stiglitz J, Sen A, Fitoussi J-P (2010) Mismeasuring our lives. Why GDP doesn't add up. The New Press, New York
Stoddart W (2009) Hindoeïsme in kort bestek. Over goden, wijzen en geschriften. Synthese, Den Haag
Szalavitz M (2012) Is human nature fundamentally selfish or altruistic? Time, 8 October 2012. http://healthland.time.com/2012/10/08/is-human-nature-fundamentally-selfish-or-altruistic/. Last consulted 16 June 2018
Tawney R (1942) Religion and the rise of capitalism. Penguin Books, Harmondsworth
Terry L (s.d.) The Bologna process and its impact in Europe: it's so much more than degree changes. Vanderbilt J Transnatl Law 41:107–228
Thatcher M (1993) The downing street years. HarperCollinsPublishers, London
The Bologna Declaration of 19 June 1999 – Joint declaration of the European Ministers of Education. http://media.ehea.info/file/Ministerial_conferences/02/8/1999_Bologna_Declaration_English_553028.pdf. Last consulted 16 June 2018
Tolstoj L (2012) De weg van het leven. Erven J. Bijleveld, Utrecht
Tulipano R (2013) America the wasteful: a detailed look into our throw-away society. https://gentwenty.com/america-the-wasteful-a-detailed-look-into-our-throw-away-society/. Last consulted 16 June 2018

Vandekerckhove S, Van Garderen F (2015a) Farmabedrijf zet regering voor blok. Hoe omstreden firma Alexion ex-minister Onkelinx chanteerde. De Morgen, 21 March 2015, p 1
Vandekerckhove S, Van Garderen F (2015b) Minister versus Big Farma. De Morgen, 21 March 2015, pp 12–13
Van der Borght K (2014) China: de rechtsorde zoals we ze kennen? Intersentia, Antwerp
van Oudheusden J (2012). Een kleine geschiedenis van Amerika. Bert Bakker, Amsterdam
Verhaeghe P (2011) De neoliberale waanzin – Flexibel, efficiënt en… gestoord. Uitgeverij VUBPRESS, Brussels
Vivekananda (1989) Karma yoga. The complete works of Swami Vivekanda (Mayavati Memorial Edition), vol I. Advaita Ashrama, Kolkata
Wauters R (2015) Onze partij houdt Michel I bij elkaar. De Morgen, 21 March 2015, pp 4–5
Westcott L (2015) Alibaba's IPO set to be biggest internet stock launch since Facebook (article of 17 March 2014). http://www.thewire.com/business/2014/03/alibabas-ipo-set-be-biggest-internet-stock-launch-facebook/359252/. Last consulted 16 June 2018
Willige A (2016) The world's top economy: the US vs China in five charts. https://www.weforum.org/agenda/2016/12/the-world-s-top-economy-the-us-vs-china-in-five-charts/. Last consulted 16 June 2018
Wolffers I (2010) Gezond. Over de mens, zijn gezondheid en de gezondheidszorg. Nieuw Amsterdam Uitgevers, Amsterdam

Chapter 4
Some Further Themes on the Outlook of the Capitalist World

4.1 Capitalism as the Driving Force of Both Economic Growth and Socio-Economic Injustice

4.1.1 Economic Growth Versus the Distribution of Welfare

It is obvious that, during the past centuries, capitalism has contributed to economic growth, be it that, in our times, the questions arise (1) at what price, (2) whether or not economic growth is really that important as the adherents of economic neo-liberalism want us to believe, and (3) whether this growth has not reached its limits.[1]

The mechanisms of capitalism discussed in the previous chapters, such as noteably the technique of private money creation based on credit provisioning by private banks, next to the capital company model, are without any doubt among the ones best catching the essence of the capitalist economic system that economic growth is a goal to be attained at all costs.

As a result, it seems that, at least in some areas in the world and, within those, for some parts of the population more than for other parts, prosperity has increased, albeit that in other areas in the world, it may be argued that prosperity, and at least welfare, has rather decreased for large groups of people.[2]

[1] Compare Harari (2014), pp. 372–373.

[2] Harari expresses this as follows (Harari 2014, p. 372):

> The economic pie of 2014 is far larger than the pie of 1500, but it is distributed so unevenly that many African peasants and Indonesian labourers return home after a hard day's work with less food than did their ancestors 500 ago. Much like the Agricultural Revolution, so too the growth of the modern economy might turn out to be a colossal fraude. The human species and the global economy may well keep growing, but many more individuals may live in hunger and want.

K. Byttebier, *The Unfree Market and the Law*, Economic and Financial Law & Policy – Shifting Insights & Values 2,
https://doi.org/10.1007/978-3-319-97382-1_4

As should be clear from the foregoing, it have mainly been the doctrines of economic liberalism and, later in history, economic neo-liberalism that have resulted in the unjust distribution of the welfare stemming from the economic "progress" that capitalism (purportedly) brought (as of the seventeenth century). Because of these mechanisms, the gaps of welfare division in our present societies may even be considered greater than ever before in history.

This in itself already implies that the doctrines of economic liberalism and economic neo-liberalism do not meet up with one of their basic starting premises, namely that in a world where everyone behaves as egoistically, selfish and greedily as possible, welfare will gradually increase proportionally for everyone.

On the contrary, the current world economy, as submitted to the doctrines of economic neo-liberalism, is characterized by a vast number of manifest injustices, some of which will be further explored in this chapter.

4.1.2 Capitalism as a System Inherently Creating an Unjust Division of Wealth and Property

4.1.2.1 General

It will be clear to anyone by now that the global world economy is more than ever before characterized by an unprecedented "worldwide unjust distribution of wealth and prosperity".

This unjust distribution of wealth and prosperity appears firstly at the level of countries themselves, where there are countries with prosperity for a large part of the population, but still also countries where a large part of the population suffers from poverty.

Moreover, the division of wealth and prosperity between countries is to a large extent distorted by public debt (in the meantime being referred to as one of the most underestimated economic problems of our times[3]), where there are countries facing high public debts, next to countries disposing of large monetary reserves.

Paradoxically there are even countries traditionally considered being rich as regards the (high) level of prosperity for a large part of their population, but who nevertheless face a large public debt, even to the extent that it could be questioned whether these countries will ever succeed in paying back these debts. This situation is increasingly becoming a threat for the level of prosperity of the general population,[4] while at the same time creditors get richer by the minute as a result of the interest the public debt positions generate.[5] (See, furthermore, under Sect. 4.6.)

This unjust distribution of wealth and prosperity is, moreover, also strongly present in interpersonal relations where, on a global scale, an increasing polarisation is

[3] Piketty (2014). See even Bush (2010), p. 471.

[4] See especially the observations of Thomas Piketty in this regard (see Piketty (2014)).

[5] See https://www.nationaldebtclocks.org/.

occurring between a small group of rich and extremely rich people and an ever increasing large group of poor and very poor people. It has in this regard even been observed that in many so-called prosperous countries, the middle class, because of the dismantling of the welfare state and the suspension of mechanisms of redistribution of wealth and prosperity, is, to a growing extent, joining the poor to very poor classes. (See, furthermore, under Sect. 4.7.)

It should hereby be clear that this unjust distribution of the welfare generated by the economic system is an inherent consequence of the mechanisms of capitalism, as described exhaustively in the previous chapters, among which, most notably, the capitalist financial mechanisms.

4.1.2.2 The Capitalist (Private) Money Creation Model as a System of Distributing Wealth in an Unjust Manner

The first capitalist financing mechanism causing an unjust distribution of wealth referred to at the end of the previous Sect. 4.1.2.1 is obviously the private money creation mechanism which causes that "the ones in need" (and this term may be applied to a very broad category of entities, going from human beings to states) have to pay a (high) price for the access to new money, in general in the form of bank interests. On top of that, within the logic of capitalism, the more one is in need, the higher the price will be for accessing newly created money,[6] ensuring that in this

[6]The reason for this is that, under the logic of capitalism, the poorer a potential credit taker is, the higher the risk for the credit giver, so the higher the price (= the interest) that will be charged for the credit will be. As a result, the poorest economic agents (going from individuals to states) will bear the highest interest burden, which in its own turn makes the richest institutions on earth (and their shareholders), mainly private banks and similar financial institutions, ever more rich.

As a result, the logic of the capitalist financial system literally implies that the rich get ever more rich to the detriment of the poor.

One may observe this logic thus the more striking as regards so-called "shark loans". (On the economic rationality behind loan sharks, see Ferguson (2009), p. 41.) Under the dictates of (unbridled) capitalism, it appears that poor people who don't have access to regular bank credits, but who are nevertheless in need of credit, are inclined to take up credit from more wealthy members of society (among which certain types of specialized financial institutions) against extreme contractual conditions. Examples are being given of loan sharks charging 100% interest over a loan period of 30 days (see https://www.investopedia.com/terms/l/loansharking.asp; last consulted on June 16, 2018).

Even the so-called micro-credits that were developed to help poor people in developing countries (by giving them access to cheap credit) have gotten contaminated by the capitalist ideas, where it has been mentioned in recent press that the interest charged for such micro-credit can also take extremely high proportions. (See for instance Máxima-bank vraagt 'woekerrentes' voor micro-kredieten. At: http://www.quotenet.nl/Nieuws/Maxima-bank-vraagt-woekerrentes-voor-micro-kredieten-145079 (last consulted on June 16, 2018).)

All this illustrates how far away the capitalist credit practices are from the Christian ideals that those who have too much should be willing to share their excess wealth with those who are in need (Luke, 3:11) and that the one giving a loan should do this without the intention of ever getting paid back (Luke, 6:35), let alone of charging a high interest. (See also Byttebier (2017), p. 94 a.f.)

Luke, 6:34–35 indeed reads as follows:

model it will be very hard for the poor (going from individuals to states) to get back on their feet from a situation of poverty.[7]

The situation many poor countries have been witnessing this for decades, not to say centuries, is illustrative for this capitalist logic.

What is perhaps even the worst is that these observations can hardly be called new, as they already have been addressed in the teachings of some of the great philosophers from classic antiquity, such as Plato and Aristotle, but also in those of early church fathers, such as Saints Ambrose en Augustine who, through their insights, have been at the base of the so-called clerical interest prohibition which has determined middle age socio-economic thinking for ages.

It is therefore not surprising that the breakthrough of capitalist loan and credit practices at the end of the Middle Ages has gone along with a resolute omission of the insights of these classical philosophers and leading religious persons, and through this, of their aspiration to advocate for a more just world for everyone.[8]

4.1.2.3 The Capital Company Model as a Further System of Unjust Division of the Added Value from Economic Activities

A second capitalist mechanism which is especially strongly responsible for the gaps between the poor and rich within capitalist societies is the earlier mentioned capital company model.

The combined use of this mechanism and that of the so-called (liberal) economic "Iron Law of the Wages" has more precisely caused that worldwide, enterprises consider the labour they employ as a cost factor which they should hence keep as low as possible in order to keep the profits the enterprise is making, ultimately intended to be divided among its capital providers, as high as possible.[9]

It is this technique which is above all responsible for the fact that a small elite of capital providers of (large) enterprises within society succeed in becoming ever more rich to the detriment of the efforts of the working classes, ergo the larger masses of mankind.

Next to that, this capitalist mechanism is also highly responsible for short term economic thinking which has been determining the outlook of the capitalist economies for ages now, where problems or difficulties are in general not solved, but on the contrary, are continuously postponed to the future. This economic logic is

---

And if ye lend to them of whom ye hope to receive, what thank have ye? For sinners also lend to sinners, to receive as much again. But love ye your enemies, and do good, and lend, hoping for nothing again; and your reward shall be great, and ye shall be the children of the Highest: for he is kind unto the unthankful and to the evil. (King James Version; http://biblehub.com/kjv/luke/6-34.htm; last consulted on June 16, 2018).

[7] Compare Stiglitz (2002), p. 23.

[8] This is yet another illustration of the turnaround of values caused by the capitalist ideologies.

[9] Compare Stiglitz (2002), pp. 10–11.

generally known as the so-called "laissez faire, laissez passer-principle",[10] with as a typical example the debt financing model of Western governments.[11]

While assessing the capitalist economy as, among others, based on the use of the capital company mechanism, one needs to further bear in mind that, under the doctrines of both economic liberalism and economic neo-liberalism, it is mainly up to the capital providers of such enterprises (next to the managers and directors they appoint) who are considered to be the most beneficial steering power within society, to appropriate the added values of such enterprises' operations. Those who (merely) provide labour can, in this approach, in the best case obtain a sufficient salary through negotiating a tolerable employment agreement (and should have no expectancy that their government, or any other entity, will be supporting them in this).[12]

As referred above, it goes without saying that this starting premise which determines the essence of the doctrines of economic liberalism and economic neo-liberalism, is one of the main recipes for all kinds of societal injustices as these are certain to occur in a game of contracting where those who are the strongest from the start, among which noteably large enterprises, will also be able to negotiate the best contractual terms and conditions.

4.1.3 *The Impact of Capitalism on Power*

Under the doctrines of economic liberalism and economic neo-liberalism, the world economy has, moreover, gotten characterised by "a globally very unfair participation in the exercise of power" where entire democracies merely still provide nothing more than lip service to democracy rather than truly living up to it.[13]

As a consequence of the large influence on the exercise of power by large capital, the capitalist mechanisms referred to in the previous Sect. 4.1.2 already inherently leading to inequality and injustice, are even furthermore reinforced. According to some, this even is one of the main objectives of economic neo-liberalism.[14]

---

[10] In this context, Galbraith has pointed out that especially when a state (or another government) establishes a commission to study a problem, the laissez faire, laissez passer-principle in general is in place, as such commissions mostly work for such a long time that, whenever they present the outcome of their findings, the problems they researched have either lost public interest or, since then, more pressing problems have arisen which need a similar postponement approach. (See Galbraith (1992), p. 20.)

[11] It has, for instance, been reported in November 2017 that the Belgian outstanding debt (= the public debt and the debt of private citizens combined) then amounted to 296% of the Belgian Gross Domestic Product. It was hereby, furthermore, mentioned that the combined private debt amounted to 190% of the GDP and the public debt to more than 100% of the GDP (See Belgische schuldenberg groter dan ooit. At: https://www.demorgen.be/economie/belgische-schuldenberg-groter-dan-ooit-bf4e2127/ (last consulted on June 16, 2018).

[12] See again also Stiglitz (2002), p. 10 a.f.

[13] See for instance Sachs (2011).

[14] See, for instance, the observations of the French Philosopher Michel Foucault, as referred to in Byttebier (2017), p. 326. See also Chomsky and Polychroniou (2017), p. 154.

Capitalism thus obtains the characteristics of the proverbial vicious circle: capitalist mechanisms have as an inherent consequence that the rich get richer, which enlarges their participation in the exercise of power, thus enabling them to even more advocate that the mechanisms that make them rich and powerful, should be further reinforced in order to make them even more rich and powerful.

First in the Western world, and later on a global scale, this trend has in the meantime been going on for ages already, albeit with certain "ups and downs", where the "downs" are often a consequence of a temporary downturn of the capitalist system, although these have, so far, not yet led to a fundamental change in the capitalist principles governing the world.

As has already been mentioned in the previous chapter (see more specifically at the end of Sect. 3.5.5.), already two and a half millennia ago Plato warned that a society which would start to choose the pursuit of money as its main societal objective, would evolve in the direction of a society where the rich classes would obtain all wealth and power.

Meanwhile, renowned economists, such as Krugman, Sachs and Stiglitz, and in the more recent past Piketty, have demonstrated that, in the current neo-liberal world, the prediction of Plato has been more than proven, as in most capitalist countries a governing model prevails that is mainly steered by large banks and enterprises and by the rich classes of society (= so-called "corporatocracy").

In such a governing model, through periodical elections, lip service may still be provided to the so-called democratic principles which support state organisation, be it that especially through the influence of the media and social e-platforms, political candidates belonging to the rich classes of society, in many cases have the best chances to sell their ideas to the voting public, while governing teams who are still somewhat striving for a certain degree of societal justice, in most cases will be strongly counteracted by many of the free market mechanisms (such as techniques of tax evasion by the rich classes, techniques of moving production to low-wage countries[15]; etc.).

A modern-day expression of "being governed by the rich" forms the contemporary social policy applied by many countries and supra-national institutions, among others aimed at dismantling the social welfare state. In a similar way, also the fiscal policy of many countries is illustrative of this phenomenon: as a result, all over the world, mainly the poor and middle classes are severely taxed, under the awareness that the exodus of the rich and the companies to countries with a fiscal policy better serving their interests, is a further motivation to leave them relatively unburdened by taxes.

---

[15] Stiglitz (2010), p. 195.

4.1.4 The Ongoing Dismantlement of the Mechanisms of Correcting Unbridled Capitalism

As explained before, over time, there has been an inclination to strongly advocate "correction mechanisms" on the free market operation (or, put otherwise, on unbridled capitalism), where different movements in societal life have attempted to give capitalism a "more human slant".

The call for more justice for the working classes became very strong during the first decades of the previous century. In some countries, especially former communist countries, this even led to true revolutions (albeit that, in those countries, these revolutionary powers would even so fail in establishing a more just societal model).

In the Western world, the efforts of the working classes to install a more just socio-economic order, have mainly been successful in the period after World War II up till the 1970s, which, in many countries led to the so-called "welfare state model" which, in terms of economics, came down to a "corrected free market system" (sometimes referred to as a "mixed economy" model).

As a result, at least in the Western world, during a few decades, efforts were made to establish a more just society where also the lower classes of the population, at least to a certain extent, were able to benefit from the fruits of economic growth and progress (not taking into account that similar efforts remained noteably lacking in most countries and areas in other parts of the world).

However, under the ever-increasing implementation of the doctrines of economic neo-liberalism, the (Western) welfare state model is getting more and more challenged. As a result, especially in many Western European countries (where the model of the welfare state was developed most), many government services, among which public education, care for the ill and elderly, next to public services such as police and justice, are since then systematically being dismantled. The types of social care and public service mechanisms that are still prevailing, are themselves moreover suffocating under ever more drastic budget cuts.[16]

Through this, economic neo-liberalism aims at realising one of its most basic mythical societal viewpoints that by not caring for those in need, general welfare will increase, while at the same time ignoring the fact that, in reality, such a world viewpoint is changing the world ever more into a jungle where the law of the strongest prevails.

Those who see this differently are invited to consider the social abuses that were taking place under the "uncorrected" type of capitalism of the eighteenth, the nineteenth and the first half of the twentieth century, occasionally even escalating into armed conflicts having gripped entire parts of the world. In the same way, it should be considered that it has only been through the breakthrough of socio-economic correction mechanisms, such as public services and social care, that, in the period after World War II, at least for a while, a somewhat more just socio-order saw the daylight, be it only in the Western world.

[16] Compare Chomsky (2017), p. 65 a.f.

Not coincidentally, the dismantling of these realisations of the welfare state has been put high on the neo-liberal agenda.[17]

To further demonstrate the devastating effects of implementing this ideology, we shall hereafter further describe in more detail some of the particularities of the outlook of the modern-day capitalist economy, as shaped (or: made "unbridled" again) in accordance with neo-liberal doctrines.

4.2 Even Further Shaping a World of Massive Exploitation of the Working Human Being

4.2.1 Starting Premise

The fact that, within (unbridled) capitalism, labour and hence the labouring human being are subjected to capital, ergo to the endless pursuit of profits by (large) enterprises and their capital providers, cannot come as a surprise, given the fact that this is exactly also one of the main goals of the doctrines that have shaped (unbridled) capitalism, namely economic liberalism and economic neo-liberalism.[18] (See already above, under Sect. 2.4.)

This has already been elaborated upon exhaustively in Chap. 2 of this book.

Under the doctrines of economic liberalism and economic neo-liberalism, the justification hereof, as also mentioned in Chap. 2, is that it is the class of entrepreneurs who are providing the economy with the impulses necessary for economic growth and progress, implying that it is not more than normal that they are to obtain a proportionally much larger part of the (neo-liberal) pie than the larger masses who, in that view, are but taking advantage of the efforts of said entrepreneurs.

As has also been explained before, economic thinking thanks this already since ages prevailing vision, to a large extent, to the works of Adam Smith himself.[19] The idea that entrepreneurs are the most wholesome power within society and that their hunger for ever more money is beneficial rather than, as Catholic doctrine had stated earlier on in history, sinful, indeed goes back to some of the writings of Smith himself,[20] as these have since then been embraced and further worked out under the doctrines of economic liberalism and economic neo-liberalism.

---

[17] See Clune (2013).

[18] In a disguised form, this is what the "trickle-down-economy" is all about.

[19] We have left open the question whether Smith himself sympathised with this vision to such an extent that he would deemed it a valid excuse for the many detrimental characteristics of modern-day capitalism.

[20] See the further references in Byttebier (2017), p. 114 a.f. Also Byttebier (2015), pp. 145–147.

4.2.2 *The Capitalist Objective of Keeping Wages at a Minimum Put in Practice Through Neo-liberal Policy Making*

An obvious expression of the subjection of labour to capital form the capitalist remuneration systems.

It should hereby be clear that the entire capitalist machinery is aimed at minimising the payments for "labour" in order to maximise business profits, at the level of a single enterprise defined as that what is left of the turnover made by this enterprise after deducting its costs, and where the salaries to be paid to the employees are to be seen as such a cost.

This principle inherently expresses one of the most characteristic "conflicts of interests" within the capitalist economy: for the working classes, wages are in most cases the only means to provide in one's livelihood (and that of one's family), while for the capital providers who above all attempt to maximise their profits, wages are a cost which should be kept as low as possible.[21]

The theoretical background of this (inherent) "conflict of interests" has already been explained above in Sect. 2.4, to which we can further refer here. We shall hereafter limit ourselves to merely illustrating the impact of these theoretical insights on present-day, neo-liberal policy making.

It will in this regard hardly come as a surprise that up to this very date, the principles set out in the previous paragraphs are stronger than ever dominating the political debate (on how the socio-economic order should function), as this debate has moreover, especially since the 1980s, to an ever growing extent been dominated by the adherents of economic neo-liberalism.

Said principles also are among the main causes of the ever increasing gaps between the poor and the rich within global societies, where only those achievements of the welfare state which protect labour and which are at present still in place, be it only in some countries, still provide some protection of labour against capital.

However, the classic liberal/neo-liberal argument that the competitive position of the entrepreneurs needs to be even more enhanced, provides to an increasing extent an excuse for neo-liberal governments all over the planet to diminish these labour protection measures.

The fact that in the contemporary globalised world the presumed impaired competitive position of Western production enterprises is mainly the consequence of the even more harrowing working conditions in low wage countries,[22] in other words of the absence of legislation protecting labour, as a result of which during the past decades production has to a large extent been moved to such low wage countries, is in this regard a factor which is barely taken into consideration in the current debate on how the socio-economic order should function.

---

[21] Stiglitz (2002), pp. 10–11.

[22] Where labour is still even provided by underaged children who barely get compensated.

As a consequence of these elements, capitalism does not make the largest part of the economic wealth flow to those who work the hardest (or otherwise put: to those being employed by capitalists at the lowest possible wages), but on the contrary to those who have no scruples to (shamelessly) exploit other people's labour at the lowest possible wages (an insight which—as explained above in Sect. 2.4—translates in Ricardo's classic "Iron Law of the Wages"[23]) and who are, moreover, often willing to sacrifice all other imaginable values (such as respect for human rights; respect for the dignity of others; respect for the environment; respect for animal rights…) to the unbridled pursuit of profits in order to get richer themselves.[24]

These observations, harsh as they may sound, are nevertheless fully in line with the starting premise of the doctrines of economic liberalism and economic neo-liberalism on which "capitalism" (or, in more modern terms: "the free market system") is based, namely that one should behave in the most egoistic, selfish and greedy way possible,[25] implying that it should not come as a surprise that, more often than not, (extremely) egoistic, selfish and greedy people flourish within this system.[26]

On writing this text passus, the world press covered how Jeff Bezos became the (purportedly) new richest man on the planet.[27]

At the same time, other press uncovered the secret behind his huge fortune, which for those understanding how (unbridled) capitalism works, is hardly a secret at all.

It more precisely appeared that the success of Amazon is the result of a strict application of the "Iron Law of the Wages" and that on a wide scale, Amazon is exploiting its labourers, for instance by underpaying them and by making then work under appalling labour conditions. All this has in the UK (where an investigative reporter has looked deeply into the working conditions within the Amazon empire) obviously been made possible thanks to the efforts of subsequent neo-liberal governments which, already since the early eighties, have done anything within their power to free the English economy from labour and social protective mechanisms, thus clearing the path for empires such as the Amazon empire.[28]

4.2.3 The Low Societal Position of the Working Classes

A further expression of the subordination of labour to capital within modern-day societies forms the lower social position the working classes hold as compared to the rich classes.

[23] Galbraith (1987), p. 84. See also the findings of Erich Fromm and Herbert Marcuse.

[24] Bruckner (2002), p. 26; see also Fromm (1979), p. 90 a.f.

[25] Smith (1979), p. 47; Berend (2006), p. 14; Bruckner (2002), p. 26.

[26] Loizou (2012), p. 32.

[27] See especially Vinton (2017).

[28] See for instance Webster (2017). See already before Daisy (2015).

Although the liberal and neo-liberal state organisation takes place under the flag of a presumed equality, in reality this equality is far from real. (See already above, under Sect. 3.1.)

In a world where, in accordance with the capitalist principles and ideals, (almost) everything can be purchased with money, it is evident that those who are rich are able to buy more (luxury) goods than those who are poor. In the same world where someone's value is to a large extent measured by external signs of luxury and wealth, it is not a great mystery that the rich get more prestige than the poor.

It is, however, even worse that financial success has become more and more decisive for government participation. Where in theory (most) capitalist countries claim to be democratic, in reality it appears that the rich classes have a much greater impact on governmental authority than may be considered legitimate from a democratic point of view. Already for decades now, prominent economists have exposed the mechanisms of "corporatocracy", a government model characterised by large enterprises (and their stakeholders) strongly determining the outcome of political decision making.[29]

It has already been indicated earlier in this book that this method of having the outcome of public policy determined by the agendas of the rich and powerful within society is probably most present in the fiscal policy of a large majority of the countries in the world. As a consequence of this, the fiscal policy of most countries is characterized by the fact that governments obtain their fiscal income mainly from the poor and middle classes and leave the rich class practically untouched.[30]

As has also already been mentioned earlier, there are moreover numerous other methods by which the rich all over the world influence governments, such as lobbying, claiming bailouts when they are in trouble, obtaining subsidies when in need…

According to some, the capitalist socio-economic order, especially to the extent that it is more and more recreated under the doctrines of economic neo-liberalism, shows all the characteristics of a contemporary feudal system.[31] Anthropologist Rik Pinxten has in this regard even claimed that because of this, the neo-liberal socio-economic order implies a break with the enlightenment concepts of "freedom", "equality", and "fraternity/solidarity" which were intended to lie at the basis of the liberal societies.[32]

As a result, the neo-liberal socio-economic order to an ever growing extent resembles the description George Orwell made in his famous short story "Animal farm". In the mean time, it also becomes ever clearer that capitalism does not meet up to its underlying promise that it provides for the highest possible prosperity for everyone.[33]

[29] See especially Sachs (2011). See already before Galbraith and Salinger (1978), p. 162.

[30] Oxfam (2014).

[31] Bruckner (2002), 25 a.f.

[32] Ongenae (2014), p. 44.

[33] Bruckner (2002), p. 20. See also Fromm (1979), p. 85 a.f.

4.3 The Sacrifice of All Values to the Golden Calf of Money Pursuit

To the extent that capitalism increasingly dominates the world economy, the (unbridled) pursuit of money has even so been put forward as the dominating value within the socio-economic order to which, during the course of the eighteenth, nineteenth and the twentieth century, gradually all other thinkable values have been systematically sacrificed.[34]

Further characteristics of capitalism becoming the dominating economic system as of the eighteenth and the nineteenth centuries are, next to the belief that all economic acting should exclusively, or at least primarily, serve one's own individual needs, a very sharp competitive behaviour (on the so-called "free market") where one is not supposed to deploy one's talents to help others, but on the contrary to build the most dominant (market) position possible[35] in order to ensure that others do not reach the same success within the own market segment (but are preferably "eliminated").[36] (See already above, under Sect. 3.3.)

For the corporate world (but to an increasing extent also for many other economic agents, next to governments and government officials who adhere the doctrines of economic liberalism and neo-liberalism), the unbridled pursuit of money has not only been alleviated to be the leading moral principle, but it has also been put higher than all other values and interests.

Through this, the care for the eco-system, at the same time the own "habitat" of the human species, next to that of all other living creatures, has to an ever increasing extent been sacrificed to the capitalist pursuit of profit, with as evident consequences the high extent of pollution which characterises the present-day world, in our times having resulted in the so-called "climate change" problem in all of its inestimable dimensions.[37]

---

[34] Kruithof (1985), pp. 56–56.

See also Ripple (2017):

> We are jeopardizing our future by not reining in our intense but geographically and demographically uneven material consumption and by not perceiving continued rapid population growth as a primary driver behind many ecological and even societal threats. By failing to adequately limit population growth, reassess the role of an economy rooted in growth, reduce greenhouse gases, incentivize renewable energy, protect habitat, restore ecosystems, curb pollution, halt defaunation, and constrain invasive alien species, humanity is not taking the urgent steps needed to safeguard our imperilled biosphere.

[35] This is the so-called "market leadership" myth. (See also Simon (2009), p. 54.)

[36] Kruithof (2000), p. 15.

[37] Stiglitz (2006), p. 17; Kruithof (1985), p. 57.

Especially in the debate of global warming, the negationism of mainly socio-economic "right" oriented thinkers takes worrying proportions.

Achenbach has in this regard pointed out that in 2015 almost half of the Americans did not believe that the use of fossil fuels contributes to global warming (see Achenbach (2015), p. 134):

> People emphasising the sense of community, are inclined to distrust large capitals and advocate strong government regulations; they usually deny the risks of climate change. People

In the same manner, also public health has to a high degree been subjected to the pursuit of profit of the corporate world. The consequences thereof are obviously numerous. An obvious example concerns the massive use of nuclear energy which as of the twentieth century has been massively been resorted to without any real worry about the fact that both nuclear waste, and the challenges of maintaining old(er)—or even outdated—nuclear energy installations sufficiently safe, keep forming an uncontrollable problem. As doubtful are certain practices of the industrial food industry,[38] next to these of the pharmaceutical sector.[39]

It needs not much further explanation that also the mineral resources of the planet have resolutely been involved in the capitalist production processes where, given the (neo-)liberal "laissez faire, laissez passer-principle", there has never been room for any planning from an elementary intergenerational perspective, which has resulted in a continuous decrease of all kinds of commodities and energy supplies (among which, in some areas in the world, even drinking water)[40] for the benefit of irrational production processes, aiming at satisfying the even more irrational consumption needs of the happy few who can afford these.[41]

Even the operation of governments has in many countries become subjected to the blind free market powers. Reference can for instance be made to the often exces-

---

> who are more hierarchical and individualistic, have respect for successful business men and do not like government involvement, they are inclined to deny warnings on climate change, recognising that accepting it, will lead to taxes or regulations to reduce greenhouse emissions. In the US the debate has become an acid test, where someone joins one group or another. When we argue about climate (...), we actually argue about who we are and to which club we belong.

See furthermore Ripple (2017):

> The earth is finite. Its ability to absorb wastes and destructive effluent is finite. Its ability to provide food and energy is finite. Its ability to provide for growing numbers of people is finite. And we are fast approaching many of the earth's limits. Current economic practices which damage the environment, in both developed and underdeveloped nations, cannot be continued without the risk that vital global systems will be damaged beyond repair.

[38] See Wolffers (2011), p. 92, on the immense power of the food industry.
See also Gore (2013b), p. 283.

[39] Wolffers (2011), p. 240 a.f.
In Western countries alone, the pharmaceutical industry is estimated to have made 10% of the population addicted to antidepressants and other "legitimate" narcotics. For instance, according to recent research by the "Christian mutuality" (a public health insurer), in Flanders alone, one out of 6 people takes sedatives on a very regular basis, which, given the very addictive characteristics of these drugs, is a very worrying high figure.
See furthermore Harari (2014), p. 368.

[40] Hartwell (2014).

[41] See also Oxfam (2017), p. 6, referring to this problem as to one of the "false assumptions" on which the capitalistic economic system is based:

> **False assumption #6: Our planet's resources are limitless.** This is not only a false assumption, but one which could lead to catastrophic consequences for our planet. Our economic model is based on exploiting our environment and ignoring the limits of what our planet can bear. It is an economic system that is a major driver of runaway climate change.

sive costs for public works which are attributed to private businesses, the latter obviously driven by an unbridled pursuit of profit, rather than by any concern for the general interest. As a result, such public works usually cost fortunes in public funds, which helps to explain the high budget deficits which many Western countries are facing. In more recent times, the massive resorting to so-called public-private partnerships where government tasks are outsourced to the private sector which itself aspires to gain high profits from this, is an expression of this same phenomenon.[42]

The list of further examples is obviously endless.

It is even more harrowing that, due to all these processes, a fundamental intergenerational injustice has manifested, causing that in many countries, younger generations, especially those from lower societal classes, find themselves in a world that has been drained by free market practices.

For Herbert Marcuse, capitalism has thus started expressing a loss of rationality (and by this a loss of its historical roots). Once triggered, capitalist rationality has turned irrationality into the leading norm. Have originally been perceived as "rational": the development of production at a breathtaking pace, the conquest of nature and the extension of wealth in the accumulation of ever more goods. However, by doing so, capitalism has become an irrational force, because increased productivity, next to the control of nature and social wealth have been turned into destructive powers, destructive not only in the figurative sense (such as in the sacrifice of all higher values to the pursuit of money), but also in a literal sense: the battle for existence becomes fiercer by the hour, both within individual countries as on an international level, and the built-up aggression discharges in the legitimation of medieval cruelty (such as warfare, torture and terrorism), and in a scientifically conducted destruction of humanity and nature.[43]

4.4 Globalisation as a Factor Magnifying the Impact of Capitalism

In the globalized capitalist word, all the abovementioned characteristics of capitalism have even been more enhanced.

As explained before, the rising "neo-liberal order" which under the impulse of the doctrines of economic neo-liberalism gained momentum on a global scale as of the 1980s, hereby unexpectedly experienced (even) better circumstances through the collapse, in the period 1989–1991, of the communist system in East-Europe and the Soviet Union,[44] which caused that the powers of capitalism, especially within the (socio-)economic context, no longer had to deal with a countervailing force.

[42] Oxfam (2014), p. 19.

[43] Marcuse (1968), p. 102.

[44] Steger (2013), p. 41.

Since then, neoliberal authors have often argued that, as a result of the collapse of the communist economies, there are no alternatives for the free market doctrines.[45] As a consequence, the belief in the free market system has since then become even more fanatic, where the free market is even seen as a necessary condition for a free society and as a condition for any individual or collective progress,[46] which implies that there cannot be any longer any alternatives for the free market system perceivable.

As a result, free marked doctrines caused an unprecedented globalisation of the world economy—to be understood as the increase of the international traffic of goods, services, capital and labour resulting in a mutual inter-wovenness between countries in the socio-economic field[47]—which was based on the earlier developed methods of (neo-)liberalisation and deregulation.[48] (See also before, Sects. 3.5–3.7.)

According to Steger, this process of globalisation has been characterized by three crucial developments in the field of the socio-economic order[49]: (1) an increased internationalisation and liberalisation of trades and finances; (2) a growing power of transnational enterprises[50] (before referred to as: multinationals[51]) and large (investment) banks and (3) an increasing role of international economic institutions, such as the IMF, the World Bank, the OECD and the WTO, many of which themselves have increasingly adopted the principles of economic neo-liberalism.[52]

Due to this increasing globalisation, the manifest imbalances which traditionally characterised capitalism in the post colonial capitalist era, have on a global scale started to take unprecedented proportions.[53]

It should be, meanwhile, very clear that (uncorrected) capitalism keeps many people in poverty.

This poverty is traditionally very visible in the North-South relations, where a large part of the population of many countries, especially on the African continent, has already since a very long time been condemned to a life in poverty.[54]

We shall deal with this topic in more detail further in the text. (See further, under Sects. 4.7–4.9.)

---

[45] Rand (2008), p. 26.

[46] Pauli (2014), p. 33.

[47] Stiglitz (2006), p. 4.

[48] Krugman (1998), p. 80 a f.

[49] See Steger (2013), p. 41; Lloyd (2012), p. 370 a.f.; Berend (2006), p. 263 a.f.

[50] Berend (2006), p. 269.

[51] Turner (1973).

[52] On this subject, see also Stiglitz (2002), p. 23.

[53] Steger (2013), p. 31.

[54] As phrased by Ripple (2017):

> But, even at this moment, one person in five lives in absolute poverty without enough to eat, and one in ten suffers serious malnutrition.

A second characteristic of modern-day globalised capitalism in the North-South relations, remains the (extremely) low price setting of the products produced in Southern countries (mainly agricultural products).[55]

Many of the (agricultural) products produced in these countries are purchased by large importers and distributors at extremely low prices, in order to be sold on the markets in the Northern countries at very high prices. During this process, the income of the original producers (especially farmers in Southern countries) remains often very low, while the consumers of the home countries of the importers/distributors in general pay high prices, causing the profit margins of the large importers/distributors to be very high (and all this is, obviously, under the doctrines of economic neo-liberalism, justified by the pursuit of profit motivating said importers/distributors).[56]

It goes without much further saying that as a result, poverty in poor(er) countries remains largely unsolved within the globalised capitalist world. In light of the prevailing doctrines of economic neo-liberalism, one may even wonder how this will ever be tackled, especially given the fact that the mechanisms of capitalism, especially when remaining uncorrected, are the main causes of this poverty.

One of the most striking illustrations of how globalised capitalism has determined the outlook of the globalised world economy, has probably been the rise, as of the 1990s, of a group of low-wage countries where, due to a high population in combination with a lack of protective labour and social legislation, enterprises have access to the production factor "labour" at the lowest possible cost, implying that enterprises based in these countries are able to produce many products much cheaper than competitors from countries where the production factor labour is much more expensive.[57]

As a result, the globalised world increasingly experiences a quasi-paradoxal situation where a multitude of labour and social protective regulations has started to represent a threat, rather than an added value, to the general wellbeing of the working population.

This may be explained due to the fact that in countries where, due to a high level of labour and social protection legislation, the "production factor" labour has become comparatively expensive, enterprises operating within a globalised economy face an increasing challenge to remain competitive, which during the past

---

[55] Stiglitz and Chariton (2005); Food and Agriculture Organization of the United Nations (2014); Lloyd (2012), p. 374.

[56] As said earlier, Harari (2014), p. 372, has phrased this strikingly as follows:

> The economic pie of 2014 is far larger than the pie of 1500, but it is distributed so unevenly that many African peasants and Indonesian labourers return home after a hard day's work with less food than did their ancestors 500 ago. Much like the Agricultural Revolution, so too the growth of the modern economy might turn out to be a colossal fraude. The human species and the global economy may well keep growing, but many more individuals may live in hunger and want.

[57] See also Stiglitz (2002), p. 10, explaining why referring to labour as a (mere) production factor is inappropriate.

decades has resulted in production to move to countries where labour and protective social legislation is less strict (and because of this, labour cost has remained lower).

As a result, especially the so-called "manufacturing industry" of the countries with traditional strong social labour and legal social legislation has during the past decades systematically declined—a phenomenon which has also been described as "de-industrialisation"—to the benefit of countries where the production factor labour, due to a lack of a similar labour and social protective legislation, has remained comparatively cheaper. Bearing in mind the economic "comparative advantages law", a certain balance remains as regards those sectors of the economy where there is still a higher need for labourers with a higher degree of specialisation (especially to the extent that in countries with a weaker labour and social protection legislation, in the past also the general educational level has remained lower), but also in such sectors, said low wage countries are catching up.[58] This has led to a situation where the traditionally strong economies of Western countries are witnessing a gradual economic decline, especially in the more traditional sectors of their industry. At the same time, certain Asian and South-American countries have made economic advance, albeit in many cases not, or hardly, to the benefit of their general population.

As a result, as is the case for all capitalistic mechanisms, also this mechanism contributes to the growing polarisation between the rich and the poor which is globally taking place.

Bearing in mind the (neo-)liberal idea of "trickle down economics", it is remarkable how in both groups categories of countries, it have been mainly the rich and extremely rich who bear the fruits of said re-allocation caused by the doctrines of economic neo-liberalism, while the poor and middle classes hardly benefit from this.

4.5 The Downward Economic Spiral of Many Western Countries

Bearing in mind certain of the starting premises of capitalism (among which its most basic principle that the stronger within the socio-economic order may—or are even supposed to—take advantage of the weaker, in the current context: that those who control capital may/should take advantage of those "merely" providing labour), it can not be a surprise that, as already referred to under the previous Sect. 4.4, capitalism has evolved into an economic system where economic production to an increasing extent is moving to countries where the production factor labour is the cheapest, most often countries where labour and social protective regulation is weak.[59]

[58] See the OECD-Country note referring to Belgium, at: http://www.oecd.org/edu/Belgium-EAG2014-Country-Note.pdf (last consulted on June 16, 2018).

See furthermore Anonymous (2013), Paelinck (2014) and Temmerman (2014).

[59] Stiglitz (2006), p. 67.

It is even to be feared that, as has also already been referred to in the previous Sect. 4.4, in those (Western) countries with strong labour and social protective models, some forms of production are threatened to gradually disappear.

This process has in literature already been referred to as so-called "de-industrialisation", characterized by the fact that in countries where labour is comparatively more expensive due to labour and social protective legislation, the economic tissue is getting more and more diluted (as under the premises of capitalism, an economy cannot function on providing services alone).[60]

It should, therefore, not be surprising that in the wake of this de-industrialisation which has been taking place in many Western (among which especially Western-European) countries, neo-liberal governments are responding by dismantling even more said labour and social protection legislation in order to make their economies again more "competitive", an evolution which can be described as a true "race to the bottom" (comparable to the similar race to the bottom in the fiscal domain).[61]

Otherwise put, the shift of economic production from Europe and the USA to mainly Asian countries which has occurred as a result of the neo-liberalisation of the world economy is, as of the 1970s, causing a global dilution of labour and social protective mechanisms which, obviously, provides a further indication that (neo-) liberal capitalism does not fulfil its underlying promise that it will result in the highest possible welfare for the general society.

Given the outlook of the current globalised world economy, and especially taking into account this "de-industrialisation" which is still going on in many Western countries, the future looks bleak.[62]

As within capitalist economies, only the manufacturing industry can result in a significant amount of export (of manufactured products)—it is, for instance, much more complicated, albeit not entirely impossible, to export services (with exceptance of special cases, such as the Indian call centers,[63] next to, more in general, tourism)—many Western Countries facing this process of "de-industrialisation" are threatened with a reduction of their export position (and through this, with a deficit on the current account of their payment balance).[64]

To the extent that these countries become more and more dependent on import, such countries are even more threatened by an increasing poverty, leaving the question, at least in light of the doctrines of economic neo-liberalism themselves, what can be done other than further dismantling the mechanisms protecting the poor from the rich (such as labour and social protective legislation) in order to attract production to one's own territory again.

Under the doctrines of economic neo-liberalism, there is clearly no willingness to seek for solutions for these ever increasing problems; on the contrary, said doctrines continue to fully propagate the continuation of these evolutions, thus provid-

---

[60] See Michielsen (2014), pp. 13–14.

[61] Stiglitz (2006), p. 67.

[62] Stiglitz (2006), p. 68.

[63] For an inside story on these, see Walker and Hartley (2012).

[64] See furthermore Stiglitz (2002), p. 23.

ing one more of the many ingredients for baking the neo-liberal pie and for ensuring its unfair distribution.

4.6 The Bankruptcy of Government Financing and the Fiscal Punishment of the Large Masses

4.6.1 The Traditional Methods of Financing Countries

The abovementioned (adverse) effects of capitalism have even been further emphasised by the evolution, during the past decades of implementing the doctrines of economic neo-liberalism, of the methods of government financing (which is, as is the case for many other elements of the capitalist economic system, characterised by an ever increasing dependence on systems of debt financing, hence by a domination of the private banking sector).

Traditionally, most countries in the world (and their governments) are primarily financed by systems of taxation and similar methods of financing state expenses based upon contributions to be paid by the general public to the state (or to other public authorities).[65]

From an economic point of view, such a method of (government) financing comes down to a periodical appropriation, by the central government (or by another government having tax authority) of a given state, of a part of the economic tissue to afterwards spend it on different (government) expenses which are purportedly more or less alleged to serve the general interest.[66]

In such a system of government financing, the income of (the government of) a given country strongly becomes function of the strength of its economy.[67] Governments of countries with a strong economy—which, within capitalism, generally implies a large gross domestic product and preferably also a strong export position—will, because of this, usually have access to a larger underlying tissue for their fiscal and "para-fiscal" skimming behaviour, while countries with a weaker economy (usually expressed by a smaller gross domestic product and, often, by a strong dependency on import) will by definition have to rely on a smaller underlying economic mass for their fiscal and para-fiscal skimming behaviour.[68]

---

[65] For instance in Belgium, there are next to the actual taxes, several so-called "social security contributions" in play which, from an economic point of view, have the same effect as actual taxes themselves.

See in this regard furthermore Stiglitz (2010), p. 197; see also Kruithof (2012), p. 76.

[66] Baeck (1972), p. 82.

[67] Hallerberg and Bridwell (2008), p. 74.

[68] Meanwhile, this is a problem which has repeatedly compromised the attempts of subsequent Belgian federal governments to balance government financing (see for instance Moerman (2014), p. 18).

On a global scale, this observation already witnesses a fundamental intrinsic unjust system of government financing which to a high degree, and this already for decades, not to say centuries, is to a large extent responsible for the traditional gaps between poor and rich in the North-South relation.[69]

Moreover, countries also determine their spending behaviour to a very high degree in a sovereign way.[70]

Mainly in function of political considerations (usually based on political and ideological ideas), there are, hence, countries with a strong government role and where the public interest has in the past been interpreted in a broad sense of the way. It concerns mainly some West-European countries where, especially during the period after World War II, government has to a large extent been based on social and Christian democratic thinking, hence on a solidarity principle (for instance the Benelux-countries, Germany, France, the Scandinavian countries…).

Next to this, there are also countries with a traditionally more weak government role. Especially those countries which have since long been adhering the principles of capitalism in its most purest sense belong to this second group, with as typical examples the USA and the UK, next to a (large) group of countries which are relying on a small economic tissue and where the government, by necessity (because it has no funds) plays a small role, such as most noteably the so-called "poor countries".

In the first group of countries, there is, on the upside, usually a strong degree of social protection in place, but on the downside, the population is subject to a generally (extremely) high degree of taxation (next to a high degree of imposing several other types of (social) contributions on the general public), while in the second group of countries, this is in most cases much less so.

Furthermore, in the first group of countries the government will usually (at least to some extent) be more concerned about the redistribution of the gross economic revenue to the general population. As a drawback, this group of countries may experience a negative effect on individual initiative, as the reward for a productive engagement in the economic field will sometimes not differ much (or enough) from a replacement income provided by the government.

The tax pressure and the pressure from similar types of contributions, such as, for instance, social security payments, will in this context also be function of the goals put forward by the government, but also from the strength of the underlying economy.

The foregoing often implies that, for instance in a country with a strong economy, it will be possible to keep the tax rates and the rates of other types of contributions at a lower level, while in countries with a weaker economy, such rates will have to be kept at a higher level in order to obtain the same income.

---

[69] Oxfam (2014), p. 16 a.f.

[70] With, for instance, the exception of countries which have called upon special financing resources provided by the IMF and which are as a result subjected to a stricter monitoring by the same IMF (see Fritz-Krockow and Ramlogan (2007), p. 38 a.f.).

The tax pressure and the pressure from other types of contributions may itself also have an effect on the strength of the economy. A heavy tax pressure (or pressure from other types of contributions) may indeed negatively influence the production costs of the enterprise sector and through this, especially within globalized markets characterized by a fierce competition, enterprises may find themselves in a worse position than their competitors from countries with a less heavy tax pressure and/or pressure of other types of contributions.

In some cases, this may contribute to the above-described process of delocating industries. (See already above, under Sects. 4.4 and 4.5.)

The tax pressure and the pressure resulting from other types of (social) contributions can, furthermore, also undermine the purchase power of the (general) population and, consequently, have a negative impact on the demand curves within the economy. In cases where the public suffers too long from heavy taxation (and/or from imposing similar contributions), this can moreover lead to fatalism, such as: the feeling that one is not able to bare the fruits of one's own efforts; the impression that being economically active does not make much difference from being inactive due to the government redistribution strategies; the decline of investment confidence…

Government financing and spending in this way obviously concerns a very complex problem which moves spirits worldwide and where ideological and other viewpoints help to colour the debate.

The complexity of the problem has only sharpened over the past decades, especially each time when an economic crisis occurs, as in recent times has obviously been the case in many Western countries in 2001 and in 2007–2008.[71]

4.6.2 The Growing Public Debt of (Some) Western Countries

As regards the period after World War II and especially as a consequence of subsequent economic problems especially as of the 1980s, countries with a traditionally large government role gradually experienced a (relative) decrease of their income from taxes and similar contributions in comparison to their spending behaviour, causing that the income derived from traditional taxes and similar contributions were in many cases no longer sufficient to cover the running government expenditures.[72]

Already since the 1970s,[73] these type of (especially Western) countries had to massively resort to (additional) credit to finance their expenditure, either from their own population (investors, among which institutional investors, and financial insti-

[71] Stiglitz (2012), p. 210.

[72] Krugman (1994), p. 156 a.f.; Streeck (2013), p. 70 a.f.; Bonner and Wiggin (2006), p. 226 a.f.

[73] Obviously, also before in history countries became endebted to the bank sector. (See Graeber (2012).)

tutions themselves), from foreign investors or, in some cases, even from supranational organisations.[74]

Next to this, also the (large) group of countries with a historically weak economic tissue has in the period after World War II[75] increasingly become dependent on credit to cover essential government spending.[76]

This has especially been the case for the so-called "poor" or "developing" countries (in IMF terminology also referred to as: "Heavily Indebted Poor Countries (HIPC)") of which the (external) debt in many cases has become a structural problem.[77]

This situation has, furthermore, been influenced by the heavy financial crisis of 2007–2008. As a result of this crisis, many countries have been faced with an even further increasing government deficit[78] and, because of this, have become even more (chronically) dependent on debt financing.

The problem of the debt burden of both the developing countries, as well as the decaying capitalist countries, is most probably one of the largest and most underestimated economic problems of our times.[79]

According to the website http://www.nationaldebtclocks.org/, as for instance accessed on 31 March 2015, the global countries' debt burden (= debt of all countries together) then amounted to over 60,653.525 USD billion USD. The debt of the USA alone represented a little less than 1/3rd of this global countries' world debt,

---

[74] Brook and Watkins (2012), p. 33.

See also Keen (2017), pointing out that (and in what way) Germany is one of the main exceptions in this regard:

> Germany is virtually the only country in the world with falling levels of both public and private debt. But this is only possible because of its huge trade surplus. Trade deficits must be financed by borrowing. Germany's trading partners are getting deeper into debt in order to buy German goods. In essence, Germany is offshoring the creation of its money supply. That can't go on forever, because it eventually results in overindebtedness in trade deficit countries.

[75] Ingham (1984), p. 48.

[76] See Streeck (2013), p. 73:

> The development of the debt state may be understood both as a retarding factor in the crisis of the tax state and as the rise of a new political formation with its own laws.

[77] See http://www.imf.org/external/np/exr/facts/hipc.htm (last consulted on June 16, 2018); Cohen (2008), p. 167; Van Meerhaeghe (1985), p. 97.

[78] Stiglitz (2012), p. 208.

[79] See especially Piketty (2014). See even Bush (2010), p. 471.

In an interview with the Duch newspaper "De Volskrant", former ECB-president Jean-Claude Trichet expressed his concerns for the huge amounts of outstanding public debt, especially of the Members of the European Union (see De Waard (2018)):

> Trichet's main concern is that the global debt burden – both public and private debt – is at present higher than before the financial crisis of 2007 and 2008. "This indicates how fragile the system still is. The IMF has pointed this out this very weak. And, to my opinion, the international community is not sufficiently aware of this fact." (Own, free translation.)

with an amount of ±18,198 billion USD. On the same date, the debt burden of Belgium amounted to 532,108,000,000 USD (being more than half a trillion USD).

When consulting the same website http://www.nationaldebtclocks.org/ on 1 December 2017, it appeared that the situation had even gotten worse. On the latter date, the global countries' debt burden amounted to over 69,007.000 USD billion USD. The debt of the USA alone still represented a bit less than 1/3rd of this global countries' world debt, with an amount of ±20,568 billion USD. The debt burden of Belgium on this date amounted to a bit more than 549,597,400,000 USD.

When consulting the same website http://www.nationaldebtclocks.org/ on 9 May 2018, it appeared that the global countries' debt burden then amounted to over 72,486.450 USD billion USD. The debt of the USA by then represented a bit more than 21.069 trillion USD. The debt burden of Belgium on this date amounted to a bit more than 557,210,446,000 USD.

Hence in a bit more than 3 years, the global countries' world debt has increased with a sum of almost 12 trillion USD and this even though, all over the world, countries have been more than ever resorting to a strict neo-liberal government budget approach,[80] implying drastic cut backs on government expenses for public services and social welfare.

This insight more than ever raises the question whether (and within what timeframe) the state of the world economy will allow the mentioned countries to skim off an amount of taxes worth more than 72,486 billion USD to pay back this immense countries' debt burden. One hereby needs to bare in mind that any postponement of this repayment, because of the running interests, makes the countries' debt burden even grow further, and this literally by the second.

Those who consult the abovementioned website http://www.nationaldebtclocks.org/ will indeed observe that during even a short visit to the website, the countries' debt burden will have accrued with several millions of USD in interests.

For instance, during said visit of the website on 1 December 2017, it appeared that within the time frame of only one minute, the combined interest burden on said global countries' world debt amounted to more than 4.5 million USD. On 9 May 2018, the combined interest burden on said global countries' world debt amounted to more than 4.766 million USD per minute.

The further question then becomes if the repayments by the countries financed through their tax income will ever take place at a faster rate than the increase of interest of the same debt burden.

In this context, one should not forget that the more than 72 trillion USD in global countries' world debt is not the only debt burdening the world economy that needs to be regained from economic growth. On a global scale, a vast number of different private economic agents (going from individuals to enterprises) are even so burdened with an immense (and in many cases increasing) debt burden.

[80] See on this for instance Friedman (1993).

It is more and more to be feared that the expectation that all this debt will ever be repaid through the income derived from economic activity, has become a utopic one.[81]

Nevertheless, in full accordance with the doctrines of economic neo-liberalism, the working methods of capitalism need to be upheld forever, so general policy making of most countries and of most supra-national institutions remains that everything should be done to pay back all these debts, which, in the recent past, has in a number of countries led to restructuring measures in accordance with the strictest guidelines of economic neo-liberalism, with as a typical example the budget discipline that the European Union is imposing onto its member states, but which do not prevent that both private and public debt continue to grow.

4.6.3 An Increasing Subjection of Endebted Countries to the Mercy of the Financial Markets

As an overall consequence of the abovementioned evolutions, several groups of countries, with on the one hand the classic "poor" countries, and on the other hand an increasing group of (former) "rich" countries, have become increasingly in need of credit.

Credits are taken with all types of private and public entities, among which local and foreign private institutions, next to certain international, public institutions (such as the IMF and the World Bank).

The dependence of some (world) countries on financing by the (private) bank sector has grown so high that detailed data on the total size of the debt burden of all countries in the world towards the private bank sector are as good as impossible to obtain.

This large dependence on credit of many countries also explains the great importance of their so-called "credit rating" which, according to some sources, is in present times considered to be more important than even the presence of natural resources. (See already above, at Sect. 2.1.7.)

This credit rating which, in full accordance with the doctrines of economic neo-liberalism, is also left over to private market players, purportedly offers an "independent" indication on the probability with which a debtor (be it a country, or a private debtor), will be able to pay back his debts. As a consequence, credit rators possess a huge power which, although not legitimated at all from a democratic point of view, (co-)determines the welfare (or the absence of such welfare) of entire countries.[82]

---

[81] See the similar concern recently expressed by former ECB-president J.-C. Trichet (see De Waard (2018)).

[82] See in general Harari (2014), p. 352.

See also Coffey (2012):

In this way, the credit rating of a country especially determines the interest rates which private banks charge to countries when providing a credit (hence: while making their decision to "out of nothing" hand out newly created money), entailing a "principle of anti-solidarity": countries already in trouble will hereby get a lower credit rating, implying that when they are in need of new credit, they will be charged higher interest rates, and because of this will further get into more difficulties.

Needless to say that it is a very worrysome fact[83] that, all over the world, (neo-liberal) governments have become so fundamentally dependent on the decision making power of private market players, and this thus the more as, because of the capitalist mechanisms of organising the corporate and financial sector, the control over economic life itself has increasingly come into the hands of a very small (financial) elite (= most noteably the capital providers of private banks and of other large enterprises), which have in this way obtained more power than can ever be acceptable in truly democratically organised societies.[84]

The system of government financing through credits supplied by private banking thus has been turned into one more system enabling a small group of people to gather extremely large fortunes to the detriment of the rest of society.[85]

A government taking a credit with a private bank will indeed, in the current, neo-liberal logic that dictates public finances, witness how a large part of its tax and other revenues are disappearing in the bottomless pit of the agreed upon bank

---

That means the real power to control the world lies with four companies: McGraw-Hill, which owns Standard & Poor's, Northwestern Mutual, which owns Russell Investments, the index arm of which runs the benchmark Russell 1,000 and Russell 3,000, CME Group which owns 90% of Dow Jones Indexes, and Barclay's, which took over Lehman Brothers and its Lehman Aggregate Bond Index, the dominant world bond fund index. Together, these four firms dominate the world of indexing. And in turn, that means they hold real sway over the world's money.

[83] This worry is moreover not new, as ancient philosophers such as Plato, already expressed it. (See Plato (1987), p. 296 a.f., dealing with so-called "imperfect societies".)

[84] Sachs (2011), p. 116 a.f.; Kruithof (2000), p. 14; Krugman (2004), p. 221.

[85] See for instance Diks (2013).

According to this author, the wealth of the Rotschild family can be estimated at 490,000,000,000,000,000 USD, or 490,000 trillion USD. The author of this article explicitly refers to the power to (privately) create money out of nothing and the fact that, because of this power, entire nations have entirely become in the grip of the private banking sector, as one of the main causes for this extreme wealth accumulation. The author, furthermore, points out that if the Rothschild family would be willing to share its extreme wealth, every human being would obtain 70 million USD.

Other sources mention a far more moderate wealth of the Rotschild family, estimated at a "mere" USD 350 billion in assets throughout the world, however at the same time indicating that much of the family's wealth is held privately, making it is very difficult to ascertain their true net worth, and that, moreover, a lot of the family's wealth is distributed among different family members across different countries and different businesses (see https://www.quora.com/Why-does-500-trillion-rich-Rothschilds-are-not-on-Forbes-richest-people-list; last consulted on June 16, 2018).

interests, a fact which, at every re-financing operation of government debt, is strengthened more and more.[86]

Galbraith has indicated this phenomenon as one of the characteristics of "the culture of contentment" which has caused that people in general (and, through this, the governments they appoint) have taken an extremely negligent posture as regards economic themes and in most cases prefer short term solutions which procrastinate problems, in favour of a durable long term economic policy.

In this neo-liberal attitude, it is assumed that the "laissez-faire, laissez-passer" principle ensures that, in the long run, everything will turn out fine.[87] It is precisely this (wrong) (semi-)religious attitude towards economic life that explains the large willingness of many countries (next to private persons) to keep engaging into credit financing at such a large scale (and more in general, to leave all economic problems over to the solutions brought forward by the private markets). The belief that there can be no (government) planning in economic matters has during the past decades even been further enhanced due to the collapse of the biggest part of the communist world. As the latter was characterized by a so-called "central planning economy", adherents of economic neo-liberalism consider its collapse as further proof that planning in economic matters cannot work.

When furthermore, as again in recent history, the governments of many countries need to take up even more credit generated by the private bank sector to help distressed banks to overcome their own financial difficulties (in the context of so-called "bail out operations"),[88] the skimming behaviour of private banks (and their shareholders) of the economic wealth generated by society, is not only gradually taking gigantic proportions, but the ethics deployed in the methods of doing so, seem to be completely lacking.

Some have rightfully remarked that the doctrines of economic neo-liberalism, especially when applied to the financial sector, have in this way led to "a privatization of gains and socialization of losses"-policy,[89] which Stiglitz has referred to as one of the greatest "moral hazard"-dilemmas of our times.[90]

Governments which, in case of budget shortages are driven to take credit from the (private) market(s), have, over the past years, when faced with problems of repaying those credits, furthermore, showed little restraint in refinancing such

---

[86] This, additionally, creates an important intergenerational shift, as the next generations will have to carry the financial burden created by the opulence and waste of the former generations.

[87] Galbraith (1992), p. 20.

[88] See for further comments on the so-called "too big to fail"-paradigm, Chomsky (2017), p. 83 (speaking of the "too big to jail"-paradigm).

With regards to Belgium, the bail-out efforts done in 2008–2009 in order to support banks in need, are reported to have been responsible for 15% of the then total government debt, a fact that for Rik van Cauwelaert represents a sufficient motive for the introduction of a special bank tax (ensuring that banks take their responsibility in supporting the re-payment of this debt, moreover because Belgian banks, in history, have always made a lot of profit on financing the Belgian government debt …). (See Van Cauwelaert (2014).)

[89] Engelen (2011), p. 27. See also Chomsky and Polychroniou (2017), p. 153 a.f.

[90] Stiglitz (2006), p. 217.

credits by taking up new credits, thus continuously shifting the remediation of government financing even more forward in time.

Needless to say that with each such every operation of "re-financing" a government debt, the negative characteristics of the capitalist financial system described above are even more strengthened. As if this is not enough, such a system of (re) financing governments through debt provided by the banking sector becomes in this way, literally by the minute, more manifestly unjust from an intergenerational point of view,[91] as each next generation gets burdened more with an increasing government debt created by previous generations. In such a system of government financing, the deficiencies of a previous generation (which has refused to compromise on its spending behavior), are, without shame, passed on to the next generation(s), which will consequently experience a reduced chance to enjoy the same luxuries of the previous generation(s) which was (were) accountable for the huge government debts built up in the past.

This phenomenon has in the mean time been confirmed by empiral research of, among others, Crédit Suisse (see further Sect. 4.7.)

The problems with the budgets of many European countries, such as obviously Greece, next to several other countries like Italy, Ireland, Spain, and Belgium, are in this regard harrowing examples of how the (neo-)liberal "laissez-faire, laisser-passer" principle has led many countries of the world in ever growing financial problems over the past decades. It is hence not a coincidence that the problematic situation of public finances of many countries is one of the biggest challenges of our times,[92] albeit that the political world in most of these countries remains completely lacking to advocate truly fundamental and just solutions.[93]

4.6.4 Some Final Reflections on the Complete Immorality of the Neo-liberal System of Government Financing

4.6.4.1 On the Correlation Between Taxing the Lower and Middle Classes and Thus Providing the Rich Classes with a Further Enrichment System

Whichever way, as is the case for any debtor, a country building up a debt burden will at one point in time also have to start to dismantle such debt.[94]

The normal scenario for reducing a debt is to repay it to the creditor, heightened with the agreed upon interests, if any. For this purpose, a country with an outstanding debt—and, in principle, the situation of such a country in debt is no different from

[91] Kruithof (1985), p. 57.

[92] See also De Waard (2018), containing an interview with former ECB-president J.-C. Trichet.

[93] The same applies to the climate change problem, one of the most important other problems of our times which the doctrines of economic neo-liberalism prefer to simply ignore.

[94] See also Piketty (2014), p. 540, who, for that reason, prefers taxation as a technique of government financing above debt financing.

that of any other economic agent who is a debtor—will have to generate enough income in the future to make such repayment(s).

Under the currently prevailing system of government financing of most countries, the natural source of income of a country in debt from which, in the end, the sums needed to repay the debt will have to be generated consists, as mentioned before (see above, at Sect. 3.3.), of the inning of taxes (and similar government imposed charges).[95]

This source of income can increase in two ways:

- either an increase of the taxable mass (= especially the global income of the underlying economy of such a country) occurs; provided that there is at the same time an unchanged tax tarification (as well as tarification of other charges), in such a case, the total tax income of the country will increase[96];
- or, in case there is a status quo or decrease of the taxable mass,[97] a country can resort to higher tax rates (or rates of similar charges), or even to new taxes (or charges).

The past decades have shown that the latter approach (based upon the increase of taxes and other charges) may be problematic, as the pressure on the (national) economy(ies) of countries applying this method of obtaining more income, tends to become too high, which, given the fact that in many Western (and Western inspired) countries the tax burden of the lower and middle classes is already extremely high, while the rich classes are above all tax avoidance oriented, over the past decades, has caused many of these countries to opt for additional credit rather, than for increasing their tax income.[98]

As a result, this (neo-liberal) attitude has caused such countries to continuously postpone any remediation of government financing (and on the contrary, to choose, again and again, for debt (re-)financing), making government finances ever more problematic.[99]

---

[95] The "reduction" of debts through new credits (so-called credit financing), obviously does not bring a solution, as it only leads to a (from an intergenerational perspective very unjust) shift of the problem.

[96] Which will take place in case of economic growth, including especially export of own products and services.

[97] This will happen in case of a stagnating or negative economic growth (which in general leads to a higher dependence on import).

[98] See also Congregation for the Doctrine of the Faith (2018), n° 32:

> The *offshore* system has also ended up aggravating the public debt of the countries whose economies are less developed. It was in fact observed how the accumulated private wealth of some elites in the fiscal havens is almost equal to the public debt of the respective countries. This highlights how, in fact, at the origin of that debt there are often economic losses created by private persons and unloaded on the shoulders of the public system. Moreover, it is noted that important economic players tend to follow, often with the collusion of the politicians, a practice of division of the losses.

[99] Piketty describes this as follows (Piketty (2014), p. 540):

> The rich world is rich, but the governments of the rich world are poor.

Moreover, the fact of hoping for a continuous economic growth in order to install a larger taxable base from the economic fabric, has also shown to be an illusory strategy,[100] a fact with which especially members of the European Union have been confronted with in the ongoing aftermath of the financial crisis of 2007–2008.

Therefore, it may be clear that a system of (uncontrolled) government debt financing easily tends to bear witness of true mismanagement, showing, at the very least, a fundamental lack of awareness that economic growth has its limits, and at the same wrongly estimating that an irresponsible creation of fictitious new money (in the form of credit lending by private banks), rather than drastically overhauling spending behavior, could offer a solution for the problem of government shortages.[101]

According to some, this situation is deemed the worst in Europe[102] where, as a result, during recent times, many countries have fiercely (albeit in many cases fruitlessly) been putting efforts into balancing government budgets.[103]

Piketty has described this as follows[104]:

> Europe is the most extreme case: it has both the highest level of private wealth in the world and the greatest difficulty in resolving its public debt crisis – a strange paradox.

It should hereby be considered that, as has already been mentioned before, a further injustice of the prevailing systems of government funding is that the vulnerability to taxation (and similar charges) mainly affects the (lower and middle) working classes of society,[105] or, otherwise put, "income from labour".

---

[100] Think tanks, such as the aforementioned "Club of Rome" have already for decades been warning about this.

[101] Compare Ronse (1992), p. 79.

The Catholic church has even put it more bluntly:

> it is good to point out how often the public debt is also created by an incautious, if not fraudulent, management of the public administrative system. These debts, those financial losses that burden the various nations, pose today one of the major obstacles to good functioning and growth of the various national economies. Numerous national economies are in fact burdened by having to cope with the payment of interest, which derives from that debt, and must therefore dutifully undertake structural adjustments to suit this need. (See Congregation for the Doctrine of the Faith (2018), n° 32.)

[102] As regards especially Europe, see Krugman (2012), p. 177 a.f.; Stiglitz (2012), p. 254. See also Dévoluy et al. (2011), p. 52.

[103] See De Boeck (2014), p. 12; Van Haver and Blomme (2014), p. 6; Haeck (2014).

[104] Piketty (2014), p. 540.

[105] Stiglitz (2002), p. 11.

See also Oxfam (2017), p. 20, catching this problem in the phrase "tax is for everyone else":

> One of the main ways that the super-rich contribute to broader society is through taxes incurred on their income, wealth and capital gains, which can pay for essential public services and redistributes wealth from the richest to the most vulnerable people. However, the IMF has found that tax systems around the world have become steadily less progressive since the early 1980s, via the lowering of the top rate of income tax, cuts to taxes on capital gains and reductions in inheritance and wealth taxes.

Indeed, within capitalist economies, "labour" is not only the least appreciated "production factor"[106] (see above, at Sect. 2.4.), but it is also the least mobile factor (for instance due to the fact that many types of labour need to be performed on a fixed physical location and that the persons performing this labour need to be located in its vicinities, and/or due to the fact that someone who looses his job often meets great difficulty of finding another job, so especially from a certain age on).[107] In practice, this also implies that income from labour is the one most easily subject to taxation (and to similar charges), and this is why, in many countries, mainly income from labour is subject to the most heavy fiscal (and "parafiscal") charges.[108]

On the contrary, especially in an economy increasingly dependent on globalized capital and money markets, as is the case for the current world economy, capital is inherently far more mobile than labour. To put it bluntly, especially in a liberalized and deregulated world economy, money is far more easily (and often precisely for the purpose of preventing taxation) transportable over country borders and, moreover, far more easily reinvestable in another business.[109]

In the same sense, financial instruments (in the end representing money which has been invested, for example either as capital or as debt of a corporation or company), are also as highly mobile and therefore easily transportable over country borders, or may easily be sold in order to reinvest the proceeds of such sale in other financial instruments.[110]

As a consequence, the levying of taxes (and of other charges) on income deriving from (large) capital, in practice, is far more labourious than the taxation of income from labour, whereby it can even be remarked that the larger a capital investment, the easier it gets to avoid taxation, for instance due to the fact that transaction costs for a potential re-allocation of capital become relatively more insignificant as the capital to be moved is larger, but also because it is easier for large enterprises to resort to big consultancy firms which provide services of fiscal optimization, next to

---

[106] See Stiglitz (2002), p. 10, rightly criticizing the use of this term.

[107] See Stiglitz (2002), p. 11.

[108] It needs to be emphasized that, when mentioning "income from labour", this not only refers to labour performed as an employee, but for instance also to labour performed as an independent worker in his own (or in a small business). Indeed, in addition to working classes in a strict sense of the word, also small independent business owners, as well as small and medium enterprises, are clearly interesting sources of income through taxation for many (Western and Western inspired) governments.

[109] See Stiglitz (2002), p. 13, furthermore pointing out that this is even more the case due to (neo-) liberalization measures:

> Capital market liberalization enhances the bargaining power of capital: effectively, it gives "capital" the right to announce that if it is taxed unduly, or if other measures that it dislikes are adopted, i will leave the country.

[110] Stiglitz (2012), p. 73:

> The rich and superrich often use corporations to protect themselves and shelter their income, and they have worked hard to ensure that the corporate income tax rate is low and the tax code is riddled with loopholes. Some corporations make such extensive use of these provisions that they don't pay any taxes.

applying mechanisms of corporatocracy of (fiscal) policy influencing, such as lobbying and blackmail.[111]

In this way, on a global scale, fiscal (and parafiscal) systems are evolved into systems which mainly impact the low and middle class, as well as the poor, while, at the same time, as a result of the earlier mentioned systems of credit financing, the amount of interests on government debt (which ultimately is carried by tax payers), entails a further source of substantial profits for the already (extremely) rich credit providers, mainly private banks (and their shareholders and managers).[112]

Stiglitz has hence rightly argued that the failure of democracy to create a fair socio-economic order, especially as regards the mechanisms of government financing, is one of the most important indications that capitalist financial mechanisms have failed.[113]

---

[111] Stiglitz (2012), pp. 73 a.f.; Stiglitz (2002), pp. 13–14; see also Oxfam (2014), 16.

For some striking examples, see Oxfam (2016), pp. 27 a.f., for instance mentioning some of the practices of Belgian beer producer "AB InBev":

> The Belgium-based Anheuser-Busch InBev (AB InBev) is the world's largest brewing company, and sells over 200 different brands of beer across Europe, Asia and America. Not only does the company dominate the market—it has a powerful political voice too. It spent $3.7m lobbying the US government in 2014, and 56 of the 141 lobbying reports it filed were on issues relating to taxation. AB InBev has used its influence to deliberately target legislation designed in the public interest, for example establishing voluntary advertising standards to avoid limitations on advertising to young people. In Brazil before the 2014 World Cup, the company was involved with FIFA in pressuring the government to change a law banning the consumption of alcohol at football matches, so that its products could be sold. Small retailers also pay a price for corporate dominance. In the US, the Justice Department is currently probing allegations that AB InBev is curbing competition by buying up distributors, making it harder for micro-breweries to get their products onto store shelves. (See Oxfam (2016), p. 28.)

[112] See also Brockmans (2014), p. 26; Bernstein (2004), p. 30.

In its study "Even it up", Oxfam for instance mentions the case of Nicaragua, where, in 2014 the poorest 20% of the population is forced to spend 31% of their income on income taxes, while the richest 20% only have to spend 13% of their income on taxes (see Oxfam (2014), p. 83).

Oxfam has in this regard even argued that, at the beginning of 2016, the global system of tax avoidance to the benefit of the rich and the powerful is sucking the life out of welfare states in the rich world, for instance denying poor countries the resources they need to tackle poverty, put children in school and prevent their citizens dying from easily curable diseases.

See also Oxfam (2017), p. 4 a.f.:

> Paying as little tax as possible is a key strategy for many of the super-rich. To do this they make active use of the secretive global network of tax havens, as revealed by the Panama Papers and other exposés. Countries compete to attract the super-rich, selling their sovereignty.

[113] Stiglitz (2006), pp. 269 a.f.; and Stiglitz (2002), p. 25.

> While we all speak passionately about the importance of democratic principles, we also recognize that our democracies are imperfect and that some groups' voices are heard more loudly than others. In the arena of international economic policy, the voices of commercial and financial interests are heard more loudly than those of labour and consumer interests. As just noted, they have tried to convince others, with remarkable success, that there is no

4.6.4.2 Some Further Data on the Corporatocratic Methods of Influencing Tax Policy

Figures provided by Oxfam in 2015 have confirmed that the most important source of income of the very rich (such as the dollar billionaires at the top of the Forbes lists) is the income derived from financial instruments granting rights towards financial institutions. The second most important source of income of the very rich were their shareholdings in the pharmaceutical sector, which has moreover been indicated as the most profitable sector. Both sectors also rank as the sectors spending most on lobbying and campaign financing.[114]

---

conflict of interests – which means that there are no trade-offs. The consequences speak for themselves: the growing dissatisfaction with reform policies is partly a consequence of the fact that so many have actually been made worse off. (Stiglitz (2002), p. 25.)

Compare Soros (1999), pp. 121–123; Hazenberg (2013), p. 136. See also Kruithof (2000), pp. 145 a.f.; Bijlo (2014), p. 63.

Michel Foucault has in this regard held that in particular the objective of big enterprises to seize political power is characteristic for the particularity of economic neo-liberalism. Where classic "economic liberalism" had been about a given economy determining a space in which the free market can grow unhindered, neo-liberalism is exactly about how the political exercise of power can be modeled to the needs of such free market economy (or, put otherwise, the selfish needs of the rich and powerful). According to Foucault, this is precisely the reason why economic neo-liberalism is much more directing than classic economic liberalism as regards market mechanisms (= neo-liberalism as so-called "intervening liberalism"), which as a result explains in more depth the tendency of economic neo-liberalism to influence politics (inter alia, in the field of fiscal decision making, but for example also in the field of monetary policy). (See Foucault (2008), pp. 247 a.f. and 270 a.f.; also Foucault (2013), p. 181. See furthermore Oxfam (2017), p. 4, confirming all of this.)

[114] Oxfam (2015), p. 5.

For instance, the large and successful enterprises operating in the financial and insurance sector each year make gigantic profits come from different activities, among which large-scale lending to states (and other public entities). These profits are mainly used for financing dividend payments to shareholders which explains the enormous wealth of the very rich. However, substantial amounts of these profits are also used for financing all types of mechanisms influencing governments (so-called "corporatocracy"). (See Oxfam (2015), p. 7.)

In 2013, the financial sector for instance spent only in the USA 400 million USD on lobbying activities and next to that 517 million USD on campaign financing, which makes it the second largest lobbyist with a share of 12% of global spending on lobbying in the USA. In the European Union, the expenditure for lobbying by the financial sector was "limited" to 150 million USD. Meanwhile, the global community of the Western economies remains burdened with the large financing cost of the bailouts of 2008–2009, which are estimated to have amounted to 21 billion USD in the USA alone. It is furthermore striking that, while the financial sector has been able to rise up again from the ashes created by the financial crisis which it had, to a large extent, caused itself and once again makes extremely high profits again, which, under the form of dividend payments, flow back to the very rich, the income of the average American had in 2015 still not been restored to the level it had before the financial crisis. (See Oxfam (2015), p. 7.)

Also in 2013, the pharmaceutical sector and the health sector spent as much as 487 million USD on lobbying expenses, which made this sector the largest lobbyist (with a share of 15% of total lobbying expenditure). During that period, the sector spent moreover 260 million USD on campaign financing. The expenditure of the pharmaceutical sector and the health sector in Europe in the same year was estimated at ±50 million USD. (See Oxfam (2015), p. 7.)

Not by coincidence, the most important item on the agenda of said lobbyists is "fiscality", a fact that has been indicated as one of the main reasons why, on a global scale, the rich and powerful proportionally contribute far less to the income of states than the poor and middle classes. This in turn translates in ever decreasing government budgets, including the budgets for public services (such as education and health care),[115] and, furthermore, helps explaining why governments so massively resort to debt financing.

This fiscal injust system which is clearly the result of the implementation of the doctrines of economic neo-liberalism[116] has meanwhile been indicated as one of the further main causes of the increasing worldwide gaps between the rich and the poor layers of society.[117]

In its report named "Even it up", Oxfam has referred to this as "the great tax failure".[118]

As a result, worldwide, fiscal policy has, especially in countries where public finances are highly dependent on taxes and similar charges, led to a system whereby especially lower incomes (a.o. from labour as an employee, or in the context of a small personal business) are taxed most, while much higher incomes, for example incomes from capital, from management services or from high public functions, tend to escape such taxes to a much greater extent.

As explained earlier, this effect is even enhanced due to the fact that capital as an economic production factor is much more mobile than labour. As also explained before, within the context of the neo-liberalized global economy, a policy of too high a taxation of income from capital, as a result, often leads to displacing such capital from countries with high taxes to countries with more favorable tax regimes.

In this way, the rich and powerful easily commit to practices which may be qualified as blackmail in their ongoing pursuit of escaping taxes (hence of not contributing to the general wellbeing of society) as much as possible.

This is precisely why neo-liberal fiscal policy has in this way turned into a shadow play of countries competing against each other in developing the most favorable tax regimes for big business and capital. As a result, fiscal policy has become the text book example of a classic "race to the bottom",[119] and this on a global scale. (See also above, Sect. 3.3.2.2.)

---

[115] Oxfam (2015), p. 9.

[116] More specifically the idea that the rich (entrepreneurs) are the driving force within society and should, therefore, be burdened by taxation as little as possible, so that they may continue their "noble pursuit" of striving for unbridled wealth, given the beneficial effects this has for the rest of society. In this, thinking of economic neo-liberalism clearly goes back to the ideas of Adam Smith, who also expressed his contempt for taxing the rich entrepreneurs as they should remain unhindered in their noble plight of bringing more prosperity to the world.

[117] Steger (2013), p. 42; Lipton (2014); see also Oxfam (2014), p. 16 a.f.

[118] Sachs (2011), p. 118.

[119] Bijlo (2014), p. 63.

As explained in Oxfam's study "Even it up" (see Oxfam (2014), p. 16):

> The race to the bottom on corporate tax collection is a large part of the problem. Multilateral agencies and finance institutions have encouraged developing countries to offer taks incen-

4.6.5 Is There Still a Way Out?

In light of the foregoing, it may be clear that the current mechanisms of government financing, based upon taxation (and similar charges) of especially the poor and lower classes, supplemented with systems of debt financing, are part of a system which is at the same time "ineffective" (as worldwide many national governments are faced with huge deficits), as well as intrinsically "unjust" (as the system is mainly impacting the poor and (relatively) neglecting the rich, but, on the contrary, especially through (bank) interests on government loans, even helps the rich get ever more rich).

As a result, (neo-)liberal public finances have, to a large extent, turned into a system of government financing which, on one hand, has confronted the governments of many (Western and Western inspired) countries with a permanent lack of funds, and, on the other hand, mainly impacts the lower and middle classes, while the true rich are not expected to show any solidarity with the rest of mankind.[120]

From a historical point of view, the latter observation is hardly new, although the neo-liberal reasoning behind it relatively is, given the fact that the intrinsic injustice of taxing (poor) people is probably as old as tax mechanisms themselves, and that, from a historical angle and on a global scale, it have usually been the lower classes of any given society that suffer the most from the pressure of taxes (and other charges) imposed on them by the richer elite.[121]

One could thus even say that the prevailing systems of government financing show all the characteristics of a (new) feudal system under which the poor and middle classes are at the complete mercy of the policy goals of the rich class.

Needless to say that any attempts to justify the present-day prevailing systems of government financing, especially to the extent that they mainly touch the welfare and wellbeing of the lower and middle classes, as leading to a fair redistribution of

---

> tives – tax holidays, tax exemptions and free trade zones – to attract foreign direct investment. Such incentives have soared, undermining the tax base in some of the poorest countries. In 2008/09, for instance, the Rwandan government authorized tax exemptions that, if collected, could have doubled health and education spending.

[120] See already Galbraith (1974), pp. 91 a.f.

See also Bijlo (2014), p. 63. Furthermore Légé (2011), pp. 89–108; Oxfam (2016), p. 5.

[121] Bernstein (2004), p. 30, also explicitly pointing out that in the post-modern (neo-liberalized) world, the weakest and poorest are the ones who are most heavily taxed.

See also in the report "Even it up" of Oxfam:

> For instance, today's lopsided tax policies, lax regulatory regimes and unrepresentative institutions in countries around the world are a result of this elite capture of politics. Elites in rich and poor countries alike use their heightened political influence to benefit from government decisions, including tax exemptions, sweetheart contracts, land concessions and subsidies, while pressuring administrations to block policies that may strengthen the hand of workers or smallholder food producers, or that increase taxation to make it more progressive. In many countries, access to justice is often for sale, legally or illegally, with access to the best lawyers or the ability to cover court costs only available to a privileged few. (See Oxfam (2014), p. 59.)

wealth, bear witness, to say the very least, of a very perverted form of irony (and even: hypocrisy), where indeed, in reality, the current systems of government financing, especially given their failure to involve the true high incomes in this so-called "redistribution exercise", have mostly shown to cause an opposite effect.[122]

When aspiring for a more just society characterized by more just and fair societal mechanisms of (re)distributing wealth,[123] there is consequently not much to say in favor of the policies of a lot of Western (and Western inspired) countries, especially within the European Union, of striving for a greater government discipline as, based upon (neo-)liberal thinking, these efforts have not succeeded in sanitizing government finances, but seem to have had an opposite effect of creating a detrimental economic climate.

It should, on the contrary, be clear that neo-liberal public policy has not in any significant way contributed to installing a sound and/or just system of government financing, as it has utterly failed to truly turn the tide of the ever increasing debt financing and tax pressure—in its largest sense—on the masses (but considerably less on the richer classes).[124]

Hence, the time seems, more than ever, ripe to reflect upon a totally different approach towards the problem of government financing[125]; a proposal thereto will me made in Sect. 5.12.

4.7 The Increasing Polarisation Between the Rich and the Poor

4.7.1 Wealth Inequality on a Global Scale

4.7.1.1 General

Given the abovementioned insights into the way economic neo-liberalism aims at reinstalling unbridled capitalism, it should come as no surprise that in the recent past, prominent academic authors from various disciplines[126] have warned that social welfare is at peril.[127]

---

[122] Oxfam (2014), pp. 16 a.f. See also Streeck (2017).

[123] On this policy goal, see Stiglitz (2002), p. 27.

[124] For further details, see Anonymous (2014).

[125] For further proposals in this regard, see Byttebier (2017), Chapters 4 and 5.

[126] Such as: J. K. Gailbraith (see especially Galbraith (1974), pp. 95–96), in addition to his numerous other publications; Amartya Sen (see especially Sen (1977, 2009)); Paul Krugman (see e.g. Krugman (2009, 2012)); Joseph E. Stiglitz (see e.g. Stiglitz (2002, 2006, 2012)); Thomas Piketty (see e.g. Piketty (2014)); Max Roser and Esteban Ortiz-Ospina (see Roser and Ortiz-Ospina (2017)).

[127] See also Stiglitz (2002), his whole contribution dealing with this topic.

Under the logic of unbridled capitalism, people other than the rich and powerful find themselves mainly involved in performing (hard) labour in order to serve the purposes of capital, and this irrespective of any concern for their wellbeing.[128]

Hence it can not come as a surprise that especially since the 1980s, the period since when the ideas of economic neo-liberalism started to get implemented by capitalist governments on a world-wide scale,[129] the capitalist economic order has more and more evolved into a system where a relatively small group of people is getting inestimably rich—the wealth of some individuals even surpasses the wealth of certain entire nations—to the detriment of the global well-being of the world population (and, by extension, of the wellbeing of the world itself).[130]

It even appears that globalisation, for people not belonging to the rich classes, has a particularly downward levelling effect, where the gaps between the poor and the (very) rich, which up till a few decades ago were mostly expressed in the North-South relations, are gradually and increasingly being extended to the traditionally capitalist countries themselves.[131]

The understanding that unbridled capitalism is above all creating gaps between the poor and the rich, is moreover far from new.

As Pascal Brucker has expressed this (already in 2002)[132]:

> We know the figures in their terrible monotony (although there are people who doubt them).

Or, as Pizzigati has phrased it[133]:

> The early twenty-first century would begin just as the previous century had begun, with astounding quantities of wealth and power concentrated at America's economic summit.

---

[128] Galbraith (1992), pp. 90–91.

[129] Oxfam (2014), p. 8.

[130] Stiglitz (2002), p. 25.

[131] Steger (2013), p. 42.

See also Turner (2016), p. 119, having pointed out:

> Inequality has grown dramatically in advanced economies over the past 30 years. Since 1980 the bottom quintile of U.S. earners has received no increase in real wages; the income of the top 1% have tripled (…). The root causes are widely debated. Globalization of product and financial markets has certainly played a significant role; the impact of new technology may even be more profound. And the growth of finance has itself produced rapidly increasing earnings at the top of distribution.

Even the Catholic church has in the recent past reached this insight:

> Although global economic well-being appears to have increased in the second half of the twentieth century with an unprecedented magnitude and speed, at the same time inequalities proliferate between various countries and within them. Moreover, the number of people who live in conditions of extreme poverty continues to be enormous. (See Congregation for the Doctrine of the Faith (2018), n° 5.)

[132] Bruckner (2002), p. 21:

> On connaît les chiffres dans leur redoutable monotonie (même si certains peuvent les contester).

[133] Pizzigati (2012), p. 319.

Already in the 1950s and '60s, authors such as Erich Fromm and Herbert Marcuse had also come to the conclusion that capitalism causes all values being sacrificed to the interests of capital, hence the rich and powerful within society.

The increasing gaps between the rich and the poor in especially the American society have, furthermore, already been warned about by Galbraith in 1958, describing this phenomenon as "the triumph of inequality".[134]

Relatively recent data in the macro-economic context have similarly indicated that, before the start of the (modern) globalisation in 1973, the income ratio between the richest and the poorest countries was more or less 44:1. Twenty-five years later, this ratio was 74:1. In spite of some progress in the alleviation of poverty worldwide (for instance in the field of the fight against hunger), in 2012, the bottom 25% of humanity needed to survive on an income of less than 140 USD per year. At the same time, the joint possessions of the world's three richest billionaires was already then higher than the combined GDP of the least developed countries and their 600 million inhabitants.[135]

In other words, since the so-called (neo-)liberalisation of the world economy, the traditional gaps between North and South have only become wider and deeper, which forms a further indication that free marketism does not uphold its basic promise that the invisible hand of the market powers will ensure that, when everyone behaves in the most egoistic, selfish and greedy way, this will best serve the general interest.

In his concise style, Christopher Lloyd has in 2013 described the problem as follows[136]:

> At the end of 2001, the richest 2 per cent of adults in the world owned more than half of global household wealth, with the super-rich 1 per cent owning more than 40 per cent. Conversely, the bottom 40 per cent owned less than 1 per cent between them. It has been estimated that the richest 10 per cent of the world's adults now own more than 85 per cent of its total wealth. North America alone houses just 6 per cent of the world's population, but accounts for 34 per cent of all household wealth.

Since then, as will be demonstrated below (see Sects. 4.7.1.2–4.7.1.5), this situation has only gotten worse.

---

[134] Galbraith (1974), pp. 95–96:

> In 1965 the one-tenth of families and unattached individuals with the lowest incomes received before taxes about 1 per cent of the total money income of the country; the tenth with the highest incomes received 28 per cent of the total, which is to say their incomes averaged 28 times as much as the lowest tenth. The half of the households with the lowest incomes received, before taxes, only 23 per cent of all money income. The half with the highest income received 77 per cent. In 1965 only about 6 per cent of all family units had incomes before taxes of more than $15,000. They received, none the less, 27 per cent of total income. At the other extreme, 25 per cent had before tax incomes of less than three thousand and received only 4 per cent of the income.

[135] Steger (2013), pp. 113–115.

[136] Lloyd (2012), p. 374.

It needs hereby to be emphasised that the growing economic inequality is not only a hard fact, but it entails several far-reaching negative consequences, such as[137]:

- It makes it very difficult to fight poverty in the world;
- It hinders economic growth (especially in countries characterized by high economic inequalities)[138];
- It highlights several other types of inequality, inter alia inequality between men and women;
- It causes unequal access to life opportunities, including the chances of a proper education and of finding a suitable job, in addition to unequal access to health and social care;
- It is one of the main hindrances for a sufficient degree of social mobility (= the "condemned to stay poor"-syndrome[139]);
- It contributes to an increasing degree of violence and insecurity[140];
- . . .

Several more detailed data as of 2014 have since then been confirming the trend that, within capitalism as made "unbridled" again under the doctrines of economic neo-liberalism, there is an increasing polarisation between the rich and the poor occurring on a global scale.

In the following sections, some of these findings will be looked into in more detail.

4.7.1.2 Findings of 2014

In 2014, economist Thomas Piketty published his book "Capital in the Twenty-First Century"[141] which records the findings of a systematic research of the problem of the growing world-wide inequal division of wealth.

---

[137] Oxfam (2014), pp. 9–11 and pp. 35 a.f.; Oxfam (2016), pp. 4 a.f.

[138] See e.g. Haeck (2014), p. 6.

[139] See also Bahree (2016):

> There is also (...) a strong correlation between extreme inequality and low social mobility.If you are born poor in a highly unequal country you will most probably die poor, and your children and grandchildren will be poor too. In Pakistan, for instance, a boy born in a rural area to a father from the poorest 20% of the population has only a 1.9% chance of ever moving to the richest 20%. In the U.S., nearly half of all children born to low-income parents will become low-income adults.

[140] This even has raised the question to what extent former outbursts of violence in American schools (see for instance the Columbine- and comparable drama's; on this: Cullen (2009), p. 417; see also van Oudheusden (2012), p. 164) have been an expression of this downward spiral in the field of public education financing and investments in social care systems. (See furthermore Galbraith (1992), p. 122.) In more recent times, a similar question arises as regards the wave of terrorist attacks that have occurred in several European cities.

[141] Piketty (2014).

The conclusion of said book is that an evolution is taking place towards a structural (extremely) high level of inequality, where the majority of the world's wealth is increasingly ending up in the hands of a small group of people.

Piketty for instance mentions that, in the USA, the 10% richest people own 72% of the country's wealth, and he warns that in Europe the situation is going in the same direction. The author describes the consequences of such an extreme inequality as disastrous, as societies characterised by such an extreme inequality are unable to further progress.[142] (On the latter, see also above, Sect. 4.7.1.1.)

The already earlier quoted profound study by Oxfam of 2014, named "Even it up – Time to end extreme inequality"[143] similarly showed that the financial crisis of 2007–2008 has only further strengthened the unequal distribution of (the world's) wealth.

According to this study, in 2014 there were twice as much billionaires than there had been in 2009.[144]

According to the same study, the number of billionaires had since 2009 grown to 1645 and their common possessions had increased by 124%, to 5.4 trillion USD. The study of Oxfam also shows that the 85 richest people in the world together then owned more money than the poor half of the world population, a wealth which in 2014 grew at a rhythm of 668 million USD per day.[145]

The study "Even it up" of 2014 further reports that, in this way, the gaps between the rich and the poor are (literally) expanding by the day, if not by the minute, which is attributed to the fact that it is easier for capital to make new money than from labour efforts:

> Once accumulated, the wealth of the world's billionaires takes on a momentum of its own, growing much faster than the broader economy in many cases. If Bill Gates were to cash in all his wealth and spend $1m every single day, it would take him 218 years to spend all of his money. But in reality, the interest on his wealth, even in a modest savings account (with interest at 1.95 percent) would make him $4.2m each day. The average return on wealth for billionaires is approximately 5.3 percent, 156 and between March 2013 and March 2014, Bill Gates' wealth increased by 13 percent – from $67bn to $76bn. This is an increase of $24m a day, or $1m every hour.[146]

According to an article based on the findings of "Crédit Suisse" which was posted on the Forbes website on October 11th 2014, total world wealth at that moment was estimated at 263 trillion USD. This (huge) wealth was however distributed in a very unequal way,[147] whereby:

- people with more than 1 million USD, represented only 0.7% of the world population, but owned 41% of all wealth in the world;

---

142 See also Pauli (2014), pp. 32–35.

143 Oxfam (2014).

144 Oxfam (2014), pp. 8 and 32.

145 Oxfam (2014), pp. 8 and 32.

146 Oxfam (2014), p. 32.

147 McCarthy (2014).

- 23% of the world population owned between 10,000 and 100,000 USD, together representing 14% of the world's wealth;
- 69% of the world population owned 10,000 USD, or less, and thus accounted for less than 3% of the world's wealth;
- An individual needed to own no more than 3650 USD (including the value of a house, if applicable) to be part of the richest half of the world's population.

According to other research undertaken by "Crédit Suisse" (and made public in the "Crédit Suisse Global Wealth Report"), in 2014, 41% of the (USD-)millionaires of the world lived in the USA; Japan was ranked second with a "much lower" 8%. Seven percent of the worlds millionaires were reported to live in France, and six percent in both Germany and the U.K. Also in 2014, 775 (USD-) billionaires were reported to live in Europe (9 more than in 2013); 609 in North-America; 650 in Asia and 40 in Africa.[148]

4.7.1.3 Findings of 2015

In 2015, it appeared from a further Oxfam-report that the moment in time where 1% of the world population would own more than 50% of the worlds wealth, was then very close.[149] One may add to this that, according to the findings of 2017 quoted below (see Sect. 4.7.1.5.), this turning point has been reached at least in 2017.

This 2015 Oxfam report moreover showed that since 2010, in the wake of the financial crisis of 2007–2008, the wealth of the richest 1% of the world population was increasingly growing, implying that the richest 1% was appropriating an ever increasing part of the global wealth.

According to this 2015-study, in 2014, 1% of the richest people owned 48% of the world wealth, implying that the other 99% of the population owned only 52%. Moreover, the distribution of the remaining 52% of wealth was as worrying, as the largest part of this 52% of the remaining global wealth was, in 2014, still in hands of 20% of the world's richest people, implying that but 5.6% of the global wealth was available for the remaining 80% of the world population.[150]

The same Oxfam study of 2015, furthermore, showed a tendency that the very rich saw their part of the global wealth growing to an ever increasing extent. It was hereby estimated that in 2010, the Forbes-top-80-billionaires together disposed of an estimated amount of 1.3 trillion USD. In 2014, this joint wealth amounted to 1.9 trillion USD, which meant an increase of more than half a trillion USD in 4 years time. Not surprisingly, in the same period a decrease occurred of the share of the poor in the world possessions. According to these figures, in 2014, the share in the global wealth of the 80 richest people on the planet was as large as the share of the 50% poorest people on earth. To the extent that the growth of the wealth of the

[148] McCarthy (2014).

[149] Oxfam (2015).

[150] Oxfam (2015), p. 2.

people not belonging to the top 80 of very rich, is much slower than the growth of the wealth of the 80 richest people, the gap between the very rich and the rest of the population was reported to be increasing.[151]

Similar figures of 2015 brought to the public's attention by "Crédit Suisse" have confirmed and even more underlined the foregoing trends.

For instance, in its "Global Wealth Databook 2015",[152] "Crédit Suisse" reported that, in the course of 2015, global inequality had been even further growing, with, purportedly for the first time in history, half the world's wealth getting in the hands of just 1% of the global population.[153]

It was hereby underlined that in recent years, worldwide, middle classes had been more and more squeezed at the expense of the very rich, and that, also for the first time, there were more individuals in the middle classes in China—109 million—than the 92 million in the US.[154]

The 2015 report of "Crédit Suisse" furthermore showed that, as regards the situation in 2015, a person needed only 3210 USD (or £2100) to be counted among the wealthiest 50% of world citizens. A personal wealth of about 68,800 USD was furthermore reported to secure a place in the top 10%, while the top 1% were reported to have a fortune of more than USD 759,900.[155] It was also reported that, as regards 2015, about 3.4 billion people—just over 70% of the global adult population—had a wealth of less than 10,000 USD, and that a further 1 billion—a fifth of the world's population—were in the 10,000–100,000 USD range.[156] Each of the remaining 383 million adults—8% of the global population—was reported to have a wealth of more than 100,000 USD, whereby this number included about 34 million US dollar millionaires. About 123,800 individuals of these were reported to have wealth of more than 50 million USD, and nearly 45,000 of more than 100 million USD.

The CS 2015 report concluded:

> Wealth inequality has continued to increase since 2008, with the top percentile of wealth holders now owning 50.4% of all household wealth.

A further surprising fact that can be derived from said "Global Wealth Databook 2015" of "Crédit Suisse" is that, measured in personal wealth (and not: "income"), there were in 2015 more poor people in America than there were in China, which is mainly due to the Western banking system being more prevailing in the USA and in Europe than in the rest of the world, as a result of which more Americans and Europeans are in debt than people elsewhere in the world (whereby such bank debt accounts for a negative factor in calculating one's personal wealth). It more pre-

---

[151] Oxfam (2015), p. 3.

[152] Crédit Suisse Research Institute (2015).

[153] Treanor (2015).

[154] Treanor (2015).

[155] The report hereby defines "wealth" as the value of assets including property and stock market investments, but excluding debt (see Treanor 2015).

[156] Treanor (2015).

cisely appeared from said report that "America" (in this study this implies both the USA and Canada) had some 10% of the poorest people in the world and also some 30% of the richest; Europe had about 20% of the world's poorest people and 35% of the richest and China had none of the world's poorest people and about 7 or 8% of the world's richest people.[157]

As a side remark, albeit a very important one, it can, furthermore, be pointed out that in 2015, Sarah Anderson devoted a research to the income of 168,000 bankers and financial analysts of Wall Street, New York.

From Anderson's research, it appeared that these bankers and analysts in 2014 each received an average bonus of 173,000,- USD (or at the time: 160,000,- EUR). Said bonuses were reported to be 27% higher than these of 2009. All together, in 2014, the Wall Street bonuses amounted to 28.5 billion, an amount which was the double of the total American incomes of the ±1,007,000 Americans in the same receiving a minimum-income. This way, the financial Wall Street-elite receives an extra income which is higher than the sums of the basic incomes which are paid to 1.2 million Americans who receive the minimum hourly wage of wage of 7.25 USD (or 6.7 EUR). According to the study of Anderson, the bonus pool would be enough to bring the hourly wage of 2.9 million American bartenders, or the 1.5 American nurses to a minimum of 15 USD per hour. Anderson warns that already in 2014 the bonuses were again approaching the level of 2006, when an extreme bonus culture caused an extreme risk behaviour in the financial sector (which has been at the base of the financial crisis of 2007–2008).[158]

4.7.1.4 Findings of 2016

In the beginning of 2016, Oxfam published a new study called "An economy for the 1%. How privilege and power in the economy drive extreme inequality and how this can be stopped"[159] which largely confirmed the findings of the 2014- and 2015-studies.

From the study of 2016, it however also appeared that the situation had even gotten worse,[160] which can hardly come as a surprise given the fact that, on a global scale, the theories of economic neo-liberalism are more and more successful of being implemented by neo-liberal governments all over the planet.

One of the most striking findings of this 2016-study was most probably that in 2015, a mere 62 individuals owned as much riches as the bottom half of mankind.

According to this 2016 Oxfam-study "An economy for the 1%":

- In 2015, just 62 individuals had the same wealth as 3.6 billion people—the bottom half of mankind.

[157] Treanor (2015).

[158] Anderson (2015a, b).

[159] Oxfam (2016).

[160] Bahree (2016).

- The study hereby mentions that this figure was down from 388 individuals as recently as 2010, illustrating the striking tempo in which the implementation of hardcore economic neo-liberalism is widening the gaps between the poor and the rich on the planet;
- Also in 2015, the wealth of the richest 62 people had risen by 44% in the 5 years since 2010, which implied an increase of more than half a trillion dollars (USD 542 billion), to an astounding USD 1.76 trillion.
- Meanwhile, the wealth of the bottom half of mankind had fallen by just over a trillion dollars in the same period, a drop of 41%.
- Since the turn of the century, the poorest half of the world's population has received just 1% of the total increase in global wealth, while half of that increase has gone to the top 1%.
- The average annual income of the poorest 10% of people in the world had risen by less than USD 3 each year in almost a quarter of a century. Their daily income had risen by less than a single cent every year.

It should be noted that studies from the OECD confirm these observations.[161]

4.7.1.5 Findings of 2017

The aforementioned trends have continued during 2017.

According to the eighth edition of the Global Wealth Report of Credit Suisse Group AG, in the year to mid-2017, total global wealth rose at a rate of 6.4%, the fastest pace since 2012 and reached USD 280 trillion, a gain of USD 16.7 trillion. This reflected widespread gains in equity markets matched by similar rises in non-financial assets, which moved above the pre-crisis year 2007's level for the first time. Wealth growth also outpaced population growth, so that global mean wealth per adult grew by 4.9% and reached a new record high of USD 56,540 per adult.[162]

However, it was even so reported that income inequality kept on skyrocketing, "further polarizing society and stoking discontent". The value of financial assets, especially company securities, was hereby mentioned as one of the key factors for this inequality, because wealthier individuals hold a disproportionate share of their assets in this form.[163]

---

[161] OECD (2013). See also https://www.oecd-ilibrary.org/social-issues-migration-health/trends-in-income-inequality-and-its-impact-on-economic-growth_5jxrjncwxv6j-en (last consulted on June 16, 2018).

[162] https://www.credit-suisse.com/corporate/en/research/research-institute/global-wealth-report.html (last consulted on June 16, 2018).

Global wealth grew at a faster pace to USD 280 trillion, the highest since the bank began tracking it in 2000. The US accounted for more than half the increase. The growth was fuelled not only by widespread gains in equity markets but also substantial increases in non-financial assets, the report said. Average global wealth grew 4.9% to a record $56,540 per adult, with the richest 1% owning about half of all household wealth (see Anonymous (2018a)).

[163] Anonymous (2018a).

Otherwise put, the increase of the global wealth in the period 2016–2017 has mainly been the result of the growth of financial assets, especially in the USA that mainly benefited the rich and the powerful. Financial assets were hereby even reported to have grown more rapidly than non-financial assets. Moreover, much of the rise in financial wealth itself was due to financial asset price inflation.[164]

Although the report itself does not point this out in explicit terms, the foregoing obviously raises the question whether the ongoing increase in wealth (in the aftermath of the financial crisis of 2007–2008) is sustainable and whether or not it is mainly caused by financial bubbles. It his were indeed the case, it appears that, once again, the egoistic, selfish and greedy behavior of the rich and powerful may be leading the world economy in yet another severe financial crisis.

The CSG 2017 report, furthermore, keeps on warning that, even as global wealth increased overall, there were as many disturbing disparities in the period 2016–2017.[165]

Of particular concern was the situation of young people (see also further, under Sect. 4.10.), next to the continuing disparities between rich and poor countries.

The CSG 2017 report in this regard pointed out that especially millennials are doing less well than their parents at the same age, mainly as a result of the financial crisis of 2007–2008. The report mentions that (1) rising student debt in developed countries; (2) a high degree of unemployment that followed in many countries after the financial crisis of 2007–2008; (3) tighter mortgage rules after 2008; (4) higher house prices, and (5) less access to pensions were creating a so-called "perfect storm" that is holding back wealth accumulation for the (entire) millennial generation.[166]

The CSG 2017 report in this regards concludes[167]:

> As a result, the Millennials are not only likely to experience greater challenges in building their wealth over time, but also greater wealth inequality than previous generations.

As has been mentioned before in this book, this is but a further illustration of the fact that the whole neo-liberal financial and government financing system has proven not only to be completely unjust as such, but to be especially completely unjust from an intergenerational perspective.

Overall, the gaps between the rich and the poor were in 2016–2017 at comparable levels to the years before. In line with the situation during the foregoing years, the 2017 CS report in this regards mentions that the top 1% of people own 50.1% of all household wealth in the world.[168]

---

[164] Crédit Suisse Research Institute (2017), p. 4.

[165] Anonymous (2018a).

[166] Crédit Suisse Research Institute (2017), p. 27 a.f. See also Anonymous (2018a).

[167] Crédit Suisse Research Institute (2017), p. 39.

[168] Crédit Suisse Research Institute (2017), p. 16.

These data are confirmed in a further report of Oxfam of 2017, "An economy for the 99 percent"[169] which, furthermore, presents an even more worrysome picture of the increasing polarisation between the rich and the poor.

According to this Oxfam 2017 report, in 2017 eight[170] men owned the same wealth as the 3.6 billion people who make up the poorest half of humanity.

Otherwise put, Oxfam's 2017 report demonstrates that the gap between the rich and the poor was even far greater than had been feared in the past. It details how big business and the super-rich are fuelling the inequality crisis by dodging taxes, driving down wages and using their power to influence politics. Especially new and better data on the distribution of global wealth—particularly in the countries with a rising economy, such as India and China—indicated that the poorest half of the world has less wealth than had been previously thought. Had this new data been available in 2016, it would have appeared that already then nine billionaires owned the same wealth as the poorest half of the planet, and not 62, as Oxfam had calculated at that time.[171]

The following figures as regards the global situation at the beginning of 2017 speak, furthermore, for themselves[172]:

- Since 2015, the richest 1% owned more wealth than the rest of the planet;
- Eight men owned the same amount of wealth as the poorest half of the world;
- Over the next 20 years, 500 people will hand over USD 2.1 trillion to their heirs—a sum larger than the GDP of India, a country of 1.3 billion people;
- The incomes of the poorest 10% of people increased by less than USD 3 a year between 1988 and 2011, while the incomes of the richest 1% increased 182 times as much;
- A FTSE-100 CEO earned as much in a year as 10,000 people in working in garment factories in Bangladesh;
- In the US, new research by economist Thomas Piketty showed that over the last 30 years the growth in the incomes of the bottom 50% has been zero, whereas incomes of the top 1% had grown 300%;
- In Vietnam, the country's richest man earned more in a day than the poorest person earns in 10 years.

Winnie Byanyima, Executive Director of Oxfam International, commented on these devastating figures as follows[173]:

> Across the world, people are being left behind. Their wages are stagnating yet corporate bosses take home million dollar bonuses; their health and education services are cut while

[169] Oxfam (2017).

[170] In the previously quoted Oxfam report of 2016, this number was 62.

[171] https://www.oxfam.org/en/pressroom/pressreleases/2017-01-16/just-8-men-own-same-wealth-half-world (last consulted on June 16, 2018).

[172] Oxfam (2017), p. 2.

[173] https://www.oxfam.org/en/pressroom/pressreleases/2017-01-16/just-8-men-own-same-wealth-half-world (last consulted on June 16, 2018).

corporations and the super-rich dodge their taxes; their voices are ignored as governments sing to the tune of big business and a wealthy elite.

Oxfam's 2017 report, furthermore, shows how the global's broken economies are funnelling wealth to a rich elite at the expense of the poorest in society. The richest are accumulating wealth at such an astonishing rate that the world could see its first trillionaire in just 25 years.[174] Seven out of 10 people live in a country that has seen a rise in inequality in the last 30 years. Between 1988 and 2011, the incomes of the poorest 10% increased by just USD 65 per person, while the incomes of the richest 1% grew by USD 11,800 per person—182 times as much.[175]

Also the Oxfam 2017 report confirms how big business and the super-rich are fuelling the inequality crisis. Oxfam's research has hereby clearly revealed that, over the last 25 years, the top 1% have gained more income than the bottom 50% put together. The report shows that, far from "trickling down", income and wealth are being "sucked upwards" at an alarming rate.[176] The Oxfam 2017 report hereby demonstrates how, in order to maximize returns to their wealthy shareholders, big corporations are (1) dodging taxes, (2) driving down wages for their workers and the prices paid to producers, and (3) investing less in their business.[177]

Corporate tax dodging was reported to cost poor countries at least USD 100 billion every year. This is enough money to provide an education for the 124 million children who aren't in school and fund healthcare interventions that could prevent the deaths of at least six million children every year.[178]

The Oxfam 2017 report even so outlines in detail how the super-rich use a network of tax havens to avoid paying their fair share of tax and an army of wealth managers to secure returns on their investments that would not be available to ordinary savers.[179]

The report also demonstrates that, contrary to popular belief, many of the super-rich are not at all "self-made". On the contrary, the analysis of Oxfam shows over half the world's billionaires either inherited their wealth or accumulated it through industries which are prone to corruption and cronyism. It also demonstrates how big business and the super-rich use their money and connections to ensure that govern-

---

[174] See however the earlier quoted extreme wealth of the Rotschild family, referred to earlier in footnote 85.

[175] https://www.oxfam.org/en/pressroom/pressreleases/2017-01-16/just-8-men-own-same-wealth-half-world (last consulted on June 16, 2018).

[176] Oxfam (2017), p. 3.

[177] Oxfam (2017), p. 3 a.f.; https://www.oxfam.org/en/pressroom/pressreleases/2017-01-16/just-8-men-own-same-wealth-half-world (last consulted on June 16, 2018).

Oxfam for instance interviewed women working in a garment factory in Vietnam who work 12 hours a day, 6 days a week and still struggle to get by on the USD 1 an hour they earn producing clothes for some of the world's biggest fashion brands. The CEOs of these companies are some of the highest paid people in the world.

[178] https://www.oxfam.org/en/pressroom/pressreleases/2017-01-16/just-8-men-own-same-wealth-half-world (last consulted on June 16, 2018).

[179] https://www.oxfam.org/en/pressroom/pressreleases/2017-01-16/just-8-men-own-same-wealth-half-world (last consulted on June 16, 2018).

ment policy (only) works for them. For example, billionaires in Brazil have sought to influence elections and successfully lobbied for a reduction in tax bills while oil corporations in Nigeria have managed to secure generous tax breaks.[180]

The increasing polarisation between the rich and the poor in 2018 even drew the attention of the 2018 World Economic Forum in Davos (which had as its theme "Creating a Shared Future in a Fractured World"),[181] surprisingly reaching some similar conclusions as those of the CSG and the Oxfam reports.

4.7.2 *Some Further Data on Wealth Inequality in the UK in Particular*

The increasing impoverishment and the increasing polarisation between the rich and the poor in the UK are of particular relevance in illustrating how the doctrines of economic neo-liberalism, aiming at making capitalism as "unbridled" (or even: "relentless") as possible again, have in a period of some mere decades, succeeded in turning a former Western welfare state, into a state where poverty is yet again one of the main political and economical challenges of the present day.[182]

This is at the same time illustrative of the true legacy of the neo-liberal governments of the late Margaret Thatcher and her successors. Indeed, the attack on the welfare state model has, as explained before, been experienced with especial severity in the UK.[183] (See above, under Sect. 3.5.2.2.)

As Taylor-Gooby has put it[184]:

> The response to the 2007–8 banking crisis, repeated recessions and economic stagnation in this country has been to balance budgets by cutting government spending rather than increasing taxes. The harshest cuts are in social provision, with the poorest groups bearing the brunt.

When consulting the website of Oxfam on May 11th 2018, one learns that the UK is, at present, one of the most unequal nations in the developed world, amongst others characterized by strong dividing lines within UK society, between young and old, between people living in the different parts of the UK and between different income groups.[185]

Economic inequality is hereby even qualified as one of the main UK problems. Not surprisingly in light of the aforementioned, said economic inequality is also

---

[180] https://www.oxfam.org/en/pressroom/pressreleases/2017-01-16/just-8-men-own-same-wealth-half-world (last consulted on June 16, 2018).

[181] Gilmore (2018). See also Knight Frank Research (2018).

[182] On the crisis of the British welfare state in general, see Taylor-Gooby (2013).

[183] Taylor-Gooby (2013), p. 2.

[184] Taylor-Gooby (2013), p. 2.

[185] Whitham (2016).

reported to have grown tremendously under the successive (neo-liberal) governments for the last quarter of a century: the poorest families have increasingly lost out on the benefits of economic growth, while the very wealthiest have seen their incomes spiral upwards.[186]

Oxfam research has moreover shown that the five richest families in the UK are wealthier than the bottom 20% of the entire population. In other words: just five households own more money than 12.6 million people—almost the same as the number of people living below the poverty line in the UK. These gaps are moreover even widening. In the last 20 years, incomes for the bottom 90% of the country increased by a quarter. In the same time, the richest 0.1% saw their income double four times the increase of the bottom 90% of the population. According to the Oxfam website, the concentration of wealth and power at the top level of society has definitively a real impact on people's lives and is a sign of economic sickness—it slows down growth, implying there is less money to go into essential services for the people who need them most.[187]

Not surprisingly in light of the foregoing, the main increase in income inequality occurred over the 1980s. Even (neo-liberal) Prime Minister Theresa May has been reported to have been talking about the need to find ways of giving people a greater stake in society through, for example, greater employee representation on company boards, at the same time criticising the "irresponsible behaviour of big business" and promising "changes in the way big businesses are governed".[188]

The Oxfam website, furthermore, points out that indeed a focus on big business is particularly relevant: while many ordinary workers are finding it difficult to make ends meet, Oxfam research conducted in 2016 revealed that a quarter of all new wealth generated in the UK is going straight into the pockets of people who are already millionaires.[189]

Even more in general, the Oxfam website reports that more than three decades of high levels of inequality have had a profound impact on politics and society, leading many people to believe that they have little stake in society and feeling locked out of both politics and economic opportunity. The inability of even employment to offer a guaranteed route out of poverty, furthermore, illustrates the extent to which the economy isn't working for everyone, while increasing concentrations of wealth and poverty supports May's view that some places haven't benefited from economic growth at all.[190]

---

[186] https://www.oxfam.org.uk/what-we-do/issues-we-work-on/poverty-in-the-uk/challenging-extreme-economic-inequality (last consulted on June 16, 2018).

[187] https://www.oxfam.org.uk/what-we-do/issues-we-work-on/poverty-in-the-uk/challenging-extreme-economic-inequality (last consulted on June 16, 2018).

[188] Whitham (2016).

[189] Whitham (2016).

[190] Whitham (2016).

4.8 Revisiting Some of the Capitalistic Mechanisms and How Their Interaction Causes the Increasing Gaps Between the Rich and the Poor

At the risk of being repetitive, this Sect. 4.8 highlights the interconnection between the several capitalistic methods of organising the economy and how these lie at the roots of the above-explained (in Sect. 4.7) increasing gap(s) between the rich and the poor all over the world.

The data mentioned in the previous Sect. 4.7 on the distribution of the global wealth themselves already provide a certain indication about the extent of poverty in the world: the fact that more than half of the global wealth is in hands of 1% of the world's population, obviously implies that less than the other half of all global wealth is what remains to the other 99% of the world population.

There is no rational argument whatsoever to contradict that such a manifest unequal distribution of wealth is by all standards completely unjust.[191]

It is, furthermore, a fact that this unequal distribution of the global wealth is but a logical consequence of the several mechanisms of capitalism (as described above). It should hereby also be taken into consideration that the doctrines of economic neo-liberalism, given their aim of making capitalism "unbridled" again, have to a large extent sharpened these inherent effects of the capitalist methods and instruments, so also especially in the field of the unequal distribution of global wealth.

This once again confirms that unbridled capitalism is basically and by all moral standards unfair and unjust.

The perception of the perverse effects of capitalism (or in modern terms: free marketism) is hence not so different as that of climate change, itself but being one of the many other adverse consequences of centuries of unbridled capitalism.

For those willing to perceive it, it should hence become crystal clear that the starting premises of both economic liberalism and economic neo-liberalism are manifestly incorrect and unjust.

As indicated earlier, one of these starting premises of both economic doctrines entails that, within the socio-economic context, people should behave as egoistic, selfish and greedily as possible and that this will result in the highest possible welfare for everyone.

By now, one can but argue that it is beyond all comprehension why so many people still believe this nonsense, as all facts demonstrate that it does not make any sense whatsoever, except for serving the interests of the rich and powerful.

One should, furthermore, consider that the only period where, under the yoke of capitalism, at least some efforts were made to establish a more just distribution of wealth, as a result of which at least some part of the human race could be held outside poverty, albeit only in certain areas on earth (roughly: in the so-called West), has been the period after World War II until somewhere in the 1970s. This was cer-

[191] Even in the Aristotelian sense of the word.

tainly not due to the intrinsic mechanisms of capitalism itself (and obviously even less to the doctrines of economic liberalism and economic neo-liberalism).

On the contrary, this was only due to the fact that in the mentioned time period, different forces in society advocated a greater justice, among others in the field of the distribution of wealth. Among these forces were, for instance, trade unions, next to some political movements, such as the socialist and socio-democratic parties, certain movements within Christian democracy (and, in the USA, to some extent, the democratic party).[192]

It has been thanks to the collective efforts of this kind of movements that, at least for some time in history, it was advocated that capitalism should be given a "more humane look", which in its own turn allowed the propagating and the making of efforts to reduce poverty, at least in the Western world.

However, especially the rich and powerful within society would soon dismay these efforts. Their criticisms that the organisation of the welfare state came down to a deterioration of their individual freedom and richnesses, hereby gradually materialised in the pseudo-scientific movement of economic neo-liberalism, where it was assumed that the system of a welfare state is highly undesirable, given the large financing efforts it requires.[193]

Indeed, the corrections to unbridled capitalism which were introduced in the socio-economic order thanks to the efforts of trade unions and "left-oriented" political parties, obviously came with a cost, which the adherents of economic neo-liberalism are not willing to pay. The main reason hereof is that, under the doctrines of economic neo-liberalism, one should leave the entirety of the profits generated by the overall economy as untouched as possible, so they can entirely flow to the entrepreneurs (be it in their capacity of CEO's, directors or shareholders) themselves.

As has been explained above, this is but the logic consequence of the idea (going back to Adam Smith himself) that entrepreneurs are the (only) benevolent force within society who therefore need to be rewarded for their efforts as high as possible, which for instance helps explaining the high salaries and related advantages of CEO's and company directors and the high dividends which are to paid to company shareholders, while at the same time the wages of (other) employees should be kept as low as possible, next to the strong (neo-)liberal aversion against any form of state interference and the even stronger aversion of the rich and powerful against paying taxes.[194]

---

[192] Compare Chomsky (2017), p. 65 a.f.

[193] See for instance Friedman (1993). See also the works of Ayn Rand referred to under "References", next to numerous other neo-liberal authors.

[194] For some recent data in this regard, see Oxfam (2017), p. 17:

> In publicly listed companies, this drive for ever-greater profit has delivered rich rewards for shareholders. For corporations in the UK, the proportion of profits going to shareholders as dividend payments rather than being reinvested in the business, has risen from 10% of profits in the 1970s to 70% today. In 2015, the proportion was 86% and 84% for Australia and New Zealand respectively, thanks in part to a tax credit that investors receive on their dividend payouts. In India, as profits have been rising for the 100 largest listed corporations,

As also already explained elsewhere in this book, this very same attitude makes the adherents of economic neo-liberalism (among whom especially the rich and powerful) most fervently in favour of eliminating all societal systems fighting poverty, which in turn gradually causes capitalism to become more and more "unbridled" again.

It is therefore not a surprise that, since the 1980s, the implementation of the doctrines of economic neo-liberalism has in a growing number of countries above all been aimed at (1) dismantling those parts of the state apparatus that ensured social protection and access to public services for the general public, next to (2) ensuring a maximum safeguard for the large fortunes (for instance through tax cuts for the rich and powerful).

However, an intrinsic weakness in this approach arises from the observation that, in order for enterprises to make (the highest possible) profits needed to allow the payment of high CEO salaries and shareholders' dividends (both aimed at making the rich ever more rich), the products and services provided by such enterprises need to find an elementary number of people being willing to purchase them and hence, more importantly, being able to afford them.

In that regard, even under the doctrines of economic neo-liberalism, the lower classes should at least be granted some piece of the neo-liberal pie in order to allow them to participate in the consumption processes.

To the extent that the "Iron Law of the Wages" causes the average income of the lower (and middle) classes not to be sufficient to be consuming enough (in order to continue to guarantee the turnovers of the large companies), since the 1980s, the answer to this annoying dilemma has been found in an extensive promotion and encouragement to take up credit for consumer purposes.

This in turn attributed even more to an excessive creation of scriptural money based on bank loans, which initially benefited both the financial sector (as the interests on credits are an important source of income for the financial sector), as well as the production sectors (as especially since the 1980s, consumer credits offered one of the breeding grounds for unbridled consumerism).

In this approach, the factor time got more and more "loosely used", which is typical for liberal and neo-liberal doctrines.[195] One hereby lost sight of the fact that any (consumer or other) credit one day needs to be paid back and that, bearing in mind the Iron Law of the Wages, a too low income of the members of the lower (and even middle) classes derived from the compensation for performed labour, may result in many of them becoming unable to pay back said consumer credits.

---

the share of net profits going to dividends has also increased steadily over the last decade, reaching 34% in 2014/15, with around 12 private corporations paying more than 50% of their profits as dividends (…). Corporations have also been hoarding cash: according to rating agency Moody's, US (non-financial) corporations held a total of $1.7 trillion on their balance sheets at the end of 2015135 and have been buying back their own shares to further increase the value for shareholders. In the US, the 500 largest listed corporations spent on average 64% of their profit on buying back shares between September 2014 and September 2016.

[195] Reference being made to the well-known "laissez faire, laissez passer"-principle.

Especially as of the eighties of the twentieth century, this concern is even further strengthened by the fact that, even so driven by the Iron law on wages, a lot of (industrial) production has moved to low wage countries, a phenomenon which caused that several types of labour, and hence (industrial) production became no longer employable in the Western world itself.

Thus, the underlying principles of capitalism have led to a vicious circle which already in 2007–2008 has attributed to one of the heaviest financial crises in the period after World War II.

This financial crisis itself would drive many people further into even more poverty, which, at least in the (Western) countries where in the period after World War II a strong protective social tissue had been developed, increased the pressure on these societal systems correcting unbridled capitalism even more.

In the aftermath of this financial crisis of 2007–2008, the response of the governments of many countries and supra-national organisations to respond to this situation has strangely enough been that the capitalist principles which have caused all these problems, should even be further strengthened.

As a result, instead of tackling the underlying causes of said financial crisis, under the impulse of neo-liberal thinking, on a worldwide basis efforts are made which lead to an even further dismantling of the mechanisms which attempt to ensure a more just distribution of welfare, as a result of which the disastrous powers of capitalism are even further strengthened.

The surprising result of the financial crisis of 2007–2008 has thus been that one did not start to advocate to tackle the underlying causes of the crisis. For instance, nowhere in the world, policy makers aimed for other systems of money creation or government financing than those developed under capitalist doctrines. Neither started policy makers working on installing a better world wide protection of labour[196] (and of the working classes), nor on further enhancing systems of care for the many people who find themselves in miserable circumstances because of the powers of capitalism. Even so, on the policy making level, no one commenced working on a truly just fiscal system, nor were any initiatives taken to challenge the people having been responsible for the financial crisis.[197]

On the contrary, it seems that, in many countries and supra-national organisations (such as the European Union), policy makers mainly aim for the further

---

[196] See also Stiglitz (2002), p. 16.

[197] Iceland being a noteable exception. (See, for instance Syrmopoulos (2015); https://www.mintpressnews.com/iceland-has-sent-26-bankers-to-prison-while-us-white-collar-prosecutions-hit-record-low/210595/; last consulted on June 16, 2018.)

As pointed out by Syrmopoulos (2015):

> Massive debts were incurred in the name of the Icelandic public, to allow the country to continue to function, which are still being repaid to the IMF and other nations eight years later by the citizens of Iceland. In contrast to the U.S., Iceland has chosen to hold the criminals that manipulated their financial system accountable under the law.

See also Chomsky (2017), p. 83 a.f.

deployment of a socio-economic order in which the many dictates of the free market operation predominate everything.[198]

Gradually, this risks to turn back the clock to the nineteenth century when poverty was a fact for a substantial part of the population and at the same time a small elite of industrials and merchants lived an extremely luxurious life.

The extent to which the latter is already happening in some countries will hereafter be dealt with in the next Sect. 4.9.

4.9 Some Figures of the Increasing Impoverishment

4.9.1 Poverty in the World in General

It does not need to surprise that, in light of the foregoing, poverty rates are skyrocketing.

As we all know, the principles of (unbridled) capitalism have been determining the traditional North-South relations for ages, with all the known suffering, amongst which even a prevailing famine in many Southern countries.[199] (See also Sect. 4.6.)

In the recent past, Stiglitz has pointed out that the world is marked by an ever intensifying race between the growth of the (world) population, and the growth of poverty, and that poverty is winning.[200] It should hereby be clear that, as the implementation of neo-liberal thinking and the dismantling of social correction mechanisms on unbridled capitalism continue to progress, the victory on poverty and exploitation is at risk to increase even more.

It has been argued before that the African Continent is increasingly characterised by ever widening and deepening gaps between the rich and the poor, where some press has described (most) African cities as "small islands of wealth surrounded by oceans of shantytowns", where people are even forced to fight for clear water and descent sewer systems.[201] In 1992, Galbraith made a similar observation about what

---

[198] Even the Catholic church has reached a similar conclusion:

> The recent financial crisis might have provided the occasion to develop a new economy, more attentive to ethical principles, and a new regulation of financial activities that would neutralise predatory and speculative tendencies and acknowledge the value of the actual economy. Although there have been many positive efforts at various levels which should be recognized and appreciated, there does not seem to be any inclination to rethink the obsolete criteria that continue to govern the world. On the contrary, the response seems at times like a return to the heights of myopic egoism, limited by an inadequate framework that, excluding the common good, also excludes from its horizons the concern to create and spread wealth, and to eliminate the inequality so pronounced today. (See Congregation for the Doctrine of the Faith (2018), n° 5.)

[199] Meredith (2014), pp. 100–103.

[200] Stiglitz (2006), p. 10.

Stiglitz' comment in question does not essentially differ from the insights of Thomas Malthus.

[201] Meredith (2014), pp. 100–103, esp. p. 103.

he called "golden ghetto's" in the metropolis Manila in the Philippines, struck by a high poverty rate (introducing the open question whether the American and European cities will, in the future, as well align to that model).[202]

Some (more or less recent) figures on the topic of poverty in the world in 2014 speak for themselves.

It has, for instance, been reported that in 2014 2.2 billion people were living in, or on the edge of multidimensional poverty, which implies that 15% of the then world population was either poor or vulnerable to become poor. Also in 2014, 80% of the world population was not covered by any type of social protection system. Still in 2014, 12% of the world population (or 842 million people) were chronically hungry. Worldwide, 1.5 billion people were working without any formal employment contract or any similar protective regulation,[203] indicating the vast degree of exploitation which characterizes the capitalist economic system.

4.9.2 The Increasing Need of Food Banks in the UK and in the USA

In light of the foregoing, it should not come as a surprise that there is not only increasing famine in Southern countries.

Even a traditionally, purportedly "prosperous country" as the United Kingdom—characterized by what Galbraith in the past referred to as an "affluent society"[204]—is increasingly faced with hunger.

As regards the year 2014, it was for instance reported by the British press that no less than 913,138 persons regularly called upon the food bank "Trussell Trust". The main cause hereof was explained to be the failure of the British social security system, which, as has already been mentioned before, has suffered severely under the dismantling efforts of the (neo-liberal) governments of Margaret Thatcher and, later on, David Cameron (2010–2016) and Theresa May (as of 2016).[205] (See above, under Sect. 4.7.2.)

By the end of April 2018, the situation had even got worse. It was then reported that food bank use in the UK had reached its highest rate on record with 1,332,952 three-day emergency food supplies delivered to people in crisis in the course of 2017, a number that was 13% higher than in 2016.[206] The Trussell Trust, the UK's

[202] Galbraith (1992), p. 129.

[203] United Nations Development Programme (2014), p. 3.

[204] Galbraith (1974).

[205] See http://www.independent.co.uk/news/uk/politics/food-banks-archbishop-of-canterbury-urges-politicians-to-face-up-to-britains-hunger-9909324.html (last consulted on June 16, 2018); See also http://www.independent.co.uk/voices/editorials/hunger-has-not-vanished-from-our-affluent-even-overweight-society%2D%2Das-archbishop-welby-has-pointed-out-9909189.html (last consulted on June 16, 2018).

[206] Moore (2018) and Bulman (2018).

national food bank provider, in this regard reported that people going hungry were often at work, in low-paid jobs, skipping meals. Low income was mentioned as the biggest single—and fastest-growing—reason for referral to food banks. Being in debt was mentioned as one of the other main causes.[207]

When evaluating these data, one should bear in mind that the abovementioned illustration is probably but the metaphorical top of the iceberg and that in the post-Thatcher United Kingdom, many similar food banks are experiencing an increasing growth of the number of people dependent on their services.

Also in the USA, (traditionally) one of the richest countries in the world, the need for food banks has been growing at an alarming rate in the aftermath of the financial crisis of 2007–2008, indicating that also in the USA, hunger is becoming an increasing problem. The high degree of poverty in the USA is, according to some, mainly the result of an exceptionally high income inequality.[208]

According to the website of the food bank "Feeding America",[209] in 2012, a troubling number of one out of six American inhabitants were reported to be more or less dependent on food help. According to this same website, in 2012, 46.5 million Americans (15% of the American population) were living in poverty (amongst which 16.1 million (or 22%) children below the age of 18).[210] In that same year, about 49 million American inhabitants were living in so-called "food insecure families" (amongst which about 16 million children).[211]

According to the findings of a similar study of 2014, 72% of American families that had been calling upon the services of the food bank "Feeding America" lived below the so-called "federal poverty line",[212] at a moment where the median of their income was reported to be 9175 USD per year. According to the same study, the food bank "Feeding America" was then supplying food help to 46.5 million people, amongst which 12 million children and 7 million elderly (through a network of 58,000 food centres).[213] In a similar study of 2014 by "Feeding America", it was stated that the vast recession of 2008 (itself created by the financial crisis of 2007–2008) was one of the main causes of the increasing poverty and hunger in present-day USA.[214]

---

207 Moore (2018). See also Bulman (2018); https://www.oxfam.org.uk/what-we-do/issues-we-work-on/poverty-in-the-uk (last consulted on June 16, 2018).

208 Roser and Ortiz-Ospina (2017).

209 http://www.feedingamerica.org/ (last consulted on June 16, 2018).

210 This was moreover reported to be the highest number in over 50 years. (See Feeding America (2014), p. 3.)

211 http://www.feedingamerica.org/hunger-in-america/impact-of-hunger/hunger-and-poverty/ (last consulted on June 16, 2018).

212 See http://aspe.hhs.gov/poverty/14poverty.cfm (last consulted on June 16, 2018).

213 See Feeding America (2014).

See also http://help.feedingamerica.org/site/PageServer/?pagename=HIA_hunger_in_america&s_src=W14CDIRCT&s_subsrc=http%3A%2F%2Fwww.feedingamerica.org%2F&_ga=1.31822968.715348318.1418886761 (last consulted on June 16, 2018).

214 See Feeding America (2014), p. 1:

> Unemployment and poverty rates have remained high since the Great Recession of 2008, and the number of households receiving nutrition assistance from the federal government's

As regards the situation in 2016, a report called "Household Food Security in the United States in 2016"[215] of the United States Department of Agriculture similarly mentioned that:

> an estimated 87.7 percent of American households were food secure throughout the entire year, implying they had access at all times to enough food for an active, healthy life for all household members. The remaining households (12.3 percent) were food insecure at least some time during the year, including 4.9 percent with very low food security, meaning that at times the food intake of one or more household members was reduced and their eating patterns were disrupted because the household lacked money and other resources for obtaining food. Changes from 2015 to 2016 in food insecurity overall (from 12.7 to 12.3 percent) and in very low food security (from 5.0 to 4.9 percent) were not statistically significant, but they continued a downward trend in food insecurity from a high of 14.9 percent in 2011. Among children, changes from 2015 in food insecurity and very low food security were also not statistically significant. Children and adults were food insecure in 8.0 percent of households with children in 2016, essentially unchanged from 7.8 percent in 2015. Very low food security among children was 0.8 percent in 2016, essentially unchanged from 0.7 percent in 2015. In 2016, the typical food-secure household spent 29 percent more on food than the typical food-insecure household of the same size and household composition. About 59 percent of food-insecure households participated in one or more of the three largest Federal food and nutrition assistance programs during the month prior to the 2016 survey (food stamps (SNAP); Special Supplemental Nutrition Program for Women, Infants, and Children (WIC); and the National School Lunch Program).[216]

When consulting the homepage of the website of Feeding America[217] on 2 May 2018, one may still learn that:

> 41 million people face hunger in the U.S. today — including nearly 13 million children and more than five million seniors. Hunger knows no boundaries — it touches every community in the U.S., including your own.

It is hardly a coincidence that both the United Kingdom (under "Thatcherism") and the United States of America (under "Reaganomics") have been among the first Western countries that adopted the theories of economic neo-liberalism in order to purify capitalism from the effect of the welfare state model that under these theories were considered devastating.

> Supplemental Nutrition Assistance Program has increased by approximately 50 percent between 2009 and 2013. Demand for charitable food assistance has also expanded. HIA 2014 finds an increased number of individuals relying on charitable assistance to access nutritious foods for themselves and their families.

See also Feeding America (2014), p. 3:

> The economy has experienced an unusually slow recovery since the deep recession in 2008 and 2009. The nation's poverty rate reached 15.1 percent in 2010, the highest rate since 1993. The poverty rate remained at 15 percent in 2012 with 46.5 million people living in poverty. This is the largest number living in poverty since statistics were first published more than 50 years ago.

[215] Coleman-Jensen et al. (2017).

[216] Coleman-Jensen et al. (2017).

[217] See http://www.feedingamerica.org/. See also Feeding America (2017).

4.9.3 *Increasing Poverty in Belgium*

In a recent book by Geysels and Vlaminck, named "De schande en de keerzijde" (which may be translated as "Disgrace and its reverse side"), it is similarly indicated that, in 2014, about 15% of the Belgian population, this is about 1.5 million people, lived in poverty. The book furthermore shows that the richest 10% of the Belgians were, at that time, 254 times richer than the poorest 10%; the top 5% owned as much as 75% of what the rest of the population owns. Otherwise put, the 20% richest families owned 61.2% of the total wealth in Belgium. The other way around, the 20% poorest families owned only 0.2% of the total wealth in Belgium. About 100,000 people in Belgium received a living wage which is below the poverty threshold, while 94,500 Belgians were euro millionaires. Of the 2.2 million Belgian children, 420,000 were socially disadvantaged.[218]

According to the fifth edition of the "Federal Annual report on poverty and social exclusion", which appeared in March 2015, in 2014, more than 15% of the Belgian population, or 1,652,000 people, lived below the poverty threshold.

This report, furthermore, confirmed that the financial crisis of 2007–2008 had worsened poverty and social exclusion in Belgium (and Europe) and that no effective measures were taken to cope with this. The poverty threshold in Belgium then implied that a single person had an income of 1074 euro per month, while a family with two children had an income 2256 euro per month. The said annual report also reached the conclusion that 5% of the population, or 561,000 people, were in a situation of "material deprivation" (amongst others: facing arrears with rent; not being able to access animal protein on a daily base; facing problems to pay heating invoices; not having a washing machine, television, telephone or car…).[219]

It has since then been reported[220] that in 2018, 2,232,000 people in Belgium were at risk of ending up in poverty or social exclusion. Both the number of people facing a shortage of income (= 14.9% of the population), as the number of people facing a risk of poverty or social exclusion (= 21.1% of the population), had remained the same in comparison to previous years, implying that for 1 out of 5 people living in Belgium, living remains equal to merely surviving.

It was also reported that on practically all levels, be it public policy, the media or the general opinion of a large part of the Belgian population, there is no longer any willingness to look for the institutional or structural reasonings for this high level of poverty, but that, to an increasing extent, the individual living in poverty himself is blamed as solely responsible for his situation.[221]

---

[218] Geysels (2014), pp. 11–59, esp. pp. 24–27. See also Raspoet (2014), pp. 51–55.

[219] http://www.hln.be/hln/nl/957/Binnenland/article/detail/2262911/2015/03/24/15-procent-van-de-Belgen-leeft-onder-armoedegrens.dhtml (last consulted on June 16, 2018).

[220] See Lahaye et al. (2017). See also Anonymous (2018b).

[221] See Anonymous (2018b).

The latter is obviously in line with the doctrines of economic neo-liberalism that also in Belgium has become the overruling socio-economic doctrine hardly ever being challenged any more.

There is a concern in Belgium that the continued implementation of the doctrines of economic neo-liberalism will further increase these poverty rates, as is the case in many other countries.

4.10 The Anti-solidarity Capitalist Socio-Economic Order

4.10.1 Reconsidering Once More Why Economic (Neo-) liberalism Is Hostile Towards Solidarity

We have already indicated above that, on a theoretical level, both economic liberalism and economic neo-liberalism do not advocate solidarity. (See already above, Sect. 3.8.)

Putting it in a more blunt way, the solidarity principle is essentially in complete opposition to one of the main starting points of liberal and neo-liber thinking, namely that within the socio-economic environment, man should behave as egoistically, selfishly and greedily as possible in order to insure that economy will be fed with sufficient impulses of productivity and innovation.

The previous Chap. 3. of this book elaborated already extensively on the impact of this axiom on the socio-economic (hierarchy of) values which characterise contemporary societies all over the world, especially since the theories of economic neo-liberalism have gotten implemented in practice as of the 1980s.

It should, hence, not be surprising that at present, in a world where the above-mentioned neo-liberal starting premise that in the socio-economic order people should behave as egoistically, selfishly and greedily as possible, has worldwide grown to one of the leading principles of human behaviour, the resulting socio-economic world order is in practice one which is increasingly characterised by a very high degree of anti-solidarity.

The neo-liberal world as it has been shaped since the 1980s is a world which is that above all based on the "every man for himself"-principle. Those who are excluded in this neo-liberal world—and as described above, this is unfortunately the case for a very large part of humanity—owe this in this construct only to themselves, especially to their own incompetence, stupidity, laziness, lack of initiative, or what other reason one may encounter when reading Rand, or when hearing any adherent of the doctrines of economic neo-liberalism uttering his (idiotic) opinion on any societal theme.

Objective factors that in reality lie at the basis of many inequalities in the socio-economic context, such as inborn talent, physical or mental health (condition), age, gender, race and sexual orientation (resulting in as many grounds of discrimination which are at present still prevailing for and by many people), other life chances related to birth (into a rich or poor family and/or society), next to factors such as coincidence or luck, are hereby not taken into account. (See already above, under Sect. 3.1.)

Within the kind of reasoning as deployed under the doctrines of both economic liberalism and economic neo-liberalism, there must not be an expectation of care or support by the community, as this would imply that the competent within society become too much burdened with the care for the incompetent, which is bound to hinder the progress of mankind and its economy (as put that bluntly by, for instance, Ayn Rand[222]).

Taking into account this neo-liberal anti-solidarity principle, the extent to which neo-liberal thinking has increasingly succeeded in getting a strong grip on the entire world, especially in the field of the socio-economic order, has also been shaping a world which is to an ever growing extent become of an "anti-solidary" nature.

This observation can be illustrated with many examples from every day life. We shall, hereafter, only refer to a few from recent events, bearing in mind that the topic more than merits further fundamental scientific research.

4.10.2 Some Further Remarks on the Tax Aversion of the Rich and the Powerful

It may be clear from what has been argued before that economic neo-liberalism opposes a large role for "the government", a theme which has already been referred to above in Sect. 2.6.

Under neo-liberal thinking, every individual should (be able to) take care for himself and this as zealously as possible, implying that there cannot be room for a (large) role of the government.[223] Expenses for systems of public service or collective care are, by definition, to be kept at an absolute minimum, a stance which for instance has been strongly defended by Milton Friedman in his dissertation named "Why Government is the Problem".[224]

This neo-liberal viewpoint obviously goes hand in hand with the neo-liberal vision on fiscal matters. It has already been demonstrated before that the rich and very rich of the planet do not happily pay taxes, because they, purportedly being the driving forces within economy, prefer to invest in prosperity and employment, read: primarily advocate their own pursuit of ever more profits (a viewpoint which goes back to the observations of Adam Smith himself).

---

[222] Rand (2008), p. 23.

[223] Gailbraith has observed that under these doctrines, the only role reserved for the government lies in spending for military reasons, for subsidies to large corporations and agriculture and for financing "bailouts" of financial institutions in need. (See Galbraith (1992), p. 122.)

[224] Friedman (1993), p. 11.

To the extent that government operation is deemed to be completely obsolete, paying taxes comes down to a type of waste which should preferably be avoided,[225] at least for the rich and very rich who in this way of reasoning deserve better than being forced to share a part of their wealth with the less fortunate in society, and moreover prefer a system of state debt financing by privately owned banks because this generates even more profits for them (stemming from the dividends they receive in their capacity of shareholders of the private banks that provide the said credits).[226]

This mindset explains why, as already argued before (see especially under Sect. 4.6.), the rich and very rich are to an ever growing extent deploying a tax evasive behaviour, mostly with the help of specialised consultancy firms. It is even the more striking that this is a known fact for a long time, but that practically no-where in the world public authorities have been inclined to cope with this.

At the best, from time to time, some of the most far reaching mechanisms of tax evasion benefiting the rich and very rich are criticised in the international press sometimes, albeit in most cases only for a very short period, at best causing some temporary social commotion or public anger. However, this has not yet stimulated or inspired many governments to take true measures in order to deal with this problem in a fair manner (with perhaps as one noteable exception the fiscal policy by the French government Hollande (2012–2017)).

The success with which the rich and very rich escape from any significant taxation is outright impressive, but obviously, also has important societal downsides.

One of these downsides is that governments who do not succeed in taxing the rich and very rich (and the enterprises owned or run by them), as explained before (see also in Sect. 4.6.) need to focus mainly on taxing the lower and middle classes who consequently, in most countries in the world, suffer from high taxation.

A second downside which has also already been dealt with above is that, as a result of the foregoing many countries of the world are faced with chronical financial deficits. In a further past, bearing in mind the neo-liberal "laissez faire, laissez passer" principle, this was tackled by means of a resort to systems of debt financing, causing a lot of countries to take up huge credits. These in turn have mainly contrib-

---

[225] See for instance some of the reactions of Bill Gates to Piketty findings (made public in Piketty (2014)), making it clear that, as a rich man, he is obviously not in favor of taxing (income from) capital more, rather of taxing consumption more:

> Piketty's favorite solution is a progressive annual tax on capital, rather than income. He argues that this kind of tax "will make it possible to avoid an endless inegalitarian spiral while preserving competition and incentives for new instances of primitive accumulation".I agree that taxation should shift away from taxing labor. It doesn't make any sense that labor in the United States is taxed so heavily relative to capital. It will make even less sense in the coming years, as robots and other forms of automation come to perform more and more of the skills that human laborers do today.But rather than move to a progressive tax on capital, as Piketty would like, I think we'd be best off with a progressive tax on consumption. (…) Like Piketty, I'm also a big believer in the estate tax. Letting inheritors consume or allocate capital disproportionately simply based on the lottery of birth is not a smart or fair way to allocate resources. (See Gates (2014).)

[226] Oxfam (2015), p. 7.

uted to a further enrichment of the financial sector, and especially to the shareholders of financial institutions, being the only one(s) benefiting from the huge outstanding government debts.

Otherwise put, the whole organisation of the neo-liberal socio-economic order is one serving best the interest of the rich and very rich who, at all cost, avoid having to share their wealth with the rest of mankind.

4.10.3 The Dismantlement of the Welfare State Model and the Thereof Resulting Breach of Generations

To the extent that, in the wake of the financial crisis of 2007–2008, many policy making bodies (among which the European Union itself as it is even so governed by the principles of economic neo-liberalism) are reaching the conclusion that the huge outstanding government debts are no longer acceptable,[227] several of these are nevertheless still mainly engaged in remediation measures which are based upon other theories of economic neo-liberal thinking, namely that too large governments should be scaled back.

Concretely, this translates into a worldwide dismantling of many types of public services (such as justice, medical care, care for the elderly, and education), but also (and obviously) in a reduction of different social care mechanisms and systems of protecting labour.

This causes the socio-economic processes to run in a downward spiral, where those who are already rich and powerful, obtain ever more wealth and power (literally) by the second, to the detriment of a lot of suffering for the rest of the global population.

Gradually, some of these elements are even evolving into a (very) sharp intergenerational conflict.[228]

An obvious illustration thereof is, for instance, the evolution of the systems of higher education in many countries/regions, such as e.g. the United Kingdom, The Netherlands and the Flemish community. These countries/regions have in common that they all strongly responded to the European call made in the so-called Bologna

---

[227] See, for instance, an interview with the former ECB-president Jean-Claude Trichet that was published in "De Volkskrant" on April 23th 2018. (See De Waard (2018).)

[228] See also the opinion expressed by Professor N. Ferguson as quoted in Knight Frank Research (2018), p. 10:

> This is an extraordinarily difficult question in political economy, because it's about generational imbalances. Right now, the dice are loaded in favour of the baby-boomers, people like me who were born in the two decades after the end of World War Two, and they're loaded against newborns, children and the unborn. This is a really striking pathology of modern times, this breach of contract between the generations. It's very hard to fix because the unborn and children don't get to vote, whereas the elderly now tend to stick around long after retirement age, and they vote in rather large numbers.

Declaration[229] to drastically "rationalize" the higher education systems prevailing within the European Union.

As a result, regarding these three countries/regions, large cut back measures have been resorted to in the more or less recent past. These probably have had the strongest impact in the UK (where generally speaking, the neo-liberalization of society has occurred the strongest), secondly in The Netherlands, which has been among the first to align its higher education model to the UK system and, thirdly, also in the Flemish community, which in its turn is aligning itself to the United Kingdom and The Netherlands. A result of this neo-liberalisation of the higher education system has been the impact on the financial organisation of universities and other instutions for higher education, to an ever growing extent forcing these to finance themselves in accordance with free market principles. It needs not come as a big surprise that access to higher education is, hence, becoming more and more subject to paying ever increasing entry or tuition fees.[230]

Through this, higher education entrance fees in at least two of these three countries/regions, namely in the United Kingdom and The Netherlands, are gradually nearing the tariffs that are already applied for a long time by a lot of the American (private) universities. When realizing that (higher) education is one of the main mechanisms—and perhaps within the capitalist socio-economic order even the only one—which can succeed in accomplishing an elementary social mobility within society, the result of this evolution is that higher education policy deployed in the abovementioned countries is increasingly giving expression to the neo-liberal anti-solidarity principle, causing that especially young people from the lower classes of society increasingly experience a reduced access to higher education.[231]

We shall come back to this issue in a further section (see further, under Sect. 4.11.).

In the neo-liberalised world order, a lot of similar problems of intergenerational injustice have manifested in numerous other domains of societal organization.

---

[229] See The Bologna Declaration (1999).

[230] Regarding the situation in the USA, it has, for instance, been pointed out in an article that appeared in The Economist of 28 March 2015 that:

> tuition fees have nearly doubled, in real terms, in 20 years. (See Anonymous (2015a), pp. 11–12.)

Furthermore, it has been argued that:

> In America, retrenchment in state budgets has pushed up tuition fees. In California, for instance, they have tripled over 15 years, and a further 28% rise is proposed. Outside America, the first big shift towards private funding happened in Australia, where tuition fees were jacked up in the late 1980s. A host of other countries followed including New Zealand, Chile, South Africa, some of the former Soviet republics, Britain and Thailand. China used to impose no fees at all, now it charges 6,000–10,000 yuan ($800–1,600) a year, not much for an urban family but a lot for a rural one. (See Anonymous (2015b), pp. 12–14.)

[231] See, for a more recent example in the geographical context of the Netherlands: Minten (2015), p. 18.

For instance in Western Europe, especially the generation of (relatively) young people who, thanks to the welfare model that was created in the era after World War II, have been raised in a societal system giving them a sufficient access to public services and social care mechanisms, to a growing extent find themselves in a world dominated by the dictates of economic neo-liberalism where, unless helped by parents or others, career and other opportunities are becoming more and more scarce (with as harrowing examples of: a high youth unemployment in many countries; increasing poverty; being forced to live longer with their parents...).[232]

4.10.4 Business as Usual for the Banking Sector

One more illustration of how the anti-solidarity principle gets more and more implemented under the doctrines of economic neo-liberalism obviously concerns the behaviour of bankers.[233]

After in 2007–2008 having caused one of the most severe financial crises in the period after World War II,[234] and taken into further consideration that a lot of the banks involved in said financial crisis only survived thanks to considerable efforts of governments of many countries (which, in many cases, has further worsened the financial problems of these countries), the financial sector has since then again been taking up its "business as usual".

It is very significant that in the study of Oxfam from 2015 which has already been referred to earlier in this book, the financial sector has in the recent past once again been indicated as one of the most profitable (in terms of generating financial profits) economic sectors, where one should not lose sight of the fact that the profits of the financial sector are mainly a consequence of withdrawing wealth from the rest of the economy and are primarily, if not exclusively, intended for making those who are already rich even richer (see above in this book, under Sects. 4.7 and 4.8, the description of how the dividends of the financial institutions are one of the main sources of income of the very rich).

Next to that, the financial sector continues to be indicated as one of the greatest lobbyists on a global scale, which helps explaining why the huge profits from the

---

[232] See already above, the earlier referred to findings by Crédit Suisse (see Sects. 4.2 and 4.7).

[233] See recently Congregation for the Doctrine of the Faith (2018).

[234] Compare Congregation for the Doctrine of the Faith (2018), n° 21, referring to:

> the fact that among the major reasons for the most recent economic crisis was the immoral behavior of agents in the financial world, where the supranational dimension of the economic system makes it easy to bypass the regulations established by individual countries [and to the fact that] the extreme volatility and mobility of capital investments in the financial world permit those who control them to operate smoothly beyond every norm that does not aim at an immediate profit, often blackmailing by a position of strength even legitimate political authority.

sector often do not need to be spent on redeeming the high costs generated by the "bailouts" that were needed to resolve the financial crisis of 2007–2008.[235]

Meanwhile, at least in the USA and probably even so on a global scale, a worrying revival of the bonus mechanisms that helped creating said financial crisis of 2007–2008 can be observed. (See, for instance, the above referred to study by Sarah Anderson, as referred to in Sect. 4.7.)

It is hereby very remarkable to witness how the financial sector, after having brought the world to the brink of economic collapse in 2007–2008, has at the same time been able to pass on its large problems to the rest of community (= a so-called "socialization of losses"),[236] to currently again being evolved into one the most profitable sectors, the profits of which again exclusively flow to the rich capital providers (= a so-called "privatization of gains").

As may be clear from several resources, the banking sector, nevertheless, shows no inclination to deal with its underlying structural flaws in a serious matter, an insight that caused former president of the ECB Jean-Claude Trichet, in an interview of April 23th 2018, to declare that the banking sector is at present in a worse shape than it was in 2008.[237]

One of the most harrowing illustrations of the neo-liberal anti-solidarity principle in the recent past, has probably been the fate of Greece in the aftermath of the financial crisis of 2007–2008.

Being a member of the European Economic Community since 1981, it appeared that Greece, like some other South-European countries,[238] has been less able to adapt to the dictates of economic neo-liberalism determining the European policy, causing that Greece, especially in the wake of the financial crisis of 2007–2008, had come in very severe financial problems. Since said crisis, Greece became reliant on financial "support" from certain supra-national organisations such as the European Union and the IMF, for which it was however forced to pay an extremely high price. This high price literally refers to the very high interest rates imposed to Greece regarding its foreign debt (which has been much higher than the interest applied to countries with less financial problems), and in a more figurative sense, to the high remediation measures to which the successive Greek governments have been sub-

[235] The fact that states are willing to bail out banks is for Chomsky an argument to hold that there is, in fact, not a free market system in place:

> Every time there is a crisis, the taxpayer is called on to bail out the banks and the major financial institutions. If you had a real capitalist economy in place, that would not be happening. Capitalists who make risky investments and failed would be wiped out. But the rich and powerful do not want a capitalist system. They want to be able to run the nanny state so when they are in trouble the taxpayer will bail them out. The convention phrase is "too big to fail." (See Chomsky and Polychroniou (2017), p. 153.)

[236] Chomsky and Polychroniou (2017), p. 153, speaking of "socialism for the rich" and "capitalism for the poor".

[237] De Waard (2018).

[238] Compare this to the recent events in Italy.

jected and who have condemned large parts of the Greek population to a life of poverty.[239]

In light of its previous far more tolerable attitude towards the practices of capitalism,[240] it is hence highly remarkable to finish this Section by mentioning that even the Catholic church (through the Congregation for the Doctrine of the Faith) has recently been pointing out that[241]:

> it is impossible to ignore the fact that the financial industry, because of its pervasiveness and its inevitable capacity to condition and, in a certain sense, to dominate the real economy today, is a place where selfishness and the abuse of power have an enormous potential to harm the community.

4.11 Some Further Thoughts on the Impact of Economic Neo-liberalism on the Academic World

In the light of what has been argued before in this book, it cannot come as a surprise that under the rise of economic neo-liberalism, also the organisation of (higher and university) education,[242] has been subjected to the goals of (unbridled) capitalism, or otherwise put the free markets.

This observation can clearly be illustrated with a (short) summary of the evolutions of the academic system during the past years.

A debate, which is probably as old as the universities themselves, relates to the question on what the goals academic education, and by extension higher education in general should focus.

For a very long time, the answer to this question sounded that university education should mainly aim at contributing to the development of both knowledgeable and critical minds, thus focusing on general development and critical thinking.

It is in this regard very typical that the university education model has grown from philosophical and religious schools from Classical Antiquity, with as one of its central themes the study of the role of man within the universe.

Since the foundation of the first European Universities of modern history, this approach of the academic education model has been determining the outlook of most (Western) universities, and by extension these of the rest of the world.

With the rise and breakthrough of capitalism as the predominating economic system, this approach towards universities has gradually changed in a thorough manner, where universities over time have been reduced from institutions for criti-

---

[239] Kuntz et al. (2015), pp. 9–13, esp. p. 11. See also Nicolson (2015), pp. 68–101.

[240] See Byttebier (2017), p. 313, n° 282.

[241] Congregation for the Doctrine of the Faith (2018), n° 14.

[242] This subject matter obviously is close to the heart of the author of this book, as he is both active in the academic sector himself and in this capacity has been a first hand witness of the destructive impact the implementation of the neo-liberal idea good, in the course of his academic career, has had on the academic sector.

cal research and education to, in modern times, institutions which are mainly aimed at delivering technical expertise and specialisation in different areas and where the intent of free and critical research has gradually made way for an emphasis on output which is usable in economic life, next to the training of labour forces which are as directly as possible employable in the capitalist machinery.[243]

Along with this, and again on a global scale, the financing model of universities and other institutions for higher education is becoming to an ever growing extent adjusted to the American model, implying that the financing of these institutions mainly by means of government funds is making place for models of private financing[244] (a transition which in the European context, especially in countries with a much higher government involvement than in the USA, is far from running smoothly and/or in a simple way).

Especially since the so-called European "Bologna Declaration" of 19 June 1999, which in essence is an action plan mainly inspired by the ideas of economic neoliberalism as applied to the academic world, this evolution has condemned the outlook of the European university landscape, where the extreme expectation is that universities should, at the lowest cost possible, produce the maximum possible economic output, both in the field of the annual number of diplomas to be delivered, as in the field of the quantifying of scientific research output which needs above all to be usable for economic purposes.[245]

---

[243] In this context, see the vision of Margaret Thatcher herself (see Thatcher (1993), pp. 597–598) which, due to many neo-liberal interventions, has since then been realised in most European countries.

See also Anonymous (2015c), pp. 6–11, esp. 6:

> Governments want top-class universities because the modern economy is driven by human capital. The goal is to nurture people who will create intellectual property and clusters of high-tech companies similar to those around Stanford and Cambridge.

[244] Anonymous (2015c), pp. 11–12; Anonymous (2015b), p. 12.

[245] In the so-called "Prague communication" of 19 May 2001 it is, for instance bluntly mentioned that one of the main goals of university education is to offer a framework for a lifetime of learning "in order to strengthen the economic competitiveness" (see http://europa.eu/legislation_summaries/education_training_youth/lifelong_learning/c11088_nl.htm (last consulted on June 16, 2018).

Even so, in the communication of Leuven and Louvain-la-Neuve of 28 and 29 April 2009, the employability of fresh university students on the (capitalist) labour markets has been mentioned as the central topic, where it was announced that:

> the interested parties need to collaborate in order to increase the initial qualifications, to renew the schooled professional population and to improve the provisioning, accessibility and quality of career and work guidance. Furthermore traineeships in the context of learning programs and on-the-job-trainings are more encouraged. (See http://europa.eu/legislation_summaries/education_training_youth/lifelong_learning/c11088_nl.htm. last consulted on June 16, 2018).

See especially under point 2 of the latter communication:

> student-centred learning and mobility will help students develop the competences they need in a changing labour market and will empower them to become active and responsible citizens.

Obviously education should also be useful, albeit the excessive emphasis of "economic usability" (in order to provide enterprises with a permanent flow of the quickest possible usable specialised labour forces which need to generate the highest possible profit in the shortest term possible) has strongly shifted away the universities from one of their most original missions to encourage critical reflection and re-sourcing within and for the benefit of society.

In the mean time, it is at the very least highly debatable if the Bologna Declaration has been the success the European Union wants its citizens to believe it was.

On the contrary, from an academic point of view, many critical voices have been raised in this regard.

For instance Paul Verhaeghe has rightly pointed out that as a result of the abovementioned evolution, in the timeframe of one generation, the academic world has changed in a fundamental manner, causing that (young) academics barely have any influence on their career path, but on the contrary are to an ever growing extent delivered to the mercy of an often invisible administration that has to ensure that they generate sufficient output in order to merit their mandate.[246]

What Verhaeghe describes is basically a typical illustration of what has already in the past been referred to by Erich Fromm as "a process of dehumanisation" to which capitalism has wilfully brought humanity, and which, especially since and due to the neo-liberal Bologna Declaration also has started determinating the activities of the (European) universities.

It is, hence, hardly surprising that in a study organised by "Education international" in 2014, Belgium, next to a number of other Western European countries, has been explicitly mentioned as one of the countries where a worrisome decrease of academic freedom can be observed.[247] An analysis of the higher education system in Flanders that was conducted by the OECD (in 2014) has similarly shown that the

---

Furthermore, the 13th point of this communication emphasizes the immediate employability of graduating university students:

> With labour markets increasingly relying on higher skill levels and transversal competences, higher education should equip students with the advanced knowledge, skills and competences they need throughout their professional lives. Employability empowers the individual to fully seize the opportunities in changing labour markets. We aim at raising initial qualifications as well as maintaining and renewing a skilled workforce through close cooperation between governments, higher education institutions, social partners and students. This will allow institutions to be more responsive to employers needs and employers to better understand the educational perspective. Higher education institutions, together with governments, government agencies and employers, shall improve the provision, accessibility and quality of their careers and employment related guidance services to students and alumni. We encourage work placements embedded in study programmes as well as on-the-job learning.

[246] Verhaeghe (2011), pp. 22–23.

Verhaeghe hereby convincingly argues that this evolution has especially been caused by the introduction of several neo-liberal inspired quantitative evaluation systems (as these prevail since and under the rule of the abovementioned Bologna Declaration).

[247] http://www.ehea.info/Uploads/%281%29/EI%20report%20Bologna%20ministerial%202012.pdf (last consulted on June 16, 2018).

Flemish higher education system is more elitist than ever before in history, even to the extent that one can barely qualify this education system as still being of a democratic nature.[248]

Even renowned American journalists have in the recent past reported that the situation of many European countries is a mess.[249]

It may be even more worrysome that the academic world is feeding this growing elitism even more. As a result, getting an academic education threatens to become (again and/or even more) a mechanism supporting the ever increasing polarisation between the rich and the poor within society.

At the same time, the historical assignment of universities is step by step reduced from institutions conducting scientific research out of a critical mindset in order to share their findings with a public of students, and, by extension, with society in general, to technical schools educating professionals who can be easily employed by the entrepreneurial world and where, to a growing extent funded by private capital, scientific research can only still take place on the condition that it benefits the interests of large capital.[250]

It may be as worrysome that similar findings occur as regards a number of institutions in other sectors of societal life, such as institutions for medical care, primary education and high schools, institutions providing social care and youth care…[251]

4.12 The Ruin of the Planet's Eco-System

To conclude with a final striking illustration of the consequences of (unbridled) capitalism, this Sect. 4.12 will hereafter address the subjection of the (moral) value of respect for the environment to the capitalist profit principle, as it has in recent times emerged in the form of the so-called "climate debate".[252]

---

[248] As regards Belgium, see http://www.oecd.org/edu/Belgium-EAG2014-Country-Note.pdf (last consulted on June 16, 2018).

[249] Micklethwait and Woolridge (2014), p. 121.

[250] See also Chomsky (2017), p. 67.

[251] See Verhaeghe (2011).

One can but express the hope that, at the very least, the following vision that in 2018 has been expressed by the (Catholic) "Congregation for the Doctrine of the Faith" will ever get through to the European universities in order to finally start some elementary public debate about the foregoing:

> In this regard, it is particularly desirable that institutions such as universities and *business schools* both foresee and provide, as a fundamental and not merely supplementary element of their curricula of studies, a formational dimension that educates the students to understand economics and finance in the light of a vision of the totality of the human person and avoids a reductionism that sees only some dimensions of the person. An ethics is needed to design such formation. The social doctrine of the Church would be a considerable help in this connection. (Congregation for the Doctrine of the Faith 2018, n° 10).

[252] Amesz (2012), p. 159.

This theme can be introduced with an ironic remark on how the powers that be deal with the subject in full accordance with the most idiotic principles of unbridled capitalism.

In the context of the so-called "Climate treaty"[253] by which the global community tries to deal with the climate change issue, an annual climate conference takes place aiming at preventing the (further) undesirable impact of human activities in general and of industrial activities more specifically on the climate.

Reference can in this regard be made to the earlier quoted remark of Galbraith that when a state (or another government) establishes a commission to study a problem, the laissez faire, laissez passer-principle in general is in place, as such commissions mostly work for such a long time that, whenever they present the outcome of their findings, the problems they researched have either lost public interest or, since then, more pressing problems have arisen which need a similar postponement approach.[254]

The climate conferences held so far, going from the one in Copenhagen of 2009 up till the one of Bonn of 2018, can hardly be called successful, with as main cause for their basic failure: the unwillingness of the global economic system driven by the neo-liberal pursuit of profits principle to compromise on certain of its strongly polluting production and transportation techniques, regardless of their disastrous effect on the environment.[255]

In other words, the somewhat "ironic" observation can be made that, periodically, strongly attended conferences take place, more often than not in exotic and through this very attractive locations from a touristic point of view, above all appealing on the services of the highly polluting airport sector. This has been going on for years already without there being a noteworthy output that would secure the protection of the environment in the long run.

Already in 1992 (again) Galbraith indicated that the refusal to engage in a true climate policy is a perfect illustration of the blind faith governments all over the world have in the neo liberal "laissez-faire, laissez-passer"-principle holding that, by doing nothing, everything will turn out fine in the end.[256]

It is at the very least remarkable that policy makers and captains of industry are still assuming that the climate change can be tackled by resorting to mainly financial contributions which Western countries (still need to) make to poor countries.

---

[253] See "UNFCCC"—"United Nations Framework Convention on Climate Change" of May 9th 1992.

[254] See Galbraith (1992), p. 20, already quoted in footnote 15 of Chap. 2.

[255] In this context, John Dejaeger bluntly held that:

> vier vijfde van de wereldbevolking geen boodschap heeft aan betekenisloze klimaatovereenkomsten en gewoon doorgaat met het verbranden van steenkool en olie. (freely translated: "four fifths of the world population is not involved with the meaningless climate agreements and just continues with the burning of coal and fossil oil".) (See Dejaeger (2014), p. 89.)

[256] Galbraith (1992), p. 23.
Phrased in a more blunt manner: Rand (1992), p. 37. See also Bell (1996), p. 187.

Meanwhile, there is still no concrete approach to combat climate change and the consequences hereof are getting more and more tangible by the day.

It even seems that since the former American candidate for Presidency and winner of the peace Nobel price Al Gore, in 2006, managed to touch the world conscience with his documentary movie "An inconvenient truth"[257] not much has been achieved to reduce global warming,[258] as Al Gore to a large extent has confirmed himself in the sequel to said documentary "An Inconvenient Sequel: Truth to Power" (2017).

It hereby seems that a large part of the human race, and certainly of its policy makers and other leading figures, hardly realizes that the (relative) success of the "homo sapiens" as one of the dominant life forms on earth has been achieved mainly by the very favourable climate conditions of the "Holocene" (the geologic era from about 11,700 years ago until now), basically being a (relatively mild) period where the climate became warmer than in the predecessing period, the last ice age, and by the grace of which homo sapiens has been able to thrive.[259]

It remains an open question what will happen to this human race in case of a drastic climate change as being predicted in certain of the more pessimist climate change forecast models.[260]

4.13 The Dazed Human Being

Already for almost 2000 years, the Gospels of Jesus Christ preach that "the Sabbath was made for man, not man for the Sabbath" (see Mark, 2:27; see also Mark, 3: 4–5).

This saying that is attributed to Jesus Christ in general implies that systems of societal order, amongst which legal rules, should, in principle, be serving humanity and especially attribute as much as possible to make people happy.[261]

As history shows, during a large part of the Middle Ages, at least the official theoretical clerical viewpoint on socio-economic processes was, as much as possible, based on this starting premise. Official (Catholic) church teaching thus learned

---

[257] Gore (2013a), p. 496.

[258] Stiglitz (2006), p. 166. See also Hazenberg (2013), p. 137.

[259] Amesz (2012), p. 61.

[260] See for instance https://www.climateprediction.net/ (last consulted on June 16, 2018).

[261] Compare this to how Stiglitz has defined the overall purpose of the economy:

> The purpose of economic activity is to increase the well-being of individuals, and economic structures that are able to do so are more desirable than those that do not. (See Stiglitz (2002), p. 9.)

See, similarly Congregation for the Doctrine of the Faith (2018), n° 6.

that economic processes had to be considered as a means of establishing Gods Kingdom on earth, and not as a goal on their own.[262]

As of the seventeenth and eighteenth century, certain ideological movements, first rationalism in general[263] and later on newly developed economic disciplines based upon rationalism, such as economic liberalism (the predecessor of economic neo-liberalism) more specifically, would over the course of but a few centuries only, succeed in turning around this premise completely and in shaping the presently prevailing societal model where a blind obedience to socio-economic processes has completely been elevated to an absolute life goal, and where the aim of achieving happiness for the (average) human being has been turned into a factor of no relevance whatsoever, at the highest only to be pursued in one's so-called "private life".[264]

This artificial division of human life in a "professional" part and a "private" part already in itself is a striking example of the high extent to which unbridled capitalism, as shaped by the doctrines of economic liberalism and later on in history economic neo-liberalism, holds the Western part of the human race completely in its grip. People in poor countries, where the struggle for survival is even more fierce, do not even have that luxury.

Furthermore have the doctrines of economic liberalism and economic neo-liberalism also in numerous other fields of societal life advocated several even more far-reaching value-reversals in comparison to the earlier in history prevailing approaches from the world of philosophy and religion.

It has even been convincingly argued[265] that the doctrines of economic liberalism and economic neo-liberalism have succeeded in qualifying the historical value of "altruism" to be "evil", and to elevate "selfishness", "egoism" and "greed" to be the basic virtues man should strive for, making it hardly surprising that in present-day societies, practically all systems of societal life have become based on these dictates of egoism, selfishness and greed.

---

[262] These theories culminated, for instance, in the writings of Saint Thomas Aquinas (1225–1244).

[263] It is remarkable that in the writings of the twentieth century mystic Maria Valtorta (1897–1961), Jesus Christ has been quoted on declaring that rationalism has been one of the main causes for the decline of Christian faith in the Western world:

> See, My soul: There are few things that I condemn as severely as this rationalism which rapes and desecrates and kills Faith -- I say Faith with a capital, in order to say true Faith, absolute, regal Faith. I condemn it as My assassin. It is this very rationalism which kills Me in hearts and which prepares and has prepared very sad times for the Church and the world. I have cursed other things. But none will I curse as this. It has been the seed from which have come other poisonous doctrines, and others, and still others. It has been the treachery which opens the door to the enemy. It has in fact opened the doors to Satan who has never reigned as much as now, since rationalism reigns.But it is said: 'When the Son of man will come, He will not find faith in hearts'. Therefore rationalism does its work. I will do Mine. (See http://www.bardstown.com/~brchrys/Ratunlsm.html; last consulted on June 16, 2018.)

[264] See especially the already before in this book quoted insights of Erich Fromm.

[265] See for instance Harari (2014), p. 348 a.f.

One of the results of this turnabout of the moral values has been that the ideal of profit pursuing has since then become prioritised in almost all domains of societal order, where everyone and everything have to be measured in terms of its financial profit or its financial cost.

For a long time already, this principle does not only dominate the economic domain, but has in an increasing manner also started dominating the operation of governments, noteworthy as regards the providing of public services, but also in the field of providing social care.

This reality is not only to be witnessed in a macro-economic context, but, on the contrary, has become more and more present in the daily life of every human being.

For those who are born in a poor family in a poor country, the reality of unbridled capitalism will hence in most cases imply a life sentence of poverty. For the average person in the Western world, the effects of capitalism are often not (yet) that dramatic, albeit that also for the Westerner, it is to be feared that as the socio-economic order is to an ever growing extent getting based on the principles of the uncorrected free market, the world is becoming a tougher, harsher and nastier place to live in, and this especially for those belonging to the poor classes of society.

Meanwhile, the understanding that under the dictates of economic neoliberalism, making capitalism unbridled again mainly leads to a polarization of global society into a small group of rich and very rich people and a much larger group of poor and very poor (see Sect. 4.7), is breaking through, making the continuing success of neo-liberal thinking thus the more difficult to grasp.

Albeit in the traditionally richer countries, an individual may still have a theoretical freedom of choice as regards the extent to which he wants to participate in the harsh logic of the unbridled fee market processes, this freedom of choice is shrinking day by day to the extent that the global dismantling of the welfare state model is gradually progressing under the influence of the doctrines of economic neo-liberalism.

The Western man who still would be willing to examine his conscience on his own participation to the unbridled capitalist processes, can perhaps start by asking himself the following questions:

- In which sector am I professionally active?
- How high is my income?
- From which economic activities am I getting this income, and what is the effect of these activities on other values, going from the environment in a broad sense of the word to the impact on the fate of other people?
- ...

An entrepreneur (or CEO or capital provider of a company) may add to these the following questions:

- How much am I paying my staff? And how am I treating them generally speaking?
- How much am I willing to pay my (less powerful) suppliers?
- At which price does my company create products or services?

- How am I behaving fiscally and para-fiscally?
- What profit am I making and how do I spend it?
- …

The answer to this type of questions (obviously next to numerous others) will provide a further insight in the extent to which an individual assists in shaping the capitalist world, where it can obviously be observed that, as more and more individuals increasingly adhere the principles of unbridled capitalism (or: free marketism), as has been the case over the past decades, it will become thus the more difficult for other individuals to avoid being subject to their devastating influence.

The answer to these type of questions may probably also indicate that, to the extent that someone has gathered more wealth and fortune, his participation to the principles and processes of unbridled capitalism will probably have been proportionally higher than his care for poorer members of society.

In any case, all of this has a particular impact on every person's day-to-day life, with as a constant factor that, day by day, egoism, selfishness and greed continuously increase. It may probably even more troublesome that, in many cases, people purportedly successful on an economic level, have no shame to admit that they are selfish, egoistic and greedy, sometimes even taking much pride in such a life attitude.

Even so, the kind of people who have succeeded in generating the most wealth and fortune are to a growing extent considered as modern-day heroes, a factor that is often strengthened by the media (and the social media), translating into a high social regard for the rich and very rich, where the methods and mechanisms by which their high wealth and fortune have been built are rarely questioned any more.

That (unbridled) capitalism has created economies of scale and a-never-before-in-history-to-be-witnessed economic growth may be obvious. In the present world, this is even so predominantly the case that it has gradually overshadowed all other dimensions of human life, a finding which has been brought to the attention already decades ago by Herbert Marcuse in his book "the one-dimensional human being"[266] and which, since then, has been confirmed repeatedly by other research.[267]

Anthropologist Pinxten has in the recent past argued that the (assumed) success story of the neo-liberal model is in reality mainly leading to an increasing level of inequality,[268] whereby (the common) man is systematically "stripped" of everything that makes life valuable and interesting, especially his ethic, religious, esthetical and political dimensions, and whereby the meaning of life itself gets evermore devaluated, and finally only the economic sphere remains as a dictatorial system in which any given individual will only be able to function as either a producer or consumer-labourer.

---

[266] Marcuse (1991).

[267] Skidelsky and Skidelsky (2013), p. 66.

[268] Chomsky and Polychroniou (2017), p. 154.

According to Pinxten, everything that is happening on earth is in this way increasingly left to the invisible hands of the free market, resulting in a societal almost perfectly mirroring Huxley's "Brave New World".[269]

It is obviously very questionable if this all contributes to the happiness and the wellbeing of the moderate man.

Meanwhile, most of us who are not belonging to the so many richest people on earth and who moreover have not yet ended up in poverty ourselves, are so busy undergoing our many socio-economic roles which (unbridled) capitalism is enforcing upon each of us, that only a lucky few may still find the time to fundamentally reflect about this.

In the current, so-called "secularised" society model that is one of the many other faces of (unbridled) capitalism and where the deploying of a religious, spiritual or even generally ethical life attitude is to a growing extent considered as non-appropriate, or at the very best as a sheer waste of time for crazy people,[270] deeply reflecting on these fundamental questions of life is not an easy venture any more.

On the contrary, life-consuming roles in the capitalist game taking all the time and energy of the average human being, especially the one belonging to the working class, are the roles of: "lifetime employee",[271] "eternal consumer", "chronically-to-be-milked tax payer", "chronical (bank) borrower", in many cases even "eternal mortgage taker", from a certain age, "constant medical patient" (or, better put: "eternal consumer of pharmaceutical products"), but even so, in many cases, that of a selfish, egoïstic and greedy creature eternally competing with others.

Through all of this, the role of a human being has mainly been turned into the metaphorical wolf to others and who perceives all other human beings mainly as a wolf to himself.

Meanwhile, the social dimension of life gets for many people to an ever increasing extent limited to the virtual realm of electronic data exchange, which only benefits the marketing and advertising industry, and where everyone can rejoice on "twitter", "facebook", "Instagram" or the likes to see how anyone else in the world is doing, or what another persons' unreflected opinion about whatever irrelevant topic may be.

---

[269] Ongenae (2014), pp. 44–45, esp. p. 44.

[270] See, for instance, Luyendijk (2015), p. 89, as regards the vision on ethical values of bank sector employees.

[271] See Galbraith (2004), p. 21:

> It remained for the often perversely articulate John Maynard Keyes to doubt on the pleasure of toil. He quotes the words of an aged charwoman that were preserved on her tombstone. She had just been released from a lifetime of work:
>
> Don't mourn for me, friends,
> Don't weep for me, never,
> For I'm going to do nothing,
> For ever and ever.

References

Achenbach J (2015) Tijd van Ongeloof. National Geographic, March 2015 (Dutch edition), pp 120–137

Amesz B (2012) Aan de knoppen van het klimaat – Het hele verhaal over de opwarming van de aarde. Fontaine Uitgevers BV, Hilversum

Anderson S (2015a) Off the deep end: the Wall Street bonus pool and low-wage workers. http://www.ips-dc.org/deep-end-wall-street/. Last consulted 16 June 2018

Anderson S (2015b) Wall Street bonuses and the minimum wage. http://www.ips-dc.org/wall_street_bonuses_and_the_minimum_wage/. Last consulted 16 June 2018

Anonymous (2013) Vlaamse onderwijs blijft top, maar vertoont dalende trend (article of 3 December 2013). http://www.hln.be/hln/nl/957/Binnenland/article/detail/1751614/2013/12/03/Vlaamse-onderwijs-blijft-top-maar-vertoont-dalende-trend.dhtml. Last consulted 16 June 2018

Anonymous (2014) Reality check: Eurozone debt looks unsustainable. The Economist, 26 October 2014

Anonymous (2015a) The world is going to university. The Economist, 28 March 2015, Special Report, pp 11–12

Anonymous (2015b) Mis and match. The Economist, 28 March 2015, Special Report, pp 12–14

Anonymous (2015c) Top of the class. The Economist, 28 March 2015, Special Report, pp 6–11

Anonymous (2018a) Gap between rich and poor reaching its peak. http://www.dailymirror.lk/article/Gap-between-rich-and-poor-reaching-its-peak-148737.html. Last consulted 16 June 2018

Anonymous (2018b) Jaarboek 'Armoede in België' bijzonder kritisch voor responsabiliserend armoedebeleid. https://nl.metrotime.be/2017/10/11/news/jaarboek-armoede-in-belgie-bijzonder-kritisch-voor-responsabiliserend-armoedebeleid/. Last consulted 16 June 2018

Baeck L (1972) Groei en onkruid in de welvaartstaat. De nederlandsche boekhandel, Antwerp

Bahree M (2016) The world's richest 1% just got a lot richer, while everyone else didn't. https://www.forbes.com/sites/meghabahree/2016/01/19/the-worlds-richest-1-just-got-a-lot-richer-while-everyone-else-didnt/#2889fa1e6b6a. Last consulted 16 June 2018

Bell D (1996) The cultural contradictions of capitalism. Basic Books, New York

Berend I (2006) An economic history of twentieth-century Europe. Cambridge University Press, Cambridge

Bernstein WJ (2004) The birth of plenty. How the prosperity of the modern world was created. McGraw-Hill, New York

Bijlo E (2014) Nobelprijswinnaar Joseph Stiglitz: 'Europese landen moeten belastingen gelijktrekken'. Knack, 19 November 2014

Bonner W, Wiggin A (2006) Empire of debt. The rise of an epic financial crisis. Wiley, New Jersey

Brockmans H (2014) Vermogenswinstbelasting treft vooral middenklasse. Trends, 27 November 2014

Brook Y, Watkins D (2012) Free market revolution – how Ayn Rand's ideas can end big government. Palgrave Macmillan, New York

Bruckner P (2002) Misère de la prospérité – la religion marchande et ses ennemis. Bernard Grasset, Paris

Bulman M (2018) Food bank use in UK reaches highest rate on record as benefits fail to cover basic costs. https://www.independent.co.uk/news/uk/home-news/food-bank-uk-benefits-trussell-trust-cost-of-living-highest-rate-a8317001.html. Last consulted 16 June 2018

Bush G (2010) Decision points. Crown Publishers, New York

Byttebier K (2015) Nu het gouden kalf verdronken is. Van hebzucht naar altruïsme als hoeksteen voor een Nieuwe Monetaire Wereldorde. Maklu, Antwerp

Byttebier K (2017) Towards a new international monetary order. In: Byttebier K, van der Borght K (eds) Economic and financial law & policy – shifting insights & values, vol I. Springer, Cham

Chomsky N (2017) Requiem for the American dream. The 10 principles of concentration of wealth & power. Seven Stories Press, New York

Chomsky N, Polychroniou C (2017) Optimism over despair. On capitalism, empire and social change. Penguin Random House UK

Clune M (2013) On masters of the universe: Hayek, Friedman, and the birth of neoliberal politics (article of 26 February 2013). http://lareviewofbooks.org/review/what-was-neo-liberalism#. Last consulted 16 June 2018

Coffey B (2012) The four companies that control the 147 companies that own everything. https://www.forbes.com/sites/brendancoffey/2011/10/26/the-four-companies-that-control-the-147-companies-that-own-everything/#432d7061685b. Last consulted 16 June 2018

Cohen D (2008) Towards a new modus operandi of the international financial system. In: Serra N, Stiglitz JE (eds) The Washington consensus reconsidered. Oxford University Press, Oxford

Coleman-Jensen A, Rabbitt M, Gregory C, Singh A (2017) Household Food Security in the United States in 2016. ERR-237, U.S. Department of Agriculture, Economic Research Service

Congregation for the Doctrine of the Faith – Dicastery For Promoting Integral Human Development (2018) Oeconomicae et pecuniariae quaestiones – Considerations for an ethical discernment regarding some aspects of the present economic-financial system. http://www.vatican.va/roman_curia/congregations/cfaith/documents/rc_con_cfaith_doc_20180106_oeconomicae-et-pecuniariae_en.html#. Last consulted 16 June 2018

Crédit Suisse Research Institute (2015) Global Wealth Databook 2015. http://publications.credit-suisse.com/index.cfm/publikationen-shop/research-institute/global-wealth-databook-2015-en/. Last consulted 16 June 2018

Crédit Suisse Research Institute (2017) Global Wealth Report 2017. http://publications.credit-suisse.com/tasks/render/file/index.cfm?fileid=12DFFD63-07D1-EC63-A3D5F67356880EF3. Last consulted 16 June 2018

Cullen D (2009) Columbine. Old Street Publishing Ltd, London

Daisy M (2015) Amazon's brutal work culture will stay: bottom lines matter more than people. https://www.theguardian.com/commentisfree/2015/aug/22/amazon-brutal-work-culture. Last consulted 16 June 2018

De Boeck E (2014) Begrotingsbesparingen in België, Frankrijk, Nederland and Eurozone. Hoeveel al gerealiseerd, hoeveel moet nog volgen. Trends, 20 November 2014

De Waard P (2018) De schuld is gegroeid, het systeem kwetsbaar, het besef ontbreekt. De Volkskrant, 23 April 2018

Dejaeger J (2014) Het eenzijdige debat over de klimaatopwarming – Het westerse fundamentalisme. Trends, 11 December 2014, p 89

Dévoluy M, Lang D, Mathieu C, Mazier J, Sterdyniak H (2011) La politique économique and Europe. In: Les Économistes atterés, Changer d'économie! Nos propositions pour 2012. Les liens qui libèrent, Paris

Diks J (2013) Voor iedereen op aarde $70 miljoen als Rotschild zijn vermogen deelt. http://www.gewoon-nieuws.nl/2013/11/voor-iedereen-op-aarde-70-miljoen-als-rothschild-zijn-vermogen-deelt/. Last consulted 16 June 2018

Engelen E (2011) After the great complacence. Oxford University Press, Oxford

Feeding America (2014) Hunger in America 2014 (national report). Feeding America, Chicago

Feeding America (2017) 2017 Feeding America annual report. A hunger for a brighter tomorrow. Feeding America. Chicago

Ferguson N (2009) The ascent of money. A financial history of the world. Penguin Books, London

Food and Agriculture Organization of the United Nations (FAO) (2014) The State of Food and Agriculture – innovation in family farming FAO, Rome

Foucault M (2008) The birth of biopolitics – lectures at the Collège de France 1978–1979 (trans: Burchell G). Palgrave Macmillan, New York

Foucault M (2013) De geboorte van de biopolitiek. Boom, Amsterdam

Friedman M (1993) Why government is the problem. Hoover Institution on War, Revolution and Peace, Stanford University

Fritz-Krockow B, Ramlogan P (eds) (2007) International Monetary Fund handbook. Its functions, policies and operations. International Monetary Fund (IMF). http://www.imf.org/external/pubs/ft/imfhb/eng/handbook.pdf. Last consulted 16 June 2018

Fromm E (1979) The sane society. Routledge & Kegan Paul, London

Galbraith JK (1974) The affluent society. Penguin Books, Middlesex (first edition of 1958)

Galbraith JK (1987) Economics in perspective – a critical history. Houghton Mifflin Company, Boston

Galbraith JK (1992) The culture of contentment. Houghton Mifflin Company, Boston

Galbraith JK (2004) The economics of innocence fraud. Houghton Mifflin Company, Boston

Galbraith JK, Salinger N (1978) Almost everyone's guide to economics. Penguin Books, London

Gates B (2014) Why inequality matters (article of 13 October 2014). https://www.gatesnotes.com/Books/Why-Inequality-Matters-Capital-in-21st-Century-Review. Last consulted 16 June 2018

Geysels J (2014) De Schande. In: Geysels J, Vlaminck E (eds) De Schande en de Keerzijde. Van Halewyck, Leuven, pp 11–59

Gilmore G (2018) The world's super rich populations are growing but where is growth strongest? http://www.knightfrank.com/wealthreport/2018/global-wealth/new-order. Last consulted 16 June 2018

Gore A (2013a) The future – six drivers of global change. Random House, New York

Gore A (2013b) Onze toekomst. Spectrum, Antwerp

Graeber D (2012) Debt. The first 5000 years. Brooklyn and London

Haeck B (2014) Ook begrotingsalarm in Frankrijk and Italie. De Tijd, 29 November 2014

Hallerberg M, Bridwell J (2008) Fiscal policy coordination and discipline: the stability and growth pact and domestic fiscal regimes. In: Dyson K (ed) The Euro at 10 – Europeanization, power, and convergence. Oxford University Press, Oxford

Harari YN (2014) Sapiens – a brief history of humankind. Penguin Random House, London

Hartwell A (2014) Sourcing mineral resources – problems and solutions. In: Goldin I (ed) Is the planet full? Oxford University Press, Oxford

Hazenberg J (2013) De machteloze staat. Hoe globalisering en individualisering de overheid uithollen. De Geus, Breda

Ingham G (1984) Capitalism divided? The city and industry in British social development. McMillan Education Ltd., London

Keen S (2017) Can we avoid another financial crisis? http://www.dw.com/en/can-we-avoid-another-financial-crisis/a-41111841. Last consulted 16 June 2018

Knight Frank Research (2018) The Wealth Report 2018. http://www.knightfrank.com/resources/wealthreport2018/the-wealth-report-2018.pdf. Last consulted 16 June 2018

Krugman P (1994) Peddling prosperity. W.W. Norton & Company, New York

Krugman P (1998) The accidental theorist and other dispatches from the dismal science. W.W. Norton & Company, New York

Krugman P (2004) The great unraveling: losing our way in the new century. W. W. Norton & Company, New York

Krugman P (2009) The return of depression economics and the crisis of 2008. W.W. Norton & Company, New York

Krugman P (2012) End this depression now! W.W. Norton & Company, New York

Kruithof J (1985) De mens aan de grens. Over religiositeit, godsdienst en antropocentrisme. EPO, Antwerp

Kruithof J (2000) Het neoliberalisme. EPO, Antwerp

Kruithof J (2012) Het algemeen belang en de overheid. In: Jaap Kruithof – Teksten voor de toekomst. EPO, Berchem

Kuntz K, von Rohr M, Ertel M (2015) De grote plannen van de Griekse premier Alexis Tsipras. Knack, 18 March 2015, pp 9–13

Lahaye W, Pannecoucke I, Vranken J, Rossem V (2017) Armoede in België – Jaarboek 2017. Skribis, Gent

Légé P (2011) Pour une nouvelle fiscalité. In: Les Économistes atterés Changer d'économie! Nos propositions pour 2012, Les liens qui libèrent, Paris
Lipton D (2014) Fiscal policy and income inequality (speech of March 13th 2014). http://www.imf.org/external/np/speeches/2014/031314.htm. Last consulted 16 June 2018
Lloyd C (2012) What on earth happened? The complete story of the planet, life & people from the big bang to the present day. Bloomsbury, London
Loizou A (2012) Het duivelspact. Een insiderverhaal over hoe het grote geld wordt verdiend. Zuidnederlandse uitgeverij, Aartselaar
Luyendijk J (2015) Dit kan niet waar zijn. Atlas Contact, Amsterdam
Marcuse H (1968) Geweld en Vrijheid (trans: Boukema H). Politieke opstellen. De Bezige Bij, Amsterdam
Marcuse H (1991) One-dimensional man. Routledge, London
McCarthy N (2014) There are more billionaires in the world than ever. http://www.statista.com/chart/2750/there-are-more-billionaires-in-the-world-than-ever/. Last consulted 16 June 2018
Meredith M (2014) Alle rijkdom verdwijnt. Knack, 26 November 2014, pp 100–103
Michielsen T (2014) Slimme fabrieken moeten Vlaamse industrie redden. De Tijd, 19 November 2014, pp 13–14
Micklethwait J, Woolridge A (2014) De vierde revolutie. Op zoek naar de overheid van morgen. De Bezige Bij, Antwerp
Minten D (2015) Wij krijgen te weinig waar voor ons geld. De Standaard, 3 March 2015, p 18
Moerman B (2014) Regering moet vijf miljard extra besparen. De Standaard, 6 December 2014
Moore R (2018) Statistics of poverty and waste that shame our society. http://www.edp24.co.uk/features/how-did-food-banks-become-the-new-normal-1-5490716. Last consulted 16 June 2018
Nicolson A (2015) Twee steden één Europa. National Geographic (editie Nederland-België), March 2015, pp 68–101
OECD (2013) Crisis squeezes income and puts pressure on inequality and poverty. OECD
Ongenae C (2014) Antropoloog Rik Pinxten roept op tot verzet – Het oude kastendenken is terug. Knack, 26 November 2014, pp 44–45
Oxfam (2014) Even it up – time to end extreme inequality. Oxfam GB, Oxford
Oxfam (2015) Issue briefing: wealth: having it all and wanting more. Oxfam (www.oxfam.org), January 2015
Oxfam (2016) An economy for the 1%. How privilege and power in the economy drive extreme inequality and how this can be stopped. Oxfam briefing paper. https://www.oxfam.org/en/research/economy-1. Last consulted 16 June 2018
Oxfam (2017) An economy for the 99%. It's time to build a human economy that benefits everyone, not just the privileged few. Oxfam briefing paper (January 2017), https://d1tn3vj7xz9fdh.cloudfront.net/s3fs-public/file_attachments/bp-economy-for-99-percent-160117-en.pdf. Last consulted 16 June 2018
Paelinck G (2014) Vlaanderen is er niet in geslaagd onderwijs te democratiseren (article of 9 September 2014). http://deredactie.be/cm/vrtnieuws/binnenland/1.2082666). Last consulted 16 June 2018
Pauli W (2014) De kloof in de democratie – Het historische belang van Thomas Piketty. Knack, 10 December 2014
Piketty T (2014) Capital in the twenty-first century. Belknap Press, Cambridge
Pizzigati S (2012) The rich don't always win. The forgotten triumph over plutocracy that created the American middle class, 1900–1970. Seven Stories Press, New York
Plato (1987) The Republic. Penguin Books, London
Rand A (1992) The virtue of selfishness. New American Library (a division of Penguin Group), New York
Rand A (2008) Capitalism: the unknown ideal. New American Library (a division of Penguin Group), New York

Raspoet E (2014) Steuntrekkers zijn luieriken, zeggen ze. Maar overleven in armoede is keihard werken. Knack, 22 October 2014

Ripple W (2017) World scientists' warning to humanity: a second notice. http://scientistswarning.forestry.oregonstate.edu/sites/sw/files/Warning_article_with_supp_11-13-17.pdf. Last consulted 16 June 2018

Ronse T (1992) Rambo op lemen voeten – Amerika in de jaren negentig. Kritak, Leuven

Roser M, Ortiz-Ospina E (2017) Global extreme poverty. https://ourworldindata.org/extreme-poverty. Last consulted 16 June 2018

Sachs J (2011) The price of civilization: reawakening American virtue and prosperity. Random House, New York

Sen A (1977) Rational fools: a critique of the behavioral foundations of economic theory. Philos Public Aff 6(4):317–344

Sen A (2009) The idea of justice. Allen Lane, London

Simon H (2009) Hidden Champions van de 21e eeuw. Successtrategieën van onbekende wereldmarktleiders. A.W. Bruna Uitgevers, Utrecht

Skidelsky R, Skidelsky E (2013) How much is enough. Money and the good life. Penguin Books, London

Smith A (1979) An inquiry into the nature and causes of the wealth of nations, as republished by Campbell RH, Skinner A, Todd WB (eds). Clarendon Press, Oxford

Soros G (1999) Het liberale fundamentalisme bedreigt de democratie. In: De Meyer R, Vervliet E (eds) Klinkende munt – De bokkensprongen van het grote geld. Year 24, n_ 3. Noord-Zuid-Cahier

Steger M (2013) Globalization. A very short introduction. Oxford University Press, Oxford

Stiglitz J (2002) Employment, social justice and societal well-being. Int Labour Organ 141(1–2):9–29

Stiglitz J (2006) Making globalization work. Penguin Books, London

Stiglitz J (2010) Freefall. Free markets and the sinking of global economy. Allan Lane (an imprint of Penguin Books), London

Stiglitz J (2012) The price of inequality. Allen Lane (an imprint of Penguin Books), London

Stiglitz J, Chariton A (2005) Fair trade for all – how trade can promote development. Oxford University Press, Oxford

Streeck W (2013) Buying time. The delayed crisis of democratic capitalism. Verso, London

Streeck W (2017) How will capitalism end? Essays on a failing system. Verso, London

Syrmopoulos J (2015) Iceland just jailed dozens of corrupt bankers for 74 years, the opposite of what America does. https://thefreethoughtproject.com/icelands-banksters-sentenced-74-years-prison-prosecution-u-s/. Last consulted 16 June 2018

Taylor-Gooby P (2013) The double crisis of the welfare state and what we can do about it. Palgrave Macmillan, Houndmills

Temmerman J (2014) Beeld dat te veel Vlaamse jongeren hoger onderwijs volgen, klopt niet (article of 9 September 2014). http://www.standaard.be/cnt/dmf20140909_01258428. Last consulted 16 June 2018

Thatcher M (1993) The downing street years. HarperCollinsPublishers, London

The Bologna Declaration of 19 June 1999 – Joint declaration of the European Ministers of Education. http://media.ehea.info/file/Ministerial_conferences/02/8/1999_Bologna_Declaration_English_553028.pdf. Last consulted 16 June 2018

Treanor J (2015) Half of world's wealth now in hands of 1% of population – report. The Guardian, 13 October 2015

Turner L (1973) Onzichtbare wereldmachten – multinationale ondernemingen en de wereld van nu. Boekenuitgeverij Keesing, Amsterdam

Turner A (2016) Between debt and the devil. Money, credit and fixing global finance. Princeton University Press, Princeton

United Nations Development Programme (2014) Human Development Report 2014. UNDP, New York

Van Cauwelaert R (2014) De schuldfactuur van de banken. De Tijd, 29 November 2014

Van Haver K, Blomme P (2014) Europees knipperlicht voor Belgische begroting. De Tijd, 29 November 2014

Van Meerhaeghe MAG (1985) Museum of grootmacht. De identiteitscrisis van Europa. Lannoo, Tielt

van Oudheusden J (2012). Een kleine geschiedenis van Amerika. Bert Bakker, Amsterdam

Verhaeghe P (2011) De neo-liberale waanzin – Flexibel, efficiënt en… gestoord. Uitgeverij VUBPRESS, Brussels

Vinton K (2017) Amazon CEO Jeff Bezos is the richest person in the world – again. https://www.forbes.com/sites/katevinton/2017/10/27/amazon-ceo-jeff-bezos-is-the-richest-person-in-the-world-again/#1d976c011948. Last consulted 16 June 2018

Walker M, Hartley C (2012) The culture shock of india's call centers. https://www.forbes.com/sites/morganhartley/2012/12/16/the-culture-shock-of-indias-call-centers/#6d38b18c72f5. Last consulted 16 June 2018

Webster T (2017) Undercover reporter reveals 'brutal' working conditions at Amazon. http://www.theblaze.com/news/2017/11/27/undercover-reporter-reveals-brutal-working-conditions-at-amazon. Last consulted 16 June 2018

Whitham G (2016) Inequality and division in the UK – ensuring the economy works for everyone. https://policy-practice.oxfam.org.uk/blog/2016/09/inequality-and-division-in-the-uk%2D%2Densuring-the-economy-works-for-everyone. Last consulted 16 June 2018

Wolffers I (2011) Gezond. Over de mens, zijn gezondheid en de gezondheidszorg. Nieuw Amsterdam Uitgevers, Amsterdam

Chapter 5
Looking for Inspiration to Escape the Chains of the Free Market

5.1 General Plea for a (More) Altruistic Approach of the Socio-Economic Order

It goes without much further saying that the vision on (unbridled) capitalism as the determining economic system on earth that has been described above, is not an optimistic one.

However, such a pessimism is justified when one realizes that, on a global scale and to an increasing extent, the several "correction mechanisms" to unbridled capitalism which, in the period after World War II, especially in the Western world, were installed in order to give capitalism a more humane outlook, have become under a severe pressure during the past years as a result of the efforts of the doctrines of economic neo-liberalism to make capitalism "unbridled" again.

Hence, the time is more than ripe for a thorough reflection on the future of the socio-economic order[1] which should become more based on the basic understanding that especially three capitalist processes are above all responsible for the many negative consequences of capitalism, amongst which the high degree of poverty that many people suffer, the increasing polarisation between the rich and the poor on a global scale and the high debt burden to which many countries (next to private persons) have become subject during the past decades.

The first of these mechanisms is the mechanism of private creation of money by the private banking system which is responsible for the fact that whoever—and this can be an individual, an enterprise or a state—is "poor", will have to pay a high price for accessing newly created money. The result of this aforementioned private money creation system (see also above, Sect. 2.1) is namely that (private) banks (and their underlying shareholders) have been able for centuries already to enrich

[1] Compare the similar plea of Stiglitz (2002), esp. p. 27.

K. Byttebier, *The Unfree Market and the Law*, Economic and Financial Law & Policy – Shifting Insights & Values 2,
https://doi.org/10.1007/978-3-319-97382-1_5

themselves to the detriment of the rest of the economic players and above all to the poor within society.

A solution to this problem could be to (again) bring money creation in the public domain, which could be part of a new monetary world order where the supply of money would rely on considerations of altruism and justice, rather than on the creeds of egoism, selfishness and greed that are currently driving the underlying dynamics of private money creation and through this, of the prevailing monetary system(s).[2]

The second of these mechanisms is the self-evidence through which capitalism relies on the shameless exploitation of others. Under the dictates of capitalism, those who want to become rich should do that by selling products and services, preferably in the highest quantities possible, on a continuous basis at the highest possible price, while at the same time keeping their costs as low as possible. More often than not, tax systems of a lot of countries even further encourage such entrepreneurs to conduct their business under the form of a company or corporation.

Unfortunately, the remuneration for the working individuals (which are necessary to enable the production and trade of goods and services) are part of the cost structure of this kind of enterprises, implying that the principles of capitalism incite them to keep the remunerations for working individuals as low as possible. This basic principle of capitalism is in traditional economic literature referred to as the so-called "Iron Law of the Wages"[3] and has been determining socio-economic relations for ages already. (See already above, in Sect. 2.4.)

Admittedly, within the so-called welfare states or care states, this "Iron Law of the Wages" has in the past been adjusted through all types of labour protecting legal measures, but these achievements of the welfare state model are in the globalised economy more and more contested due to the interference of the doctrines of economic neo-liberalism. To the extent that such labour protecting measures increase the cost of labour, there is moreover a high risk that, within a globalised world, a shift of economic production will occur to those countries where such labour protecting measures are not, or to a far lesser extent, available.

As a result, the group of countries where such protecting mechanisms still prevail are in a globalised context faced with a difficult choice: (1) either to witness the dismantling of their (manufacturing) industry; or (2) to make the latter more and more specialised (assuming that the countries where such labour protecting measures are not, or to a lesser extent, present, themselves will not succeed in realising such a high degree of specialisation, an assumption which more and more seems to be of an illusory nature); or (3) to simply abandon their labour protecting measures.

Driven by the neo-liberal dictate that markets should be as free as possible, more and more countries have resorted to the latter choice, implying that, as regards the policy goal of protecting labour, a true race to the bottom has been engaged.

---

[2] See the plea in the Chapters 4 and 5 of Byttebier (2017).

[3] The term is surprisingly not that much used in contemporary economic literature any more, even though the economic principle it denominates prevails at present stronger than ever. (See also Stiglitz (2002).)

An alternative approach to this catch 22 dilemma will call for a global approach that would strive for the establishing of a global equalisation of labour protection measures at a (sufficient) minimum level.

Obviously, this will only be possible by states entering labour protection treaties, where the question arises if (a sufficient amount of) countries will ever be willing to enter into such treaties, albeit that only in case such a willingness will occur, it will be possible to diminish the shameless exploitation of the working human being as is presently happening under the dictates of (unbridled) capitalism.

The third set of fundamentally unjust mechanisms on which capitalism is based, are the prevailing mechanisms of government financing.

As has already been elaborated upon earlier on in this book, the (central) governments of most countries in the world are primarily financing themselves by means of raising taxes (next to similar forms of "duties", such as, for instance, so-called social security contributions). Besides, especially during the past decades, many countries have massively resorted to (additional) credit as a means of dealing with the deficits they are facing (and this instead of aiming at establishing effective and more just tax systems and/or the dismantling of intrinsically useless government expenditure, such as, for instance, expenses of a military nature).

As has also been demonstrated in the previous chapters of this book, the way a lot states apply said mechanisms of capitalism in practice in itself bears witness of many further manifest injustices. For instance, in most capitalist countries, income taxes are relatively much more imposed on the poor and middle classes, while the rich classes (and the enterprises they own/run), often remain relatively undisturbed. (See above, under Sect. 4.6.)

Another as disturbing factor is that the techniques of credit financing by states have become an important source of income for the financial sector, resulting in a biased system of government funding where (big) financial institutions have high stakes in making states chronically dependent on credit financing, as the interests of these credits are ultimately funded by the average tax payer and this for the sole benefit of a small financial elite owning and running the financial institutions.

Phrased differently, it should be clear that, in most countries, also the systems of state financing help shaping the present-day unjust world in which the rich are continuously getting richer and the poor and middle classes either stagnate or get poorer.

A solution to this problem could exist in creating an alternative system of government financing, where one would abandon the model of government funding based on taxing the poor and middle classes and on financing deficits through debt funding, and instead opt for a model where states would be assigned allocations out of a system of public money creation by a supra-national monetary institution. Such a system could be part of international agreements establishing a new monetary world order, as proposed by the author of this book in one of his other books "Towards a New International Monetary Order".[4]

---

[4] See Byttebier (2017).

Obviously the question arises to which extent the world community would ever be willing to make such a fundamental swift in monetary and, moreover, general economic practices.[5] The most important challenge in this regard will most probably be to finally start using the instruments of democratic governance to control and direct the economy to meet both the individual and collective needs of people, rather than those of an impersonal market mechanism (that itself only benefits the rich and very rich).[6]

In order to find further answers to the question what further principles should lie at the basis of the urgently needed reforms to the prevailing socio-economic order,[7] additional inspiration can (and should) be found in several other fields of human interest than economics in the strict sense of the word, including for instance religious and philosophical systems, but certainly also in socio-economic ideologies other than those of economic liberalism and economic neo-liberalism that have been dominating the debate for decades already.

Some of these are already part of the world heritage for thousands of years, although they have hardly been given the attention they deserve as a source of inspiration for establishing a more just and fair socio-economic (and, by extension, societal) order.[8]

Because the content of some of these philosophical and religious doctrines have in the past been misunderstood, it may useful to first continue this chapter of this book with paying some attention to their content, especially as regards the topics of a socio-economic nature.

5.2 On the Question Whether or Not a New World Socio-Economic Order with a Humane Face May Still Be Considered Conceivable

5.2.1 Introduction

It should be clear that, in the course of the past three to four centuries, it have mainly been the theories and doctrines of economic liberalism and economic neo-liberalism that have determined the outlook of the global economy.

---

[5] See again Byttebier (2017), Chapters 4 and 5.

[6] See Stiglitz (2002) in Polanyi (2001), p. xxxviii.

[7] Reference can, again, be made to the call for such changes to the prevailing socio-economic order, made by Stiglitz (2002), esp. p. 27.

[8] Compare Congregation for the Doctrine of the Faith (2018), n° 8:

> It must be noted that the systems that give life to the markets—before deploying the anonymous dynamics made possible by ever more sophisticated technologies—are in fact founded on relationships that involve the freedom of individual human beings. It is evident therefore that the economy, like every other sphere of human action, "needs ethics in order to function correctly — not any ethics whatsoever, but an ethics which is people-centred."

Under the dominance of these theories and doctrines, practically all other lines of thinking, especially those advocating more societal justice and fairness, next to a higher degree of altruism within the socio-economic order, have become almost completely marginal.

We shall illustrate this finding hereafter by especially exploring how some of (the most important of) these other thought systems have fared under the implementation of the doctrines of economic neo-liberalism during the past decades.

5.2.2 *The Sad Fate of Communism*

It has of course to be acknowledged that, especially during the period from 1917 until the end of the 1980s, attempts have been undertaken to base societies and economies on so-called Marxist thinking.[9]

However, especially the application of the ideas of Marxism within the communist countries during said period, barely have aimed at implementing the economic ideas of Marx himself (or, in addition, those of other, similar so-called left-thing scholars), but on the contrary, soon have degenerated into other types of totalitarianism with similar effects as those of unbridled capitalism itself.[10]

The fact that during the first half of the twentieth century communism broke through in a number of countries, furthermore soon met a severe opposition by the powers of capitalism.

Among the biggest antagonists of the teachings of Karl Marx, and by extension "left" thinking in general were, for instance, the Catholic Church, which stigmatised communism, and by extension socialism, as the source of all evil, next to many Western political parties and the governments composed by them, not least in the purportedly "open-minded" USA (and this notwithstanding its lip-service to the principle of "freedom of expression"), where especially in the 1950s, under the impulse of the former American senator Joseph McCarthy, a true witch-hunt for alleged communists was unleashed.[11]

The economic isolation in which at the time newly established communist countries were driven by a hostilely responding world, in combination with internal problems of organising a democratic society, would further contribute to the failure of implementing the ideologies of Marxism. Given this huge resistance to said

---

[9] See especially Marx' main book "Das Kapital". See Marx (1982/1983) (edition in three volumes).

[10] One can, for instance, refer to the philosophy of Levinas who refers to these systems (amongst which capitalism itself) as to systems of "Ontology".

[11] Galbraith (1979), p. 32.

It is in this context very illustrative that the lip service to the freedoms of opinion and expression as they are preached in a lot of the capitalist countries of that time, would not preclude that even a famous artist as Charlie Chaplin, got accused of being a communist and had to flee from the USA to spend the rest of his days in exile in Switzerland, in a similar way as Jewish people had been driven out of nazi-Germany in the period before World War II. (See http://nl.wikipedia.org/wiki/Charlie_Chaplin (last consulted on June 16, 2018).)

ideas, it did not come as a surprise that, already by the end of the 1980s and the early 1990s, most communist regimes appeared to have failed.[12]

5.2.3 *Ideological and Other Factors Contributing to the Decline of the Welfare State Model in the Western World*

In the Western World, especially socialist and socio-democratic ideologies would in the period after World War II lead to different corrections to unbridled capitalism in the form of, amongst others, legal measures aiming at the protection of labour, next to different systems of social protection and of care for the weak within society.

Presumably, the favourable economic situation of the 1950s, when Western Europe was rebuilt out of the ashes of the second World War, helped creating the (economic) climate for introducing these types of correction systems to unbridled capitalism, albeit the fear that communist parties would get a too strong grip on the Western world has also been indicated as an important factor which would motivate the powers that were to allow some modifications to unbridled capitalism.

The building, upon this variety of ideological systems, of more just welfare states would however meet its end as of the 1970s onwards, and even more so during the 1980s, when the doctrines of economic neo-liberalism got more and more established and implemented in the Western world.

A number of factors further contributed to the bankruptcy of social thinking within the Western capitalist countries.

In short, the severe economic problems caused by the oil crisis of the 1970s[13] a.o. confronted the Western entrepreneurial world with a strong increase of the prices for energy. This obviously endangered the profit margins of said entrepreneurial world and hence would turn into a first reason why a former present willingness of large capital to share some of its wealth with the working classes, would as soon become at peril.

---

[12] As of today, it nevertheless remains an open question to what extent capitalism which has taken the place of communism in the countries involved, has brought that much more salvation and improvement for their population, where it can be observed that, even in the unified Germany, the territories of the former D.D.R. still face numerous disadvantages within the socio-economic context. It is perhaps even a bigger mystery what the exact socio-economic situation is in the group of countries that have emerged from the ashes of the collapsed Soviet-Union, albeit that the information that is available in the West does not leave room for much optimism.

See, in this regard, Stiglitz (2002), p. 26:

> The interplay between politics and economics has been most dramatically in Russia, where the privatization process resulted in the devastation of the middle class, and the creation of huge inequalities and an oligarchy which, if it seeks to establish a rule of law, will use its wealth and power to try to ensure that that rule of law favours itself.

[13] Which obviously does not mean that capitalist economies did not repeatedly face several other problems as well.

As a further consequence of the oil crisis of the 1970s, the governments of many Western countries themselves faced more and more problems to keep their budgets in balance. As a result, expenses for public services (such as public education, but later also justice) and for establishing systems of social security, became highly targeted. For instance in the USA, the neo-liberal/conservative economist Milton Friedman would, in that period, bluntly write that the problem of public spending is not that government does not dispose of enough financial means, but that there is simply too much government spending for utterly useless purposes, such as public education and social care.[14]

The neo-liberal answer to the problem of the waning economies of the Western countries has since then been (and has continued to be) that the role of government within the economy should be as little (or inexistent) as possible, which in many countries has led to an ever increasing dismantling of states (amongst which a systematic dismantling of public services, with the exclusion of military expenses, and of social care mechanisms, or, put more briefly, of the welfare state model).

As has been elaborated upon earlier in this book, the ideas of economic neo-liberalism would in the Western world also get a powerful grip on a large part of the public opinion, and lead to the installation of neo-liberal governments all over the world that, since then, have mainly aimed at dismantling the welfare state model even more through different measures of "(neo-)liberalisation" and "deregulation" of the economy in order to free it from the impact (deemed disastrous) of the above-mentioned mechanisms of correcting unbridled capitalism.

5.2.4 *The General Decline of Left-Wing Thinking*

Socialism (or, by extension, left-wing thinking) has (so far) not succeeded in providing a significant answer to the neo-liberalisation of the world socio-economic order as described so far.

Obviously, within the USA, communist, socialist or left-wing thinking has never had any significant impact, partly even because of its identification with "demonic" practices.[15]

---

[14] Friedman (1993).

[15] See Smith (2014):

> Communism was very dominant through much of the 20th century, controlling countries in every region of the world. For a few years, the Throne of Satan mentioned in Revelation 2:13, was housed in the old communist Soviet Union. And though the fall of the Berlin Wall and the collapse of the Soviet Union suggest communism was on its way down, recent events show it may not be as dead as we hoped.

See also Stiglitz (2010), p. 197:

> In America, words like socialism, privatization, and nationalization carry with them emotional baggage that makes clear thinking difficult.

In Western European countries, left-wing political parties have probably made the mistake to be too willing to participate in governments which, from a socio-economic viewpoint, mainly had a neo-liberal agenda. It can, for instance, not be neglected to what extent the policies of the European Union are influenced by the doctrines of economic neo-liberalism. This in itself is one of the (many) consequences of the (intrinsically undemocratic) dynamics characterizing European policy making, leaving European member states in many domains no other choice than to implement the dictates of the European Union within their national, legal systems.

For instance, the legal tool of "(European) directives", in essence a method of aristocratic/corporatocratic policy making, has during the past decades turned out to be a very fruitful method of executing the European neo-liberal agenda. Also the monetary policy of the ECB (and by extension the ESCB) has strongly assisted in subjecting the European economy to the principles of economic neo-liberalism; reference can, for instance, be made to the stringent (neo-Friedmanian) budget logic of the ESCB which has turned monetary policy in yet another tool of dismantling the welfare state.

Otherwise put, to the extent that, in many European countries, socialist parties have participated in governments that have assisted in executing the neo-liberal European agenda, they have themselves contributed to the ongoing increasing neo-liberalisation of the European socio-economic order, and this is probably why they have lost a large part of their political credibility.

From a more academic point of view, reference can again be made to the insights of Erich Fromm who has (rightly) argued that socialism (like communism), in spite of all high-flow rhetoric, in reality has been constructed against the background of traditional materialistic thinking. According to this author, in order to disguise this materialistic interpretation of socialism, extracts out of context of the writings of Marx had become modified to political platitudes without any true societal impact any more, let alone the force to make social changes.[16] This insight helps explaining why the ideas of socialism have lost a lot of their appeal to the large masses.

Notwithstanding the foregoing, one can furthermore but observe that while the lower social classes in many countries are paying an increasingly higher price for the failure of the capitalist economic model,[17] the world is more and more heading for an increasing polarisation between the rich and the poor and an increasingly growing part of the world population are living in poverty. (See above, under Sects. 4.7–4.9.)

[16] Fromm (2014), p. 193.

[17] For a recent example, see De Rijke (2015), pp. 68–75; Kuntz et al. (2015), pp. 9–13.

5.2.5 A Grimm Prognosis of the Future

At least in light of the foregoing observations, the question more and more becomes whether the only thinkable approach towards organising the socio-economic order is indeed the one dictated by economic liberalism and economic neo-liberalism, coming down to a blind adoration of the free market mechanism, as it is shaping a world in which the "everyone for himself" principle is gradually determining all aspects of societal organisation.[18]

An affirmative answer to this question basically comes down to the fact that one can but assume that the human being, as economic liberalism and economic neo-liberalism preach, is indeed eternally condemned of being as egoistic, selfish and greedy as possible.

Continuing this approach could furthermore imply that, in a somewhat near future, states should better be repealed and that large enterprises and their rich capital providers would best withdraw in (literally) fortified cities, or other secluded areas, and mobilise large private militias to protect their wealth from the rest of the world population. The rest of the world population could then, largely abandoned to itself, be condemned to spend the rest of their lives outside of these demarcated areas and to have as sole life purpose to provide a "pool" of the cheapest possible work forces for the rich classes. As the inhabitants of the poor areas will not be provided with means of education or health care, let alone other public services or (social) care mechanisms, because this is not possible in a neo-liberalised world economy, their life conditions will most probably be appalling and, due to a lack of access to education, there will not be any vertical mobility at all. At most, the rich classes might still be willing to pay for an elementary law enforcement in order to prevent that the discontent poor classes would disturb life in the rich areas all too much.

It is hardly a coincidence that the paragraph above seems to reflect recent science fiction literature or movies.[19]

Nevertheless, authors such as Micklethwait and Woolridge have already pointed out that in the USA, the construction of what they call "gated communities", provided with own security officers, health services and schools is already taking places for a long time now.[20]

---

[18] Compare Chomsky (2017), p. 65.

[19] See, for instance, the Mexican-Argentinian-Spanish movie, "La Zona" from 2007 of director Rodrigo Plá. (See http://www.imdb.com/title/tt1039652/; last consulted on June 16, 2018.) See similarly the motion picture "Elysium" (2013) (see https://www.imdb.com/title/tt1535108/; last consulted on June 16, 2018).

[20] Micklethwait and Woolridge (2014), p. 122.

See also Donnell (2017), mentioning how some of the (very) rich of the planet (who have caused most of the problems the world faces today because of their behaviour of acting in accordance with an ideology that holds that one should behave as egoistically, selfishly and greedily as possible) are at present buying such secluded areas in New Zealand. As Donnell has pointed out:

> Recent reports in Bloomberg and the *New Yorker* suggest dozens, if not hundreds, of Silicon Valley futurists are secretly prepping for doomsday. These apocalypse-fearing survivalists

Other sources similarly refer to cities in poor countries in which enclaves of areas populated by the (very) rich are surrounded by ghetto's in which poverty and misery predominate.[21]

The question even becomes whether the global establishment of such an extreme selfish society can still be prevented.

If this still would be possible, it will most probably only be the case to the extent that humanity becomes prepared for a resolute reversal in the choices of values which lie at the base of the current neo-liberal, socio-economic order. This obviously implies abandoning the idea that man has to behave as selfishly, egoistically and greedily as possible and that, instead, (more) room for altruism and solidarity would be created.[22]

> are stocking up on canned goods. Investing in solid gold currency. Keeping helicopters fuelled up. Purchasing apartments in nuclear bomb-proof bunkers. And if a SHTF ("shit hits the fan") scenario unfolds, many have an escape route already in mind: south, south, all the way to New Zealand.
>
> If you want to ride out the apocalypse, there's no better place. When the rest of the world is imploding, isolation – often thought to be New Zealand's greatest weakness – becomes its biggest strength. The island nation is too far away to invade, separated from its nearest neighbour by the 2,800km width of the Tasman Sea. Its most serious predator is the possum. If it's a political revolution you fear, the climate is a far cry from the intractable antagonism of the US. One recent parliamentary debate featured Māori party leader Marama Fox singing a light-hearted politicised version of Santa Baby, accompanied by her colleague on ukulele. Everyone stood up to applaud afterwards.
>
> Tech leaders seem particularly smitten by New Zealand's reputed immunity to Armageddon. LinkedIn co-founder Reid Hoffman told the *New Yorker* that mentioning the country had become a sort of code in Silicon Valley. "Saying you're 'buying a house in New Zealand' is kind of a wink, wink, say no more," he said.
>
> Speaking at the World Economic Forum in Davos, Robert Johnson, president of the Institute for New Economic Thinking, said that he knew "hedge-fund managers all over the world who are buying airstrips and farms in places like New Zealand because they think they need a getaway".
>
> One entrepreneur estimated 50% of his peers have bought property in New Zealand or elsewhere. Figures from 2016 show that US buyers were second only to Australians in the amount of New Zealand land they purchased. In the year to June last year, 1,288 Americans gained residence in New Zealand, while another 11,873 were issued work or student visas. (See Donnell (2017).)

[21] Galbraith (1992), p. 131; Meredith (2014), p. 103.

[22] See furthermore Stiglitz (2002), p. 27:

> If we, as an international community, are to promote equitable, sustainable and democratic development – development that promotes societal well-being and conforms to basic principles of social justice – we must reform the international economic architecture. We must speak out more loudly against policies which work against the interests of workers. At the very least, we must point out trade-offs, we must insist on democratic processes for determining how economic decisions are made. We have remained silent on these issues for too long – and the consequences have been grave.

See, in a similar sense, Congregation for the Doctrine of the Faith (2018), n°6:

> For this reason, the competent and responsible agents have the duty to develop new forms of economy and of finance, with rules and regulations directed towards the enlargement of

Knowing that in the past, many have advocated altruism and solidarity as basic principles of societal construct, it is worth spending some time exploring some of the most important doctrines in which this approach has had a central place. These doctrines stem from different areas, such as mainly (albeit not exclusively) the domains of religion and philosophy, next to economy itself.

5.3 Socio-Economic Thoughts Stemming from the Religious Domain

5.3.1 The Doubtful Success of the Modern-Day Religion of Economic Neo-liberalism

A version of the Hindu myth of "Parashurama", the sixth avatar of the Supreme Lord Vishnu, starts with a complaint by "Bhūmī-Devī", the goddess of the earth, about the behaviour of the Kshatriya's, the cast of rulers who were shamelessly exploiting her. This makes the Supreme Lord Vishnu incarnate as the avatar Parashurama, with as mission to end this exploitation of "Mother Earth". This in its own turn entails a fierce battle which goes on through many generations of Kshatriya's, and which finally leads to the entire extinction of the (former) cast of the rulers.

It may appear that, since then, a new similar cast of rules has arisen which evenly shamelessly indulges in exploiting the earth and its resources, namely the cast of modern-day "capitalists".

The triumph of capitalism as the predominating socio-economic system, is essentially also the triumph of greed, egoism and selfishness. It is, therefore, not surprising at all that the historical rise of capitalism has gone hand in hand with an increasing secularisation of societies in the countries who have adopted capitalism as their determining socio-economic system, as obviously strongly advocated by liberal and neo-liberal thinking. This has, moreover, hardly been a coincidence, as the value scale of liberal thinking is fully opposed to the value scale of most religious systems, especially when going back through the basic idea good of the latter.

> the common good and respect for human dignity along the lines indicated by the social teachings of the Church. (…) It is especially necessary to provide an ethical reflection on certain aspects of financial transactions which, when operating without the necessary anthropological and moral foundations, have not only produced manifest abuses and injustice, but also demonstrated a capacity to create systemic and worldwide economic crisis.

See also Cole (1937), p. 256 (on the dangers of having a society based on the principles of unbridled capitalism):

> My final moral, then, is that unless we want the world to convert into armed camps of impoverished people, we must plan for plenty (…) in ways which are quite inconsistent with the retention of the capitalist system.

Neither astonishing is the fact that many contemporary authors stemming from several scientific disciplines have pointed out that economic neo-liberalism itself in this regard holds all the characteristics of a new religion which has brainwashed the minds of its disciples, implying that, in the countries where capitalism prevails, all other ideologies and religions have gradually been pushed backwards under the (at least implicit) axiom that only neo-liberal thinking itself may determine socio-economic relations.

It may even seem that, under the dictates of economic neo-liberalism, the world socio-economic order has made the choice which was left by Jesus Christ in the Gospels between a life dedicated to God, or a life dedicated to the money devil (see Matthew, 6:24), resolutely in favour of a blind adoration of the money devil.

5.3.2 *On the Difficulties of Acknowledging How the World's Leading, Traditional Religions Could Still Form a Source of Inspiration for a New Socio-Economic Order*

A good understanding of the basic messages of these world religions, most of which propose a scale of values in complete opposition to the central values of "greed", "egoism" and "selfishness" which prevail within economic liberalism and economic neo-liberalism, may nevertheless still form an important source of information for socio-economic change.

The currently largest religion in the world, which is also the most familiar to the Westerner, is Christianity.[23] In the course of its existence, Christianity has been split up in different quasi-separate religions, such as Catholicism, the different forms of Protestantism and, in Eastern parts of Europe, the orthodox churches. Each of these branches itself is the result of historical evolutions, leading to large religious movements that in modern times often but provide lip service to the underlying teachings of Jesus Christ.

This is not much different for some of the other world religions.

Those who are by nature critical towards religion, and especially those who show no willingness to explore the core inspiration source of the prevailing world religions, will, as a result, in many cases not feel any attraction to the (socio-economic) ideas they represent.

Finding any serious answer in these religions to the economic doctrines preaching an unbridled selfishness and materialism, among which especially economic neo-liberalism, is therefore not an easy task.

When, for instance, looking at Catholicism only in a superficial manner, what will mainly stand out is the extreme level of institutionalisation of a (very) rich institution that is based upon an outdated hierarchy and that is, furthermore,

---

[23] It is estimated that ±32% of the world's population is said to be Christian. (See Anonymous (2015a); Bertrand (2015), pp. 14–15.)

characterized by many discriminations, amongst others towards women and minority groups, such as homosexuals.[24] Given the immeasurable wealth which the Catholic Church, often by questionable means, has gathered over the centuries, the call it makes on an ongoing basis for more "charity" and "brotherhood" may even be considered utterly hypocrite.

Those who take a closer look at the protestant Christian doctrines may, at the socio-economic level, moreover, notice the strong inter-wovenness with conservative and (neo-)liberal economic thinking, even so raising the question how these doctrines still relate to the teachings of Jesus Christ. This is certainly the case within the traditionally capitalist countries, among which the United Kingdom itself, next to numerous of its former colonies, albeit also in the Calvinist Netherlands, a socio-economic thinking prevails where, in an even so contradictory way, an attitude towards life that is essentially selfish, is still defended under the cloak of Christian wrapping.

In other words, when comparing the current appearances of religion systems calling themselves "Christian", especially in their socio-economic dimension, with the message of Jesus Christ Himself, it may seem that they have completely betrayed the historical root of He who above all contested everything unjust, and instead have themselves contributed to establishing an intrinsically unjust, socio-economic world order.[25]

---

[24] Although one could acknowledge that, under the leadership op Pope Francis I (as of 2013), there are some small efforts being made of treating homosexuals better within Catholicism (see Duffy (2018)), be it on a very moderate scale as, basically, the Catholic church keeps on condemning any form of homosexual lifestyle (see Robertson (2018)).

As Robertson puts it:

> The Catechism of the Catholic Church (a summary of official church teaching and doctrines, the latest of which was compiled by Pope John Paul II in 1992), does acknowledge that the "number of men and women who have deep-seated homosexual tendencies is not negligible", advocating that they "be accepted with respect, compassion, and sensitivity" (Catechism 2358).
>
> (…)
>
> "Basing itself on Sacred Scripture, which presents homosexual acts as acts of grave depravity, tradition has always declared that 'homosexual acts are intrinsically disordered'. They are contrary to the natural law. They close the sexual act to the gift of life. They do not proceed from a genuine affective and sexual complementarity. Under no circumstances can they be approved" (Catechism 2357).
>
> So – homosexual acts apparently constitute grave depravity, are "intrinsically disordered", contrary to the natural law, and should never be approved. What does the church suggest these sorry individuals do? Chastity. Catechism 2359 states that "homosexual persons are called to chastity". It's there in black and white. (See Robertson (2018)).

[25] Compare to Tolstoj (2012), p. 96:

> We are astonished about how far what is called Christianity is away from what Jesus preached, and how far our lives are from Christianity. But how could things be any different with a belief teaching that all men are equal, that all men are children of God, that all are brothers and that the life of every human being is sacred, and this was preached among people who believed that God had divided people in lords and slaves, in believers and non-believers, in poor and rich. The people following the doctrine of Christ, had two choices: change the entire order of things, or change the doctrine. They chose to do the latter.

An extreme expression of such a distortion can be found in the biased opinion that Margaret Thatcher was a heroine of Christian virtue,[26] while she, in reality, in her role as government leader of the United Kingdom in the period 1979–1990, mainly conducted an economic policy aimed at making the socio-economic order of her country more selfish than ever before in history and, in doing so, has devoted her life to the establishment and enforcement of the most aggressive capitalist methods of oppression and exploitation of the UK's poorer population groups. (On some the consequences of her devastating policy, see above, under Sect. 4.7.2.)

It is impossible to grasp how this could ever be reconciled with the teachings of Jesus Christ Himself.

A similar observation may be made as regards, for instance, Hinduism,[27] which, as has already been explained in in Chap. 3 of this book, at first glance mainly seems to have contributed to an unjust societal system (as this prevails for centuries already), namely the notorious Indian caste system.

5.3.3 Justification for Still Attempting to Find an Inspiration for a More Just Socio-Economic Order in the Traditional World Religions

Those who, notwithstanding that what has been explained under Sect. 5.3.2 above, would still be willing to make the effort to dig under the surface of the abovementioned religion systems may be surprised to encounter, in each one of these religions, a line of thinking completely opposite to the currently dominating values of selfishness, egoism and greed, and will most probably reach the conclusion that, if all people in the world would make an honest effort to live in accordance with their basic teachings, the world would probably evolve to a true "paradise on earth".

The tragedy of the abovementioned religions is therefore the tragedy of humanity itself.

It hereby mainly seems that, throughout history, within each of the abovementioned religious traditions, only a limited number of people have succeeded in adopting the real underlying religious values and that, on the contrary, the institutionalised experience of it by the large masses often but witnesses the constraint of

[26] See the quote in Byttebier (2015), p. 525:

> We will remember the Iron Lady for her remarkable achievements, but more importantly she modeled a strong and clear belief in Christ and His Word, giving her courage and decisiveness in times of crisis. She left a legacy of leadership that transformed her nation and the world, inspiring many generations to come.

[27] Estimated to be practiced by 15% of the world's population (see Anonymous (2015a), p. 24; Bertrand (2015), pp. 14–15).

human kind that does not succeed in overcoming its animal impulses of own preservation and serving its own interest.[28]

This is exactly why even a but elementary investigation of the basic values of some of the abovementioned religious systems may help us in gathering the building blocks for a new societal order hardly to be neglected.[29]

It is, hence, more than worthwhile to elaborate upon some of the basic doctrines of the abovementioned religion systems, especially those who relate to questions of a socio-economic order. This exploration will start with one of the religions which is perhaps the least understood in the Western world, but which, at closer inspection, nevertheless may be one of the most valuable religious systems, namely Hinduism.[30]

5.4 On Some of the Socio-Economic Messages of Hinduism: Selfless Labour and Fulfilling One's Dharma

5.4.1 The Complexity of Hinduism

To the average Westerner, Hinduism is perhaps almost impossible to understand.

At first glance, the religious system known as "Hinduism"[31] has the appearance of a melting pot of, in some cases even conflicting myths and superstitions, populated by a magnitude of gods and other mythological figures of the rich Hindu pantheon.[32]

Through the eyes of a Westerner, it may even seem that Hinduism, within the socio-economic context, has mainly contributed to a societal order which is not that

[28] This has on many occasions been pointed out by the enlightened Master Osho, in many of his books. (See for instance Osho (2006), p. 4 a.f.)

[29] See also Sapir and Statman (2005), pp. 470–471:

> (…) thanks to its ability to act as a counterweight to the power of the state, religion makes a critical moral and social contribution to society. In the modern state, religion remains one of the last remaining forces able to fulfill this role, a role vital to the democratic play of checks and balances. Religion also contributes to the moral level of society by providing inspiration for social and moral behavior. (…) A further possible advantage of religion stems from its constant preoccupation with the major questions concerning human existence; the meaning of life, good and evil, death and immortality, and so on. By constantly raising these issues, religion plays a part in preventing society from sinking into a form of hedonistic materialism.

[30] We shall not explore Islam basically due to a personal unfamiliarity with the Islamic religion of the author, be it without expressing any value judgement on its intrinsic merits.

[31] See Das (2012), p. xxxiv:

> Hinduism is not a 'religion' in the usual sense. It is a civilization based on a simple metaphysical insight about the unity of the individual and the universe and has self-development as its objective.

[32] Tardan-Masquelier (2015), pp. 68–69.

much better than the one of Western capitalism itself. (See already above, in Sect. 3.1.2.)

The experience of Hinduism by common Westerners, especially those who wallow in the (neo-) liberal ideologies of unbridled materialism, presumably may further entail the image of the "Hare Krishna" people who, in the best case, will be considered to be a relatively harmless group of eccentrics who live at the edge of society and who, from time to time, can be seen in the streets of cities, as regularly occurs in London, chanting mantra's while dancing, or to scuff all types of books or leaflets on obscure Indian guru's to those who have been addressed by them.

It is hence hardly a coincidence that, for instance in Belgium that conducts a passive-oppressive policy against minority religions, the Hare Krishna-movement, next to other religious movements that find inspiration in Hinduism, has been stigmatised as a sectarian movement.[33]

However, those who are willing to take the effort to dig deeper into the Indian culture and, for instance, to search for the basis of the worship of Krishna as one of the perfect manifestations of the Divine, will not only discover a treasure of stories and myths which in variety and fantasy are at the very least of equal worth of those of Ancient Greek and Roman mythology,[34] but which nevertheless are much more than entertainment and, on the contrary, express a spiritual vision of life which is the perfect antipode of the values of selfishness, egoism and greed as defended by the doctrines of economic neo-liberalism.

Those having only a superficial knowledge of the Indian culture in general, and of its main religion, Hinduism, more specifically, will probably be, moreover, surprised that, in spite of the confusing magnitude of gods which are worshiped in Hindu countries, Hinduism is in essence as monotheistic as for instance Judaism and Christianity.

Within Hinduism, it is indeed assumed that there is also but One Divinity, manifesting itself in an endless number of ways and in an endless number of forms.

As regards the material world, to which the planet earth and all creatures living on it belong, everything that exists is even so but a manifestation of this Divinity (which may be referred to in different terms, such as "the (higher) Self"; the "Paramatman"…).

Also in the spiritual realms, there are several manifestations of the Divine, with the three highest appearances of the Divine being the Lords "Shiva", "Brahma" and "Vishnu".

Each of these highest Divine manifestations moreover represents certain aspects of the Divine. For instance, Shiva represents the aspect of destruction, albeit a con-

[33] See the Report published by Duquesne and Willems on behalf of the investigation committee, with the view to policy making to prevent the illegal practices of sects and the dangers the impose to society and to the individual, especially to minors (at: Belgische Kamer van Volksvertegenwoordigers, Kamer, 1996–1997, 28 April 1997, 313/7- 95/96).

[34] Compare to Osho (2017), p. 367:

> (…) the Hindus have written wonderful stories that are unequaled to this day, but it is very difficult to understand an interpret these stories.

structive destruction which creates room for renewal,[35] but also the destruction of the lower impulses and motives, amongst which obviously egoism, selfishness and greed, in each (individual) human soul itself. Brahma furthermore represents the Divine power of creation, while Vishnu is considered to be the manifestation of the conserving aspect of the Divine.

One of the permanent assignments of Vishnu is to, for the benefit of everything that exists, conserve the eternal doctrine, as this is for instance written down in the Veda's (referring to a vast series of sacred Hindu scriptures stemming from different periods in history).

Hence, when things go wrong in creation, especially when somewhere in the Universe imbalances appear, Divinity is bound to come to help and when doing so, the three highest manifestations of the Divine may take different shapes, even physical shapes in the material world. Not coincidently, it is often Vishnu who, as the custodian of existence and the order of things, comes to the rescue, which in some cases happens in the form a so-called "avatar".

5.4.2 *Rama and Krishna*

The fortunes of ten of the avatars of Lord Vishnu lie at the base of a magnitude of mythological stories, among which two of the most important epics from Indian literature (and, by extension, world literature), namely the "Ramayana" and the "Mahabharata".

Both of these epics describe the whereabouts of each one of the avatars of Vishnu having a human form (while some of the other avatars of Lord Vishnu had forms of a non-human nature).

The "Ramayana" tells the story of the avatar Rama and his companions, some of them being in their own accord a manifestation of Vishnu (for instance: Hanuman), be it in a less perfect way than Rama Himself.[36]

Next to a magnitude of other holy scriptures, myths and legends, the "Mahabharata"[37] narrates of the fortunes of Krishna, probably the most popular avatar of Vishnu and, by extension, within the Indian culture, one of the most popular manifestations of the Divine.[38]

---

[35] Given the fact that everything which exists, is constantly evolving, the Shiva-aspect from Hinduism is closely related to the Buddhist idea holding that everything that exists is impermanent and evolving.

In Ancient Greece, this idea for instance lied at the basis of the teachings of Heraclitus of Ephesus who even so held that everything is permanently changing/evolving. (See Mansfeld (2012). See also Osho (SD).)

[36] Within Hinduism, this is not a contradiction, bearing in mind that everything that exists is a manifestation of the Divine.

[37] On the beauty of the Mahabharata, see also Das (2012), p. xxxviii.

[38] See also Das (2012), p. 192.

It should, however, be clear that these scriptures offer much more than entertainment.

On the contrary, parts of these epics have brought an understanding to humanity on important spiritual doctrines, especially the different types of yoga prevailing within Hinduism.

One of the central pieces of the "Mahabharata" (which could be literally translated as "the Big World", referring to India itself, implying that the Mahabharata is, literally considered, the story of India) describes the heroic battle[39] for the throne of the kingdom belonging to the Kuru clan, between two branches of the same family, the Kaurava's and the Pandava's. When looked at it from a spiritual viewpoint, this battle reflects, in the terrestrial realm, the battle between the powers of light (represented by the Pandava's) and the powers of darkness (represented by the Kaurava's), as this battle is continuously ongoing in the material world in general, but also especially in the inner world of every human being. The latter does not only make the story of the Mahabharata the story of India, but also the story of every human being.

During the most decisive episode of said battle, the avatar Krishna is to be found at the side of the Pandava's, where He takes up the role of charioteer of Arjuna, one of the Pandavic princes.[40]

At the moment when the armies of the Kaurava's and the Pandava's line up to go to battle, Arjuna hesitates to engage, as he does not wish to fight his relatives, let alone kill them; Krishna responds by making a plea known as the "Bhagavad Gītā" (literally "the Song of the Lord"), a set of spiritual teachings which, although it is part of the Mahabharata, also leads a life of its own.

The spiritual insights contained in the "Bhagavad Gītā" even belong to the core of Hindu religion.[41]

One of the most central themes of the Bhagavad Gītā is that every human being is born with a specific, sacred task, his so-called "dharma". It is the highest duty of any human being to find out what is his dharma and to consequently fulfil it. The execution of one's proper dharma brings one to the experience of one of the highest forms of yoga, so-called "karma-yoga", or the yoga of action, where man, regardless of which action is dictated by his dharma, through selfless action, needs to strive for a better and more just world and to avoid being led by other, selfish goals, such as the pursuit of personal wealth or welfare. Every man hereby needs to fulfil his own duties, and not be tempted to take over another person's sacred duties.[42]

---

[39] At least as literal genre to be compared to the description of the battle of the Old Greeks against the Trojans, as narrated by Homer in the Ilias.

[40] It is narrated that Krishna, as avatar of the Divine who can hardly take sides, lets each of the two clans choose to be assisted in the battle by either Himself, or by His army. The Kaurava's choose to be aided by Krishna's army, while the Pandava's make the smarter choice of being aided by Krishna Himself.

[41] For some works commenting on the Bhagavad-Gita, see for instance Yogananda (2012); Bhaktivedanta Swami Prahbupada (1976).

[42] See furthermore Vivekananda (1989).

5.4.3 *Vamana*

The fact that the pursuit of personal wealth cannot be considered as a (sacred) duty on itself, even though the possession of wealth—or even the acquisition thereof through the execution of one's dharma—can become a means to fulfil one's dharma,[43] is, moreover, in an as beautiful manner, explained in a set of stories describing the fates of one of the other avatars of Vishnu, namely that of the dwarf "Vamana".

In the stories surrounding the avatar Vamana, the latter has to face the asura Bali. Bali, because of his noble intentions and notwithstanding the fact that he is a "demon" (= asura) had managed to conquer the three known worlds, namely the underworld of the asura's or demons, the world of the humans and the upper world of the deva's, or the lower gods. When they encounter, Bali, out of the nobility of his heart, grants Vamana a favour (without realising that Vamana is in fact an avatar of Vishnu, hence of the Supreme Lord). Vamana responds by asking for a piece of land of the magnitude of three of his steps. Notwithstanding warnings of his teacher who suspects a ruse of Lord Vishnu, Bali allows the requested boon, after which Vamana grows extra-dimensionally and captures the three worlds with but two of His steps. After this, there is no more room for a third step, but Vamana still urges Bali to keep his promise. Bali who wants to hold his word, then realises that Vamana is an avatar of Lord Vishnu and sees that his pursuit of material prosperity, symbolised by the conquest of the three worlds, does not lead to anything. Coming to this realisation, Bali kneels before Vamana and asks Him to make the third step on his head, thus acknowledging his subjection to the Supreme Deity.

In the same manner that Jesus Christ resisted the temptations of the devil at the beginning of His public appearance as described in the Gospels, amongst which the promise to be put in possession of the whole world (see Luke, 4: 5–8), the actions of Lord Vishnu bring Bali to the realisation that one may not expect any benefits from material wealth, albeit that in Bali's case, this insight only came after he has first effectively ruled these three worlds and, through the intervention of Vishnu, lost them again.

---

[43] Compare this insight to a recent similar vision expressed by the Catholic church:

> When human beings recognize the fundamental solidarity that unites them with all of humanity, they realize that they cannot keep only for themselves the goods that they possess. When one habitually lives in solidarity, the goods that he or she possesses are used not only for one's own needs, but they multiply themselves, also producing unexpected fruits for others. It is here that we clearly notice how sharing may not be "only the *distribution* but also the *multiplication* of goods, the creation of new bread, of new goods, of new Good with a capital "G"". (See Congregation for the Doctrine of the Faith (2018), n° 20).

5.4.4 Lessons of Hinduism on a Socio-Economic Level

These are just a few illustration on how Hinduism, in its numerous tales and myths, teaches mankind a spiritual doctrine, which in the dimension of the socio-economic order is characterised by values as "selfless labour" and the sacred duty to fulfil one's own "dharma" in order to help ensuring a better and more just world, and hereby not to fall in the trap of endlessly pursuing personal wealth, but to perceive material wealth only as a means to fulfil one's own sacred duties.[44]

The vast set of other stories of Hinduism deal with numerous other aspects of the Divine (such as the other Supreme manifestations of the Divine, Shiva and Brahma, but also the female counterparts of the three highest divine manifestations, namely Lakhsmi, Vishnu's companion, Parvati, Shiva's companion, and Saraswati, Brahma's companion, as well as the countless lower gods and goddesses, all being themselves but manifestations of the One Divinity).

The female deities often play an as important role as their male counterparts—implying that God is in essence genderless—so for instance in the both beautiful and popular myth of the creation of Ganesh (or: Ganapati), as Krishna one of the most popular deities within Hinduism. The story of the creation of Ganesh more in detail narrates how Parvati, because she wants her own servant and does not want to depend only on the servants of Shiva who ultimately only obey him, brings forth her own son, Ganesh, who subsequently, when Shiva wants to obtain access to the private quarters of Parvati at a moment when She wants to be in private, gets involved in a ruthless battle with the other male manifestations of the Divine, containing the founding message that male arrogance needs to know its limits.

Hence, those who are willing to make the effort to go beyond the first impression that Hinduism may make to the average Westerner, will be surprised get to know some of the richest spiritual doctrines in the world.

It is therefore not a coincidence that the true teachings of Hinduism have formed an important inspiration for both the thinking and the acting of many historical figures, such as Mahatma[45] Gandhi.[46]

Throughout history and up to this very date, Hindu religion moreover has produced many other saints or saintly people, some of them worthy to be mentioned because of their aspirations of creating a more just societal order, causing some of them even to become cult-figures in the West, such as Maharishi Mahesh Yogi (1918–2008),[47] probably better known as "the Guru" of the Beatles, next to A.C. Bhaktivedanta Swami Prahbupada (1896–1977), the founder of the Hare

---

[44] It is interesting to read Das' book "The difficulty of being good. On the subtle art of dharma", which in essence is the result of a profound self-reflection by the author on these matters (See Das (2012)).

[45] Literally: "Great Soul", a concept comparable to the denomination "Saint" in Christian religions.

[46] The way that Gandhi has been influenced by the teachings of the Bhagavad Gita in its own turn has formed the inspiration for the beautiful opera of Philip Glass "Satyagraha" (1980).

[47] Also appearing on the famous cover of the Beatles LP "Sgt. Peppers Lonely Hearts Club".

Krishna's who also became known as the spiritual Master of one of the Beatles, George Harrison. In a more contemporary context, reference can for instance be made to the remarkably active Mātā Amṛtānandamayī Devī, better known as Amma (1953) who on a global scale has set up many charity projects.[48]

Those who want to know more about the doctrines of selfless labour (so-called "karma-yoga") and of, through this, fulfilling one's dharma, can be further referred to the many sacred scriptures of Hinduism. For a more modern-day description of the doctrines of Hinduism, one may, for instance, consult the books of Vivekananda (1863–1902) whose dharma it has been to make the different types of yoga more accessible to the Western world.[49]

5.5 On One of the Socio-Economic Messages of Buddhism: The Control of One's Desires

Far more than is the case for Hinduism, Buddhism[50] goes back to one central inspiring historical figure, namely Siddhartha Gautama Buddha (ca. 450 a.C. tot ca. 370 a.C.), often referred to as (just) Buddha.[51]

Not so different from Hinduism,[52] Buddhism holds as one of its basic truths that everything that exists, is basically one.[53]

It will hence not come as a surprise that this observation implies a high standard of conduct which also determines socio-economic relations.

Certain Buddhist viewpoints, furthermore, hold that all problems in the world are caused by "trishna"¸ which could be translated as "thirst": (or "craving" or "desire"), in the sense of a thirst for all kinds of material possessions, power and sex. Just as is the case with a drug addict, "trishna" influences the spirit and the mind of the

---

[48] See http://amma.org/global-charities (last consulted on June 16, 2018), where already on the introductory page of this website, reference is made to the notion of "selfless action":

> Amma teaches that everyone — rich or poor — has the power to make a difference in the life of another, and that no selfless gesture is insignificant. Rather, it is the selfless actions we perform for one another that hold the keys to true peace — peace in the individual, peace in the community and peace among diverse cultures, nations and faiths. Amma's centers in many countries contribute to this humanitarian effort by inspiring people to serve selflessly in the building of a better world.

[49] See Vivekananda (1989).

[50] 7% of the world's population is estimated to practice Buddhism (see Anonymous (2015a), p. 24; Bertrand (2015), pp. 14–15).

[51] Andries (1996), pp. 62–63.

[52] According to some, Buddhism is indeed rooted in Hinduism.

Remarkably enough, within Hinduism, Buddha is considered to be one of the avatars of Lord Vishnu.

[53] In a similar way, Hinduism holds that everything that exists is a manifestation of the Divine (also expressed in the sutra: "The Creator is His Creation.")

human being who suffers from it, causing him to act accordingly. This then results in suffering which goes on continuously, as man who is caught by "trihsna" undertakes an ongoing quest to satisfy ever more new desires in order to compensate for the disappointment of not have been sufficiently satisfied in the past. This then leads to an endless circle of rebirths in a world of illusion, called "samsara", which cannot come to an end, unless when the senseless pursuit of satisfying all imaginable desires is stopped.

Hence, the right attitude to life consists of containing the pursuit of satisfaction of desires. It is crucial to do so by accepting that not a single form of desire satisfaction can ever be of such a nature that a full satisfaction will be reached. This should then lead to the awareness that, when (or as long as) unsatisfied, a desire causes pain, and when a desire is satisfied in an imperfect way, new desires will arise. In its own turn, this awareness should result in an attitude to life that one should better not desire at all.

The basic teachings of Buddhism are in a beautiful manner explained in the well-known "Dhammapada", a selection of verses which are attributed to the historical Buddha Himself.[54]

Many contemporary Buddhist authors, for instance Thich Nhat Hanh, next to, obviously, the Dalai Lama, have furthermore provided practical guidelines on how to realise this goal of releasing a life of desires in modern day-to-day life.[55]

It goes without saying that the teachings of Buddhism are entirely opposite to a number of the central values of economic neo-liberalism, such as greed, egoism, selfishness, the unbridled pursuit of wealth, consumerism and (unbridled) materialism.

For completion's sake, it needs however to be remarked that one of the most central themes of Buddhism holding that man should not surrender to his unlimited desires, is also clearly present within Hinduism, which, given the (historical) close relationship between both religious teachings, is hardly a coincidence. As said, Hinduism contains in this regard many stories of the "deva's" (= the lower gods) being engaged in battle with the "asura's" (= the race of demons). These terms usually are (also) meant as metaphors for the noble principles in every human being (= represented by the deva's) which are continuously engaged in battle with one's lower desires and instincts (= represented by the asura's). It is hereby remarkable that in most stories the deva's initially loose the battle, until the moment where the Divine comes to the rescue in one of its manifestations (mostly: Shiva, Vishnu, Durga of Kali), or, when things tend to get out of hand too much, as an avatar (i.e. embodied in the material world).

---

[54] See for instance the edition of Styles, in the translation of Juan Mascaró (see Styles (2015)). For a profound, modern-day comment, see Osho (1989).

[55] Reference should also be made to Osho who has commented on numerous holy scriptures and sutras of Buddhism, and to the French Buddhist monk Matthieu Ricard.

5.6 On Some of the Socio-Economic Messages of Christianity: Loving One's Neighbour and Charity

Just as is the case for Buddhism, Christianity also goes back to one central historical figure, known as "Jesus Christ", or also as "Jesus of Nazareth" (5 a.C.(?)-30 a.C. (?)), whose appearances as a spiritual Master are described in many sacred scriptures, such as the "official" four Gospels contained in the New Testament, next to many so-called apocryphal scriptures.

For a lot of Westerners, Christianity is the world religion with which they are most familiar, which is certainly not a coincidence when one realizes that Christianity, from a historical perspective, provides one of the main cultural reference patterns of the Western world. Regretfully, this familiarity has, in many cases, taken the shape of true aversion and this due to many reasons, such as the fact that many people still calling themselves Christians today, can hardly effectively be considered as true disciples of Jesus Christ, next to many clerical and other church related abuses with which many people have either personally been faced, or become acquainted as a result of a massive press coverage.[56]

Furthermore, the contemporary aversion towards Christianity (especially in Europe), can to a high extent be further explained by the strong secularisation to which the capitalist, socio-economic order has lead, as moreover deliberately staged during the eighteenth and the nineteenth centuries by several political and economic doctrines, among which economic liberalism, socialism and communism.

Given the further observation that, under the impulse of economic neo-liberalism, Western countries who clearly had their historical roots in Christianity, strongly prioritise values such as greed, selfishness, egoism, unbridled materialism, consumerism and the pursuit of money, it could be somewhat surprising that the historical Jesus Christ Himself has, in very clear wordings, mainly opposed a society which would prioritise said values.

Similarly to Hinduism and Buddhism, true Christianity thus provides a doctrine which, were it truly put into practice by people, or at least by people calling themselves Christians, would help turning the world into a metaphorical paradise.

In the (embryonic) economic viewpoints of Jesus Christ, at least in as far as they can be inferred from the Gospels, every man basically faces the fundamental life choice between God and the "mammon" (a term that could be translated as the "money devil"). According to Christ's teachings, it is obvious that man should choose a life in the service of God and not in the service of "the mammon", whilst it is impossible to choose for both (see Matthew, 6:24).

---

[56] See, for instance, the opinion of André Truyman:

> that being catholic, practicing catholic behaviour, catholic values and catholic authority can be so hypocrite that it can hardly be taken seriously for a large part of the population, within and outside of the church. (See Truyman (2015), p. 179).

Surprisingly in line with certain findings of modern anthropology and psychology,[57] the choice for unlimitedly pursuing money (or, put otherwise, for a life of greed), has been explained by Jesus Christ in the next verse of Saint Matthew's Gospel (see Matthew, 6:25; see also Luke, 12:22), more specifically the fear of an uncertain future.[58]

In further parts of the Sermon on the Mount, Jesus Christ furthermore held that man shall not gather treasures on earth, where they will decay from worms and moth, or be stolen by thieves, but that on the contrary, man should gather treasures in heaven (see Matthew, 6:19).

Hence, the correct religious attitude to life of the followers of Jesus Christ consists of not allowing the abovementioned fear and concern for one's own insecure future to take hold, thus avoiding the need for a life led by egoism and greed in general and money pursuit more in particular (hence: focused solely on satisfying materialistic desires), and that, on the contrary, man should be focused on achieving the Kingdom of God.

Jesus Christ left little room for misinterpretation on how a true altruistic life should look like when He held that those who have "too much" must be willing to share freely with those who do not have enough. This viewpoint can, for instance, be concluded from Jesus Christ's reply to the question of the rich young man about what to do "to become part of eternal life" (see Luke, 18:18; Mark, 10:17). Jesus Christ's answer to this question was: "You still lack one thing. Sell everything you have and give to the poor, and you will have treasure in heaven. Then come, follow me." (see Luke, 18:22[59]; see also Mark, 10:21), which in the then prevailing Jewish society that explained wealth as a gift of God, was an unexpected answer.[60]

One can, moreover, highlight the parable of the Good Samaritan, whose care for a seriously injured man Jesus Christ referred to as the ideal of altruistic behaviour, certainly in comparison to the improper, egoistic behaviour of the priest and the Levite who, in spite of their higher social and/or religious standing had walked by past the same man earlier on and had left him to his ill fate (see Luke, 10:30–37). It is very notable that in this parable, the Good Samaritan did not expect any compensation for his help to the abovementioned seriously injured man but, on the contrary, paid the innkeeper into whose care he had left said injured man, with his own money in advance while announcing that, if the sum provided would turn out not to suffice

[57] See for instance Kasser (2002).

[58] Matthew, 6: 25:

> Therefore I tell you, do not worry about your life, what you will eat or drink; or about your body, what you will wear. (NIV, at https://www.biblegateway.com/; last consulted on June 16, 2018.)

[59] NIV, at: https://www.biblegateway.com/.

[60] A similar illustration of the Christian socio-economic viewpoint can be found in a further verse from the Gospel of Saint Luke, where Saint John the Baptist is quoted on saying:

> Anyone who has two shirts should share with the one who has none, and anyone who has food should do the same. (See Luke, 3:11; NIV, at: https://www.biblegateway.com/.)

to completely cover the cost of the treatment, the Samaritan would be happy to pay the balance on his return (see Luke, 10:35).

It is hard to envision a sharper contrast between these ideals of Jesus Christ and the doctrines of (neo)liberal thinking where any human interaction, including the care for the elderly and ill, has been reduced to a mere method of pursuing money.[61]

Notwithstanding the fact that, in early Christianity, attempts were undertaken to put the abovementioned teachings of Jesus Christ into practice, not many of these seems to be left in our present-day times, especially not in the countries still considering themselves Christian. This may be explained due to the fact that, already early in the history of Christianity, the messages of Jesus Christ was gradually reduced to performing lip-service to mere rituals.[62]

Although the different protestant movements within Christianity, from the sixteenth and seventeenth century on, aimed at reacting against certain abuses within the catholic church itself, from a socio-economic viewpoint, they can hardly be called revolutionary at all. On the contrary, said protestant movements would mainly be in support of the rise of (unbridled) capitalism, and of the values of greed, egoism and selfishness it stands for. It hence should not be a surprise that the mix of early capitalist practices and protestant thinking would soon in history degenerate in some of the largest possible economic abuses in history, namely slavery and colonialism, next to numerous types of massive exploitation of the working classes. Moreover, up till today, especially within the USA, protestantism remains having a very fruitful effect on the doctrines of economic neo-liberalism and (political) conservatism.[63]

Nonetheless, Western societies have undoubtedly also been positively influenced by Christianity, with as striking examples the installation of education systems accessible to the broad public (instead of the previously prevailing systems of private education in Ancient Greece and Rome which had only been accessible to a limited number of privileged people) and of (public) hospitals and similar medical care institutions.

---

[61] See, similarly, Congregation for the Doctrine of the Faith (2018), n° 9:

> In this sense, our contemporary age has shown itself to have a limited vision of the human person, as the person is understood individualistically and predominantly as a consumer, whose profit consists above all in the optimization of his or her monetary income. The human person, however, actually possesses a uniquely relational nature and has a sense for the perennial search for gains and well-being that may be more comprehensive, and not reducible either to a logic of consumption or to the economic aspects of life.

[62] Nevertheless, there have been attempts by some of the most remarkable figures of Christianity to live in accordance with the teachings of Jesus Christ in a more pure way, albeit also these have had a modest impact all-by-all. One can, for instance, refer to the beginning of Christianity (as further elaborated on in the book "Acts" of the New Testament). Another striking example has been the movement started by St. Francis of Assisi in the twelfth century.

[63] See also Galbraith (1979), pp. 23–24.

5.7 On One of the Socio-Economic Messages of Judaism: Humility

5.7.1 A Very Brief Overview of the History of the Jewish People

Although it seems that the history of mankind, both from an individual and collective perspective, is mainly one of suffering, throughout history, the Jewish people are most probably one of the people having suffered most.[64]

The Old Testament narrates of the many occasions in ancient times that the Jewish people found themselves in situations of oppression. Even if one is to reject this evidence by dismissing the Old Testament as a mere collection of stories and myths,[65] one can hardly deny that, also in more recent history, suffering has unfortunately remained one of the central themes in the fortunes of the Jewish people.

A central fact in the documented path of the suffering of the Jewish people has undoubtedly been the so-called "Diaspora" (or even Diaspora's),[66] the purported dissemination of the Jewish people outside of its traditional home territories (Judah/Palestine). The historically best known Diaspora, which occurred due to some extreme reactions of the Roman Empire to the revolutionary acts of certain groups within the Jewish people, is the Diaspora which took place in the course of the two first centuries of our era.[67] Since then, the further history of the Jewish people has remained one of being prosecuted, albeit that the Jewish people at the same time continued to hold on to its national, cultural and especially religious identity.

Especially in Middle-Age Christian Europe, the breeding ground for the hatred towards Jews has been massive.

A socio-economic factor which has contributed to this hatred was a direct result from the so-called (medieval) "ecclesiastical interest prohibition" (see already above, in Sect. 2.1.2.) which, especially in catholic regions, has determined the economic landscape of middle age financing for more than a millennium. Going back to an edict of Louis The Pious, the Jews living in the European regions, being non-Christians, were themselves exempted from this ecclestical interest prohibition (at least as regards the providing of loans to non-Jews),[68] and there was, the other

[64] See also Galbraith and Salinger (1978), p. 101, mentioning this fact in an ironic way in response to the fact that Milton Friedman had at the time been appointed as special adviser of the government of Israel.

[65] The reality is probably such that the Old Testament mixes historical truth with a high degree of narrative freedom prevailing in older civilisations, in a way not that different from the literary genre deployed in the abovementioned classical epics from Indian literature. (See above, under Sect. 5.4.)

[66] Goldfarb (2012), p. 146.

[67] Especially the second destruction of the Temple of Jerusalem in 70 a.C. by the Roman Emperor Titus (39–81 a.C.) and a failed rebellion from 135 a.C., after which the Jews were denied access to the city of Jerusalem by death penalty, have been important, as these initiated 1800 years of Diaspora (see Goldfarb (2012), p. 146; Poulain (2015), p. 28).

[68] Evers (1999), p. 135.

way around, under the doctrines of Judaism, not an impendent for interest charging towards non-Jews.[69] As a consequence, it have been mainly Jewish lenders who lied at the root of the development of professionalised lending based on levying interest which has risen in the late middle ages.[70]

Because in a lot of Christian territories, Jews were, furthermore, denied access to many professions—with, for instance, bans on holding a government position, on possessing land, on becoming a member of merchants and traders guilds…—in many cases, there were not many professional outways other than money trade.

This helps explaining why money trade, and later on credit lending (based on the charging of interest), throughout the Christian world, got to a growing extent handled by the Jews. It is a fact that, in many European regions, this contributed even more hatred towards the Jews who hence were increasingly seen as so-called "usurers". Next to different other accusations such as the murder on God('s son); host breach; infanticide; allying with the devil; causing epidemics, such as the plague; etc., the assimilation of Jews with "money usurers" created a climate of increasing prosecutions (in most cases: going hand in hand with the forfeiture of all material possessions). Ecclestical or worldly edicts that forced the Jews to live in separate districts (so-called "ghetto's") would even further stimulate a growing breeding ground for anti-Semitism.[71]

It is therefore hardly remarkable that, in the course of the history of the West, many incidents of prosecution and even extinction of Jews have been reported, especially in periods during which other disasters occurred, such as the breakout of a contagious disease (with as a typical example the plague), or the occurrence of an economic recession (sometimes leading to periods of starvation), and the Jewish people were blamed for this. In some (Eastern-European) areas, these forms of prosecution got referred to under the denomination "pogrom".[72]

The in recent times undertaken attempt to systematically extinguish the Jewish people by nazi-Germany, also known as "the holocaust",[73] has therefore not been an unprecedented event in history, even though the size and the systematic, almost industrial approach the nazi's deployed, could be categorized as such.

---

[69] As a consequence of this, for instance in Flanders, up till the second half of the thirteenth century B.C., lenders were exclusively Jews (see Vandewalle (1976), p. 8).

[70] Evers (1999), p. 135; Bogaert et al. ([2000] 1991), p. 77; Bogaert et al. (2000), p. 77; Wieviorka (2014), p. 24.

See also Goldfarb (2012), p. 51. Goldfarb points out that borrowing money is always a humiliating activity and therefore a source for resentment. The author mentions that the small (Jewish) lenders were often at the same economic edge as the people to whom they lent the money and were often desperate if they had to legally enforce repayments and interest charges (see Goldfarb (2012), p. 51). This author also mentions that the Jewish lenders were very often forced to pay high taxes and "protection money" to the local nobility and other rich families (see Goldfarb (2012), p. 52).

[71] Evers (1999), p. 135; Wieviorka (2014), pp. 25–26.

[72] Goldfarb (2012), pp. 159 and 298.

[73] Goldfarb (2012), p. 15.

5.7.2 Humility As One of the Central Themes of Judaism

It is in light of the foregoing thus the more astonishing that ages of oppression have apparently provided the Jewish people a breeding ground for advocating humility as one of the central values of the Jewish religion.[74]

The Jewish view on humility has probably nowhere been better described than in the "Parsja Choekat 5773", a historical Jewish scripture where the relation between "no anger," "humility" and a "correct religious attitude" is drawn by means of reference to a letter of Nachmanides (also known as: Rabbi Mosjé ben Nachman[75]) to his son Nachman.

According to tradition, Nachmanides expressed the wish that his son would read said letter on a daily basis in order to develop a correct religious attitude towards life.

In the quoted letter, there has amongst others been written:

> Remember where you come from and where you are going and that during your life you are nothing but a worm; this is certainly the case after death.[76]

On the question who is truly rich, the letter moreover states the following:

> My son, understand and realise that those who regard themselves as being above others, is revolting against the Heavenly Kingdom, as he dresses with heavenly clothes, as it is written "Hasjeem rules, He wears clothes of pride." Why would one feel proud? Because one is wealthy? Hasheem makes rich or poor.[77]

For completion's sake, it should also be mentioned that the virtue of humility is not only propagated within the Jewish religion. Also in Catholicism, the topic has been raised at numerous occasions. Reference can in this regard, for instance, be made to some of the most popular catholic saints of all times, on the one hand, Saint Francis of Assisi, for whom humility was such an important central theme that he even named the monk order he created "(fratres) minores" (literally: the "inferior"

---

[74] It is estimated that only 0.2% of the world population is Jewish (see Anonymous (2015a), p. 24; Bertrand (2015), pp. 14–15).

On the (Jewish) virtue of humility, see furthermore Levinas (1988), p. 139.

[75] Gerona 1194; + Palestine 1270.

[76] http://www.nik.nl/2013/06/parsja-choekat-5773/#sthash.uwa05rKa.dpuf (last consulted on June 16, 2018).

Thanks to the findings of modern biology, the qualification of man as (a far descendant of) a worm(-like creature) which has been the far predecessor of, amongst others, the human being, can even be taken literally, which may even further highlight said call for "humility" (See Dawkins (2005), pp. 449–471). To be more precise, reference can be made to "rendezvous 26" or "The velvet worm's tale" (Dawkins 2005, pp. 449–471) and "rendezvous 27" or the "Acoelomorph flatworms" (Dawkins 2005, pp. 472–476).

[77] http://www.nik.nl/2013/06/parsja-choekat-5773/#sthash.uwa05rKa.dpuf (last consulted on June 16, 2018).

brethren),[78] and, on the other hand, Saint Theresia of Lisieux who preached the so-called "small path" ("la petite voie").[79] Humility is moreover the central theme in one of the most important writings of Christianity, namely Thomas à Kempis' "The Imitation of Christ".[80]

Obviously, the (correctly interpreted) Jewish viewpoint on humility is in direct opposition to the opposite values of pride, selfishness and greed propagated under the doctrines of economic neo-liberalism.[81]

The latter may even be clear from studying the book of Exodus, more specifically where it deals with the fortunes of the Jewish people in its exile though the desert. At the moment when the Israeli people got fed with manna, the heavenly bread God provided them, it was instructed that everyone could only take as much as needed to still his immediate hunger, but that nothing could be kept for the next day (Exodus, 16: 16). Those who proudly ignored this warning by setting manna aside for the next day, then only found worms and a horrible stench (Exodus, 16: 19–20).[82]

---

[78] Russell (1948), p. 408; Moorman (1976), p. 39.

In one of the original rules of the Order of the « fratres minores » that was issued by Saint Francis Himself, the essence of this insight has been phrased as follows:

> None of the brethren shall have any power or domination, especially among themselves. As our Lord says in the Gospel : *The princes of the Gentiles exercise dominion over them, and they that are great exercise authority over them, but it shall not be so among* the friars : *but whosoever would be the greatest among them let him be their minister* and servant ; and *he that is the greatest among them let him be as the younger.* And no one is to be called prior, but all alike shall be called Friars Minor. And let each wash one another's feet. (See Moorman (1976), p. 51).

[79] See Sainte Thérèse de l'Enfant Jésus (1957), p. 237, referring to a letter of Saint Theresia of Lisieux to Mother de Gonzague of June 1879, in which Saint Theresia explains her "small path" ("la petite voie", also referred to as "la grande épreuve intérieure").

See also Descouvemont and Loose (1991) p. 22; De Meester (1997), pp. 147–154; de Wit and Steenvoorde (2008), p. 220.

[80] For the full text (in English), see http://www.documentacatholicaomnia.eu/03d/1380-1471,_kempis._thomas,_the_imitation_of_christ,_en.pdf (last consulted on June 16, 2018).

For instance, in the second Chapter of Book 2 of "The Imitation of Christ", humility is explained as follows:

> It is the humble man whom God protects and liberates; it is the humble whom He loves and consoles. To the humble He turns and upon them bestows great grace, that after their humiliation He may raise them up to glory. He reveals His secrets to the humble, and with kind invitation bids them come to Him. Thus, the humble man enjoys peace in the midst of many vexations, because his trust is in God, not in the world. Hence, you must not think that you have made any progress until you look upon yourself as inferior to all others.

[81] See Rand (1992), p. 29. According to Rand, "pride" is the true virtue, and humility detrimental.

[82] This example is given by Fromm (2014), p. 67.

5.8 Religious Systems as an Inspiration for Socio-Economic Reform

When considering the true essence of the teachings the abovementioned religions, it is striking to observe how they all are in full opposition to those of (unbridled) capitalism as the prevailing economic system on earth that emerged out of the doctrines of economic liberalism, and later on in history economic neo-liberalism.

Opposed to the teaching of Hinduism that, especially through selfless labour, one should aim at fulfilling one's dharma, capitalism presents the principle of the unbridled pursuit of wealth that, already for ages, keeps offering an excuse for all types of mechanisms of social exploitation of the weak within society and that, on a global scale, is moulding societies into a system where a person is only still willing to do something for another person in exchange for as much money as possible.

Opposed to the central teaching of Buddhism that one should above all aim at controlling one's desires and cravings, capitalism presents the values of materialism and (unbridled) consumerism which, especially since the implementation of neo-liberal thinking as of the 1980s, have taken outrageous proportions and even are to a large extent responsible for all kinds of distortions of the world economy which have occurred since then.

Even so opposed to the value of charity as preached by Christianity, neo-liberal capitalism swears by the basic values of selfishness, egoism and greed. As a result, even institutions for medical (and other) care and (public) education, as in the early periods of Christianity originally established by Christians for reasons of practicing charity, are in the present-day neoliberal societies going through serious identity crisis's: as a result of the blind submission of these in origin most noble institutions to the dogma's of profitability and cost control, the type of care they provide are, in the most paradoxical manner, to a growing extent still only accessible to those who are sufficiently wealthy to pay (a lot) for them.[83]

[83] For an illustration, see http://m.nieuwsblad.be/cnt/dmf20150330_01606896?_section=63022519&utm_source=nieuwsblad&utm_medium=newsletter&utm_campaign=regio-nb&M_BT=1792793260018&adh_i (last consulted on June 16, 2018).

This newspaper article points out a warning from the "Association of Hospital Directors" stating that, along with the price increase for living in retirement homes, also the prices for staying in a hospital were drastically increasing. The quoted article mentions that this is a consequence of an announced saving on subsidies for building new hospitals, causing the sector to be forced to resort to private funders which obviously increases the prices in the sector.

The website of the "Association of Hospital Directors" furthermore bluntly pointed out "the Flemish Infrastructure Fund for Personal related occasions" ("het Vlaams Infrastructuurfonds voor Persoonsgebonden Aangelegenheden" (VIPA)) had no more budget for financing any new construction or renovation of hospitals. (www.ziekenhuisdirecteurs.be/nl/ (last consulted on June 16, 2018)); see for the quoted message posted on the same date: http://www.ziekenhuisdirecteurs.be/sites/default/files/Persbericht%20BVZD-whitepaper_final.pdf (last consulted on June 16, 2018).

Compare this to the ill fate of Rebecca Zeni, a former renowned model and US TV star who was eaten alive by scabies in her Georgia care home (see Rogers (2018)), illustrating how also in the USA, the living conditions in some retirement homes are dreadful.

Opposed to the value of humility stemming from Judaism, the doctrines of economic neo-liberalism preach the values of elitism and supremacy of especially entrepreneurs (and rich capital providers). Under the teachings of economic neo-liberalism, it has even bluntly been argued that entrepreneurs and capital providers are the only ones providing societal prosperity and progress, a belief dogma which justifies that an ever increasing part of global wealth has come in their hands and that there cannot be a moral duty whatsoever to share the wealth that the economic system accumulates with the less fortunate. Under the teachings of economic neo-liberalism, the latter have only their own incompetence and laziness to blame for the fact that they remain poor, and certainly not the capitalist methods of shameless exploitation and oppression.

In light of all the foregoing, it remains nevertheless surprising that, notwithstanding the impressive numbers of people who are supposed to be members of the abovementioned religions, the true basic values of these religions but had such an extremely small impact on the contemporary socio-economic processes.

A possible explanation for this observation could be the fact that economic neo-liberalism has by its own accord all the characteristics of a religion, with the majority of the population of the capitalist countries—and, at present, this concerns practically all world's countries—as its followers. Even people still perceiving themselves as "Christian", "Buddhist", "Jewish" or "Hindu", are not showing much tendency to truly live in accordance with the basic principles supporting their religion. In many cases, those adhering said religious systems, more often than not, restrict their purported religious conduct to the blind practice of rituals, while their hearts, their thoughts and their actions remain as subjected to the dominating values of egoism, selfishness and greed as those of non-believers.[84]

It even seems that, within the quoted religious frameworks, only from time to time an individual shows a sufficient amount of courage to sufficiently embrace the central values of the religious system of his choice (in both words and actions).

Oddly enough, some of the individuals having made such a daring life choice, after some time sometimes become role models of outstanding human behaviour. Well-known recent examples hereof are Saint Theresa of Calcutta who committed her life to charity works in accordance with the teachings of Jesus Christ and Mohandas Karamchand Gandhi, better known under his spiritual name "Mahatma Gandhi", who through his words and actions aimed at living in accordance with the

[84] It is as remarkable that more modern-day experiments to set up new types of societies which are not based upon the capitalist principles of egoism, selfishness and greed, in most cases even so fail. One can for instance refer to the experiment of the followers of Osho (formerly: Bhagwan Shree Rajneesh) to establish a commune in Ontario that, even on a socio-economic level, would be based upon the principles of love and mutual care. How this experiment fared within the context of a hostile, American environment, amongst others by the inhabitants of the neighboring town Antelope, can be seen in the award winning documentary "Wild wild country" (see https://www.imdb.com/title/tt7768848/) (last consulted on June 16, 2018).

For Osho's own account on these events, see Bhagwan Shree Rajneesh (1989). For an account of the hand of one of the residents of Antelope at the time, see Quick (1995). Even the at the time sheriff of the Wasco Counting wrote his own book on these events; see Labrousse (2016).

teachings of Hinduism (but also of Jainism) (resulting in a contemporary doctrine of non-violent resistance against colonialism, imperialism and other forms of societal exploitation).

It is even more remarkable that such figures often encounter a strong admiration, not only from the followers of their own religion, but also among followers of other religions or even among atheists.

These rare examples thus illustrate how a true experience of the basic teachings of the abovementioned religions, may become a source of true societal change. Unfortunately, up till today, this mainly takes place on the edge of societal organisation, raising the question if it could not be as perceivable, or at the very least desirable, that said basic teachings of the quoted world religions, given the values they advocate, could not as well provide the basic ingredients for a new, socio-economic order driven by altruism.

At a moment in time when (unbridled) capitalism has globally degenerated into a system which threatens the future of both the planet earth itself, as the creatures that inhabit it, the time is more than ever ripe for serious further reflection on this topic.

5.9 Some Further Moral Philosophical and Economic Inspirational Sources

5.9.1 Introduction

Also in the domain of philosophy in general, and of moral philosophy more specifically, there have throughout history been numerous advocates for more justice in the field of the socio-economic order.

This book does obviously not have as a goal to present a detailed descriptions of all these philosophical systems. We can here refer to the vast literature giving an overview of the several philosophical systems that have prevailed throughout history.

On the contrary, we shall limit ourselves here to a number of striking philosophers who have formulated outspoken calls for more justice in socio-economic relations.

5.9.2 Plato and Aristotle

Already in classical antiquity, philosophers such as obviously Plato and Aristotle made it their lives' work to reflect on the ideal societal organisation.

As a consequence, they have left humanity with several scriptures in which they reflected on what a (more) just society could look like.

It is hereby thus the more striking to observe how outstanding many of the insights of these philosophers from classical antiquity have been, which however immediately brings up the thought on how little societal progress human civilisation has made since (and despite) their writings.

Plato was in general all but sympathetic to the sectors of trade and industry, because it is exactly the mechanisms of these sectors that create the deepest gaps between the poor and the rich within society. Hence Plato was more in favour of having an agricultural society where every citizen, by means of a draw, would be assigned an equal share in the land (in order to cultivate it).[85]

We shall further limit the description of Plato's ideas to the following quote from Plato's "The laws"[86] that speaks clearly for itself:

> But the intention of our laws was that the citizens should be as happy as may be, and as friendly as possible to one another. And men who are always at law with one another, and amongst whom there are many wrongs done, can never be friends to one another, but only those among whom crimes and lawsuits are few and slight. Therefore we say that gold and silver ought not to be allowed in the city, nor much of the vulgar sort of trade which is carried on by lending money, or rearing the meaner kinds of livestock; but only the produce of agriculture, and only so much of this as will not compel us in pursuing it to neglect that for the sake of which riches exist – I mean, soul and body, which without gymnastics, and without education, will never be worth anything; and therefore, as we have said not once but many times, the care of riches should have the last place in our thoughts. For there are in all three things about which every man has an interest; and the interest about money, when rightly regarded, is the third and lowest of them.

A clear message: the pursuit of money should not dominate society; circulation of gold and silver should be prohibited, interest may not be levied and possession needs to be seen continuously as a means, never as a goal.[87] Instead, man should strive for other ideals and not pay too much attention to wealth accumulation, thus avoiding that society becomes too nasty (a.o. characterized by people fighting law suits instead of aiming at friendly relationships).[88]

One can but wonder why this message, truthful as it may be, has hardly ever been listened to, as societies have throughout history evolved in a completely opposite manner, culminating in the present-day societies being based on what may very well be one of the ugliest socio-economic systems ever, namely unbridled capitalism.

Also for Aristotle, in his work "Ethica Nicomachea" (= The Nicomachean Ethics), the (unbridled) pursuit of money and profit clearly had the characteristics of a vice, being the vice of "dishonourable pursuit of profit".[89]

It is somewhat ironic to observe that the portrait Aristotle draws of the (virtue-less) "skinflint", being the type of man takes too much (or: who takes more than is reasonable), perfectly matches the (neo-)liberal ideal image of the "homo (neo-)

[85] Polak (1928), p. 88.

[86] Plato (1994–2000).

[87] Compare this to the similar message of Hinduism (see Sect. 5.4.4).

[88] See also Byttebier (2017), p. 92, with further references.

[89] Aristotle (1996), p. 124.

liberalis", i.e. the human being who, at an economic level, makes every effort to obtain as much (wealth) as possible (at any cost). The characteristics are the same, what is different is their moral perception. In the teachings of Aristotle such a "greedy person" is virtueless while, within the doctrines of economic liberalism and economic neo-liberalism, such a "homo neoliberalis" on the contrary sets the standard for an ideal economic behaviour.[90]

Furthermore, Aristotle put forward a very simple, and hence at present still very convincing definition of the concept of "injustice" which he describes as follows[91]:

> to act unjustly meaning to assign oneself too large a share of things generally good and too small a share of things generally evil.

In this Aristotelian approach, a (disproportionate degree of) "inequality"—in the way it, worldwide, determines socio-economic relations today (as described above; see especially in Sect. 4.7.)—is "unjust" by definition, where there is mention of "injustice" on the part of those who, disproportionately "have too much" of what is good and/or "have too little" of what is bad, and of "suffering from injustice" on the part of those who, equally disproportionately, "have not enough" of what is good and/or have too much of what is bad.[92]

It is clear that the present societies as governed by the dictates of (unbridled) capitalism, would but be viewed very unfavourably through the eyes of both the abovementioned great philosophers from Classical Antiquity.

It is hereby thus the more remarkable that the philosophical scriptures of both these great historic philosophical intellectuals are still eagerly being studied and even taught all over the world, while at the same time barely any or no attention is given to the contents of their doctrines in the practical organisation of the socio-economic order.[93]

5.9.3 Some Further Christian Thinkers from History

Notwithstanding the fact that already during the Roman era, numerous prominent clerical figures strongly advocated more justice at a socio-economic level, they would neither be able to steer society into the direction of more altruism and justice.

The last important (philosophical) movement in Christian thinking who has attempted this, has been the movement of the so-called "scholastics" (with as one of its notorious figures Thomas Aquinas), albeit that, generally speaking, their efforts

---

[90] This is, yet again, one more illustration of how economic neo-liberalism has succeeded in causing a complete turnaround of moral values.

[91] Aristotle (1996), p. 126.

[92] Aristotle (1996), p. 127.

[93] Brook and Watkins (2012), p. 77.

mainly led to inspirational writings, but neither would achieve the goal of establishing a fair and just socio-economic order.[94]

In protestant Europe, a crucial turn-around in Christian thinking on topics of a socio-economic nature was caused by the ideas of Martin Luther (1483–1546) and, maybe even more by those of John Calvin (1509–1564). The impact of their teachings may even be considered extreme in light of the economic growth the German territories (during the sixteenth century) and The Netherlands (during the seventeenth century, also known as "the golden age of Holland").[95]

Luther for instance stated that the organization of a society based on the teachings of Jesus Christ was illusory. In particular, as regards the interest-debate, Luther held that there is a need for a governmental power making the repayment of credit enforceable (even when a real Christian is not allowed to expect such repayment).[96]

Luther, who through his doctrines closed behind him the door of the Catholic Church, would at the same time open a new door in the world of ideas, especially, through his opinion that the teachings of Christ are not feasible at a socio-economic level, making it possible to develop a purportedly still Christian doctrine which no longer was based on a literal reading of the Gospels. This undoubtedly contributed to the emergence of capitalism, and moreover of economic doctrines presenting themselves as part of a new and independent science freed from ecclesiastical dogma defending it. For the sake of completeness, it needs however also to be mentioned that Luther occasionally also took a stand against the greed of the rich, for instance against the German banking family Fugger,[97] but also against the mechanism of the charging of interest in general.[98] For this reason, Tawney has argued that Luther's statements were often but temporary expressions of anger, and that it is very difficult to recognize in them a truly coherent social economic doctrine.[99]

Shortly later, Calvin would completely reject the ecclesiastical prohibition of interest, although he did advocate "moderate" interest rates (first of 5%, later of 6.667%)[100] anticipating (from a social angle) on the potential detrimental effects of credit lending and interest charging.

At the same time, Calvin preached that the accumulation of wealth was a permissible life goal for those who worked hard and zealously, provided that such saved wealth would be reinvested in economic growth and not be used for luxurious (meaning "sinful") expenditure.[101] Over time, the Protestant Churches would come

---

[94] See Byttebier (2017), pp. 123–124 and 126.

[95] Bell (1996), p. 287.

[96] van Genderen et al. (1965), p. 173.

[97] Tawney (1944), pp. 82–83.

[98] Tawney (1944), p. 95.

[99] Tawney (1944), p. 88.

[100] Tawney (1944), pp. 81 a.f. and 120.
See further Bieler (1961), p. 168; Beaud (1994), p. 19.

[101] Bell (1996), p. 289; Weber (1967), p. 209.

to an agreement that the charging of a "reasonable" interest (of 5%) was acceptable (and not sinful).[102]

As mentioned before, this turnabout of values attributed to defending the emergence of some of the most immoral (pre-)capitalist practices of (early) capitalism, such as colonialism, imperialism and slavery. (See above, in Sect. 2.2.1.)

5.9.4 *The Schools of Rationalism*

5.9.4.1 Adam Smith

The validation of capitalism in the world of ideas would, obviously, reach a height in the works of the Scottish moral philosopher Adam Smith.

As has already been explained before, his works would set the scene for the breakthrough of capitalism, as it has gradually progressed since the eighteenth century to become the dominating economic system in the West in the course of the nineteenth century and on a global scale in the course of the twentieth century.

His works moreover are up till today still a major inspiration source for neoliberal thinking, as it has strongly determined the face of the world economy during the past decades.[103]

5.9.4.2 The French Social School of Rationalism

The impact of Adam Smith has not prevented that some of his contemporary authors, among whom philosophers who are like Adam Smith himself to be situated in the philosophical school of rationalism, have taken completely opposite positions in a plea for a greater justice in the context of the socio-economic order of society, even to that extent that many of the arguments developed by these remain as relevant in the current debate, which is why it may be interesting to put a light on these historically forgotten philosophers.

The following quote from Jean-Jacques Rousseau's treatise "Discours sur l'origine et les fondements de l'inégalité parmie les hommes"[104] (1754),[105] already sets the scene for the reasoning developed among the French school of enlightened philosophers (of the pre-revolutionary era)[106]:

---

[102] Graeber (2012), p. 322.

[103] See furthermore Byttebier (2017), p. 153 a.f.

[104] See http://classiques.uqac.ca/classiques/Rousseau_jj/discours_origine_inegalite/discours_inegalite.pdf (last consulted on June 16, 2018).

[105] About Rousseau in general, see Beaud (1994), pp. 72–73.

[106] In the original French version, the text reads as follows:

> Le premier qui, ayant enclos un terrain, s'avisa de dire: Ceci est à moi, et trouva des gens assez simples pour le croire, fut le vrai fondateur de la société civile. Que de crimes, de

> The true founder of the civil society: that was the one who was first in fencing a parcel of land and had the guts to say: "this is mine", to the one who was naive enough to believe him. How many crimes, wars, murders, suffering and atrocities would not have happened to humanity, if someone had just withdrawn the poles or had filled the ditches and had shouted to his fellow-men: "Do not listen to this imposter, you are lost if you forget that the fruits of the earth belong to everyone and that the earth belongs to no-one!" But apparently at that time evolution had already reached the stage where things could not remain anymore as how they were.

More in general, Rousseau held that society had degenerated as a consequence of so-called "civilization". According to Rousseau, this degenerated civilization started when human beings began to produce more than they needed and, in this way, initiated a since then ever expanding artificial stimulation of needs, beyond the level of their natural needs. The excesses to which this led, became moreover distributed in a unequal and unfair manner, resulting in a division between "rich" and "poor" people, or put otherwise between the "powerful" and the "powerless".

In Rousseau's reasoning, all wealth and power basically come down to an "usurpation", which in itself is a consequence of angered passions. Rousseau saw two models to solve this, knowingly, on one hand "education" (see especially his book "Émile, ou De l'éducation") and, on the other hand, a just and fair state mechanism (see especially his book "Du contrat social").[107]

Claude Adrien Helvétius (1715–1771) also protested against the vast social and economic injustices which characterized the French "Ancien Régime" of his time.

Helvétius for instance held that in most countries, there were only two categories of people (left), namely, on one hand the (largest) group of people owing nothing, and, on the other hand a (minority) group of people thriving in excess, whereby the first group may (or even: may in the best case) provide for its basic needs only by working extremely hard, resulting in making the other group as rich as possible. Hence, it becomes completely justified to expect from government that it would install mechanisms aiming at creating a more just and fair distribution of (societal) wealth.[108]

> guerres, de meurtres, que de misères et d'horreurs n'eût point épargnés au genre humain celui qui, arrachant les pieux ou comblant le fossé, eût crié à ses semblables : Gardez-vous d'écouter cet imposteur ; vous êtes perdus, si vous oubliez que les fruits sont à tous, et que la terre n'est à personne. Mais il y a grande apparence, qu'alors les choses and étaient déjà venues au point de ne pouvoir plus durer comme elles étaient. (See furthermore Arenas (2016), p. 41.)

[107] See Rousseau (1966). See also Delfgaauw (1960a, b), p. 54; Talmon (1966), p. 56.

For Rousseau, the end goal of state organization should consist in the safeguard and the welfare of its population. As Rousseau phrased it himself (in French):

> Quelle est la fin de l'association politique? C'est la conservation et la prospérité de ses membres. (See Rousseau (1966), p. 124).

[108] Beaud (1994), p. 74.

It may be obvious that, given the increasing gaps between the rich and the poor in our present-day societies, one cannot but help observing that the insights of Helvétius may have (once more in history) become more valid than ever.[109]

In his work "Théorie des lois civils ou principes fondamentaux de la société" (1777–1792), Simon-Nicholas Henri Linguet (1736–1794) argued in general that greed and violence control the world, and that the concept of "ownership" is relying on one of the most outrageous forms of usurpation. This author, furthermore, held that the living conditions of the working classes (of his time) were worse than ever before in history, to such an extent that misery had "forced the poor to their knees in front of the rich to beg for their permission to make them even more rich" (a statement which could as well apply to some of the behavior of many a present-day private bank or capitalist employer).[110] Also noteworthy is Linguet's statement that "the grandiloquent language [of the rich] concerning slavery (…) is similar to the squeak of a raptor ripping apart a dove with its claws", a quote which could as easily be applicable to many a contemporary neo-liberal author or policy-maker.[111]

More in general, Linguet demonstrated a strong understanding of the doctrines of economic liberalism, leading to his viewpoint that mankind is being cheated by economists who promise an increase in wealth, where in reality market forces are only providing more wealth to the rich (an insight which also in the current context is experiencing a true revival among many scientists in various domains).

Significantly in contrast with the present-day (neo-)liberal doctrine of "voluntary association", Linguet furthermore argued that the working classes are caught in what he described as "the trap of the free market". Given the fact that the working classes can only offer their labour on the market (the use of which an employer can easily postpone, and which is moreover, in many cases, perfectly "fungible"[112]), labourers are bound to be forced to accept low prices (wages) for their labour[113] as they cannot live one day themselves without food or a roof above their head and, as a result, are completely dependent on their wages for their daily living.[114]

It is in this regard very significant (especially given the degree of understanding Linguet already demonstrated in the eighteenth century), that for instance Stiglitz, in his book "Making globalization work", has indicated the fear "of losing his job"

[109] Compare Kruithof (2000), p. 60.

[110] Beaud (1994), p. 74.

[111] Beaud (1994), p. 75.

[112] As may be illustrated, in the current context, by the practice of the re-allocation of factories and other production units to other countries, as well as by the practices of importing cheap labour from other (poorer) countries.

[113] It can be observed that this insight basically concurs with the insight of for example Ricardo (see his famous "Iron Law of the Wages"), although the latter derived other conclusions from this insight.

[114] Beaud (1994), p. 75.

as one of the most serious economic problems of the globalized world economy,[115] an understanding which is in line with the writings of Herbert Marcuse (describing this as the compulsion resulting from the risk of having a complete lack of facilities for themselves and for [once' s] relatives (children, spouses, eventually parents) for whom only one person is caring).[116]

Linguet who, through his opinions, presented himself as the advocate of the interests of "the fourth class" (at his time), reached the conclusion that for the working classes, there is no freedom,[117] causing the poor to be, in truth, the slaves of the rich.[118]

5.9.5 *Karl Marx*

Throughout the further history of philosophy, the debate pro and contra capitalism as an overruling economic system has been ongoing.

Obviously, reference in this regard should also be made to Karl Marx (1818–1883).

As this author's entire works may be considered to be an accusation against capitalism (in its many disastrous shapes), it is far from evident to summarize his doctrine in but a few paragraphs; nevertheless, it is possible to point out some of the most striking elements of Marx' teachings.

In essence, the Marxist doctrine is a plea for more humanity and altruism in interpersonal relations (even to that extent that this aspect of Marxist thinking is, according to some, more important than his socio-economic dimension).[119]

Marx for instance held that capitalism and the unbridled pursuit of profit on which it is based, are both physically and psychologically extremely violent and morally bankrupt and that, because of this, capitalism is containing its proper downfall.[120]

---

[115] Stiglitz (2006), p. 67. See also Stiglitz (2002), p. 9.
Stiglitz has explained this as follow:

> (…) is that for a large fraction of the world's population, work – employment – is important. For individuals who lose their jobs, it is not *just* the loss of income that matters, it is also the individual's sense of self. Unemployment is associated with a variety of problems and pathologies, from higher divorce rates, higher suicide rates to higher incidences of alcoholism. And the relationship is not just a correlation: there is a causal connection. (Stiglitz 2002, p. 9).

[116] Marcuse (1962), pp. 91 a.f.

[117] Observe that this is one of the main conditions for the aforementioned neo-liberal doctrine of "voluntary association" to be ever able to claim any credibility.

[118] Beaud (1994), p. 75.

[119] Fromm (2014), p. 192; Skidelsky and Skidelsky (2013), p. 58.

[120] See Lloyd (2012), p. 359; Vandewalle (1976), p. 97; Beaud (1994), p. 148.

Well-known is the so-called Marxist "impoverishment doctrine" stating that, as a consequence of a sequence of economic crisis's and of the growth of "the army of proletarians", the life conditions of the working masses will gradually deteriorate. According to Marx, this will ultimately result in strikes and rebellions which will lead the working classes to a massive revolution. This revolution is bound to take place when due to continued economic depressions, the life circumstances of the vast masses will have become unbearable. At that time, the proletariat will confiscate all capital, abolish inheritance law, hand over the credit system to the powers of government and submit everyone into an equal obligation to work.[121]

After Marx himself, Marxist thinking has been further elaborated and predicated by many Marxist economists, albeit that this thinking has in practice not led to a (durable) just society.

On the contrary, the communist regimes which, based on Marxist thinking, emerged in certain countries in the course of the twentieth century, themselves soon got characterised by their own dynamics of inequality, unfreedom and injustice.[122] This helps explaining the collapse of communism in many countries by the end of the 1980s and the beginning of the 1990s.

Erich Fromm has in this regard stated that the fact that the ideas of Marx have mainly been applied in practice in a distorted way, may be due to the fact that he has expressed his ideas too early in history. According to Fromm, Marx (just as his partner-in-writing Engels) had wrongly assumed that capitalism had already exhausted all of its means during his own lifetime, implying that the revolution against capitalism was soon to start. Fromm has argued that Marx was wrong in this regard and that Marx, on the contrary, announced his doctrine exactly at the height of capitalism, hence without being able to foresee that it would take more than one century more before capitalism would decline at such a rate that it was bound to collapse.

As a consequence, the most striking tragedy of Marxism has been that its implementation had to take place through some major adaptions, in a capitalist-like sense, resulting in so-called "communism".[123] It is even more remarkable that these insights of Fromm may be demonstrated in a similar manner by referring to the current participation of China in the globalised world economy.

5.9.6 And, Post-Marx?

It seems that in our times the call for more justice, in word and deed, has since then mainly been taken over by a number of NGO's (such as Oxfam, 11.11.11 and Greenpeace, next to many other fair trade movements and charity organisations),

[121] Galbraith (1987), pp. 136–137; Vandewalle (1976), p. 101; Beaud (1994), p. 149; Skidelsky and Skidelsky (2013), p. 59.

[122] At least this has brought forward a masterpiece of literature, namely George Orwells "Animal farm".

[123] Fromm (2014), p. 192.

albeit that none of these has up till now been able to essentially turn the tide of unbridled capitalism.[124]

Nevertheless, on occasion, a new philosopher surfaces in the debate pro or contra capitalism.

For instance in France, Emmanuel Levinas, Michel Foucault and Pascal Bruckner have in the course of the second half of the twentieth century strongly emerged as advocates of a more just society which would prioritise a sufficient amount of altruism, next to paying more attention to the environment, as central values.[125]

Remarkably, also a number of prominent, especially Anglo-American economists have questioned the dominance of capitalism. A little more back in the past this was, for instance, clearly the case for John Maynard Keynes and John Kenneth Galbraith. Among more recent authors, it is without any doubt important to mention Noble Prize winners Joseph Stiglitz and Paul Krugman, albeit that also other authors, such as Jeffrey Sachs and Thomas Piketty, have been able to loudly raise their voices in the ongoing debate.

5.10 From the Illusion of Equality to a Reality of Equal Opportunities

5.10.1 On Two Opposing Forces Determining the Outlook of the Socio-Economic Order Throughout History

If history teaches us one thing on the evolution of socio-economic processes, it may very well be that there appear to be two main forces which are simultaneously influencing them.

One force is the power of egoism, selfishness and greed causing that a (small) group of people takes ownership of as much wealth and power possible in order to subject the rest of mankind to the fulfilment of their own selfish needs.

The other is the power of altruism advocating more justice and equality.

The ongoing play between these two forces has been determining the outlook, on a socio-economic level, of societies throughout history, where the first force has historically been translated into, amongst others, society models based on slavery, serfdom and caste systems, next to more modern-day similar models of exploitation, but also, as regards the level of the relations between countries, into systems of colonialism, imperialism and other forms of suppression of one people by another people, while the second force has mainly manifested through emancipation struggles against the societal systems imposed by the first force.

---

[124] In the political world, altruist thinking can barely count on any true experience.

[125] For an attempt of summarising the philosophy of Michel Foucault, see Achterhuis (1988), pp. 256–276.

About the vision of Michel Foucault on the different neo-liberal systems, see especially Foucault (2013), p. 427.

Even in the contemporary world, these forces still help determining the outlook of the socio-economic order, where, within (unbridled) capitalism mainly the first force plays a dominating role in the development of all types of mechanisms of economic exploitation, extortion and suppression.

Since the rise of economic neo-liberalism, it furthermore seems that the second force has become completely absent in the socio-economic organisation of society, with as possible exceptions the occurrence of an occasional academic or religious scripture,[126] or of an occasional protest action organised by a trade union or a similar organisation, taking a stand for more altruism in socio-economic relations.

It has already been explained above that the dominating socio-economic philosophy that economic neo-liberalism has turned into during the past decades, hereby, in the most hypocritical way, keeps on providing lip service to an illusory principle of equality, while in practice it is based upon and helps creating, sustaining, supporting and enhancing a variety of systems of high inequalities.

As an example, reference can once again be made to the fact to what extent capitalism is based upon differences of life opportunities. Indeed, the success or failure in the capitalist socio-economic order of any human being is very strongly determined by the life chances he gets, especially in his youth, which to a large extent determine the way he will be able to develop later on in life.

5.10.2 The Extreme Immorality of the Doctrines of Economic Neo-liberalism Further Illustrated with the Example of Nepotism, and What To Do About It

A striking illustration of the abovementioned inequalities that continue to prevail within the capitalistic socio-economic order is its continuing adherence to systems of nepotism which themselves are in essence in complete opposition to the principle of equality (and of equal chances in life).

Obviously the question on how to handle nepotism is a (very) old question, on which already Plato (apparently unsuccessfully) reflected, resulting in his radical proposal for a society where children would at birth be removed from their natural parents in order to entrust their upbringing and education to specialised and neutral educators, ensuring that people, at a later (adult) age, would be deployed in society solely because of their talents and skills, instead of motivations of nepotism.[127]

It goes without saying that this idea of Plato is of no relevance at all in our present-day capitalist society(ies), where nepotism is probably among the most decisive factors as regards life chances in general and as regards career opportunities more specifically.

---

[126] See recently, for instance, Congregation for the Doctrine of the Faith (2018).

[127] Plato (1987), p. 181 a.f.; Popper (1966), p. 145.

Propagated by Judaic-Christian thinking, especially from the fourth century on,[128] Western society models[129] would, since that time period, more than ever before in history, be based on the (niche—or core) family model that even got to be considered of being of a "saintly" nature (see for instance the idea that marriage is a so-called "sacrament"). On a micro-level, the niche family model would since then evolve into the dominant relationship type, which would only further fortify the breeding ground for unbridled nepotism within socio-economic relations.[130]

There are probably branches of (human) sciences that investigate to what extent nepotism is a natural phenomenon, given the fact that almost every animal species shows a tendency to defend its own offspring.[131] So it should not come as a surprise that also the human species, after all still a mammal species, shows a tendency to do the same, albeit that this should not prevent civilisation to be entitled to correct such animal impulses.

Most tools of societal-order are themselves but such a product of human civilisation.

When for instance considering the example of money, one will reach the conclusion, that in the whole animal world, there is not a single comparable mechanism which may bring any animal in a position where it can make such a claim on its environment (and to pass it on to its predecessors) the way money allows to do in the human world. (See the for themselves speaking figures mentioned in Sect. 4.7.)

Be as it may, the fact that still in 2018, the one person, by birth, enters a world of the highest possible luxury (often without any obligation to do something in return),[132] while another person, also by birth, and even when working himself to death, remains condemned to lead a life of poverty and starvation[133] (= the so-called "condemned to stay poor-syndrome")[134] is extremely harrowing in light of the pretense that men are supposed to be equal.

In his "Discours sur l'origine et les fondements de l'inégalité parmie les hommes", already in 1754, Roussau had reached the same conclusion and even held this in contradiction with the laws of nature. More than a quarter of a millennium later, one can but observe that not that much has changed within global society in this regard.[135]

It may even more horrifying that in the Western culture, a socio-economic system keeps on prevailing where such fundamental injustices are still being defended

---

[128] This is from the moment when Christianity became the state religion of the Roman Empire. See further Maddison (2007), p. 80; Pinxten (2009), p. 94.

[129] As they would, later on in history, also instigate other cultures.

[130] On the decline of the (core) family model, see also Osho (1991), p. 28 a.f.

[131] Dawkins (2006), p. 6.

[132] Bruckner (2002), p. 21.

[133] Byanyima (2014), pp. 4–5 and 11.

[134] Oxfam (2014), p. 47.

[135] Beaud (1994), p. 72.

by referring to theoretical witticisms holding "that everyone enjoys equal opportunities", or "that by working hard, everyone can become evenly successful".[136]

It, hence, needs not come as a surprise that, after decades of implementing the doctrines of economic neo-liberalism, it appeared from IFS figures that as regards the UK, by 2012, the income gaps between people from rich and poor backgrounds had almost doubled in a period of but a decade and that someone from the richest fifth of households earned an average of 88% more than those from the poorest families, with the equivalent gap in 2000 being just 47%.[137]

In light of the further awareness that the present-day world food production is largely sufficient to feed every person in the world in the proper way, while at the same time hundreds of millions of people are still facing hunger, more than one billion people are living in harrowing poverty, and that this is only due to the prevailing socio-economic system, otherwise put to the system of capitalism,[138] one can but hope that every person who has ever expressed or defended any of the abovementioned viewpoints of economic neo-liberalism will soon come to his senses[139] and, instead, will help looking for more just societal models than those prevailing under unbridled capitalism.[140]

5.11 Towards a System of Altruistic Money Creation?

5.11.1 The Problematic Nature of the Prevailing Money Creation Systems Once More Revisited

5.11.1.1 Introduction

As explained above, the capitalist system of money creation, in a nutshell, comes down to leaving money creation to a large extent in the hands of the private bank sector which, by granting credit that is booked on a scriptural account and that has to be paid back enhanced with interest, pumps new money into the economy.

As has been explained in a more detailed manner elsewhere in this book (see especially Sect. 2.1.), this private money creation system does not at all contribute to a just society, but primarily serves the private interests of the rich and very rich capital providers of said banks (and other financial institutions).

---

[136] Oxfam (2014), p. 15.

[137] Chu (2017).

[138] Habets and Gloudemans (2011), pp. 29–36.

[139] This has ultimately even happened to Ebenezer Scrooge in the famous story "A Christmas Carol" by Charles Dickens, be it that this required the midnight visits of the ghost of his late colleague Jacob Marley and the three ghosts of Christmas-past, Christmas-today, and Christmas-future.

[140] See also the similar call for a profound reform of the international economic architecture of Stiglitz, already in 2002 (see Stiglitz (2002), p. 27).

The latter is mainly due to the fact that the creation of scriptural money is part of the credit provisioning activity of said private bankers, and hence represents an important source of income for these. However, this method of creating new money through loans (or credit) puts at the same time a large burden on the borrowers of such loans, even to the extent that the entire global economy, in all its layers, suffers from this.

As any borrower (obviously) needs to succeed in repaying the credit received in principal, where applicable increased by the interests that have been agreed upon, the further functioning of such a borrower who does not succeed in fulfilling his repayment obligations under the credit agreement, will become problematic.

From a historical point of view, this has for at least two groups of borrowers not always been that obvious.

5.11.1.2 The Problematic Nature of Private Bank Credits to Individuals or Households

The first group of borrowers to whom especially the payment of bank interests may represent a severe burden, is the groups of individual borrowers who take up a credit in order to provide in a (more or less) basic need of life.

On a global scale, individuals indeed find themselves often in need to finance an elementary living expenditure, without (pre-)disposing of the means to finance this. An obvious example is a credit that is taken to provide for decent housing, albeit that also other types of consumer credits (in a broad sense of the word), next to, for instance, credit that is taken up to cover the costs for an education (e.g. "student loans"[141]) clearly belong to this category.[142]

In many cases such an individual borrower moreover barely realises the extent of the obligations he enters into when taking up such a credit, especially as regards the agreed upon interest payments.

The entering into such a bank credit agreement nevertheless implies that the borrower will have to ensure to dispose of a sufficient income in order to be able to repay the capital received, increased with the agreed upon interests.

[141] The debts related to student loans in the US in 2014 were estimated to approach 1 trillion USD (see Micklethwait and Woolridge 2014, p. 121). The Economist of March 28th 2015 mentioned that:

> student debt, at nearly $1.2 trillion, has surpassed credit-card debt and car loans. (See Anonymous (2015b), pp. 11–12.)

On the dangers of relying on student debt as a means of financing education, see furthermore Chomsky (2017), p. 67, phrasing his concern as follows:

> It means that students, if they don't come from very wealthy families, they're going to leave college with big debts. And if you have a big debt, you're trapped.

[142] On the practices in the airline industry, see for instance Smout (2014), p. 3. See also Anonymous (2015c), pp. 4–5; Meeussen (2015), p. 17.

Given the fact that borrowers are in most cases (by definition) not part of the rich or very rich classes of society—in the opposite case they would not be in need for a credit for an elementary expenditure—the persons belonging to this category will in most cases depend on income from performing labour in order to be able to repay the credit, increased with the agreed upon interests.

Through this, the sum of all the credits taken up by individuals to provide in an elementary expenditure, puts a very high pressure on the economy, as there will a continuous need for a sufficient employment in order to provide all the borrowers with a sufficient income that allows them to pay back said credits (enhanced with the agreed upon interest).

Moreover, this technique makes the borrowers extremely vulnerable of being affected by an unfortunate turn of fate, such as an accident, an illness, or even a situation of unemployment, and this thus the more in countries where not enough social safety nets prevail to counter the effects of such types of unfortunate events.

The capitalist mechanism of scriptural money creation based on credit that banks grant to their customers, is moreover clearly based on the optimistic (liberal and neo-liberal) vision that the (global) economy will grow forever and that such growth will benefit all economic players. Nevertheless, at many occasions in history, it has appeared that this implies a too high overestimation of the capacity of the economic tissue, implying that, when the economic situation worsens and, as a consequence, too many such borrowers are no longer able to fulfil their credit obligations (for instance due to reasons of high unemployment), the scriptural money creation mechanism itself may come under a high pressure.

As regards recent history, this can again be illustrated by making reference to the heavy financial crisis of 2007–2008.[143]

It should therefore not come as a surprise that in the course of Western history, especially in times when clerical leaders still openly advocated for more charity in society, at various occasions, there have been attempts to prohibit, or at the very least temper the interest mechanism, under the righteous observation that the interest mechanism mainly consists of a method by which the rich get richer to the detriment of the poor.

---

[143] The Belgian press regularly reports on the problems around the re-payment of these individual credits.

In March 2015, it was reported that a record number of Belgians could not pay back their credits (http://www.hln.be/hln/nl/942/Economie/article/detail/2252439/2015/03/15/Recordaantal-Belgen-kan-krediet-niet-terugbetalen.dhtml (last consulted on June 16, 2018)).

According to this article, at the end of February 2015, 352,270 Belgians, representing 3.13 billion euro in late payments, could not re-pay their credits (especially mortgages). To reach this conclusion, said news article based itself on date stemming from statistics provided by the "Central for Credits to Individuals" of the (Belgian) National bank. These figures show that, at the end of February 2015, exactly 352,270 Belgians had at least one credit contract for which payment was late. This represented an increase of 2.5% in one year, while during that same period, the number of credits had decreased with almost half a percent. Due to the fact that a high number of Belgians facing payment problems had more than one credit running, the total number of "problematic credit contracts" amounted to 526,504. These were related to both ordinary consumer credits, and mortgage credits and represented a total in belated payment of 3.13 billion euro.

It is in this regard remarkable that this reasoning still prevails under the legal rules of Islam dealing with (bank) credit.

Neither will it be surprising that the rich in such societies have more often than not attempted to either circumvent such interest prohibitions, or to have them removed from the legal systems.[144]

5.11.1.3 The Problematic Nature of Private Bank Credits to States

A second group of borrowers for whom it has appeared that relying on bank credit can pose severe problems, consists of states (next to other public borrowers).[145] (See already above, in Sect. 4.6.)

It has already been explained before that the doctrines of economic liberalism and economic neo-liberalism are not favourable towards states (unless in case it comes down to supporting large capital itself, such as in the field of military expenditure and in the field of subsidies for moribund economic sectors,[146] with as typical example the bailouts of private banks themselves).

This negative attitude towards the role of states helps explaining the detrimental nature of the mechanisms states have to resort to in order to finance their activities.

As has already been analysed in more detail in Chap. 2 and in Sect. 4.6 of this book, in capitalist economic systems, basically two types of mechanisms of state financing prevail.

On one hand, there is the income that states derive from taxes (in a broad sense of the word).[147] Based on its sovereign authority, a state may indeed oblige its inhabitants to, at regular intervals, concede a part of their economic income (or even part of their assets) to the state, in order to ensure that the latter is able to finance its expenditure. As a historical constant factor, especially within societies reshaped in accordance with the doctrines of economic neo-liberalism, mainly people from the poor and middle classes are burdened by such taxes, while the rich, through means

---

[144] In Western societies, the dismantling of the ecclestical interest prohibition that had been a leading principle of the socio-economic order until deep in the middle ages, first in practice, and later in Christian thinking itself (see especially certain protestant doctrines), has not unsurprisingly gone hand in hand with the final breakthrough of capitalism as the overruling economic system.

[145] See also Stiglitz (2002), p. 22 a.f.

[146] According to Stiglitz (2010, pp. 199–200):

> One might have thought that the oil industry, with its seemingly unbounded profits, would not turn to government for assistance; bud greed has no bounds, and money buys political influence: it has received large tax subsidies. (…) The mining industry too receives billions in hidden subsidies; they take minerals from government-owned land virtually for free. In 2008 and 2009, America's automobile and finance industries joined the long list of the subsidized.

[147] From an economic viewpoint, systems of taxation in the narrow sense of the word and comparable systems, such as social security contributions, may be both considered as tax systems in the broad sense of the word.

of all kinds of mechanisms of influencing power, are themselves to a high extent exempt from paying taxes.

On the other hand, it is clear that in practice, for many states, the income derived from taxes is in many cases not sufficient to bear their expenditures, in which case they have to resort to mechanisms of borrowing (or: credit financing).

Especially over the past decades, states (and other public authorities) had to resort to such credits on a massive scale in order to finance their deficits. In full accordance with the liberal and neo-liberal "laissez faire, laissez passer"-principle that holds that all economic problems are bound to solve themselves (or, put otherwise: to get magically solved by the invisible hand(s) of the free markets), it is hereby (at least in an implicit manner) assumed that after any economic "dip", there will be a period of economic growth that will allow states to once again collect higher tax revenues.

This optimistic attitude (obviously next to an insufficient willingness to cut back on expenditure patterns form the past) is one of the main causes why the debts of many countries have taken such immense proportions.[148]

As a result, throughout history, states facing shortages have very often resorted to credits granted by the rich and powerful (at high interest rates), while the latter have very rarely shown any willingness to establish more just fiscal mechanisms in the framework of which state financing would be mainly supported by taxes paid by them. (See already above, in Sect. 4.6.)

As it appears from several studies, within the currently prevailing systems of state finance as shaped under the doctrines of economic neo-liberalism, this kind of behaviour is dominating stronger than ever before in history, with as its most striking example the tax evasive behaviour of the rich and powerful and of the (large) enterprises they own and run.

Moreover, under the rise of capitalism, the granting of credit to states has become increasingly institutionalised, with the financial and banking sector having become one of the largest institutional credit providers of said states.[149]

[148] See at https://www.nationaldebtclocks.org/.

[149] The historical rise of certain banks, such as, in the German regions of the sixteenth and the seventeenth century, the famous "House of Fugger", has often gone hand in hand with the rise of (worldly) governments. In the example of the House of Fugger, this was the case for the Habsburgs family which had risen to power both in the German-Austrian regions, as well as in Spain (and through this, in many more European regions), to a certain extent thanks to the financial support of the House of Fugger.

History at the same time teaches us that the alliance between state authority and the bank system has not always been a happy one. In the referenced example, the financial empire of the House of Fugger would come to an end mainly when the Spanish side of the Habsburgian family decided to no longer pay back its credits. (See Bogaert et al. ([2000] 1991), pp. 158–168; Bogaert et al. ([2000] 1991), pp. 158–168; Bogaert et al. (2000), pp. 158–168; Byttebier (2001), pp. 362–363; Tawney (1944), p. 90. For an overview of the history of the house of Fugger, see Häberlein (2006), p. 257.)

Ever since, the interwovenness between states and the financial sector has remained, with states increasingly becoming dependent on the financial means provided by private banks, even to the extent that one may argue that, under the reign of capitalism, a power switch has occurred as a

From a conceptual point of view, this capitalist financing system is very bewildering. States who, by definition, advocate the public interest have become totally dependent on private financial institutions which are driven by the capitalist pursuit of profit principle, especially on private banks which, through the mechanism of private money creation, moreover control the supply of money within the economy.[150]

States in need of financing—whereby it hardly matters whether this is caused by a shortage of tax income, or by an excess of expenditure—thus need to rely on expensive (private) loans, which at the same time are an important source of income for the private banking sector, and, hence, for their rich shareholders.

One hereby always needs to remind the fact that the amounts of interest the states-borrowers owe to the banks-lenders, at least ultimately, must be financed through tax income as well.

In this way, the (capitalistic) mechanisms of state financing have above all been turned into a means of redistributing wealth from the lower and middle classes to the rich classes of society, as it is clear that it are mainly the poor and middle classes that are most burdened by taxes, while the rich and powerful are the ones who mostly participate in the private banking sector that derives (substantial parts of) its profits out of said state loans.

It is hence very clear that, as has already been argued before (see especially in Sect. 4.6.), the capitalist methods of state financing are both very "inefficient" and "unjust". In recent history, Greece has been among the countries having suffered very severely from this.

5.11.2 *An Invite to Further Reflect on a New International Monetary Order*

In light of the foregoing, it appears that the time is more than ripe for a thorough reflection on alternative systems of government financing.

In my previous books "Towards a New International Monetary Order"[151] and "Nu het gouden kalf verdronken is",[152] such an alternative has already been thoroughly elaborated upon.

In a nutshell, the proposed alternative approach towards monetary issues holds that, based upon international treaties establishing a new, international monetary order, state financing should be approached from a completely different angle than propagated under the doctrines of economic neo-liberalism.

---

result of which states got, to an ever growing extent, governed by the dictates of the financial markets.

[150] The impact on this process of the so-called steering effect by the monetary authorities can meanwhile be called "marginal".

[151] See the Chapters 4 and 5 of Byttebier (2017).

[152] See the Chapters III and IV of Byttebier (2015).

Instead of relying on mechanisms of taxation and debt financing by the private banking sector, the national governments of the states participating in said treaties would obtain access to financial means that would directly be provided out of mechanisms of public, international money creation. More specifically, a newly to be established Monetary World Institute would be granted the authority to, at regular intervals, grant "allocations" of financial means to the national governments of the participating states. These allocations would not take place under the form of repayable credits, but on the contrary, would consist of definitively obtained operational financial means, implying that the participating countries would no longer be submitted to repayment obligations.

States would under such a system even be prohibited to finance themselves by means of other methods, among which taxation and debt financing, but would solely have to rely on the aforementioned allocations, in this way also becoming incited to a strict budgetary discipline instead of the "laissez-faire, laissez-passer" monetary approach prevailing within capitalism.

Based on such a system of government financing through public allocations, a more just societal system could be worked out, where the strength of one's economy (often caused by mere coincidence, such as the presence of oil or other natural resources on one's territory), would no longer be decisive to determine the operational budgets of a given government and where such government could no longer be held hostage by the business sector in general and by private banks more especially. As, based upon such a system, developing countries would have access to a better and more just financing system, this could also blow new life into their development.[153]

Otherwise put, said allocation model on behalf of states would take the international monetary system back to the original mission of the IMF, i.e. ensuring global liquidity, to enable sustained global growth for all countries in the world, and, with that growth, full employment and prosperity on a global scale.[154]

Finally, the system would allow states to no longer burden the poor and middle classes with all kinds of unfair taxes, which would allow these classes, on a global scale, to at last build out a worthy and prosperous life themselves.

---

[153] Further arguments for such a system of money creation on behalf of states can be found with Stiglitz (2002), p. 23, from which the following quote:

> There is a simple remedy. As has just been observed, problems of insufficiency of global aggregate demand were very much on the minds of Keynes and others at the time the IMF was established. There is framework for enhancing aggregate purchasing power, namely through the creation of Special Drawing Rights (SDRs). (…) The SDRs could be used to pursue global interests – from helping the poorest countries to improving the global environment.

It should hereby be noted that the in this book (and more in detail in Byttebier (2017), Chapters 4 and 5) proposed allocation system is taking the Keynesian SDR-mechanism (but) a step, be it a big one, further.

[154] See again Stiglitz (2002), p. 24.

Obviously, under such an alternative system of government financing, it will be important to avoid reckless money creation,[155] raising the need for appropriate systems of "checks and balances" in the decision making process on the allocations to be provided to governments, along with solid mechanisms of control and budgetary discipline. In the books "Nu het gouden kalf verdronken is" and "Towards a New International Monetary Order", ample consideration has been given to these elements.

Under this newly proposed system, also the level of money creation for the benefit of individuals could be entrusted to the same central monetary authority, albeit supplemented by a system of national central banks that would be ensured of a physical presence in each of the countries participating in this new monetary order.

Under this newly proposed monetary system, the supply of new money within the economy could furthermore be turned into a tool serving the general interest (hence serving the underlying goal of establishing a global society where every human being gets a—truly—equal chance to build a worthy life) instead of, as is the case with the currently prevailing systems of private money creation, mainly serving the pursuit of profits by the private banking sector.

As said, for all of this, further reference is here made to my book "Towards a New International Monetary Order".[156]

The question obviously is if the world community will ever be prepared to work towards such a more just mechanism of money creation.

5.12 The Need for a New Perspective on Fiscal Matters

5.12.1 Monetary Allocations Replacing Taxation

An additional benefit of the proposed system of money creation as referred to in the previous Sect. 5.11, is that there will, in principle, no longer be a need for imposing taxes, as the governments of the participating states will be able to rely on allocations out of the hands of the (newly to be created) international monetary authority.

To the extent that, in such a monetary system, it would be still considered necessary to impose taxes, this could be the case, on the one hand, as a method of avoiding an extreme polarisation between the rich and the poor within society and, on the other hand, as a method of encouraging the rich and very rich to a sufficient degree of solidarity, by offering them a choice between either having their surplus wealth

[155] Also referred to as the "easy money" paradigm (which at regular intervals creates huge problems for the capitalistic monetary order). (Again, reference can be made to Greenspan (2007).)

[156] See especially the Chapters 4 and 5 of Byttebier (2017), and the Chapters III and IV of Byttebier (2015).

taxed away, or attributing it in support of a system of socio-cultural participation for the benefit of the global society.[157]

Such a new taxation system should, of course, be the subject of an international tax treaty between as much countries in the world as possible. The objective of such a treaty should be the creation of a globally harmonised taxation system that not only should be of a fair and just nature, but also should be putting an end to all incentives for fiscal competition between countries.

5.12.2 *Reflecting on a New Four Pillar Based Tax System*

As has been further explained in the book "Towards a New International Monetary Order",[158] such a new global tax system could be based on four pillars:

- The first pillar of said tax system should be that it will be based on a "true solidarity".
  It should thereby be avoided that this solidarity would merely be one which the rich classes of society (by means of undemocratic systems of government influencing) impose on the middle and poor classes, and to which the rich classes do not participate as a consequence of all forms of tax evasion techniques. On the contrary, the solidarity principle should be such that mainly the rich would be encouraged to share their excess wealth with the less fortunate people within society.[159]
  This first goal of the new fiscal system could translate into reducing the multitude of the presently prevailing tax systems to two types of income taxes, and to one type of (harmful) transaction taxes, with the explicit exclusion of all other taxation systems in the broadest sense of the word.
  The first type of income tax which could still be retained would be an income tax for natural persons. An elementary characteristic of this income tax system should be that taxation will only involve persons who have already gathered a sufficient wealth, with exclusion of all other people whose gathered wealth is still below such a threshold.
  Such a system would obviously imply defining (a) wealth threshold(s) below which there will not be any income tax and above which the income of the natural person disposing of such a wealth, will become eligible for taxation. In the latter case, there should be no further distinction based upon the nature of the income, implying that all types of income will be taxed as soon as the person getting the income has gathered a fortune that reaches the (to-be-defined) wealth threshold.

[157] For a further elaboration upon such a system, see Byttebier (2017), p. 406 a.f.
[158] See Byttebier (2017), p. 400 a.f.
[159] See also Oxfam (2014), p. 20.

The second type of income taxes could be an income tax on business profits. Here as well, one could make use of thresholds ensuring that small businesses would be (totally) exempt from taxes and that bigger business would become subject to the income tax once they reach a certain (to-be-defined) size and/or maturity. One could diversify the business tax system even further by means of several other criteria, such as the (advantageous or disadvantageous) impact of the business on society, on the environment...

Next to these two types of income taxes, one could, furthermore, think of a transaction tax which would be limited to either transactions of a (very) luxurious nature, or transactions qualified as harmful (albeit not harmful enough to completely forbid them).

- The second pillar of the new tax system would be that the new tax system should allow a "sufficient degree of individual wealth accumulation" in order to ensure that every human living anywhere in the world (and not only a select elite of rich people) will be able to gather a basic fortune, this also from an intergenerational perspective.

  Given the fact that under the abovementioned, newly proposed system of money creation on behalf of the national governments of the participating countries, public authorities will no longer depend on taxes for their own income, they will henceforth be able to accept that also persons belonging to the lower and middle classes within society will also be able to acquire a certain degree of personal wealth.

  This is why the newly proposed tax system should mainly aspire to be of an altruistic nature and be based upon a full transparency of both gathered fortune and income.
- The third pillar of the new fiscal system would be its intention to be of a "fair" and "just" nature. It would, hence, not impact the middle and poorer classes, but only impact the rich and very rich (to be defined as those people that have acquired a personal fortune reaching the abovementioned threshold(s)).
- The fourth pillar of the new fiscal system would be its relative simplicity, implying that only a limited number of tax systems would still prevail.

  As said, this would firstly be the case for the previously described income tax system for individuals whose personal fortune would exceed the abovementioned threshold(s), and which will have to be neutral as regards the "source" of income (consequently being imposed on any form of income, be it from labour or from capital). The second tax system would consist of transaction taxes with regards to goods and services of either a very luxurious nature, or of a purportedly harmful nature (which would, however, not be considered of such severity that it would be deemed necessary to completely ban the transactions in question). The third tax system would deal with the operational profits of business entities.

  Especially this third tax system could prove its use as a true public policy tool; it could, for instance, allow for diversified tax tariffs based upon the business ethics of the business entities involved.

Given the fact that taxation will no longer considered as an instrument for financing government expenditure, it should also be further reflected upon what will be done with the taxes thus imposed (and received).

One could, for instance, reflect on the installment of a system that leaves the tax payer the option to either pay the due taxes, or to attribute these on "projects of socio-cultural participation" of his own choice. The rich and very rich who under the new tax system will (still) owe taxes will, otherwise put, be invited to attribute these taxes-to-be-paid to (to-be-defined) social or cultural projects.

This would also imply that the rich within society will no longer benefit from excessive hoarding behaviour, but on the contrary will be invited to spend their excessive wealth for the benefit of the whole society. As regards the taxes due by those rich people who would not be compelled to accept this invitation, the received taxes could flow back to the monetary authorities (in order to either redistribute or destroy them).

The here proposed tax system built on the abovementioned four pillars will, obviously, only be feasible in a global context. It will need the involvement of all countries in the world who will moreover have to make the firm commitment to abandon all sovereignty in the field of creating new taxes.

5.13 Aiming for a True Solidary World

As described in the Sect. 5.11 above, the newly proposed monetary system will imply that the newly to be created central monetary authority will periodically have to decide on providing allocations of newly created money to the national governments of the participating countries.

This obviously will imply a coherent vision on the role of these governments.

There will hence be a need for a worldwide unitary vision on the future role of governments within society.

Provided that the world community could ever be convinced to install such a new monetary system, this will hence necessarily also imply that it would reach a consensus on the tasks that will be considered crucial government tasks for which the allocations referred to under Sect. 5.11 will be granted.

The most essential of such tasks will most probably concern systems of public education and systems of medical[160] and social care in a broad sense of the word.

According to the doctrines of economic neo-liberalism currently holding the global socio-economic order in its grip, it is generally assumed that governments

[160]The cost for a universal health care may not even be that high, so accomplishing it should be considered as a reachable goal. (See Anonymous (2018), p. 9).

> Universal basic health care is also affordable. A country need not wait to be rich before it can have comprehensive, if rudimentary, treatment. Health care is a labour-intensive industry, and community health workers, paid relatively little compared with doctors and nurses, can make a big difference in poor countries. (See Anonymous (2018), p. 9).

should spend nothing, or as little as possible, on both education and medical and social care. Under neo-liberal thinking, every individual human being must himself take responsibility on these matters and ensure that he disposes of enough financial means to pay for his own medical care or for his education or that of his children. Advocates of the doctrines of economic neo-liberalism, in this regard, usually refer to models of private insurance as an alternative for public social security systems.[161]

It goes without much further saying that this approach is in contradiction with the basic idea of solidarity itself.[162] Hence, within the newly to be established societal order which could be a part of the abovementioned newly proposed monetary system, both education (at least to a certain age) and social and medical care (lifelong), should become fully free of charge for any person in need of it.

In order to obtain this goal, the approach could be such that as part of the periodical allocations to be assigned to each of the participating countries, the estimated expenditure for the universal free education system and for a solid universal system of free social and medical care, would become elementary budget items.[163]

A separate item of these government budgets could, moreover, enable each of the participating countries to grant to its citizens a so-called fixed "basic income". The main idea hereby would be that every citizen, irrespective of any further differentiating criteria, would be assigned a basic income which, on the one hand, would be high enough to provide every such individual with a sufficient level of individual freedom, including the freedom to (at least temporarily) withdraw from the pressure of the capitalist production processes, but which, on the other hand, would not be that high that everyone would simply stop working (as in such a case the global economy could come to a stop).[164]

---

[161] See furthermore Chomsky (2017), p. 66.

[162] Compare Chomsky (2017), p. 65.

[163] Compare Taylor-Gooby (2013), p. 84 a.f.

[164] As Keen has pointed out, this could also help creating a solution for the problem of (too much) private debt:

> The challenge is to reduce the accumulated debt mountain, especially the private debt mountain, in an elegant way. The best way, in my view, is actually fairly simple in principle: Central banks could distribute debt-free money in appropriate amounts to citizens on a per capita basis, with a stipulation that they have to use the money to pay down existing debts first. In effect, the central bank would take excessive debt onto its own balance sheet, and then write it off.
>
> They could do this because central banks are the only banks that can legally run negative net asset balances, i.e. whose liabilities are allowed to exceed their assets.
>
> So for example, if the European Central Bank were to set up an account for every adult eurozone citizen and credited each of those accounts with 10,000 euros, overindebtedness would suddenly decline. People who were debt-free before getting their 10,000 euros would be free to spend the money on consumer goods, stimulating real-economy demand and employment.
>
> (…)
>
> Everyone would be much better off if the ECB had given out a few hundred billion euros directly to European households instead. It could still do this, there's no good reason not to. But don't hold your breath. (See Keen (2017)).

Obviously, enough attention will need to be given to systems attributing a replacement income for those whose life has taken an unfortunate turn. Ideally, such a system should be no longer based on abstract categories (such as health insurance, unemployment benefits, pension systems...), but rather on an approach where every human being is treated as an individual. In this approach, those who are struck by an unfortunate life condition would have access to a (socio-economic) life course coach who, where and when needed, possibly by co-operating with medical experts—such as physicians, psychologists, next to others—will be able to determine which impact the unfortunate life condition has on the socio-economic employability of the individual concerned. The outcome of such an intervention could be that the basic living income of this individual would (either temporarily or permanently) be increased in order to take into account the increase in living costs because of the said unfortunate course of life.

Such a system will evidently require a very high organisational effort from the participating states, albeit that the new societal system will most probably, and at the very least on the mid-long term, generate a sufficient amount of savings in the domains of tax administration, justice, police and army, in other words, causing governments expenditure to shift from its current expenditure of organising a repressive state model, especially as regards the poor and ill-fortunate, towards a state system that takes care of people and where every human being is considered at its full value.

In such a new societal model, one could even question the presently prevailing uniform employment models that expect everyone to more or less undergo the same (high) employment pressure without taking into account distinguishing factors such as the type of work (for instance physically or mentally demanding or not), the health of the individual concerned... Such a system could, in other words, allow a sufficient degree of differentiation so that, again, central attention could be given to treating every human being as an individual, taking into account both his abilities and limitations.

On a deeper level, such a new approach of organising global society will obviously need to go hand in hand with a gradual dismantling of the pursuit of profits principle as the prevailing socio-economic principle. Also the role of the government will have to be completely turned around; it will at the least imply an approach where "civil servants" would be transformed into a type of (socio-economic) "life coaches" who support the members of society in leading a tailor-made course of life, especially in the domain of the socio-economic order.

5.14 A Modern-Day Approach to the Principle of Economic Self-sufficiency

It needs not much explanation that the new economic (world) order will, above all, also imply a new hierarchy between "labour" and "capital" (or otherwise put: between (working) "people" and "(excessive amounts of) money (that are) invested".

As has already been mentioned several times before in this book, one of the essential characteristics of (unbridled) capitalism is (up to this very date) that it is based on a strong hierarchy of values. More precisely, the pursuit of money of the rich and powerful has been elevated above all other values, especially the value accorded to the labour performed by the working people, hence to people themselves.

This understanding even may provide an entirely new meaning to certain verses of the Gospels, such as the warning of Jesus Christ that one should not choose for a life of subjection to the money devil, a choice which (unbridled) capitalism is nevertheless still advocating through all conceivable means of a socio-economic nature, even to such an extent that one can hold that, at present, this biblical mammon is truly dominating as good as all levels of societal, capitalistic organisation.

A new vision on the economy (and more in general: on the outlook of the socio-economic order) should be such that this historical mistake would be reversed and that, as resolutely as possible, a new societal model would become advocated where the human being, and especially the labour performing human being, would again be put at the center in lieu of the pursuit of profits principle.

Such a new societal order will obviously have to avoid to degenerate in a system of mere "profiteering" or, otherwise put, in a system where a too large part of humanity would withdraw from any form of participation in societal life.[165] This new societal model should hereby above all ensure that everyone, in accordance with his talents and abilities, will participate in building a truly just society under which the capitalistic systems of exploitation and extortion will have to make place for the ideal of true solidarity.

Obviously, a sufficient amount of stimuli will have to be installed within this newly to be established socio-economic order in order to ensure this goal, be it that the main instrument of achieving this goal will, most probably, have to be the enhancement of the general awareness of the necessity to do so.

It may even come as a surprise to some that the here presented ideal is not completely new, but has already several times in history been attempted.

This was for instance clearly the case with the first Christian societies aiming for a new society model in which everyone would, in a spirit of mutual solidarity, contribute to building a new world of solidarity.

The latter can, for instance, be derived from the different letters of the Saint Paul as recorded in the canon of the New Testament. Saint Paul's ideal was that a world of Christian communities would emerge where nobody would be needy and where the desire to do good would increasingly trickle down to a world outside of the Church. From "2 Tessalonians, 3:6–12", it is clear that this principle of "practical

[165] Galbraith (2004), p. 19:

> In the United States and, if less so, in other of the developed countries, no individuals invite as much criticism as those who escape the obligation to work. They are lazy, irresponsible, a burden – simply no good. This condemnation becomes severe when the alternative to work is public support. Nothing is publicly so unacceptable as going from work to welfare. The letter is the least reputable of all public expenditures.

reciprocity" was a leading principle in the socio-economic relations between and within the Christian communities. Saint Paul would, in this regard, call upon every Christian to, by performing labour, provide his own living and not depend on anyone else, because a Christian must above all be a "benefactor" and not a "protégé".[166]

In more recent times, one may for instance refer to the similar experiment that was undertaken by the spiritual Master Osho and his disciples of establishing a new kind of community, based upon the ideals of love and altruism, in the State of Oregon (USA).[167]

5.15 Reorganising the Labour Markets in Accordance with a More Correct Vision on Man

5.15.1 Problem

In order to establish the new, more altruistic socio-economic order referred to in the previous sections, there will obviously be a more correct vision on who and what man is.

Future methods of labour organisation could, for instance, take into account the findings of biological and medical science, such as the insight that man goes through life cycles, with as a consequence that there are certain phases in human life during which man can be more productive than during other life phases.[168]

In the Western world, this could translate into more humane career paths than the ones which are currently prevailing under unbridled capitalist exploitation and extortion practices, where one may observe that more and more people are no longer able to cope with the high expectations of the over-competitive free market system (unless, perhaps, through means of resorting to addictive drugs provided by the overly profit driven pharmaceutical industry, amongst which all types of antidepressants, stimulants and sedatives[169]).

---

[166] See 1 Tessalonians, 2: 1–12 and 4:9–11; see also Jones (2011), pp. 115–116.

[167] See https://en.wikipedia.org/wiki/Rajneeshpuram (last consulted on June 16, 2018).

See also the already abovementioned Netflix documentary "Wild wild country" (see https://www.imdb.com/title/tt7768848/; last consulted on June 16, 2018).

For Osho's own account on these events, see Bhagwan Shree Rajneesh (1989). For an account of the hand of one of the residents of Antelope at the time, see Quick (1995). Even the at the time sheriff of the Wasco Counting wrote his own book on these events; see Labrousse (2016).

[168] Compare Das (2012), p. xxxii.

[169] Coen (2015), p. 11.

From an investigation that has been conducted by the Belgian newspaper "Het Laatste Nieuws", the results of which appeared in said newspaper on May 12th 2018, it appeared that as a result of severe cutbacks that Belgian hospitals had to undergo during the past years, one of three nurses is at present reliant on medication in order to still be able to perform their jobs. Said investigation was conducted by "Het Laatste Nieuws" in close co-operation with the professional organisation "NVKVV" and the trade union "ACV", a.o. by means of interviews with 2,560 nurses. It appeared

The goal to advocate a more just socio-economic order will in other words only be achievable by even so advocating, on a global scale, career and productivity paths in accordance with the individuality and the limitations of human nature itself.

5.15.2 *Towards a Career Path Taking into Account Man's Phases of Life*

The approach referred to in the previous Sect. 5.15.1 could, for instance, be that every human being will have the opportunity, during roughly the first 20–25 years of its life, to shape and develop himself to the fullest extent through means of an appropriate education and a matching professional training. (See also Sect. 3.1.2.)

As mentioned before, education and professional training should hereby, on a worldwide scale, become one of the main public services, implying that everyone should have access to such a proper education and training entirely to be financed out of government budgets (from the abovementioned allocations countries will receive out of the hands of the newly to create monetary world authority; see above, under Sects. 5.11 and 5.12.).

The proposed age limits should, obviously, not become a strict dogma, as the goal of the new approach on education and training should be that it will be as custom-tailored as possible with full respect of everyone's individual talents and skills.

Denying access to a fitting education or professional training because a person stems from a poor class, or making this access dependable upon entering into expensive student loans,[170] should become practices which will belong to the past for good.

---

from said investigation that, as a result of severe cutbacks, the sector is facing a huge shortage of personnel, which makes the work pressure unbearable. 88% of the nurses hereby complained that the work pressure they are facing is too high on a daily basis, with huge repercussions on their health. 15% of the nurses admits of taking medication on a daily basis in order to be able to cope with their jobs and another 15% does the same on a weekly basis. Among the most commonly used medication are: painkillers, inflammatory agents and sleeping pills. The sector of hospital replied to the results of said investigation by pointing out that a similar high medication use is characterizing the whole of society and not only the sector of hospitals itself. (See Bossaert (2008a). See also Grymonprez (2018), p. 7.) It moreover has appeared from the same investigation that the underfunding and understaffing of Belgian hospital costs human lives, for instance, due to errors being made by too exhausted hospital staff members (see Bossaert (2008b)).

[170] See as regards the late Margaret Thatcher, her deliberate policy of, among others, high university entrance fees to push students towards student loans, under the argument that this would result into more rational study choices (see Thatcher (1993), pp. 597–598).

In reality, these higher entrance fees erode the democratisation of university education as student loans are above all a mechanism by means of which the rich (namely the financial institutions providing the loans and their capital providers ultimately receiving the profits from this) are getting more rich to the detriment of the poor (being the students in need).

Once an individual will have developed into maturity and will have finalised the phase of education and professional training, his entry to a professional life may follow. A more humane approach towards entering into the labour market could imply that, in many professional sectors, a younger person would become initiated in the job he chooses by a more senior person, on condition that it will be avoided that this would lead to systems of extortion (as currently prevailing within capitalism, for instance, to a very high degree, in the free professions sectors).

The largest participation to professional life could hereby be expected from people between the ages of 25 and 50 (or, according to recent research, even younger, namely 40[171]).

These are indeed the years during which the average person is vitally peeking. These could also be the years when the working individual will receive the highest income out of his labour efforts in order to gather a sufficient personal fortune allowing him to lead a worthy and prosperous life.

Between the ages of 50 (or even: 40) and 60, there could be a period of a gradual reduction of one's professional activities, where as much as possible a handover of one's professional duties and responsibilities would be organised towards the people between the ages of 25 and 40/50 (as mentioned earlier). This phase of life between the ages of somewhere between 40 and 50 until 60 could hence go hand in hand with less stressing expectations, both in the field of the number of working

---

[171] A recent study issued in the Melbourne Institute Worker Paper Series (see Kajitani et al. 2016) demonstrates that people who are older than 40 perform best at work when they work only 3 days per week. It appears from this research that "older people" (above 40) perform significantly better when they only work 25 h per week. From this study, it furthermore appears that working 40 h a week is linked to a smaller cognitive deficit, but working 55 h or more appears to be worse than being retired or unemployed. (See Anonymous (2016a, b).) From this research, one may hence conclude that working full time until the age of 67 is not as beneficial as the Australian government (next to many other neo-liberal governments all over the globe) make(s) people believe. (See Anonymous (2016a, b).)

As the authors of said study have phrased it themselves:

> Our empirical evidence shows that there is non-linearity in the effects of working hours on cognitive functioning. When working hours are less than around 25 hours a week, working hours have a positive impact on cognitive functioning. However, when working hours are more than 25 hours per week, working hours have negative impacts on cognition. These results suggest that people in old age could maintain their cognitive ability by working in a part-time job that requires them to work around 20–30 hours per week. (See Kajitani et al. (2016), p. 4.)

The reason for this is stress and fatigue:

> Work can be a double edged sword, in that it can stimulate brain activity, but at the same time, long working hours and certain types of tasks can cause fatigue and stress which potentially damage cognitive functions. (See Kajitani et al. (2016), p. 3, referring to several other similar research.)

hours to be performed, as in the field of hard productivity output that is expected.[172]

The latter expectations could be replaced by an expectation of guidance with and the passing on of knowledge and expertise to the younger work force. In the field of remuneration, one could expect from this category of workers that they would accept a lower financial remuneration (to the benefit of the younger generation), this in the awareness that, in a principally tax free society, everyone should be able to have gathered a sufficient personal fortune in the period between the ages of 25 and somewhere between 40 and 50.

Furthermore, such a reduction of the remuneration from performed labour could go along with an accrual of the basic living income which everyone will receive anyhow (see Sect. 5.13).

The amount of the basic living income could hereby be modified in function of the course of life, where it could be rather modest for children (still living with their parents), in order to be increased from the moment when someone starts living independently until the moment of a full-time employment. During the years of high productivity (between the ages of 25–40/50), at least for working people earning a sufficient income out of their labour, the basic living income could again be lowered, and at the moment when someone would gradually start retiring from professional life (between the ages 40/50–60), it could again be (gradually) increased.

In case the abovementioned proposals would meet the classic criticism by those blinded by the free market doctrines that they are of an unrealistic or utopian nature, it should nevertheless be observed that in older societies the approach to life from which they have been derived, has not been that uncommon.[173]

Anyway, this newly proposed approach would be much more compliant with the natural life cycle of the human species than is the case with the way the labour market functions under the rule of unbridled capitalism where everyone, up till a very high age (and in many cases literally till one drops dead), should keep on working as hard as possible in order to allow enterprises to keep on going on making as much profits thinkable.

One can however but doubt if mankind will ever be ready for such a new approach to the organisation of the labour markets, especially in light of the fact that in many neo-liberalized countries, heated political debates are taken place where neo-liberalist and conservative authors and policy makers take the stand that the average age of retirement should be made higher and higher, and the pensions of retired people lower and lower,[174] while at the same time many Western countries face sky-

---

[172] See again Kajitani et al. (2016), p. 13, who in their abovementioned research came to the following conclusion:

> This indicates that the differences in working hours is an important factor for maintaining cognitive functioning in middle and older adults. In other words, in the middle and older age, working part-time could effective in maintaining cognitive ability.

[173] See in this regard Das (2012), p. xxxii.

[174] A viewpoint that is clearly contradicted by the empirical research of Kajitani et al. (2016). (See also Anonymous (2016a, b).)

rocketing rates of youth unemployment, and, at the background of these debates, with the blessings of the many adherents of economic neo-liberalism, the rich and the powerful of the planet are literally still getting richer by the second.

Nevertheless, when combined with the other abovementioned proposals for creating a new socio-economic order, the foregoing proposal could also remedy all of the consequences of what one might refer to as the increasing "intergenerational employment conflict" that capitalism has caused, albeit, once more, the question arises if humanity will ever be sufficiently willing to do so.

References

Achterhuis H (1988) Het rijk van de schaarste. Van Thomas Hobbes tot Michel Foucault. Ambo, Amsterdam

Andries C (1996) Les chemins du Bouddha. Le Monde – hors-série – L'Atlas des religions, Édition 2015

Anonymous (2015a) De grootste godsdiensten. Knack, 21 January 2015, p 24

Anonymous (2015b) The world is going to university. The Economist, 28 March 2015, Special Report, pp 11–12

Anonymous (2015c) Getuigenis. Jonge copiloot van lagekostenmaatschappij getuigt over de moeilijke werksituatie. Ik hou van job maar ik haat sector. De Morgen, 28 March 2015, pp 4–5

Anonymous (2016a) People over 40 should only work 3 days a week, experts say. https://successfulflow.co/people-over-40-should-only-work-3-days-a-week-experts-say/. Last consulted 16 June 2018

Anonymous (2016b) Three-day week best for over-40s. https://www.telegraph.co.uk/news/2016/04/17/3-day-week-best-for-over-40s/. Last consulted 16 June 2018

Anonymous (2018) Within reach. The case for universal health care is a powerful one – including in poor countries. The Economist, 28 April 2018, p 9

Arenas L (2016) Rousseau. L'homme est bon par nature. C'est la société qui le corrompt. In: Apprendre à philosopher. RBA, Paris

Aristotle (1996) The Nicomachean Ethics (trans: Rackham H). Wordsworth Classics of World Literature, Hertfordshire

Beaud M (1994) Geschiedenis van het kapitalisme van 1500 tot heden. Het Spectrum (Aula) Utrecht

Bell D (1996) The cultural contradictions of capitalism. Basic Books, New York

Bertrand J-R (2015) Le poids de le démographie. Le Monde – hors-série – L'Atlas des religions, Édition 2015, pp 14–15

Bhagwan Shree Rajneesh (1989) Jesus crucified again. This time in Ronald Reagan's America, 1st edn. The Rebel Publishing House GmbH, Cologne

Bhaktivedanta Swami Prabhupada AC (1976) De Bhagavad-Gita zoals ze is. The Bhaktivedanta Book Trust, Amsterdam (3 volumes)

Bieler A (1961) La pensée économique et sociale de Calvin. Librairie de l'Université, Genève

Bogaert R, Brion R, Jurgan-Van Hentenryk G, Moreau LJ, Van Der Wee H (2000) A history of European Banking. Mercatorfonds and European Investment Bank, Antwerp [also: Bogaert R, Jurgan-Van Hentenryk G, Van Der Wee H (1991) De Bank in Europa. 25 eeuwen Bankgeschiedenis. Mercatorfonds, Antwerp; Bogaert R, Jurgan-Van Hentenryk G, Van Der Wee H (1991) La banque and Occident. Mercatorfonds, Antwerp]

Bossaert J (2008a) 1 op de 3 verplegers slikt pillen om job aan te kunnen (article of May 12th 2018). https://m.hln.be/nieuws/binnenland/1-op-de-3-verplegers-slikt-pillen-om-job-aan-te-kunnen~a46b86b6/. Last consulted 16 June 2018

Bossaert J (2008b) Personeelstekort in ziekenhuizen eist levens (article of May 14th 2018). https://www.hln.be/wetenschap-planeet/medisch/personeelstekort-in-ziekenhuizen-eist-levens~a8d14edd/. Last consulted 16 June 2018

Brook Y, Watkins D (2012) Free market revolution – how Ayn Rand's ideas can end big government. Palgrave Macmillan, New York

Bruckner P (2002) Misère de la prospérité – la religion marchande et ses ennemis. Bernard Grasset, Paris

Byanyima W (2014) Foreword. Oxfam, pp 4–5

Byttebier K (2001) Handboek financieel recht. Kluwer Rechtswetenschappen, Antwerp

Byttebier K (2015) Nu het gouden kalf verdronken is. Van hebzucht naar altruïsme als hoeksteen voor een Nieuwe Monetaire Wereldorde. Maklu, Antwerp

Byttebier K (2017) Towards a new international monetary order. In: Byttebier K, van der Borght K (eds) Economic and financial law & policy – shifting insights & values, vol I. Springer, Cham

Chomsky N (2017) Requiem for the American dream. The 10 principles of concentration of wealth & power. Seven Stories Press, New York

Chu B (2017) Income gap between people from rich and poor backgrounds has almost doubled, IFS figures reveal. https://www.independent.co.uk/news/business/news/income-gap-uk-ifs-research-rich-poor-divide-widening-latest-figures-a7886756.html. Last consulted 16 June 2018

Coen S (2015) Test-Aankoop: dokters grijpen véél te snel naar medicatie. U Slaapt slecht? 94 op 100 artsen schrijven pilletje voor. Het Laatste Nieuws, 28–29 March 2015, p 11

Cole G (1937) Practical economics. Penguin Books, London

Congregation for the Doctrine of the Faith – Dicastery For Promoting Integral Human Development (2018) Oeconomicae et pecuniariae quaestiones – Considerations for an ethical discernment regarding some aspects of the present economic-financial system. http://www.vatican.va/roman_curia/congregations/cfaith/documents/rc_con_cfaith_doc_20180106_oeconomicae-et-pecuniariae_en.html#. Last consulted 16 June 2018

Das G (2012) The difficulty of being good: on the subtle art of Dharma. Penguin Books, New Dehli

Dawkins R (2005) The ancestor's tale. A pilgrimage to the dawn of life. Orion House, London

Dawkins R (2006) The selfish gene. Oxford University Press, Oxford (30th anniversary edition)

De Meester K (1997) Op zoek naar de kleine weg. Van Lisieux T Leven. Leer. Milieu, Ghent, Carmelitana

De Rijke J (2015) Wij hebben al zoveel meegemaakt. Wij geloven niets meer. Knack, 25 February 2015, pp 68–75

de Wit A, Steenvoorde R (eds) (2008) Christendom. Lannoo, Tielt

Delfgaauw B (1960) Beknopte geschiedenis der wijsbegeerte – II. De moderne wijsbegeerte. Het Wereldvenster, Baarn

Descouvemont P, Loose HN (1991) Thérèse et Lisieux. Éditions du Cerf

Donnell H (2017) Silicon Valley super-rich head south to escape from a global apocalypse (article of 29 January 2017). https://www.theguardian.com/technology/2017/jan/29/silicon-valley-new-zealand-apocalypse-escape. Last consulted 16 June 2018

Duffy N (2018) Catholic Church demands apology from BBC over video challenging religious homophobia. https://www.pinknews.co.uk/2018/04/27/catholic-church-demands-apology-from-bbc-over-video-challenging-religious-homophobia/. Last consulted 16 June 2018

Evers L (1999) Jodendom voor beginners. Een heldere inleiding. Forum – De Boekerij BV, Amsterdam

Foucault M (2013) De geboorte van de biopolitiek. Boom, Amsterdam

Friedman M (1993) Why government is the problem. Hoover Institution on War, Revolution and Peace, Stanford University

Fromm E (2014) Marx's concept of man. Bloomsbury, London

Galbraith JK (1979) Annals of an abiding liberal. A Meridian Book New American Library, New York

Galbraith JK (1987) Economics in perspective – a critical history. Houghton Mifflin Company, Boston
Galbraith JK (1992) The culture of contentment. Houghton Mifflin Company, Boston
Galbraith JK (2004) The economics of innocence fraud. Houghton Mifflin Company, Boston
Galbraith JK, Salinger N (1978) Almost everyone's guide to economics. Penguin Books, London
Goldfarb M (2012) De weg uit het getto. Drie eeuwen van emancipatie van de Joden in Europa. Meulenhoff, Amsterdam
Graeber D (2012) Debt. The first 5000 years. Brooklyn and London
Greenspan A (2007) The age of turbulence. Adventures in a new world. The Penguin Press, New York
Grymonprez S (2018) 'Trop is te veel', zeggen verpleegkundigen. Stijgende werkdruk, reorganisaties en loonhervorming. De Standaard, May 12th–13th, p 7
Häberlein M (2006) Die Fugger: Geschichte einer Augsburger Familie (1367–1650). Kohlhammer, Stuttgart
Habets J, Gloudemans H (2011) De voedselparadox. Over grootschalige honger in een wereld die (meer dan) genoeg voedsel produceert. Stichting Werelddelen, Tilburg
Jones S (2011) De wereld van de vroege Kerk. Boekencentrum, Zoetermeer
Kajitani S, McKenzie C, Sakata K (2016) Use it too much and lose it? The effect of working hours on cognitive ability. Melbourne Institute Working Paper N° 07/16
Kasser T (2002) The high price of materialism. A Bradford Book/The MIT Press, Cambridge/London
Keen S (2017) Can we avoid another financial crisis? http://www.dw.com/en/can-we-avoid-another-financial-crisis/a-41111841. Last consulted 16 June 2018
Kruithof J (2000) Het neoliberalisme. EPO, Antwerp
Kuntz K, von Rohr M, Ertel M (2015) De grote plannen van de Griekse premier Alexis Tsipras. Knack, 18 March 2015, pp 9–13
Labrousse A (2016) Elected through terror. The Rajneesh through the eyes of a local sheriff. Between the Presses, LLC, Great Britain
Levinas E (1988) In de tijd van de volkeren. Garant, Leuven
Lloyd C (2012) What on earth happened? The complete story of the planet, life & people from the big bang to the present day. Bloomsbury, London
Maddison A (2007) Contours of the world economy, I – 2030 AD – essays in macro-economic history. Oxford University Press, Oxford
Mansfeld J (2012) Aldus sprak Heraclitus. De Fragmenten. Historische Uitgeverij, Groningen
Marcuse H (1962) Eros and civilization – a philosophical inquiry into Freud. Vintage Books (A division of Random House), New York
Marx K (1982/1983) Das Kapital – Kritik der politischen öconomie (edition in three volumes). Dietz Verlag Berlin, Berlin
Meeussen G (2015) Nepstatuten piloten gevaar voor veiligheid. De Tijd, 8 March 2015, p 17
Meredith M (2014) Alle rijkdom verdwijnt. Knack, 26 November 2014, pp 100–103
Micklethwait J, Woolridge A (2014) De vierde revolutie. Op zoek naar de overheid van morgen. De Bezige Bij, Antwerp
Moorman J (1976) Saint Francis of Assisi. SPCK, London
Osho (1989) The Dhammapada. The way of the Buddha. The Rebel Publishing House, Cologne (12 volumes)
Osho (1991) Het nieuwe kind. Osho Publikaties, Amsterdam
Osho (2006) Come follow to you. Reflections on Jesus of Nazareth (1). Tao Publishing Pvt. Ltd., Pune
Osho (2017) The true name. Talks on the Japuji-Saheb of Guru Nanak Dev. Full Circle Publishing, New Dehli
Osho (SD) The hidden harmony. Discourses on the fragments of Heraclius, 2nd edn. The Rebel Publishing House, Cologne
Oxfam (2014) Even it up – time to end extreme inequality. Oxfam GB, Oxford

Pinxten R (2009) Mensen. Een inleiding in de culturele antropologie. Lannoo, Tielt
Plato (1987) The Republic. Penguin Books, London
Plato (1994–2000) The laws (Nomoi) (trans: Jowett B). http://classics.mit.edu/Plato/laws.mb.txt. Last consulted 16 June 2018
Polak S (1928) Beknopte Geschiedenis der Staatshuishoudkunde. Maatschappij voor goede en goedkope lectuur, Amsterdam
Polanyi K (2001) The great transformation. The political and economic origins of our time. Beacon Press, Boston
Popper K (1966) The open society and its enemies. Routledge, London
Poulain H (2015) Les diasporas juives. Le Monde – hors-série – L'Atlas des religions, Édition 2015, p 28
Quick D (1995) A place called Antelope. The Rajneesh story. August Press, Washington
Rand A (1992) The virtue of selfishness. New American Library (a division of Penguin Group), New York
Robertson D (2018) Don't applaud Pope Francis's stance on homosexuality – it's still in line with Catholic teachings. https://www.independent.co.uk/voices/pope-francis-homosexuality-stance-catholic-church-same-sex-marriage-catechism-a8361821.html. Last consulted 16 June 2018
Rogers J (2018) **'Eaten alive'** Who was Rebecca Zeni? Former model and US TV star 'eaten by scabies in her Georgia care home' (article of 30th April 2018). https://www.thesun.co.uk/news/6169196/rebecca-zeni-model-eaten-alive-scabies-mites-georgia-lafayette/. Last consulted 16 June 2018
Rousseau J (1966) Du contrat social. Garnier-Flammarion, Paris
Russell B (1948) Geschiedenis der westerse Filosofie in verband met politieke en sociale omstandigheden van de oudste tijden tot heden (trans: Limburg R). Servire, Den Haag
Sainte Thérèse de l'Enfant Jésus (1957) Manuscrits autobiographiques. Office central de Lisieux
Sapir G, Statman D (2005) Why freedom of religion does not include freedom from religion. Law Philos 24:467–508
Skidelsky R, Skidelsky E (2013) How much is enough. Money and the good life. Penguin Books, London
Smith D (2014) Was Karl Marx and the rise of communism influenced by Satan? https://opentheword.org/2014/07/30/was-karl-marx-and-the-rise-of-communism-influenced-by-satan/. Last consulted 16 June 2018
Smout L (2014) Black-out is erg slechte publiciteit. Het Laatste Nieuws, 29–30 November 2014, p 4
Stiglitz J (2002) Employment, social justice and societal well-being. Int Labour Organ 141(1–2):9–29
Stiglitz J (2006) Making globalization work. Penguin Books, London
Stiglitz J (2010) Freefall. Free markets and the sinking of the global economy. Allen Lane (an imprint of Penguin Books), London
Styles H (2015) The Dhammapada (Penguin Little Black Classics). Penguin Books, London
Talmon JL (1966) Les origines de la démocratie totalitaire. Calmann-Lévy, Paris
Tardan-Masquelier Y (2015) Hindouisme une culture et des dieux. Le Monde – hors-série – L'Atlas des religions, Édition 2015, pp 68–69
Tawney RH (1944) Religion and the rise of capitalism. John Murray, London
Taylor-Gooby P (2013) The double crisis of the welfare state and what we can do about it. Palgrave Macmillan, Houndmills
Thatcher M (1993) The downing street years. HarperCollinsPublishers, London
Tolstoj L (2012) De weg van het leven. Erven J. Bijleveld, Utrecht
Truyman A (2015) Paus Franciscus, erfenis en toekomst. Acco, Leuven
van Genderen J, Veenhof C, Nauta D, Hage L, van der Linde S (1965) Zicht op Calvijn. Buijten & Schipperheijn, Amsterdam
Vandewalle G (1976) De geschiedenis van het economisch denken. Kluwer, Deventer

Vivekananda (1989) Karma yoga. The complete works of Swami Vivekanda (Mayavati Memorial Edition, vol I). Advaita Ashrama, Kolkata
Weber M (1967) L'éthique protestante et l'esprit du capitalisme. Plon, Paris
Wieviorka M (2014) Het antisemitisme uitgelegd aan jongeren. De Bezige Bij, Amsterdam
Yogananda (2012) God talks with Arjuna – the Bhagavad Gita. Royal Science of God-Realization – Self-Realization Fellowship, Los Angeles (2 volumes)

Chapter 6
Final Conclusions

6.1 Bearing in Mind the Past

Since the transition from nomadic to agricultural societies that, roughly spoken, started some 10 to 11,000 years ago, the organisation of societies has gradually been subject to the dictates of economics.

The rise of cities that followed from this agricultural revolution more precisely led to "the invention of money" and to the development of indirect barter trade economic systems.[1]

An important side effect of this evolution has been that it has enabled practices of saving and lending, and through this, of wealth gathering. This in its turn went hand in hand with the development of economic systems that got gradually based on egoism, selfishness and greed.

It is, hence, hardly a surprise that some of the first "systematic thinkers" from Western history, such as the renowned philosophers from Ancient Greece Plato en Aristotle, uttered strong warnings against these then newly occurring economic developments, and more specifically against the values of egoism, selfishness and greed on which they got based.

In the course of the further socio-economic history, a duality between the use of money in practice and the moral reflection on this money use has for a long time been characterising the Western world, where, on the one hand, practices of economy increasingly promoted the pursuit of money as its central economic value and, on the other hand, prominent thinkers fought this by calling for more altruism in interpersonal relations.

In the Western world, the call for altruism as the determining principle of interpersonal relations probably reached a historical peak in the teachings of Jesus Christ who literally held that the pursuit of money was equal to serving the devil. Out of

[1] For further reading, see for instance Lloyd (2012) and Harari (2014).

K. Byttebier, *The Unfree Market and the Law*, Economic and Financial Law & Policy – Shifting Insights & Values 2,
https://doi.org/10.1007/978-3-319-97382-1_6

Christ's teachings, the world religion of Christianity would emerge to become the largest world religion in our present times.

For a long time, the policy of the Catholic church within the Western world contributed to shaping a socio-economic order more or less in line with some of Jesus Christ's basic teachings.

However, especially in the course of the sixteenth and seventeenth century, new Christian thinkers would make such strong concessions to the emerging practices of pre-capitalism that this would ultimately contribute to a clerical schism from which the protestant churches emerged. Protestantism hereby bore witness of such a tolerant attitude towards the pursuit of money principle that it helped creating a true turnaround of the moral perception on money gathering, thus clearing the way for the breakthrough of capitalism as a socio-economic system that would completely abandon the teachings of Jesus Christ by turning the pursuit of profits (hence: of money) into its basic moral value.

In this way, capitalism is probably the system most in contradiction with the message brought by Jesus Christ to the extent that He literally did not want a society in which the mammon (or: the money devil) would be put before God, while on the contrary (unbridled) capitalism obviously does so.

The seventeenth and eighteenth centuries testified to the breakthrough of several so-called enlightened philosophies, in the wake of which, ultimately, the doctrines of economic liberalism emerged. This economic doctrine would since then start playing a decisive role in the further development of the economy.

The theories of economic liberalism in particular offered an ideological validation to the emerging capitalist practices, such as the creation of money based on interest-generating credits granted by private banks, the use of the capital company as a technique for doing business in a "deresponsibalised" manner and the use of new production processes which were mainly characterised by a massive exploitation of the cheapest workforce possible.

All this resulted in the course of the nineteenth century into the so-called industrial revolution, the definitive breakthrough of (unbridled) capitalism as the overall dominating socio-economic system on the planet.

In the field of socio-economic thinking, the result of these evolutions has been that one no longer had dismissive thoughts on the pursuit of money, but on the contrary, the unbridled pursuit of money was soon given the highest social (and societal) status.

The powers of (unbridled) capitalism would hereby gradually gain grip on the entire world economy, causing the genesis of a society which is strongly characterised by an exploitation of the large masses by a small elite of rich to very rich entrepreneurs and of the capital providers of the enterprises led by them.

Albeit initially being formed in the Western territories, mainly the European regions and their former colonies, the capitalistic socio-economic order would in the course of the twentieth century and until the present date, gradually be exported all over the world that in this way became gradually subjected to the techniques of capitalist exploitation.

It, hence, needs not surprise that the century of the industrial revolution was also the century during which colonialism and slavery practices flourished. The grandeur of the streets of European cities such as London, Paris and Vienna up till this very day keep on testifying of the lifestyle which the most devastating practices of colonial exploitation have made possible. The European colonial powers would hereby not even shrunk from literally stealing historical art treasures from their original territories to exhibit them ostentatiously in museums or, in some cases, even in the streets of their own ample cities.

In light of this, it may be considered thus the more remarkable that, soon after their own independence for which they had fought battle under the most noble ideals, certain American states of that time would not hesitate to re-introduce slavery in its purest form, in this way giving expression to the most strict application of one of the toughest capitalistic principles, namely the "Iron Law of the Wages".

After the new socio-economic order in the first half of the twentieth century resulted in two devastating world wars, at least for some time, some policy makers realised that the application of unbridled capitalism is disastrous for humanity and the planet earth itself. In light of this insight, an era arose where different societal powers advocated to give unbridled capitalism a more humane face. As a result, at least in the Western world, certain "left-wing" political movements, supported by the actions of trade unions and similar organisations, gave shape to the so-called welfare state model, be it with large variations amongst the different Western countries.

States thus introduced certain corrections to unbridled capitalism, such as certain types of public services (for instance education and certain forms of medical care), next to systems of protection of labour and social care in a broad sense of the word.

The oil and energy crises of the 1970s would turn out to cause a breaking point, as the increasing oil prices caused an important skimming of the profits of the large (Western) enterprises, in its own turn causing the rich and powerful within society to fundamentally question the principle of solidarity on which the welfare state model was based. Their vision that cuts were needed in the too expensive apparatus of the welfare state model would be gradually wrapped in different pseudo-academic doctrines which, today, are often placed under the denominator of "(economic) neo-liberalism", which itself is mainly a collective term for different lines of conservative economic thinking aimed at making the markets as free as possible from all kinds of influences, especially all forms of government involvement.[2]

During the 1980s, on a worldwide scale, the doctrines of economic neo-liberalism got gradually implemented in practice. In many countries, this led to a gradual (and up to this date still ongoing) dismantling of public services and systems of labour protection and social care that the welfare state had provided.

Even so, the world economy got gradually submitted to the several theories of economic neo-liberalism, resulting to the presently prevailing globalised free market order.

[2] See also Chomsky and Polychroniou (2017), p. 157.

The "sub-doctrine" of economic neo-liberalism known as "consumerism" pretended that by stimulating consumption, production would increase, which would lead to more economic growth, employment and prosperity. Another sub-doctrine of economic neo-liberalism, known as (Friedmanian) "monetarism", aimed at fighting inflation, while at the same time ensuring a sufficiently cheap money supply. The combination of both doctrines would turn out to be disastrous for the Western world which, as a result, came overdependent on (bank) debt.[3]

This cocktail of economic factors would already in 2007–2008 culminate in probably the worst financial crisis the Western world has known since the depression of the 1930s, where it can be observed that especially the financial sector has been able to remain on the ground thanks to a massive state support (known as "bailouts"), causing that the financial deficits which were created by the financial institutions have largely been shifted towards the government budgets. This in its own turn provided a new excuse for those adhering economic neo-liberalism to even further dismantle welfare states, an approach that, strangely enough, has hardly met any noteworthy societal turmoil.[4]

Meanwhile, the polarisation between the rich and poor is taking proportions exceeding the human imagination, where, due to the capitalist mechanisms, a small group of extremely rich people continue to get richer by the second (accumulating assets worth tens of billions USD), while at the same time, two billion people have to make ends meet with 2.5 USD per day (or 912.5 USD/year, or 63,876 USD/lifetime[5]).

The manifest injustices caused by (unbridled) capitalism should, by now, be more than evident for those who are willing to understand them. It may be far less comprehensible, albeit bearing witness of the disappointing low level of the degree of civilisation of mankind that the development of a more just socio-economic order has nevertheless barely been propagated so far.

Even renowned American economists, in the past stigmatised as "(too) liberal", such as Galbraith, Stiglitz and Krugman, have suggested that there is no real alternative for the free market system, but that one can only aim for installing correction mechanisms.

[3] See in this regard the concern expressed by former ECB-president J.-C. Trichet in an interview with "De Volkskrant" of April 23th 2018 (see De Waard (2018)), rightly referring to the problem of both private and public debt as one of the main, underestimated problems of our time.

[4] See also Congregation for the Doctrine of the Faith (2018), n° 5.

[5] In light of a (most probably too optimistic) assumption that the poor effectively would have an average life expectation of 70 years and that every poor person would be able to continue to receive this yearly salary from the age of 0 to 70, and not taking into account inflation and other effects. By means of comparison: this hypothetical life income would not even be sufficient to pay for the entrance fees at an average American university.

6.2 Looking at the Future

One may however wonder if the latter pessimism is truly justified, as, in the course of history many models of organising society on the level of socio-economics have risen and collapsed, implying that it is hard to understand why capitalism and the "selfish economy" which it shapes, should be an exception to this reality and should be kept in place forever.

What is above all needed, is that as many people as possible would take a different stand towards the socio-economic processes.

There is, in other words, above all need for a new way of "socio-economic thinking". This should mainly come down to resolutely abandoning the value choice made by capitalism which alleviated egoism, selfishness and greed to be the determining socio-economic principles, in favour of choosing for altruism and mutual affection as the new driving forces of the socio-economic order, and of (finally) activating the dynamics of democracy in order to put these in practice.

In doing this, one does not even need to "invent" a totally new set of moral values, as an elementary study of the most important religious and philosophical teachings from the past, themselves the result of ages of reflection on what is fair and just, may already lead to very enriching insights.

To paraphrase Levinas[6]: after centuries of reflection, it is by now sufficiently known, or at least knowable, where to find "holiness", albeit that there may be an urgent need that humanity, in sufficient numbers, really starts looking for it.

Under reference to what that has been elaborated upon earlier in this book, it could even be sufficient that every man on earth, starting immediately, would resolutely start living in accordance with the four earlier quoted values stemming from the world religions (see Sects. 5.4–5.7), namely:

(i) the Hindu principle of fulfilling one's "dharma" through selfless labour (see Sect. 5.4);
(ii) the Christian principle of (true) charity (see Sect. 5.6);
(iii) the Buddhist principle of stopping desiring (see Sect. 5.5), and,
(iv) the Jewish principle of applying humility in all interpersonal relations (see Sect. 5.7).

On a macro-level, these principles could translate into a fundamental transformation,[7] on a worldwide harmonised scale, of the socio-economic order on at least three levels, namely the level of money creation, the level of taxation and the

---

[6] Goud (1992), p. 176.

In one of his interviews, Levinas summarised this observation as follows (see Forié and Nemo (2006), p. 69):

> Yes! The other is more important than me, I am there for the other. The duties of the other towards me, are his business, not mine!

[7] See also Stiglitz (2002), p. 27.

level of providing public services and installing labour and social protection measures.

On the first level, the currently prevailing system of private money creation to the benefit of (read: the money pursuit goals of) a small number of financial institutions and their (extremely) rich capital providers, should resolutely be replaced by a system of public money creation which would be run based on public interest considerations and out of concern for the wellbeing of all human beings and by extension, of everything alive.[8]

To the extent that states, in such a new global system of public money creation, would acquire their financial operating means by means of allocations, there will be a much lower need for taxation systems which could henceforth be transformed into systems by means of which the (extremely) rich would be encouraged to display a (true) solidarity with the rest of society.

Thirdly, based on the public creation of money, one could advocate a worldwide balancing, at sufficiently high levels, of systems of public service, labour protection and social care (including medical care) which would guarantee that every human being, born anywhere in the word, will be able to lead a worthy life.

One can, hence, conclude that the noble ideas to establish a more just society are conceptually perceivable, albeit it remains an open question if there will be ever a sufficient willingness to put them into practice.

Without any doubt, this will at the very least require a fundamental reversal of the "sclerosis of the heart" caused for decades already by the doctrines of economic neo-liberalism.

References

Byttebier K (2017) Towards a new international monetary order. In: Byttebier K, van der Borght K (eds) Economic and financial law & policy – shifting insights & values, vol I. Springer, Cham

Chomsky N, Polychroniou C (2017) Optimism over despair. On capitalism, empire and social change. Penguin Random House UK

Congregation for the Doctrine of the Faith – Dicastery For Promoting Integral Human Development (2018) Oeconomicae et pecuniariae quaestiones – Considerations for an ethical discernment regarding some aspects of the present economic-financial system. http://www.vatican.va/roman_curia/congregations/cfaith/documents/rc_con_cfaith_doc_20180106_oeconomicae-et-pecuniariae_en.html#. Last consulted 16 June 2018

De Waard P (2018) De schuld is gegroeid, het systeem kwetsbaar, het besef ontbreekt. De Volkskrant, 23 April 2018

Forié F, Nemo P (2006) 11 gesprekken – Emmanuel Levinas aan het woord. Ten Have, Kampen

Goud J (1992) God als raadsel. Peilingen in het spoor van Levinas. Kok Agora, Kampen

Harari YN (2014) Sapiens – a brief history of humankind. Penguin Random House UK, London

Lloyd C (2012) What on earth happened? The complete story of the planet, life & people from the big bang to the present day. Bloomsbury, London

Stiglitz J (2002) Employment, social justice and societal well-being. Int Labour Organ 141(1–2):9–29

[8] See Byttebier (2017), Chapters 4 and 5, for a detailed blueprint of such a new monetary system.

The manufacturer's authorised representative in the EU is Springer Nature Customer Service Centre GmbH, Europaplatz 3, 69115 Heidelberg, Germany. If you have any concerns regarding our products, please contact ProductSafety@springernature.com

Printed and bound by CPI Group (UK) Ltd, Croydon, CR0 4YY
30/09/2026
02225653-0019